Brides and Doom

University of Pennsylvania Press
MIDDLE AGES SERIES
Edited by
Edward Peters
Henry Charles Lea Professor
of Medieval History
University of Pennsylvania

A listing of the available books
in the series appears at the
back of this volume

Brides and Doom

Gender, Property, and Power
in Medieval German Women's Epic

Jerold C. Frakes

University of Pennsylvania Press

Philadelphia

Library of Congress Cataloging-in-Publication Data
Frakes, Jerold C.
  Brides and doom : gender, property, and power in medieval German
women's epic / Jerold C. Frakes.
     p.   cm. — (Middle Ages series)
  Includes bibliographical references and index.
  ISBN 0-8122-3289-5
  1. Epic poetry, German—History and criticism.   2. German poetry—
Middle High German, 1050–1500—History and criticism.   3. Women—
Germany—History—Middle Ages, 500–1500.   4. Feminism and
literature—Germany—History.   5. Women and literature—Germany—
History.   6. Power (Social sciences) in literature.   7. Sex role in
literature.   8. Property in literature.   I. Title.   II. Series.
PT202.F73   1994
831'.03209352042—dc20   94-28092
                                                              CIP

The alternative readings I will propose should not be considered as yet another, superior interpretation that overthrows all the others. My goal is rather to show, by the sheer possibility of a different reading, that "dominance" is, although present and in many ways obnoxious, not unproblematically established. . . . It is the possibility of dominance itself, the attractiveness of coherence and authority in culture, that I see as the source, rather than the consequence, of sexism. For one thing, it allows for deviance to a certain extent, because deviance can be so easily accommodated, recuperated.

— Mieke Bal

What is at stake, then, is clearly the nature of reading; the question is not whether to be or not to be philological but how to read in such a way as to break through preconceived notions of meaning in order to encounter unexpected otherness — in order to learn something one doesn't already know — in order to encounter the other.

— Barbara Johnson

To date, philology has been a Western and male-dominated preserve. . . . While the study of etymologies, semantic changes, morphological and syntactic structures, and the interrelatedness of different languages and language groups can never become obsolete, a broadening of perspectives must surely follow the steady increase in the numbers of women and minority practioners in Western universities, and the incipient increase in the quality and quantity of scholars from outside the hallowed Western seats of learning, who are beginning to question the origins of our civilization from the comparativist perspective of their own — often equally ancient and civilized — past. There will be a new awareness of the relevance of issues such as gender, nationism, and race.

— Margaret Alexiou

This book will argue the priority of the political interpretation of literary texts. It conceives of the political perspective not as some supplementary method, not as an optional auxiliary to other interpretive methods current today . . . but rather as the absolute horizon of all reading and all interpretations.

— Fredric Jameson

Contents

1. Introduction

In the title of the present study I designate the focal texts, the *Nibelungen-lied, Diu Klage,* and *Kudrun,* by the unconventional term "women's epic." Perhaps it would then be useful to begin with a word on titles and the politics of naming. The Middle High German *Nibelungenlied* has survived and been transmitted in some three dozen manuscripts. *Diu Klage,* a "sequel/quasi-commentary" on the *Nibelungenlied,* is appended to that text in almost all extant manuscripts.[1] *Kudrun* survives in a single, early modern manuscript, commonly called the *Ambraser Heldenbuch* because, on the one hand, of its long-time repository (Ambras) and, on the other, of early scholarly perceptions of its contents (heroic epic).[2] The manuscript, copied by the customs official Hans Ried on commission by the Emperor Maximilian I in the years before and after 1510, is an anthology of Middle High German "heroic" literature. In the middle of this anthology of tales of the deeds of heroes is this trio of narratives that, while also featuring heroes and their deeds, focuses to a surprising degree on female characters. These three narratives, sandwiched between the manuscript's Dietrich and Wolf-dietrich epics, form, as it were, the centerpiece of the collection. Their focus on women is acknowledged by the titles given them in the manuscript:

---

1. On some of the problems of determining the genre of *Diu Klage,* see Hans Szklenar, "Die literarische Gattung der *Nibelungenlied* und das Ende 'alter maere,'" *Poetica* 9 (1977), 41–61.

2. Cod. Vindob. s.n. 2663 (fol. 140r–166r); in *Nibelungenlied* scholarship, often designated the d-manuscript. On this manuscript, see especially *Ambraser Heldenbuch. Vollständige Faksimile-Ausgabe im Originalformat des Codex Vindobonensis Ser. nova 2663 der Österreichischen Nationalbibliothek,* commentary by Franz Unterkircher (Graz, 1973). *Diu Klage* was composed around the 1220, according to Werner Hoffmann's dating; see "Die Fassung *C des Nibelungenliedes und die 'Klage,'" in *Festschrift Gottfried Weber: Zu seinem 70. Geburtstag überreicht von Frankfurter Kollegen und Schülern,* ed. Heinz Otto Burger and Klaus von See, Frankfurter Beiträge zur Germanistik 1 (Bad Homburg: Gehlen, 1967), p. 142. That *Kudrun* was composed in the thirteenth century within a generation or two of the *Nibelungenlied* is doubted by few scholars, despite the conditions of its transmission: late, unique manuscript, early modern German linguistic form, etc. On the specifics of *Kudrun's* transmission, see Franz H. Bäuml, ed., *Kudrun: Die Handschrift* (Berlin: de Gruyter, 1969), pp. 7–14; a useful analysis of the problems of dating the text in Frenkel, Кудруна (Moskva: Nauka, 1983), pp. 292–296.

"Ditz Puech Heysset Crimhilt" ["this book is named Kriemhilt"], "Ditz Puech haysset klagen" ["this book is named Klage ('Lament')"], "Ditz puech ist von Chaûtrun" ["this book is about Kudrun"].

Since relatively few medieval literary works have been transmitted with titles as unambiguously given them by their authors, most such works have been named by modern editors. In the case of the *Diu Klage* and *Kudrun*, the titles found in the Ambraser manuscript have been adopted by scholarship. With respect to the *Nibelungenlied*, however, the case is not so simple, for outside the Ambraser manuscript there is almost no evidence of a title at all.[3] Almost all editors have taken their titles from the last line of the poem: *Der Nibelunge Nôt* (B text), *Der Nibelunge liet* (C), or simply *Das Nibelungenlied*. While the medieval colophon often indicated the "title," and we might so designate these final lines here, the title appearing in the Ambraser manuscript (and, admittedly, very possibly given the text by its sixteenth-century copyist) dissents, as it were. In his "first edition" of the *Nibelungenlied*'s A-text in 1756, J. J. Bodmer also gave the poem the title *Chriemhilden Rache*. Since that time there has been no dearth of scholars who agree that Kriemhild is the "main character" and that the book somehow "is" Kriemhild's.[4] Be that as it may, since the D- and d-manuscripts and Bodmer's edition, the flow of the role in question, conception, and interpretations has not been "The Book of Kriemhild." Rather, scholarship has, as noted above, renamed the text with the more general title that designates it not as Kriemhild's book, but that of the enigmatic Nibelungs. The renaming is not so simple and perhaps not so innocent as it seems at first glance. Günther Schweikle comments on the external influences on the renaming of the text: "Sowohl bei der modernen Titelgebung ('Nibelungenlied') als auch bei Definition des Begriffes 'Heldendichtung' wirkte sichtlich die hauptsächliche Ausrichtung der Nibelungenforschung im 19. Jahrhundert auf vermutete 'heldischere' Vorfassungen der Sage nach" ("in both the modern naming of the text [*Nibelungenlied*] and the definition of the concept 'heroic poetry,' the primary direction of nineteenth-century Nibelungen scholarship has had an aftereffect on conjectured 'more heroic'

3. The D-manuscript of the *Nibelungenlied* (Munich MS 341, first third of the fourteenth century) names the text *Das ist daz Chreimhilden Puech*.

4. Recently, for instance, Werner Hoffmann has argued that the book may legitimately bear the title found in the two manuscripts noted; in *Das Nibelungenlied*, p. 50. Walter Seitter draws a rather different kind of conclusion concerning the entire genre from the fact of Kriemhild's role as primary character: "Die Hauptfigur aber ist Kriemhild — was wiederum zeigt, daß die Bezeichnung 'Heldensage' auf Einbildung beruht" ("the main character is, however, Kriemhild — which again demonstrates that the term 'heroic saga' is based on a misconception") (*Versprechen, Versagen*, p. 137).

prior stages of the saga."[5] This renaming, which is today taken for granted, was a single element in a larger scholarly project (however unconscious) that also transformed the possibilities of reading the work. An insightful recognition of the potential significance of the placement and the titles of the Ambraser manuscript is to be found in Inga Wild's examination of the immediate conditions of transmission and reception, such as they have survived for *Kudrun*.[6] The placement of the *Nibelungenlied, Klage,* and *Kudrun* together, she suggests, indicates a recognition of their thematic unity and essential ethical antithesis to the male Dietrich heroes of the surrounding texts (pp. 41, 43). Wild designates them "Frauen-Epen" ("women's epics," p. 8). In taking up her introduction of this term in my title, I am less interested in adding yet another generic category to our already burgeoning stock of analytically imprecise terms, than I am in simply recalling the arresting and insightful usage of the Ambraser manuscript and in suggesting that such a conception may well be more representative of both *interpre-*

---

5. "Das 'Nibelungenlied'—ein heroisch-tragischer Liebesroman?" in *De poeticis medii aevi quaestiones. Käte Hamburger zum 85. Geburtstag,* ed. Jürgen Kühnel et al., Göppinger Arbeiten zur Germanistk 335 (Göppingen: Kümmerle, 1981), p. 60. The significance of the title is perhaps even more far-reaching, however, for according to Hermann Schneider and Wolfgang Mohr the *Nibelungenlied* is the text that defines the entire genre, *Heldendichtung,* in *Reallexikon der detuschen Literaturgeschichte,* ed. Werner Kohlschmidt and Wolfgang Mohr, 2nd ed. (Berlin: de Gruyter 1958), 631. Some of the essential problems inherent in the conventional generic terminology and the conceptions that have constructed it are discussed by Heinz Rupp in " 'Heldendichtung' als Gattung der deutschen Literatur des 13. Jahrhunderts," in *Volk, Sprache, Dichtung. Festgabe für Kurt Wagner,* ed. Karl Bischoff and Lutz Röhrich (Gießen: Wilhelm Schmitz, 1960), pp. 9–25. Here he argues: ". . . und notwendig scheint mir zu sein, den Begriff 'Heldendichtung des 13. Jahrhunderts' möglichst zu meiden und sich auch nicht mehr auf germanische Restbestände zu versteifen" ("it seems necessary to me to the extent possible to avoid the term 'thirteenth-century heroic poetry' and also no longer to insist on the presence of surviving Germanic material," p. 9); and "Wir müssen uns von dem uns lieb gewordenen Begriff 'Heldendichtung' trennen und uns vor allem davon freimachen, germanische Vorstellung in die Literatur des 13. Jahrhunderts hineinzuprojizieren. Man wird dann manche Wertung ändern müssen, aber man wird dafür bessere und echtere Einsichten in das literarische Leben des 13. Jahrhunderts gewinnen" ("We must free ourselves from the concept 'heroic poetry' that we have come to hold dear, and above all we must give up projecting Germanic concepts onto the literature of the thirteenth century. It will then become necessary to change many valuations, but as a result a better and more authentic insight into the literary life of the thirteenth century will be obtained," pp. 24–25). Rupp points out that essentially the only "Germanic" notions that remain in thirteenth-century literature are courage, loyalty, and vengeance, all of which, of course, exist commonly in Arthurian as well as "heroic epic" (p. 16). Building on Rupp (or reacting against him) in recent years many scholars have made plausible the simple abandonment of the conventional genre classifications for medieval (German) literature, especially in the case of "heroic" vs. "courtly" epic. For obvious reasons, I wish to tiptoe around this omnivorous abyss of genre criticism here.

6. Inga Wild, *Zur Überlieferung und Rezeption des "Kudrun"-Epos: Eine Untersuchung von drei Europäischen Liedbereichen des "Typs Südeli,"* Teil 1. (Diss., München 1976; Göppingen: Kümmerle, 1979). Hers is one of those arguments that seems perfectly, almost self-evidently, obvious, but only after the argument has been so splendidly made.

tandum and (also thirteenth-century) *interpretatio*. I am at the same time quite aware of the potential political hazards inherent in the use of this term and its more general relative "women's literature" for the medieval period. For reasons that will become clear as the study progresses, I find both designations as they have been used in studies of medieval German literature particularly problematic, not because of their acknowledgment of the (predominant) narrative focus on female characters, but rather because they are susceptible to being constructed as denigrating or trivializing the text as not "real" epic, but only "women's epic," or, more insidious still, to be constructed as *necessarily* progressive, emancipatory, quasi-feminist, since "women's epic." Precisely this problematic, especially the general masculist identification and acceptance of *Kudrun* as a *Frauenroman,* and the rabidly anti-feminist signification that the term thereby gains as a result of the conventional interpretation of Kudrun and the *Kudrun* as pro-female and quasi proto-feminist will be one of the focal points of the analysis of *Kudrun*. In any case, however, the physical proximity of the three texts in the Ambraser manuscript does not constitute their close relationship but rather merely acknowledges the thematic proximity of their narratives, particularly with respect to their treatment of the issues of what we now designate gender construction. If the *Klage* is a sequel-like, quasi-commentary, corrective (and rather facile) response both to specific aspects of the plot and the issues of individual guilt and responsibility in the *Nibelungenlied,* then *Kudrun* is a full-scale attempt to subvert the ideological position established by the *Nibelungenlied* with respect to gender issues. That is, all three texts present calculated political arguments.

The discipline of medieval Germanic studies has in recent decades begun to acknowledge the political implications of its texts. As Heinz Rupp among others has demonstrated, the fact that the *Nibelungenlied* is a blatantly propagandistic political text is not to be denied. Hugo Kuhn also suggested *Kudrun* as a political poem several decades ago.[7] That sexual politics is among the political issues addressed by the texts has in recent years also been suggested both inside and on the margins of the academy.[8]

7. Heinz Rupp, "Das 'Nibelungenlied' — eine politische Dichtung," *Wirkendes Wort* 35 (1985) 166–176; Hugo Kuhn, "Kudrun," repr. in *Text und Theorie. Kleine Schriften,* vol. 2 (Stuttgardt: Metzler, 1969), pp. 200–216.

8. On the *Nibelungenlied,* see Berta Lösel-Wieland-Engelmann, "Verdanken wir das *Nibelungenlied* einer Niedernburger Nonne?" *Monatshefte* 72 (1980), 5–25; and "Feminist Repercussions of a Literary Research Project," *Atlantis: A Women's Studies Journal* 6 (1980), 84–90; Günther Schweikle, "Das 'Nibelungenlied' — ein heroisch-tragischer Liebesroman?" in *De poetics medii aevi quaestiones; Käte Hamburger zum 85. Geburtstag,* ed. Jürgen Kühnel et al., Göppinger Arbeiten zur Germanistk 335 (Göppingen: Kümmerle, 1981), pp. 59–84; and

That the *Nibelungenlied, Diu Klage,* and *Kudrun* enable a reading that addresses gender relations as an inextricable element in the political formations of the societies represented by the narratives is both an assumption on my part, and also my thesis. I am therefore myself heavily and consciously engaged here in a political project. On the other hand, it is nonetheless neither my assumption nor my thesis that the literature of the hegemonic culture of thirteenth-century central Europe is feminist in any common sense of that term — which is semantically still so very much bounded by primarily "first-world" cultural determiners of the middle to late twentieth century. Furthermore, since the complex sociological problematics of the social status of women is not linear, progressive, or capable of being plotted, and since there is no unitary status of women cross-culturally and diachronically that would legitimize a teleological, historicist comparison and ranking of the status of women, without sacrificing all of its identifying complexity, both inter- and intra-culturally,[9] I will neither compare the apples of thirteenth-century gender relations with the corresponding twentieth-century pears nor cite precursors nor plot a pretended developmental rise and fall in the status of women. Instead I propose to address what seem to me far more interesting problems by attempting to articulate both selected issues of sexual politics as represented in the texts of the *Nibelungenlied,* the *Klage,* and *Kudrun* and the equally political attempts by modern patriarchal[10] scholarship to prevent, subvert, deny, or coopt such a reading of the texts.

Otfrid Ehrismann, *Nibelungenlied: Epoche — Werk — Wirkung* (München: Beck, 1987). On *Kudrun,* see esp. Theodor Nolte, *Das Kudrunepos — Ein Frauenroman?* (Tübingen: Niemeyer, 1985); Barbara Siebert, *Rezeption und Produktion. Bezugssysteme in der "Kudrun"* (Diss., Freiburg. Göppingen: Kümmerle, 1988); and Barbara Siebert, "Hildeburg im 'Kudrun'-Epos: Die bedrohte Existenz der ledigen Frau," in *Der frauwen buoch: Versuch zu einer feministischen Mediävistik,* ed. Ingrid Bennewitz (Göppingen: Kümmerle, 1989), pp. 213–26. And, most recently, the masculist backlash of Thomas Grenzler, *Erotisierte Politik — Politisierte Erotik: Die politisch-ständische Begründung der Ehe-Minne in Wolframs "Willehalm," im "Nibelungenlied" und in der "Kudrun"* (Göppingen: Kümmerle, 1992).

　9. See, for instance, Michelle Zimbalist Rosaldo, "The Use and Abuse of Anthropology: Reflections on Feminism and Cross-Cultural Understanding," *Signs: Journal of Women and Culture in Society* 5 (1980), 389–417.

　10. Gayle Rubin argues, in her classic article on the male control of marriage and the exchange of women, that the term "patriarchy" is a particular type of male dominance, derived from the pastoral nomads represented in the Hebrew Bible and that its use should be confined to such groups and relationships ("The Traffic in Women: Notes on the 'Political Economy' of Sex," in *Toward an Anthropology of Women,* ed. Rayna R. Reiter [New York: Monthly Review Press, 1975], p. 168). Ann Ferguson, on the other hand, argues: "[My] use of the concept of patriarchy is somewhat broader than its original use, to mean 'control by the father.' I use the term *patriarchy* rather than the vaguer concept *male dominance* as my technical term because in my view the origin, persistence, and potential undermining of the male power and domination

In his recently published *Preface to the Nibelungenlied*, Theodore Andersson comments on another scholar's work: "If true, [his] observations would not so much clarify as complicate our understanding of the poem." Herewith Andersson inadvertently voices a tenet of *Nibelungenlied* research (and a general tendency of much positivistic scholarship) — that the best solution is necessarily the simplest one, the one that reduces and controls complexity rather than accepting it as the "normal" state of social formations.[11] In some types of research, especially certain constructions of the natural sciences, it may be true that the simple answer is the best (or it may simply be that this rule is there too part of a certain tradition of scholarship), but cultural criticism is gradually teaching us that more often than not simple interpretations are the result not of accuracy but of ideological constraints imposed by the interpreter's own cultural determinants. While complex analyses are not necessarily less ideological, cultural phenomena are most often complex and even complicated, and their analysis will be effective and useful to the degree that it at least acknowledges that complexity and tries to account for, rather than deny it.

One of the salient features of research on medieval literature has been its pre-, full-scale, and post-positivistic denial of certain kinds of complexity, manifested in the assumption, for instance, that an interpretation that does not explain all aspects of the text is not just incomplete but flawed by nature, for the "correct" interpretation would necessarily explain the poem's plenitude. Today, after two centuries of successive waves of final solutions to the problems of the *Nibelungenlied* — whether textual, historical, or otherwise — comprising literally thousands of books, monographs, reviews, and essays (and substantially fewer, but generally like-minded research publications on *Diu Klage* and *Kudrun*), there are few who would claim to have come across the ultimately convincing and satisfying comprehensive interpretation of the poems, and not many more who cling to the notion that literary scholarship is making progress toward an ultimately

---

of women in all the institutions of society stems from the relative strength or weakness of male dominance and exploitation of women in the family and/or associated kin networks," in "Sex and Work: Women as a New Revolutionary Class in the United States," in *An Anthology of Western Marxism: From Lukacs and Gramsci to Socialist Feminism*, ed. Roger S. Gottlieb (Oxford: Oxford University Press, 1989), p. 358. While Rubin's argument clearly has the merit of sociological and anthropological precision, unfortunately, her lead has not been followed, and users of English have not devised a viable alternative to the generalized use of the term *patriarchy*. Thus I, too, will use it in the broad sense of socially instituted male dominance.

11. (Stanford, CA: Stanford University Press, 1987), p. 151. One might also note that the interpretation I place on Professor Andersson's remark (here taken out of context) does not characterize his own complex and nuanced research.

satisfactory interpretation. Perhaps twentieth-century humanists have become jaded, disillusioned by the realization that absolute scientific knowledge is an illusion under which natural scientists themselves have rarely operated; perhaps they are simply able to acknowledge relativity or pluralism; or perhaps, finally, they (we) have simply come to accept the necessity of the historical conditioning of any and all interpretive activity. Or have we finally been convinced by sheer numbers? If ten generations of scholars of medieval German literature, including the likes of Lachmann, Heusler, and the Schröders, have not cracked the code of the *Nibelungenlied,* the *Klage,* and *Kudrun,* what hope remains for the likes of us? At any rate, we have become more modest in prefaces, book and article titles, and thesis statements. Attempts to reduce the *Nibelungenlied,* the *Klage,* and *Kudrun* to, for instance, a pastiche of (supposed) sources or their characters to allegorical figures, is no longer (or rather rarely still) done, and less obsolete but equally absolute theses are correspondingly rare.

To say that the *Nibelungenlied, Diu Klage,* and *Kudrun* are complex and complicated is, however, merely to voice a banality, and to pretend that no one has thus far dealt with the texts as complex works would be either naive or a blatant misrepresentation. Nonetheless, the topic I propose to address here, the problematics of gender, is one that is necessarily fraught with both subtle and complex issues of political, sociological, and economic development over the course of centuries. In addition, it is one that has thus far hardly been explored, even though it permeates the entirety of the *Nibelungenlied,* and the *Klage* and *Kudrun* as responses to the *Nibelungenlied,* and in subtle and not so subtle ways determines all conceptions of these works. The present analysis seeks to articulate some few strands of this complicated cultural web.

The present study addresses narrative texts written by educated, (probably) upper-class, white, christian (most likely, *pace* Lösel-Wieland-Engelmann) males of Western European culture. Those texts set their narratives in cultures that are not only male-dominated but male-conceived; the characters are primarily male, white, apparently heterosexual[12] christians of the ruling class in a literary society predicated upon the feudal mode of production.[13] The female characters, far fewer in number, are also white,

12. While such a designation certainly has less definitive meaning in a medieval context than in a modern one, it seems to me still useful to note that it is a marked and not an inevitable or automatic feature of cultural production and reception.

13. See, particularly, Barry Hindess and Paul Q. Hirst, *Pre-Capitalist Modes of Production* (London: Routledge and Kegan Paul, 1975); here, especially, p. 242 on the problems arising from the non-specific uses of the term *feudal.*

christian, apparently heterosexual, and (associate) members of the ruling elite. These texts are written for a mixed-gender audience, but, according to modern criticism they are (not unproblematically) claimed to adhere to a generic type more aligned with male than female reception, namely "heroic epic." Otherwise the audience was also generally uniform: white, christian, (predominantly) heterosexual and feudal-aristocratic. Modern criticism of the texts has been, characteristically for literatures of this type in this culture, written almost exclusively by well-educated, white, middle- and upper-class, ostensibly heterosexual and predominantly christian males of Western cultures. My own "historico-politico-economico-sexual determinations"[14] initially differed from that "norm" only in their working-class origins, but have since developed political deviations from it, as well. Obviously my project would hardly be politically viable if its goal were merely to point out cultural bigotry and sexism in the texts, in the culture that produced them, and in the scholars (and their cultures) who have interpreted them.[15] Such a litany of sins would be neither very interesting, very enlightening, nor any longer very useful for contemporary political projects, feminist or otherwise, except insofar as their general articulation had not yet reached the particular modern audience of the *Nibelungenlied, Diu Klage,* and *Kudrun.*

Conversely, it would be neither fair nor accurate to claim that the thirteenth-century hero-narrative provides *liberating* texts, in the sense that revolutionary narratives in all periods, and particularly as feminist texts of recent decades, have done. The canon of medieval heroic narrative is, as Peter Rose has observed about the classical Greco-Roman canon, "a canon of texts which, whatever their virtues, are strikingly elitist and misogynistic as well as more subtly racist."[16] They also (in almost all cases) uncritically accept the legitimacy of violence, rape, pillage, and mass murder as essential attributes of the value system of the elite class represented. Furthermore, these texts — like the Classics — have always been the intellectual property of the educated elite, and access to them has thus been controlled by the

14. Gayatri Spivak's coinage, *In Other Worlds: Essays in Cultural Politics* (New York: Methuen, 1987), p. 15.

15. To recognize the contours of Homer's sexism and its political context and effects, for instance, is a necessary scholarly task, but to complain of its non-conformity to emerging late twentieth-century mores in the United States, for instance, as if they formed a standard, would be as ahistorical as to complain of Hector's apparent preference for the spear over the assault rifle (as Elizabeth V. Spelman has pointed out); it would, additionally, be hardly more significant politically.

16. Peter W. Rose, *Sons of the Gods, Children of Earth: Ideology and Literary Form in Ancient Greece* (Ithaca, NY: Cornell University Press, 1992), p. 3.

hegemonic institutions of that elite.[17] A project such as the present one, then, must steer a course between the pious valuation of the "classic" for its own sake and the revisionist temptation to recuperate that repressive text for a modern political project that clearly would have easier and politically more nourishing fruit to pluck elsewhere.

Nonetheless, as will become clear in the course of the analysis, interwoven in the dominant pattern of the overt bigotry of the *Nibelungenlied, Diu Klage,* and *Kudrun,* there is a complex and pervasive texture of issues of property, gender, class, power and political authority, all of which enable these narratives to be read not merely as highly charged political texts, but also as texts that themselves signal that complex contemporary problems may not be resolved by simplistic *fiat.* The *Nibelungenlied* refuses to succumb to the pressures of dominant literary culture (of the thirteenth or twentieth centuries) to de-, circum-, and re-inscribe those problems in a traditional tale of the dominant gender, class, and culture. That the *Nibelungenlied* supports such a reading "against the grain" is suggested by the two other "women's epics" of the Ambraser manuscript: *Diu Klage* and *Kudrun,*[18] both of which respond deliberately and with politics aforethought to these aspects of the *Nibelungenlied,* although rarely directly, precisely, and analytically.[19]

17. Cf. also Antonio Gramsci's view of the classics in this sense, *quaderno* 12 (1932), *Quaderni del Carcere,* ed. Istituto Gramsci, Valentino Gerratana (Torino: Einaudi, 1975), III, 1531.

18. I do not, of course, pretend that the thirteenth-century reception of the *Nibelungenlied* is the necessarily legitimate one or that the coincidence of that interpretation with any other interpretation, including my own, guarantees its accuracy.

19. Thus after noting the "determinations" obtaining both for myself and generally for the *Nibelungenlied* and the medieval reception of its problematization of gender politics, I see no reason either to disqualify myself from engaging in such cultural and gender analysis as that proposed here, or to dwell further on my (lack of) qualifications for doing so, for they will soon become clear (or not) to the reader. For as Elizabeth V. Spelman points out, scholars' self-flagellation for their sins and their still unperceived and not yet abandoned cultural and gender blindnesses, simply continue to concentrate attention on themselves as privileged subjects rather than on the issue at hand (*Inessential Women: Problems of Exclusion in Feminist Thought* [Boston: Beacon Press, 1988], p. 5). This problem is especially acute with male feminists, as has been addressed by Elaine Showalter among others. One of the primary problems is that most male feminist criticism has been written about male texts (see her "Critical Cross-Dressing: Male Feminists and the Woman of the Year," in *Men in Feminism,* ed. Alice Jardine and Paul Smith [London: Methuen, 1987], p. 131). She formulates her barb by appropriating the words of her adversary in debate, Jonathan Culler: "As Culler predicts, patriarchal criticism tends to disclose whatever it values in the maternal by assimilating it to the paternal function." And she then continues (pp. 131–132): "Unless male feminist critics become more aware of the ways they too have been constituted as readers and writers by gender systems, their books may continue to be written for men and in behalf of male literary

The implications of gender relations for the *Nibelungenlied, Diu Klage,* and *Kudrun* may be approached via the articulation of economic relations as codeterminative of power hierarchies, the analysis of feudal wiving practices of the ruling elite, and the investigation of gender-based communication constraints and oppositional strategies. But to understand the basis for and controlling agents of such constraints, we must begin with an examination of the discipline into which such critical intervention is being made and from which it has long effectively been excluded; particularly important in this context are the specific conditions of exclusion. Chapter two provides a brief analysis of some of the salient features of "Philology and/as Patriarchy," followed by a second necessary foundation for the articulation of gender relations as refracted and represented in thirteenth-century literature: the sociology of women during the feudal period of the high Middle Ages in central Europe, specifically their site of participation in the feudal economic formation. For economic participation offers one key to an understanding of human beings' access to power and control of their lives. This holds true whether they live in a South Central Los Angeles systematically exploited and neglected for decades by racist and sexist ꞏꞏꞏ ꞏ ꞏ ꞏ ꞏ ꞏꞏ ꞏ ꞏꞏꞏꞏ ꞏ ꞏꞏꞏ ꞏ ꞏ ꞏꞏꞏꞏꞏꞏꞏ ꞏꞏꞏꞏ ꞏꞏꞏꞏ ꞏ ꞏꞏ [20] ꞏꞏ ꞏꞏꞏꞏꞏ ꞏꞏꞏ ꞏꞏ ꞏꞏꞏꞏ ꞏ ꞏ ꞏꞏꞏꞏ ꞏꞏꞏꞏ ꞏ ꞏ ꞏꞏꞏꞏꞏꞏ ꞏ ꞏꞏꞏꞏ ꞏ ꞏ ꞏꞏꞏ ꞏꞏꞏ ꞏ ꞏ ꞏꞏꞏꞏ ꞏ ꞏꞏꞏꞏ ꞏꞏ ꞏꞏꞏꞏꞏꞏ ꞏꞏꞏꞏꞏꞏ ꞏꞏꞏ thus power, as reflected in the property and power relations of the *Nibelungenlied* (Chapter three).[21] Here the focus will be primarily on the property relations of the ruling class, since it is to that class that the

---

traditions." While I agree completely with Showalter's legitimate demand for good faith among male co-workers, it is hard to imagine that "male *feminist* critics" (my emphasis) in any authentic sense can be unaware of their engendered constitution as readers; such would be a *contradictio in adiecto*: if they are so aware, they *may* in addition be(come) feminist; if they lack such awareness, they are quite simply not feminist. The theoretical and practical debates concerning male feminism have generally been enlightening for all parties concerned, they have also become lengthy, at times partisan, often self-serving, sometimes destructive. While such debate is essential in defining my own work, it cannot and need not be summarized or rehearsed here. To the extent that my own determiners and my own ignorance do not undermine the articulation of the topic then, let us treat them as no more than a steady ideological hum in the background; and when they do obstreperously intrude, I adjure you to take them as examples of the problems herein addressed.

20. It seems pertinent to make occasional reference to more concrete politico-economic events of the recent past and present in order to remind ourselves that our occupation with the study of medieval cultures, whether momentary or long-term, is not an apolitical, irrelevant, antiquarian hobby, but one whose politics are only the more blatant the less they are acknowledged.

21. Cf. Barry Hindess and Paul Q. Hirst: "Political dominance provides the conditions of existence of feudal exploitation, but the form of that exploitation is necessarily economic," *Pre-Capitalist Modes of Production,* p. 242.

characters of the *Nibelungenlied* belong.[22] Thereafter, in Chapter four, one type of female communication, its constraints and results will be examined: circum-coital male-female communication, both verbal and physical. Chapter five argues that as a consequence of the hegemonically imposed obstacles to female property control, power, direct communication, and thus public, political action, the two female protagonists of the *Nibelungenlied* reject such constraints and thus instigate a terminological and retributive response of patriarchy to that rebellion. For ultimately rebellion is the common, if not inevitable, result of such systemic and institutionalized repression: by Brünhild, by Kriemhild, and, in the spring of 1992, by a great number of individuals in oppressed neighborhoods of color across the United States.[23]

Chapter six examines the construction by the *Nibelungenlied*'s male characters and modern scholarship of Kriemhild and Brünhild as monsters, and *Diu Klage*'s response to the thirteenth-century reflex of that interpretation.[24] Finally, the analysis turns to a consideration of the literary-political backlash of *Kudrun,* where the carefully articulated case of the *Nibelungenlied* is dismantled, not point-by-point, not issue-by-issue, for that would be difficult, even argumentatively problematic, since the initial reception of the *Nibelungenlied* in the C-text and the *Klage* already indicate that some sector of the thirteenth-century literary audience not only understood but somehow supported the gender analysis of the *Nibelungenlied.* Rather *Kudrun* defers, deflects, and diverts our attention from the constellation of property-power-communications-gender issues of the *Nibelungenlied* and reduces it to a simpler, though not yet simple, allegory of intra-class status conflicts that subsume, coopt, and ultimately (when successful) erase gen-

22. Ihlenburg points out: "Es ist die Welt des hohen Feudaladels, die im Epos eingefangen ist, und es sind Grundprobleme der feudalen Wirklichkeit, die künstlerisch gestaltet wurden" ("it is the world of the upper feudal aristocracy that is depicted in the epic, and it is basic problems of feudal reality that are artistically developed") (*Das Nibelungenlied*, p. 20). Even so, or perhaps precisely because such is the extent of the class depiction, *relational* class analysis as such is made quite difficult in a study of the *Nibelungenlied,* for only the ruling class is depicted and little of the relations to other classes is intimated.

23. Although the national news media downplayed — this is, censored — the extent of the rebellion outside Los Angeles, and even there pretended that it was all but over after forty-eight hours. See, for instance, the spectrum of incisive analyses included in the collection: *Inside the L.A. Riots: What Really Happened and Why it Will Happen Again,* ed. Don Hazen (n.p.: Institute for Alternative Journalism, 1992).

24. Thus, while I wish to view the *Klage* here as a participant in the thirteenth-century debate concerning the gender issues problematized by the *Nibelungenlied,* that is in this context my only interest in that text; thus my attention to it is strategic to the interpretation of the *Nibelungenlied* and *Kudrun* and does not pretend to offer a full interpretation of the *Klage.*

der as a significant and even identifiable issue. The examination of the
scholarly construction championing *Kudrun's* heroine as sovereign (Chapter seven), cultural reformer (Chapter eight) and the text as "Frauenroman" (Chapter nine) comprises the final sections of the investigation,
especially as that text and its reception constitute an insidious masculist
backlash masquerading — both in the text and its modern interpreters — as
progressive politics.

As is clear from the preceding outline of the study, this feminist
analysis (as do all others) both subsumes other discrete analytical modes
and participates in a larger political project, for the repressive structuring of
gender codes — whether in thirteenth-century literature, twentieth-century
minority employment demographics, or anywhere else — necessarily articu-
lates with other hierarchies of power and authority, of economics and
politics, and ultimately of class. Peter Rose's comment in the introduction
to his recent analysis of one ideological construction in ancient Greek
literature is appropriate here:

> Although I am wary of the aberrations of some twentieth-century Marxist
> system builders, nonetheless one of the deepest attractions of Marxism paral-
> lels Gramsci's grounds for admiring the old classical edition — namely, its
> invitation to make connections, to bring some coherence to the understanding
> of phenomena that bourgeois analysis seems bent on keeping separate in ever
> more refined and narrow categories. (Rose, p. 16)

Despite the (at least) initially conflictual and unproductive relationship of various feminisms with various marxist political projects, recent
decades have seen a growing number of committed theorizations of the
inextricable inter-determinations of gender and class analysis and thus of
the necessity of allied oppositional political projects.[25] The political and
intellectual underpinnings of marxist feminism in the West have been
produced in recent decades by a wide range of critics, among them the
broadly-based and trenchant theorists Sheila Rowbotham, Michele Barrett,
and Gayatri Spivak, whose work is essential to any such project.[26] Under-

25. And despite the recent turmoil in (especially Western intellectual) marxisms due to
the collapse of Stalinism; see, among the enormous amount of recent material, the excellent
collection of essays dealing with the problems confronting anti- and post-Stalinist marxism in
After the Fall: The Failure of Communism and the Future of Socialism, ed. Robert Blackburn
(London: Verso, 19991).

26. See especially Rowbotham's *Women's Consciousness, Man's World* (New York: Pen-
guin, 1974); Barrett's *Women's Oppression Today* (London: Verso, 1980; rev. ed. 1988);
Spivak's recent collection of essays: *In Other Worlds.* In medieval literary studies the work of
Sheila Delaney might be mentioned, a selection of which is collected in *Medieval Literary*

standably in the chapters that follow, the arguments here advanced most often find their direct support in specialist research in feminist sociology, historiography, and anthropology, much of which also grows out of the theorization of a feminist confrontation with marxism. A pointed formulation of the political alliance of feminism and marxism recently has come from the perhaps unlikely pen of Fredric Jameson:

> In our present perspective, it becomes clear that sexism and the patriarchal are to be grasped as the sedimentation and the virulent survival of forms of alienation specific to the oldest mode of production of human history, with its division of labor between men and women. . . . The analysis of the ideology of form, properly completed, should reveal the formal persistence of such archaic structures of alienation — and the sign systems specific to them — beneath the overlay of all the more recent and historically original types of alienation — such as political domination and commodity reification — which have become the dominants of that most complex of all cultural revolutions, late capitalism in which all the earlier modes of production in one way or another structurally coexist. The affirmation of radical feminism, therefore, that to annul the patriarchal is the most *radical* political act — insofar as it includes and subsumes more partial demands, such as the liberation from the commodity form — is thus perfectly consistent with an expanded Marxian framework, for which the transformation of our own dominant mode of production must be accompanied and completed by an equally radical restructuration of all the more archaic modes of production with which it structurally coexists.[27]

A project informed by and committed to the politically necessary alliance of gender and class analysis, when focussing on gender construction in medieval German narrative, runs a number of inter-, cross- and simply

---

Politics: Shapes of Ideology (Manchester: Manchester University Press, 1990). On the conflictual relations of marxism and feminism, see, for instance, Heidi Hartmann's taking stock: "The Unhappy Marriage of Marxism and Feminism: Towards a More Progressive Union," in *Anthology of Western Marxism,* ed. Gottlieb, pp. 316–337. And, as the geo-political modifier in the text sentence indicates, "marxist or socialist feminism" has an astoundingly *and* comprehensibly different sense in the West and the East; see the collection *Gender Politics and Post-Communism: Reflections from Eastern Europe and the Former Soviet Union,* ed. Nanette Funk and Magda Mueller (London: Routledge, 1993); and the conference report, *Free and Equal: Female Voices from Central and Eastern Europe,* ed. Ellen Sofie Baalsrud (Oslo: Equal Status Council, 1992), whose participants (except for its Norwegian organizers and two other Scandinavian participants, and despite the title, from the former Soviet sphere of Eastern Europe) inadvertently reveal or manifest many of the problems more than problematize them.

27. Fredric Jameson, *The Political Unconscious: Narrative as a Socially Symbolic Act* (Ithaca, NY: Cornell University Press, 1981), pp. 99–100. Of course Jameson's general lack of attention to specifically feminist issues does not disqualify the importance of much of his political analysis for feminist projects, as demonstrated, for instance in Tania Modleski's fundamental use of Jameson's double hermeneutic in her *Loving with a Vengeance* (Hamden, CT: Archon, 1982).

extra-disciplinary risks on the theoretical level. To mention two aspects of just one such hazard: feminist historiography of the medieval period, while certainly not lagging behind allied disciplines, is still making up for decades and indeed centuries of masculist neglect of relevant gender issues, and is thus on many levels still very much engaged in (more or less) empirical foundational study. Likewise, the traditional philological method which dominated all literary study until (relatively speaking) very recently, and still constitutes the norm in medieval studies, is also by definition a positivistic discipline. But the necessity — according to such dominant modes — of basing one's critical work on the "hard facts" of actual *historical* conditions of medieval women's lives and on the "hard facts" of the *meaning* of the literary text "itself" conveniently overlooks what the discipline of the sociology of knowledge has taught us in recent decades about the inevitably social construction of knowledge. It pretends toward facticity only by ignoring the inevitability of overdetermination in all matters of cultural production. In their closely argued and densely freighted study of *Pre-Capitalist Modes of Production,* Barry Hindess and Paul Hirst also have occasion to deflate this recurringly remounted empirical facade and at the same time provide a clear indication of the Marxist employment and deployment — not avoidance — of "facts".

> Concrete conditions are not "given" to theory in order to validate or to refute its general concepts. On the contrary, it is the general concepts that make possible the analysis of the concrete. [p. 4]. . . . The general concepts of Marxist theory are theoretical means for the production of knowledge of concrete social formations and of concrete conjunctures. They are not a substitute for concrete analysis. They are the tools that make it possible. . . . Concrete conditions do not validate concepts, it is the concept which makes possible and validates analyses of the concrete. (pp. 9, 180)[28]

That theoretical concerns shape the form of argumentation, the definition of what constitutes evidence, and how that evidence can be deployed, will become clear both in the development of my own argument and in its representation of the theses that have come to constitute the scholarship on the texts here addressed. While there is not exactly a lengthy and broad tradition in medieval studies to serve as the basis for the specific politics of the current project, it is certainly not the first marxist intervention into the

---

28. Cf. also Jameson's observation regarding Althusser's conception of historiography, that the purpose is not to "elaborate some achieved and lifelike simulacrum of its supposed object, but rather to 'produce' the latter's 'concept'" (*The Political Unconscious,* p. 12).

field of medieval studies (nor into medieval German studies), nor is it by any means the first feminist one. Nonetheless, the field of marxist-feminist studies that specifically focuses on the medieval German heroic literature is sparsely planted indeed.[29]

As most scholars do when writing for audiences not just in their field of specialization, I too generally have adopted the modern forms of the medieval names of the characters (e.g., Siegfried for Sîvrit) when there are common modern forms generally known to readers of English and German. All translations included are my own. In translating poetic texts I make no attempt to preserve either formal features of the verse or poetic expression, for Dante was in this case, as in so many others, obviously right that "nulla cosa per legame musaico armonizzata si può de la sua loquela in altra transmutare, sanza rompere tutta sua dolcezza e armonia" (*Convivio* I, vii, 14). Instead I have always striven against those constraints and toward what Jerome called *ad sensum* translation, even if it has occasionally required the rather untidy listing of alternative connotations, all of which may have resonated for the original medieval audience, as does great and even not so great poetry for *original* audiences in every tradition. I may choose to emphasize one such alternative in my own interpretation, but not from any intent to be contentious.[30]

This study has developed over the course of several years of teaching medieval Germanic literature in university courses in the United States. I would like to express my thanks to my institutional employer, the University of Southern California, for a one-semester sabbatical leave in 1990 at a time when the *Nibelungenlied* sections of the book were nearing completion. A research fellowship provided by the Alexander von Humboldt Stiftung in 1993 made possible the completion of the *Kudrun* sections. My thanks to both institutions, and particularly to Professor Dr. Ekkehard Krippendorff at the Otto-Suhr-Institut of the Freie Universität Berlin who sponsored my tenure as a Humboldt fellow. Ray Wakefield first encouraged my interest in the *Nibelungenlied* many years ago, although neither of us foresaw a study in cultural criticism as the eventual result of that initial interest. Cristanne Miller, Franz Bäuml and James Schultz read the entire

29. One should mention the (albeit *not* feminist and rather strictly orthodox) Marxist analysis by Karl Heinz Ihlenburg, *Das Nibelungenlied: Problem und Gehalt* (noted above), as one of the most important studies of the text in recent decades.

30. I am also fully cognizant of the cliché of translator's prefaces, also from the Italian: *traditore traduttore,* and acknowledge its inevitability despite (and directly as a result of) all honest and sincere efforts toward accuracy.

manuscript at various stages and offered much appreciated general encouragement and detailed critique. My anonymous readers at the University of Pennsylvania Press also provided both excellent and useful suggestions for revisions large and small. I thank them all. Finally it is necessary to acknowledge the labors of several generations of medievalists and Germanists with whose politics and interpretations — literary and otherwise — I may often disagree, but without whom our knowledge of things medieval would be much narrower and shallower. If the bridge between their understanding of the Middle Ages and the projects of contemporary feminism and cultural criticism is to stand, it will be at least in part on the foundations laid also by them.[31]

31. The ever-changing critical contours of the field and thus of its content and definition was noted a quarter of a century ago by Werner Hoffmann: "Wer — um es ebenso konkret wie zugespitzt zu formulieren — im Jahre 1967 eine Arbeit über die "Kudrun" veröffentlicht, tut dies sozusagen über eine andere 'Kudrun' als sie ihm zum Beispiel vor fünfzig Jahren vorgelegen hätte," in *Kudrun: Ein Beitrag zur Deutung der nachnibelungischen Heldendichtung* (Stuttgart: Metzler, 1967), p. viii. And how much more so are the *Nibelungenlied* and *Kudrun* different today from the 1967 "versions" with which Hoffmann worked!

2. Philology and/as Patriarchy: The Conventions of *Nibelungenlied* Scholarship

In order to make the general outline of my thesis concerning the *Nibelung-enlied* clear from the outset and thus to direct my readers' reading of my reading, let me indicate its major prejudices by way of thumbnail plot summary. Vastly oversimplified, the fabula of the *Nibelungenlied* is thus:

> A woman is bartered as wife by her weak oldest brother to a strong foreigner in exchange for his raping into submission a foreign wife for that brother; the husband of the bartered wife is then murdered by one of her brothers' gang, whom she then brings to justice.

All initial interpretive problems for traditional patriarchal scholarship derive from this last clause (which also summarizes over half the poem). For in a feudal social formation ultimate judicial authority devolves on the highest instance in the order, generally the king, in this case Gunther, who is party to the murder.[1] In a traditional (conventionally termed a "primitive") society without police detectives, public defenders, district attorneys, judges and penitentiaries, justice in cases of murder is conventionally served by means of blood-vengeance carried out by those specifically duty-bound to do so—the kin, specifically the male relations, of the victim. The *Nibelungenlied* seems in this respect to be a "mixed" text, for the text sometimes seems ready to delegate responsibility for justice to the highest public

---

1. Cf. Perry Anderson, *Passages from Antiquity to Feudalism* (London: Verso, 1974), p. 153: "Thus political power came for a period to be virtually identified with the single 'judiciary' function of interpreting and applying the existing laws. Moreover, in the absence of any public bureaucracy, local coercion and administration—policing, fining, tolling and enforcing powers—inevitably accrued to it. It is thus necessary always to remember that mediaeval 'justice' factually included a much wider range of activities than modern justice, because it structurally occupied a far more pivotal position within the total political system. It was the ordinary name of power." In general Anderson's materialist economic, structural and class analysis of the feudal system is a necessary complement to the classic study of feudalism by Marc Bloch, *La société féodale* (Paris: Michel, 1939).

instance — the Burgundian king. Generally, however, in Siegfried's case that responsible instance is assumed to be his father Siegmund, who is the next of kin and designated blood avenger, but who is nonetheless prevented from carrying out his duty by the victim's wife, Kriemhild, who recognizes that any such attempt at the Burgundian court would be suicidal. Even modern scholars admit that, according to the text's assumed and overt mores, the only culturally appropriate response to the murder — legal, moral, and otherwise — is blood vengeance; at least they are ready to admit this so long as it is a matter of *Siegmund's* carrying out the act in direct and immediate response to the murder. It only becomes a problem — for the Burgundians and their modern scholarly advocates — when Sigmund, as the responsible male relative, abandons this course of action, while the course of action itself is not abandoned but rather assumed by — *a woman*. According to this society's codes, women may not act independently, but rather only through their male guardians: father, brothers, husband.[2] In this case, however, the woman's father is dead; her brothers are themselves both the judicial system, such as it is, and the criminals; her husband is their victim and his father too weak to be effective. She is in this sense alone, without recourse except to herself, in spite of the fact that by virtue of her sex she is also disqualified from political and until then unprecedented to even take any public action. Therefore, no matter what she does about Siegfried's murder, it will be — in the eyes of the society — illegitimate, illegal, monstrous. This fact, that Kriemhild has only the two choices — to accept injustice perpetrated on her openly and unashamedly by men, or, by acting independently, to counter that injustice and simultaneously become "monstrous," soon becomes apparent in the text, which makes this issue one of the primary focal points of the second half of the narrative.

Ursula R. Mahlendorf and Frank J. Tobin have investigated the medieval legal implications of the situations in the *Nibelungenlied*. The results are of great interest in general, but are of restricted relevance to the present investigation of *literary* signification. Mahlendorf and Tobin argue that Hagen engineers the murder to have as few legal repercussions as possible:

---

2. This despite M. Schwarze's claims a century ago to the contrary: "Wenn der gatte eines gewaltsamen todes gestorben ist, so ist die unabweislichste pflicht der witwe, wie die der kinder, die blutrache" ("When the husband has died a violent death, blood vengeance is the unavoidable duty of the widow and also of the children"). As evidence she notes the *wishes* of both Kriemhild in the *Nibelungenlied* and Hilde in the *Kudrun* (M. Schwarze, "Die Frau in dem *Nibelungenlied* und der *Kudrun*," *Zeitschrift für deutsche Philologie* 16 [1884], 450). Here the *wish* of Isolde might also have been mentioned, as well as her attempt to *act* on her wish, while Tristan was in the tub. But Kriemhild sets herself apart from these other women not by her desire alone, but by the fact that she also acts on her desire to execute vengeance.

he involves Kriemhild as an informer in order to dissuade her from bringing charges or disclosing her revelation to Siegmund, and he implicates Gunther in order to protect himself. He dare not be caught in the act and must return the body after Kriemhild's charge of murder can no longer be legally valid—*handhafte tat* presupposes that the murderer is either caught in the act or found with body on the same day as the murder. Hagen precludes both by staging the hunt away from Worms and away from witnesses at the hunt, by coming back after nightfall, and by having the body found in the morning. Since Hagen is not guilty of *handhafte tat,* he can be cleared by oath, which is even executed by Gunther, the king and supreme judge (1045,4). Hence, "Kriemhild has no recourse but to desist from further legal redress, as in fact she does. Nevertheless, a medieval audience would be keenly aware that the entire court had put itself outside the framework of the valid social order."[3] This interpretation presents an interesting interface of the text with medieval legal codes, but seems not altogether successful. Kriemhild's role as "informer" seems to implicate her in the murder only in the minds of modern critics: her "intent"—insofar as it can be *imagined*—is not culpable, and the apparent situation (impending war) would have rendered her action commendable had there been no evil intent on Hagen's part. No matter how scholars try to lighten Hagen's burden of guilt, he remains the one who singlehandedly planned and in large part executed the entire elaborate deception, and in the end it was he alone who set the stage and he alone who carried out the act of murder. Gunther's complicity does not lessen Hagen's culpability, nor does the fact that Gunther alone witnessed the murder, nor that the body was not discovered until the next morning. Rather, the *literary* events of the *Nibelungenlied,* the *fact* of Hagen's guilt, the "evidence" of the bleeding corpse, and his own admission of guilt far outweigh any extra-literary, historical legal practices. This is, however, not to say that these practices become irrelevant, for they clearly are the social substrate on which the text's deviation is constructed and which it refracts. No one doubts Hagen's full guilt when it is a matter of Siegmund's taking legitimate vengeance, but only when Kriemhild so acts.

If this second half of the narrative belongs to Kriemhild, then the first half is Brünhild's. Viewed in a larger narratological frame, the first section functions to construct the circumstances that allow the second; it creates the problems of part two and also indicates the only possible solutions to them. Viewed in terms of female participation, on the level of event, the

---

3. Mahlendorff and Tobin, "Legality and Formality in the *Nibelungenlied,*" *Monatshefte* 66 (1974), 225–38, here pp. 234–35.

two sections are also complexly related in the form of a narrative chiasmus: at the beginning of the narrative Kriemhild is a sequestered, powerless non-participant in society; by the final scenes of the tale she has become openly powerful, an all but ruling queen, and a full and finally independent actor.[4] Brünhild, on the other hand, begins as the *regens regina* of an independent kingdom who is the physical superior of all men who have dared to challenge her; she nonetheless soon becomes a physically weak, politically dependent, courtly *regis uxor,* who disappears from the narrative in the second half of the text.[5] Thus Brünhild is disempowered as the empowerment of Kriemhild proceeds.[6] In *aventiure,* 14, as they both have assumed (or had forced on them) their expected status in the mediated literary courtly culture produced by twelfth and thirteenth-century feudal society (*regis uxor*), and thus in each case have moved a substantial distance from their original positions on the extremes toward the center on their way to their final positions at the opposite extremes, they pass, or rather inevitably confront each other in the center, in the infamous *senna*-scene, the "railing of the queens."[7] The one begins extra-courtly and becomes courtly; the other begins courtly and becomes extra-courtly; each is labeled a monster precisely insofar as she oversteps the strict bounds of conventional courtly female behavior. This chiastic structure may function as a key to an interpretation of the *Nibelungenlied,* for both parts of the narrative are dominated by the women, a graph of whose public and private actions intersects as χ, divides the narrative in half, and focuses attention on the empowerment and disempowerment of women as those processes determine their roles in society.

From this political perspective of power relations, the decades-long

---

4. Walter Seitter calls this transformation of Kriemhild "Die Brünhildisierung Kriemhilds," in *Das politische Wissen in Nibelungenleid* (Berlin: Merve Verlag, n.d.), p. 176.

5. Although the final fate of Brünhild is susceptible of another interpretation as well; see below, Chapter six.

6. Seitter notes also that in Thea von Harbou's and Fritz Lang's film *Die Nibelungen* Kriemhild starts out as *tumbe Maid* and as time goes on gradually takes on the form of Brünhild ("nähert sich der Gestalt Brunhilds"); see *Versprechen, Versagen: Frauenmacht und Frauenästhetik in der Krimhild-Diskussion des 13. Jahrhunderts* (Berlin: Merve Verlag, 1990), pp. 84–85.

7. In the scholarly literature on the *Nibelungenlied,* this scene has been all but essential to any analysis of "the role of women," but not such that the socially-constructed, gender-based problems confronting the two queens are addressed, but rather for the sake of analysis of the strategies and power constellations of the men; the general tenor being that such a bitter quarrel by women (of no matter what class: here, even queens) was simply characteristic of the female sex and a further demonstration of the pettiness and selfishness of women in general and these women in particular. Here I do not address this scene, for my focus is rather on the social forces that make this quarrel inevitable.

debate concerning the *causa finalis* of Kriemhild's *leit*[8] is necessarily introduced into a larger context: why must she suffer *leit* at all? The most useful answer now seems that she must do so because her society will not allow her, as a nonconforming female, to do otherwise. *Leit* is not primarily "insult," as Friedrich Maurer maintains with all the tenacity that positivism can muster, nor "heartache," as Schröder just as adamantly counters. *Leit* certainly includes those connotations, but it is caused by a much larger problem, one that signifies — on the individual level of personal pain and grief, but also on the larger scale of the inevitable contradictions inherent in the social formations of the culture — the disempowerment and exclusion from public life and independent action that is the lot of women in the *Nibelungenlied*. This it is that causes Brünhild to reject suitors so monstrously, if monstrous it is, and this it is that makes Kriemhild rave in Hunland, if rave she does; it is this that causes the *senna*. In coming to terms with the mentalities that try to coerce us into condemning their actions, we will also account for the forces that coerced them into acting thus. For they are, not surprisingly, essentially the same, in the thirteenth-century text and the nineteenth- and twentieth-century scholarship.

Conversely, it is also possible to isolate and identify the forces that enable a reevaluation of Hagen's character over the course of the poem. In part one, for instance, Hagen treacherously murders Siegfried in what would from many (but not all) perspectives be termed cowardly fashion; in the course of part two, however, Hagen is depicted as a hero in the text and treated as such by Dietrich, among others. Modern critics most often also add a third voice, when they implicitly or explicitly maintain that, despite the fact that Hagen wielded the spear that killed Siegfried, Hagen is — proven by the poet's "intention" — a hero, and thus culpability must, apparently, be assigned to someone else — perhaps Siegfried himself, although since he too is a hero, the guilt is most often ultimately assigned to Brünhild or even Kriemhild herself.[9] Few critics of the *Nibelungenlied* have made

8. Cf. Friedrich Maurer, *Leid: Studien zur Bedeutungs- und Problemgeschichte besonders in den großen Epen der staufischen Zeit* (Bern/München: Francke, 1951), pp. 13–28, and Werner Schröder, "Die Tragödie Kriemhilts im Nibelungenlied," *Zeitschrift für deutsches Altertum und deutsche Literatur* 90 (1960–61), 41–80, 123–160.

9. On Hagen as hero, see, for example, among recent work, Winder McConnell, *The Nibelungenlied*, pp. 23–24, Michael Batts, "The *Nibelungenlied* (Thirteenth Century)," in William T. H. Jackson, ed., George Stade, ed. in chief, *European Writers: The Middle Ages and the Renaissance, I: Prudentius to Medieval Drama* (New York: Scribner's, 1983), p. 234; On Kriemhild as culpable, see McConnell, *The Nibelungenlied*, pp. 16, 19; Karl Heinz Ihlenburg, *Das Nibelungenlied: Problem und Gehalt* (Berlin: Akademie-Verlag, 1969), p. 82; and Batts, "The *Nibelungenlied*," p. 224.

distinctions among the *fabula* or events of the plot, the narrator's evaluation (if any), and their own interpretations, but rather amalgamate all these and present them as authorial intent. And thus the inherent sexism of the thirteenth-century, male-authored, and primarily male-received text becomes not only the text to be interpreted but also the co-text of the interpretation.

But the problem is deeper, for the text problematizes Hagen's behavior and also (especially) the societal restrictions on female behavior. Brünhild and Kriemhild are called monsters by Hagen and especially by (male) critics, in the interest of both of whom it is that the women be viewed as the villains. The narrator however seems to take a more complex view: after the initial introduction of Kriemhild as the courtly princess par excellence, the narrator never pretends that she is one-dimensional, but rather takes as one of the prime narrative tasks the presentation of the ambiguity of her character in great and nuanced detail. If Hagen calls her a she-devil, if scholars call her inhuman and monstrous, it is obviously a result not simply of *their* ideologies or of her actions, but of the overdetermined interplay of the two.

In discussing the strong arm power games that permeate the plot of the *Nibelungenlied*, scholars have, since the turn of the last century, regularly identified deception as the mainstay of the plot. Recently Lana Rings stated it simply: "deception is a major factor in the behavior of the characters in the *Nibelungenlied:* people say things they do not mean, often avoid saying what they think, or tell only part of what they know."[10] Two generations ago Ernest Tonnelat went so far as to identify deception as the ultimate cause of the deaths of the deceivers.[11] Regarding Siegfried's return from the skiff after the contests in Iceland, he comments:

> Ainsi les rapports des Burgondes et de Brünhild sont, dès la première heure, fondés sur la tromperie et le mensonge. Gunther, Siegfried, Hagen avaient l'illusion de ne pas commettre un acte bien grave en organisant la petite intrigue dont Brünhild vient d'être l'inconsciente et loyale victime. C'est là pourtant ce qui causera un jour, par une logique terrible, leur propre mort.[12]

10. Lana Rings, "Kriemhilt's Face Work: A Sociolinguistic Analysis of Social Behavior in the *Nibelungenlied*," *Semiotica* 65 (1987), 317.

11. Such an interpretation is still uncommon today; cf., however, Schweikle's parallel remark ("Das 'Nibelungenleid,'" p. 78).

12. "Thus the relations of the Burgundians and Brünhild are from the outset based on deception and lies. Gunther, Siegfried, Hagen are under the illusion of not having done anything particularly serious in arranging the little intrigue of which Brünhild had just been the unknowing and loyal victim. It is, however, just this that one day by a terrible logic will cause their own deaths." Ernest Tonnelat, *La chanson des Nibelungen: Étude sur la composition et*

Czerwinski observes:

> In der Nibelungen-Forschung ist wohl nie bezweifelt worden, daß die Be-
> gebenheiten auf Isenstein als Täuschung Brünhilds und Hinterlist Siegfrieds
> zu interpretieren seien. Es läßt sich jedoch zeigen, daß im Text mit der Alterna-
> tive "Gewalt oder List" nirgendwo negative Urteile verbunden werden, daß
> also List als eine mögliche Verhaltensweise erscheint und als eben die, die aus
> der Sicht Gunthers und Siegfrieds in diesem Fall angemessen ist, zu der sie sich
> außerdem — im Gegensatz zu Brünhild — in der Lage sehen.[13]

Michael Batts notes as well: "At the root of the conflict is the fraud practiced
on Brunhild."[14] Bostock (p. 205) concedes: Siegfried behaves "disgrace-
fully" to Brünhild in deceiving her; she could, he contends — confusing
literature with an apparently unmediated history — have gotten an annul-
ment of the marriage due to "deception and duress."

Fraud, deception, betrayal: at the most basic level, such actions are
predicated on the assumption that communication is possible, that lines of
communication are open and functioning and that the parties to communication are able to play the roles necessary for communication to take place,
but especially also that they are simultaneously unwilling to do so. In the
Nibelungenlied these preconditions for communication are then regularly
undermined by the practice of deception. A decade ago Gerd Steckel
outlined for me the thesis of an essay on which he was working, which
suggested that at strategic points in the *Nibelungenlied* opportunities for
vital communication occurred and were consistently, recurringly, and deliberately passed over or even subverted: whenever the point arrived at
which a certain something had to be said, the characters either said something else or nothing at all.[15] Steckel's thesis identified communication and

---

la formation du poème épique, Publications de la Faculté des Lettres de l'Université de
Strasbourg 30 (Paris: Les Belles Lettres, 1926), p. 47.

13. "In Nibelungen scholarship it has never really been doubted that the events in
Isenstein were to be interpreted as a deception of Brünhild by Siegfried. It may however be
demonstrated that nowhere does the text associate negative values with the alternatives
"violence or deceit," and thus that deceit appears to be a possible mode of behavior, in fact
precisely the one that seems most appropriate to Gunther and Siegfried in this case, and one,
moreover, that they, as opposed to Brünhild, are in a position to carry out" (p. 71).

14. Batts, "The *Nibelungenlied,*" p. 235.

15. So far as I know, Steckel's essay has never appeared, but its guiding concept has
nonetheless born fruit, for I passed it on (with attribution) in a seminar some years ago, where
it prompted Lana Rings to the research that led to the article noted above. It has also obviously
influenced my own thinking on numerous aspects of the *Nibelungenlied.* Walter Seitter cleverly
designates this communicative block "der Mechanismus des 'Vertagens des Sagens'" ("the
mechanism of the postponement/adjournment of speech") (*Versprechen, Versagen,* p. 42),
which despite its cleverness does not seem quite accurate, however, for postponement implies
at least an intended resumption in the future, which here does not seem to be the case.

possibilities for communication as significant issues in the *Nibelungenlied,* but those issues are further complicated and in fact defined by the issue of gender, for the primary communicative problems are those arising directly out of constraints imposed by the definition of gender roles. And, as Theodore Andersson has demonstrated,[16] the commonplace disguises, contests, and deceptions of bridal-quest tales and *Spielmannsepen* (where they are generally accepted without problem) become highly marked in the *Nibelungenlied,* where they lead to disaster. Those who continue to operate on the unquestioned assumption of male dominance and freedom to control communication strategies, it seems as a direct result of their blind adherence to the notion of male dominance, mercilessly slaughter each other. The women, on the other hand, skillfully elicit not always the actions they immediately desire, but at least those leading indirectly to their goals. The male marionettes engage in their traditional rites of heroic combat to the bitter, bloody, and nationally suicidal end, but we may not condemn the women as the responsible "puppeteers." That role too is played by the traditional male conceptions of honor and valor, that drive the men to martial excess as almost the only form of public action known to them — that is, by the social formations of feudalism and the courtly and/or heroic code of conduct. Conduct is the only response that the patriarchal, feudal social formation makes available to them in such situations of conflict.

The cultural coercion that makes it impossible for the (male) society of the *Nibelungenlied* to respond to gender threats in a more nuanced or at least more reasonable way is part and parcel of traditional patriarchal sexism in the West. It spawned, among other things, an entire literary tradition of more and less destructive Siegfried tales; and they have, in the course of the centuries, fed into a tradition of patriarchal scholarship. The legend of

---

16. *Preface to the Nibelungenlied,* p. 88.

17. Karl Heinz Ihlenburg points out (*Das Nibelungenlied,* pp. 40–41) that, in view of the destruction, cruelty, and brutality of aristocratic feuds, the petty wars, the destruction of property, peasants, crops, and so on characteristic of the feudal period, we see in the cold-hearted destruction represented in the *Nibelungenlied* no idealized world as in medieval romance but rather a society much closer to historical reality. We might, however, also note that in the *Nibelungenlied* only a single class is represented. In addition, however, the common notion that the courtly romance is somehow less violent and generally more pleasant is perhaps also simply an apologia from the hegemonic center about the margin: while there may be a smaller "body-count" in courtly romance, the quotidian violence large and small on which the depicted feudal society is predicated is just as capable of slavery, racism, senseless destruction of life and property for the sake of male, feudal honor, and rigid, debilitating class and gender prejudice as can be found in the literature of repression of any hegemonic culture known: whoever does not belong to the ruling elite and has the misfortune to appear in a courtly romance almost inevitably suffers violence.

Siegfried, or Sigurðr, the dragonslayer, has through the centuries been the focus of sporadically intense artistic and popular interest. The *Nibelungenlied* itself enjoyed enormous popularity in the three centuries following its composition around the end of the twelfth century, as witnessed by the three dozen complete and fragmentary manuscripts extant. The text exists in three differing versions, indicating, if nothing else, that it was reworked for specific reasons for particular audiences. Soon after the *Nibelungenlied* was written down, a second text, *Diu Klage,* appeared, as a quasi review-corrective-response-continuation-commentary. It was appended to the text in almost all preserved manuscripts of all three manuscript traditions. The Scandinavian literary tradition includes older examples of the tale in the *Prose Edda* and the *Poetic Edda,* and later ones in the prose sagas *Þiðreks saga af Bern* and the *Vǫlsunga saga.* In German there also exist, among other works, the late medieval *Der Hürnen Seyfrid,* and Hans Sachs's early modern *Der Hürnen Seufrid.* Since the rediscovery of the manuscripts of the *Nibelungenlied* in one of the first waves of that brand of medievalism characteristic of European Romanticism, the legend has spawned scores of stories, novels (such as William Morris's verse romance *The Story of Sigurd the Volsung*) and dramas (among them Ibsen's early "Hermændene på Helgeland"), a number of operas (including Wagner's *Ring* cycle); several hours of celluloid (Fritz Lang's *Die Nibelungen*); reams of nationalistic propaganda, especially during the final stages of the Napoleonic wars (when there was a *Feld- und Zeltausgabe* for [German] soldiers to carry)[18] and the Nazi period; and more recently radio plays, a pornographic comic book, and a quasi-Yiddish off-Broadway parody.

The scholarly and quasi-scholarly interest has been no less enthusiastic, prolific, and pervasive in the last century and a half.[19] The text has been

---

18. August Zeune, ed. Berlin 1815.

19. See especially Mary Thorp's older but still useful survey, *The Study of the Nibelungenlied: Being the History of the Study of the Epic and Legend from 1755 to 1937* (Oxford: Clarendon Press, 1940), but also particularly Otfrid Ehrismann's recent studies of the reception, especially in *Das Nibelungenlied in Deutschland: Studien zur Rezeption des Nibelungenlieds von der Mitte des 18. Jahrhunderts bis zum ersten Weltkrieg,* Münchner Germanistische Beiträge 14 (München: Fink, 1975). An excellent brief political analysis of the major trends in *Nibelungenlied* scholarship may be found in Karl Heinz Ihlenburg's *Das Nibelungenlied: Problem und Gehalt,* pp. 9–34. See also W. Krogmann and U. Pretzel, *Bibliographie zum Nibelungenlied* (Berlin: Schmidt, 1966); Francis G. Gentry, "Trends in 'Nibelungenlied' Research Since 1949: A Critical View," *Amsterdamer Beiträge zur älteren Germanistik* 7 (1974), 125–139; Gottfried Weber and Werner Hoffman, *Nibelungenlied,* 3rd ed. (Stuttgart: Metzler, 1968) (the more recent edition is by Hoffman alone). No attempt will be made in this book to survey the vast research literature on the *Nibelungenlied,* for to do so, as Quintilian reaches across the millennia to remind us, *aut nimiae miseriae aut inanis iactantiae est et detinet atque obruit ingenia melius aliis uacatura* (*Inst.*1.8.18–19). The literature on the *Nibelungenlied* is all but infinite,

called the national epic of the German people not just by anti-Napoleonic and Nazi propagandists, but by Germanists and non-Germans alike.[20] Helmut Brackert has cogently summarized the ideological reception of the *Nibelungenlied* as having passed through three phases. First, the period in which the poem was viewed as a symbol of a unified German nation in a time when that unity had not yet been achieved. Second, after the *Reichs-gründung,* it formed the central text of the newly established nation's national literature. The third period was that of the Nazi mythification of the Nibelungen and their pretense of restoring that allegedly pristine Teu-tonic realm. In all three phases there was a simplistic conception of Sieg-fried, Kriemhild, and Hagen as incarnations of the German spirit, which was constantly besieged by the forces of evil: dragons and Huns, and, in the Nazi construction, Jews and Communists. Brackert views the modern German reception as a single developmental unity: while the Nazi perspec-tive, culminating in the colossal insanity of Goering's tirade in the Sport-palast in Berlin in 1943, is extreme, it is no more than yet another, sequen-tial perversion of the text in the progression from national, to nationalistic, imperialistic, and racist interpretation.[21]

Even now general intellectual interest in the *Nibelungenlied* shows no sign of abating. In a recent ten-year period, nine book-length studies of the *Nibelungenlied* appeared in Germany and the United States.[22] This is re-

and like each such scholarly corpus, bludgeoningly repetitive and tendentious, especially concerning issues now more often than not relevant only for cultural historians and scholars of the reception itself.

20. Freidrich Heinrich von der Hagen was the first to call the *Nibelungenlied* "das deutsche Nationalepos," in *Der Nibelungen Lied in der Ursprache mit den Lesarten der ver-schiedenen Handschriften* (Berlin, 1810); von der Hagen's words may not be understood solely for their nationalistic import; they too have their own historical context: they were spoken in a rabid anti-imperialistic (anti-Napoleonic) cause; see Ehrismann, *Das Nibelungenlied in Deutschland,* p. 73. In the midst of the insanities of National Socialism in 1942, however, Friedrich Naumann expressed doubts about the appropriateness of the *Nibelungenlied* as national epic: "angesichts der überreichen Todesernte dieser Dichtung, die mit einem hoff-nungslosen Massentode alles germanischen Kriegsvolkes endet, . . . erwacht doch wohl unser Widerspruch. . . . [K]ann solches Übermaß von tragischem Untergang unseres adeligsten Blutes wirklich ein deutsches Nationalepos bilden?" ("in view of the abundant death-harvest of this poem, which ends with the hopeless mass death of the entire Germanic military, . . . our opposition cannot but be awakened. . . . Can such an excess in the tragic destruction of our most noble blood really be a German national epic?") in "Das Nibelungenlied—eine stau-fische Elegie oder ein deutsches Nationalepos? *Dichtung und Volkstum* 42 (1942), 54. The slaughter at Stalingrad was set to begin by the time Naumann's article was in print.

21. Helmut Brackert, "Nibelungenlied und Nationalgedanke. Zur Geschichte einer deutschen Ideologie," in *Mediævalia litteraria, Festschrift für Helmut de Boor zum 80. Geburtstag,* ed. Ursula Hennig and Herbert Kolb (München: Beck, 1971), pp. 361–364.

22. In alphabetical order, Theodore M. Andersson, *A Preface to the Nibelungenlied*; Otfrid Ehrismann, *'Nibelungenlied': Epoche-Werk-Wirkung*; Peter Göhler, *Das Nibelungenlied:*

markable enough, considering that the language and genre of the text alone require appreciable study even for the well-educated, modern English- and German-reading elite that largely form the audience, and that several years of effort are also needed to survey the main peaks of the scholarship. Although the *Nibelungenlied* is primarily of interest to a select group of elite scholars engaging in esoteric research, none of the recent books is a scholarly monograph, addressed primarily to professional colleagues. Instead they all participate to a greater or lesser degree in the recurring attempt to "popularize" the Nibelungen legend, for they take as their task the introduction of the *Nibelungenlied* to a student audience (at the U.S. undergraduate or German pre-Staatsexamen level) that has little acquaintance with literary analysis, medieval culture, and heroic epics. Why this sudden explosion of undergraduate introductions? To answer that the Middle Ages are fashionable is merely to propagate a recurring and eternally false rumor, usually voiced by medievalists in the throes of relevancy crises.[23]

It may be that the *Nibelungenlied* (or should we say, its reception) is itself undergoing a relevancy crisis, perhaps also an identity crisis. Other traditional bastions of medieval studies and philology fall about our (by training) positivistic medievalist ears before the triumphant onslaught of "theory," which has now penetrated close enough even to our disciplinary outback that its existence can no longer be denied. Thus the appearance of several of the texts in this group may well be considered the rearguard, attempting to prevent the erosion of the neo-romantic philologist's territory in which the *Nibelungenlied* resides by once again reviewing the traditional *communis opinio* about this text as disciplinary citadel. Lachmann's *Liedertheorie,* Heusler's *Aufschwellungstheorie,* the *ältere Nôt,* the *Meiri*-construction are all reviewed once more, for the sake of educating a new generation of students, who in almost no cases assume that literary criticism has anything to do with source reconstruction, and not all of

---

Erzählweise, Figuren, Weltanschauung, literaturgeschichtliches Umfeld (Berlin: Akademie-Verlag, 1989); Edward R. Haymes, *The Nibelungenlied: History and Interpretation* (Urbana: University of Illinois Press, 1986); Joachim Heinzle, *Das Nibelungenlied: Eine Einführung,* Artemis Einführungen 35 (München: Artemis, 1987); Winder McConnell, *The Nibelungenlied*; Lutz Mackensen, *Die Nibelungen: Sage, Geschichte, ihr Lied und sein Dichter,* Schriften zur Literatur- und Geistesgeschichte 1 (Stuttgart: Ernst Hauswedell, 1984); Walter Seitter, *Das politische Wissen im Nibelungenlied*; Walter Seitter, *Versprechen, Versagen: Frauenmacht und Frauenästhetik in der Krimhild-Diskussion des 13. Jahrhunderts.* Three doctoral theses also appeared in dissertation presses during these years, but for obvious reasons I disregard them on this present point; see, in the bibliography, Hilde E. Hansen, Ellen Bender, and Bernhard Burger.

23. Or perhaps German, French, or British (etc.) city councils suffering a declining tourist influx.

whom simply assume that a New Critical close-reading is the unmarked "natural" form of literary criticism, unencumbered by what their professors might think unnecessary and intrusive theory. After all, even some beginning students are clever enough to realize that a denial of theory is itself a theoretical position. At any rate, the result is that some undergraduates, and more commonly still, graduate students, despite — in the United States, at least — the profession's best efforts to prevent it, are beginning to view medieval texts through post-structuralist (marxist, feminist, semiotic, and narratological) eyes.[24]

Of course inquiries of such kinds have been appearing for two decades in medieval French studies, thanks to Zumthor, Le Goff, Kristeva, Köhler, Vinaver, Vance, and Jauß, and to a far lesser but still significant extent in medieval English studies. Even in German studies there were some early critical stirrings generally, and there has already been theoretically sophisticated work appearing for some few decades on courtly romance, lyric, literary patronage, and the cultural implications of literacy, especially, from the pens of Joachim Bumke, Günther Schweikle, Helmut Brackert, Franz Bäuml, and more recently from Peter Czerwinski and James Schultz. But the *Nibelungenlied* itself has thus far avoided a prolonged and direct attack of the very exacting post-philologists.[25]

For four of these books, however, such a characterization is not quite accurate. The two volumes by Viennese psychoanalyst Walter Seitter comprise an entertaining series of lectures delivered over the course of several years by a non-Germanist who knows his Lacan and Foucault well and delights in giving an irreverent Barthesian twist to his attempts to draw connections between the *Nibelungenlied* and contemporary popular and learned culture. To declare his often insightful, sometimes precious views

24. Structuralism itself seems to have been pretty much passed over in silence, for the New Criticism in the United States, the "werkimmanente" method (in some ways the corresponding form of New Criticism) and an utterly depoliticized (and thus thoroughly political) post-war "Geistesgeschichte" in the German-speaking countries so dominated the possibilities of critical response, that with some few exceptions the brief fashion of structuralism outside of France passed before it could penetrate to, much less breach, the disciplinary walls of medieval Germanic studies.

25. Although Brackert's work on the *Nibelungenlied,* one example of which was noted above, indicates the socio-literary ramifications of some research into *Rezeptionsgeschichte*. He counsels, for instance: "Der Älteren Germanistik im besonderen ist aufgegeben, sich zum mittelalterlichen Werk 'theoretischer' als bisher zu verhalten und das fälschlich Vertraute wiederzuentdecken als das uns ganz fremde Bewußtsein" ("it is the especial task of medieval German studies to approach the medieval work 'more theoretically' than heretofore, and to rediscover the deceptively familiar as the consciousness that is completely foreign to us"), "Nibelungenlied und Nationalgedanke," p. 364.

"non-philological" and thus irrelevant to Germanistic research is — in this revisionist age — almost to condemn one's own research to irrelevancy. On the other hand, Otfrid Ehrismann's and Theodore Andersson's books are well within the bounds of literary, and even more narrowly philological work, and specifically from a Germanistic perspective; both are introductions to be sure, but are challenging ones for beginners. While Andersson's scholarly research has concentrated for some time on that most traditional of philological issues — source study and reconstruction — and such topics also dominate in this book, there are recurring glimpses of concrete political commitments that are anything but conservative, particularly with respect to gender politics. Ehrismann is here more obviously than most of the others concerned to introduce the *Nibelungenlied,* but also devotes some attention to the topic for which he is best known: the reception, medieval and modern, of the *Nibelungenlied,* the constitution of the text through reading, text production and distribution, revision through the manuscript traditions, the deformations by modern critical ideologies, and so on.

Which brings me back to my own project, for it too necessarily affords great significance to the notion that a literary text is constituted less by any fictions of its own ontological identity than by the latent contents and contexts that render its productions and interpretations possible. One of those contexts is obviously the historical late twelfth and early thirteenth centuries, the period in which the various versions of the *Nibelungenlied* were written (down). Whatever significance there is in the previous literary and pre-literary stages of this text (and I doubt that there is very much *recoverable* significance, except insofar as it derives from the romantico-patriarchal obsession with them as origins and progenitors), it is only their [re]constituted form that has survived. Almost all questions about such pre-literary topics are ultimately irrelevant, because we cannot now and, barring discovery of a written record of one of these alleged poems, will never know the answers. Genetic criticism is necessarily "modern," for it recreates or simply creates the potential nineteenth- and twentieth-century horizon of expectations, for only we, and not the twelfth- or thirteenth-century authors and audiences, have access to some restricted body of sources and analogues of a work. These are irrelevant to later medieval writers and audiences, since unknown to them; in any case no knowledge of sources was a necessary pre-condition of the comprehension of the narrative. The *Nibelungenlied* as it appears in the manuscript traditions is — let it be reiterated into the now abating storm of source-searching denials — a work of literature, and neither a learned nor popular commentary on earlier legendary material, although some such material was known certainly by the author and *probably* also by *some* part of the audience in *some* form.[26] Whatever that form was, it almost certainly was not the (albeit occasionally entertaining) concoctions composed qua "reconstructed" by nineteenth- and twentieth-century philology, nor would it matter to us if it had been, for whatever the snatches of fourth-century historical "fact," whatever reminiscences of sixth-century Franconian heroic lays, whatever "quotations" from eighth-century *Burgundenlieder,* the thirteenth-century audience of (mostly) illiterate court personnel knew — and there was little that they could have known in these forms — the fact is, the audience of the *Nibelungenlied* could have identified such "sources," as they appear in the *Nibelungenlied,* no more accurately than we can, that is, providing that we could get them to understand such notions of source and originality in the first place. The Siegfried of the *Nibelungenlied* was no fourth-century Teutonic hero, its Gunther no Merovingian Gundharius, its Brünhild no mythical prehistoric valkyrie, its Etzel no Asian warlord. They are rather all literary characters in a swashbuckling (early) thirteenth-century tale of "long ago and [usually] far away"; they are all thirteenth-century characters and their situations are thirteenth-century situations or they are at least recreated as characters in a work of historical fiction from a thirteenth-century narrative perspective. Similarly, the *Nibelungenlied* itself is not to be viewed in the context of the *Völkerwanderung,* real or imagined, but rather as the general cultural contemporary of Bernard Silvester, Peter Abelard, John of Salisbury's *Policraticus,* Hildegard of Bingen, Wolfram's *Parzival,* and the early scholastic work on the Greek texts of Aristotle. Often this seems to have

---

26. Schweikle shrewdly notes: "Einem mittelalterlichen Hörer oder Leser konnte lediglich der gegebene Erzählzusammenhang gegenwärtig sein nicht der genetische Aspekt" ("a medieval hearer or reader could only have been aware of the given narrative context, not the genetic aspect," p. 74). See also Ihlenburg, who points out (*Das Nibelungenlied,* p. 30) that already in the 1920s there were two scholars who insisted on the strict limitations on the value of *Sagengeschichte* for scholarly work on the *Nibelungenlied:* Josef Körner, *Das Nibelungenlied* (Leipzig: Teubner, 1921) and Ernest Tonnelat's *La chanson des Nibelungen,* noted above. Heinz Rupp makes what would seem a matter-of-fact comment: "Die Dichter des 13. Jahrhunderts sehen mit ihren Augen" ("the poets of the thirteenth century see with their own eyes") and "Von den Germanen und vom Germanentum haben sie sicher weniger gewußt als wir, wahrscheinlich gar nichts" ("they [poets of High Middle Ages] certainly knew less about Teutons and things Germanic than we, probably nothing at all"); both citations from "'Heldendichtung' als Gattung der deutschen Literatur des 13. Jahrhunderts," p. 15. Such opposition has not abated. See, even among scholars of the center, Karl Stackmann's skepticism: "Das einzige, was wir ohne die Zuhilfenahme gewagter Hypothesen miteinander vergleichen können, sind die tatsächlich uberlieferten Fassungen der Sage" (*Kudrun,* 5th ed. [Wiesbaden: Brockhaus, 1980], p. lxxii), and even Werner Hoffmann's guarded caution (*Kudrun: Ein Beitrag zur Deutung der Nachnibelungischen Heldendichtung,* pp. vii, 3).

been forgotten by conventional scholarship, which treats the *Nibelungenlied* as if its cultural context were that of pre-literate, iron-age nomads.

The social and intellectual contexts that enable such historically informed and uninformed interpretations are themselves also relevant. In working through the research literature on any text about which we publish, we necessarily grapple with the scholarly opinions of others, and commonly we do so in print. Obviously, other levels or strands of analysis also inform our reading of any text, for interpretations, as Lévi-Strauss has taught us à propos Oedipus and Freud,[27] are also part and parcel of an informed reading of the text, are "versions" of the tale. Heusler and Andersson, Schröder and Weber, Beyschlag, Bäuml, and Bekker are not exactly "texts" of the *Nibelungenlied* (there we already have enough trouble with the manuscripts!), but certainly they are "versions" in this sense, and they are in general relevant texts in the sense of "post-texts." This term is Mieke Bal's, turned to brilliant use in her analysis of aspects of imposed coherence in the book of Judges, where she establishes a set of narratological categories that nonetheless have great relevance for other types of analysis as well. She designates a *post-text* "any rewriting of a previous text which is always a reading, be it a commentary or a different version of the text"; an *ante-text* "refers to a prior text which resonates in the text under scrutiny"; a *pre-text* refers to the "sociohistorical reality on which a given text plays"; while an *architexte* (a term she borrows from Gerard Genette) is the "generic type underlying a given text." *Intertext* "is the general term which encompasses the others . . . ; *intertextuality* is used for any type of relations between a text and any of its post-, ante-, pre-, or archi-texts."[28] In an analysis of the *Nibelungenlied* and its ideological and literary environs, all such terms are useful, insofar as they differentiate types of textual relationships in the morass of manuscript versions, contemporary and quasi-contemporary reception, adaptation, and scholarly response. As post-texts would be included later versions and interpretations of the tale, such as *Diu Klage, Kudrun,* and Lachmann. When I reread in *aventiure* 7 of Siegfried's pretending to be Gunther's vassal, I do so according to, in opposition to, or somehow otherwise in relation to Beyschlag. When I read of Wate claiming to be the Hegelings' treasurer just before he "pays" Gerlint by murdering

27. "L'étude structurale des mythes," in *Anthropologie structurale* (Paris: Plon, 1958), often reprinted.

28. See Mieke Bal's summary of these terms and her use of this principle in *Death and Dissymmetry: The Politics of Coherence in the Book of Judges* (Chicago: University of Chicago Press, 1988), p. 254, n. 1.

her, one of the guiding ante-texts is the calculated disempowerment of Brünhild by Gunther's vassals in their emptying of her treasury. Likewise Maurer and Schröder are ever-present whenever a representative lexeme of the semantic field *leit* appears. As ante-texts I would include not so much the alleged, non-extant source texts of the *Nibelungenlied*, as I would, for instance, the *Spielmannsepen* of the twelfth century with which the *Nibelungenlied* shares so many motifs, which, since they are employed in such radically different ways in the *Nibelungenlied*, are recurringly foregrounded. The pre-text of the *Nibelungenlied* figures greatly in my analysis, since I seek to establish a connection, however delicate (not to say tenuous), between the social contradictions depicted in the text and the contemporaneous social preconditions of the feudal social formation both enabling and re-fracted by those mediated literary representations. Finally, the problem of archi-text with respect to the *Nibelungenlied* is an ongoing concern, especially if any part of my thesis is accepted as legitimate; if the "heroes" of the text are Brünhild and Kriemhild, and one of the main topics problematized is gender relations as reflected in the impossibility of this feudal society to cope with women except as either (passive) chattels or deviants, then one would be hard put still to retain the text in the genre of heroic epic as traditionally defined.[29]

At any rate, in identifying the scholarly literature as post-texts, I simply admit the necessary intertextuality that obtains among the *Nibelungenlied*, other interpretations, and my own. Not surprisingly, my own analysis of the *Nibelungenlied* sometimes seems to consist in as large a part of attention to critical texts as to the *Nibelungenlied* per se, for I view this "*Nibelungenlied per se*" as only an *ad hoc* construct necessarily to be placed under derridean *rature*.[30] Even so, I make no attempt to respond to that body of work on *all* issues having to do with the female characters of the *Nibelungenlied*, primarily because so very little of traditional philological scholarship addresses

29. Moreover, as Franz Bäuml has pointed out (private communication), heroic epic is necessarily pre-literary; as soon as it is written down, it becomes something else again, perhaps "pseudo-heroic epic," as he terms it.

30. Cf. also Jameson (*The Political Unconscious,* pp. 9–10):

We never really confront a text immediately, in all its freshness as a thing-in-itself. Rather, texts come before us as the always-already-read; we apprehend them through sedimented layers of previous interpretations, or — if the text is brand-new — through the sedimented reading habits and categories developed by those inherited interpretive traditions. This presupposition then dictates the use of a method (which I have else-where termed the "metacommentary") according to which our object of study is less the text itself than the interpretation through which we attempt to confront and appropriate it.

the issues I choose to focus on here. As a result, most of the scholarly work treated at any length in the following essays appeared in the relatively recent decades when issues of gender had begun to surface, even if not yet so named; and much of that scholarship is in English not German, for the simple reason that institutionalized scholarship in German-speaking Europe is still primarily a product of university systems which remain the patriarchal citadels of male privilege. Not surprisingly, *relatively* little scholarship on topics of gender relations has been encouraged at any level from *Seminarreferat* to *Habilitationsschrift,* especially in the generally archconservative field of medieval studies.[31] A decade ago, Sigrid Bauschinger and Wolfgang Paulsen, in their individual introductory remarks to the proceedings of an Amherst colloquium on German women's literature, both commented on the distinct and distinctive isolation of German culture from both a tradition of women's literature and a tradition of successful feminist political action.[32] Paulsen further notes, that based on the concrete experience of the women's movement and its relative successes in North America, as opposed to Germany, up to that time, Germanists who had spent time in North America could analyze, reveal, and use methodological approaches still hidden to their German colleagues, but likely someday to be seriously discussed by them as well. While Paulsen's philo-U.S. interpretation of the situation was more accurate in 1979 than it is today, only in very recent years, outside of Amerikanistik, has German-speaking Europe begun to recognize the legitimacy of feminist studies. Still there is little effective *institutional* support for its existence.[33] In any case it is neither because of cultural or linguistic prejudice nor from any pretended Anglophone superiority in things feminist that I cite as much from the smaller body of scholarship in English as I do from the vast corpus of German scholarship

31. Nonetheless, one must recognize that in western Germany in the years immediately preceding the "Wende" there was great progress made in securing at least the institutional mechanisms that may eventually aid in attaining more equitable gender relations in the industries of higher education and research: hiring, retaining, and promoting female academics, examination practices, and so on. This at the same time that enormous ground was lost in the United States and Great Britain during the Reagan-Bush-Thatcher era of the eroding, frontal assault on, and outright dismantling of women's and minority rights.

32. Bauschinger, "Weitere Perspektive," pp. 11–13 and Paulsen, "Vorbemerkung," pp. 7–10, in *Die Frau als Heldin und Autorin. Neue kritische Ansätze zur deutschen Literatur,* ed. Wolfgang Paulsen (Bern: Francke, 1979).

33. But there are in Germany, as elsewhere, dedicated and tenacious feminists holding together study and research programs whether with generous, miserly, or no institutional support, for instance, in Berlin, the Zentraleinrichtung zur Förderung von Frauenstudien und Frauenforschung of the Freie Universität and the rather smaller unit for Interdisziplinäre Frauenforschung in the Fachbereich Kulturwissenschaft at the Humboldt-Universität.

on the *Nibelungenlied*, but rather simply because in this case there is (still) more of relevance to cite.[34]

One of the reasons, probably the main reason, that *Nibelungenlied* scholarship has focused for such a long time on the two problems that have dominated it — posited sources and narrowly conceived character analysis — is the presence in both the text and its interpretive context of bedrock patriarchal ideology and thus of almost insurmountable intellectual obstacles to overcoming the disciplinary conventions of what constitutes scholarship in the field. "Logocentrism" and "phallogocentrism," the brilliant poststructuralist coinages for the privileging of the *logos* — the explanatory word, the singular and authoritative voice, the *auctor* and *faber* and *pater*, the male and thus phallic progenitor of meaning — define the philological project as it developed in the late eighteenth and early nineteenth centuries out of the traditionally philological study of Greek and Latin into the fledgling university-level study of the vernacular literatures. The first steps after the rediscovery of the manuscripts of the *Edda*(s) and the *Chanson de Roland*, *Beowulf* and the *Hildebrandslied*, *Sir Gawain* and the *Nibelungenlied*, were to decode, describe, and become master of the language(s) of the texts, and thus appropriate and control the alterity of the texts by making them one's own. In the absence of the scholarly tradition (already in or of two millennia that classicists already had available, vernacular philology's initial task was of a "lower" order: the explication at the level of morpheme, lexeme, and basic syntax (although actually few of the works even of the master philologists, the Neogrammarians, dealt with syntax), and codification of these rules in grammar and lexicon. This is the absolute realm of the *logos*.

It was an academic realm in which the logos ruled and with few exceptions still rules; one's scholarly worth as a medievalist is (for instance, and primarily) measured in the length and girth of one's (e.g., Latin, Greek, Gothic, Norse, Old English, Old High German) vocabulary and ability to cite on the spot and verbatim from the canonical texts. It is, as the

34. Having said as much, it is immediately necessary to note the committed, informed and important multi-disciplinary work accomplished by and documented in the journal *Feministische Studien* for more than a decade now. In general it is necessary to bear in mind, first, that the drastic increase in recent years of published studies on "women's issues" does not always signal *feminist* work as such; and, second, even when such work is feminist, that in itself is not necessarily an indication of any correspondence between the scholar's research interests and her or his institutional field of employment and/or teaching. Finally, one should recall that the two most nearly feminist analyses of the *Nibelungenlied* (see below) — Lösel-Wieland-Engelmann's first article and Schweikle's essay — were both published in German. Cf. also the excellent volume: *Der frauwen buoch: Versuch zu einer feministischen Mediävistik,* ed. Ingrid Bennewitz (Göppingen: Kümmerle, 1989), in which, characteristically, only one of the dozen-and-a-half essays deals with "heroic epic."

implied metaphor of the previous sentence intimates, a masculist realm and most often still a masculine one. The hallowed traditions of philological scholarship, passed down from generation to generation, from *Doktorvater* to *Doktorsohn,* sometimes find themselves mirrored not just in the genealogical methods of philological scholarship, but also in its means: in some such cases many of the publications of the Professor derive from the research, often even the pen, of the generations of students, research assistants, "Hiwis," doctoral candidates, and *Assistenten* that pass through his [and in the rare case also, her] seminars.

The vernacular philological project was/is to uncover a stage of the cultural past, a verifiable, concrete, empirically accessible "historical reality." But, as the recent work by Martin Bernal on the Egyptian and Semitic origins of ancient Greek culture — and the racist project of classical philology during the last two centuries to deny such origins — has again reminded us, positivistic philology as practiced in modern Europe has always been less engaged in reconstructing the cultural past than in constructing it according to its own cultural and aesthetic prescriptions and prejudices.[35] Thus, in a fashion not at all unlike the similar project of classics in nineteenth-century England, France, and Germany, though certainly with

35. Martin Bernal, *Black Athena: The Afro-Asiatic Roots of Classical Civilization,* Vol. 1: *The Fabrication of Ancient Greece, 1785–1985* (New Brunswick, NJ: Rutgers University Press, 1987). Bernal's thesis, as expressed in this first of (now) four projected volumes, is, as he takes pains to document, not brilliantly new and original, but rather a recurring one in and on the margins of classical studies, and one that has been recurringly denied, mocked, or simply ignored by mainstream classicists. That which sets Bernal's project and its success apart from his iconoclastic predecessors is, however, not simply the fact that his book was published during a period of radical debunking of the intellectual results of political ideologies in many fields, but also, necessarily, his meticulous research, stunning command of the requisite languages, and clear and engaging style. See further the papers from a section of the APA conference devoted to the "Bernal thesis," published in a recent special issue of *Arethusa: The Challenge of Black Athena,* Special Issue of *Arethusa* (Fall 1989), guest ed. M. M. Levine. Cf. also Jonathan Culler's remarks in a recent issue of *Comparative Literature Studies* devoted to the topic of "Philology":

> A fourth example might be the question of how far the construction of philology as a scientific discipline in the late eighteenth and early nineteenth century was complicitous with or was based on the invention of an Aryan Greece that would serve as origin for modern cultures in northern Europe. The invention of that Greece involves the rejection or elimination of the idea of Greece's dependence on Semitic cultures and on Egypt in particular. This is another case in which one could argue that the supposedly foundational enterprise of philology is in fact dependent on cultural and aesthetic constructions. Clearly it seemed much more satisfying to European cultures to have Greek rather than Egyptian origins" ("Anti-Foundational Philology," in *What is Philology,* ed. Jan Ziolkowski, Special Focus Issue of *Comparative Literature Studies* 27 [1990], 51; also published as a separate volume).

Curiously, Culler does not acknowledge Bernal's essential role in instigating the recent discussion of this issue.

much greater intensity, the interest in the vernacular cultural tradition is obviously and necessarily also a familial, genealogical, and ultimately also ideological one: to recover not just a past cultural period, but indeed the earlier historically documented period of one's own culture and thus one's cultural ancestors, as one might wish that culture to have been. It is in a great many ways a search for the lost father, for the originator of the "race" as both the early Anglo-Saxon chroniclers and the Romantics a millennium later did in fact recurringly express it. That this project has unselfconsciously and unashamedly continued without effective methodological and ideological reform for a century and a half has at various points along the way aroused protests and in recent decades has made the mere name of philology itself a term of opprobrium.[36]

One of the parallel effects (certainly not coincidences) arising from the same historical causes as did the larger philological project is that the scholar's ultimate task is defined exclusively as the identification and description of the author's intention in composing the given text. The scholar, is thus charged with providing the often anonymous, historically decontextualized, orphaned 800- or 1000-year-old text with an origin, an intention, a creator, an author and father. The "purpose" would then be assured, for all fathers, it is presumed (by patriarchy), create their offspring, literary and otherwise, for the purpose of reproducing themselves, in the flesh and in intent. In some cases this task of identifying and biographically describing the author was a relatively easy empirical chore. A great deal of biographical information about some few medieval authors exists external to their literary works. But relatively few facts are ascertainable concerning, for instance, Chaucer's life. Wolfram von Eschenbach exists only as a name mentioned in *Parzival* as the alleged author of the text. The biography of Heloise exists only as "reconstructed" out of the largely fictional realm of the *epistulae*.[37] At the extreme the authors of many works, including the *Nibelungenlied*, are named neither in the text nor elsewhere, and no further information casts any direct light on the task of identifying them. This situation is then by necessity utterly unlike scholarship on Dante's *Commedia*, for instance,

---

36. See especially the proceedings of the conference just noted: "What is Philology," *Comparative Literature Studies* 27 (1990), ed. Jan Ziolkowski. It is, however, also necessary to remember, as Margaret Alexiou obliquely indicates in one of the epigrams to this study: that it is also still generally from these early philologists that we (medievalists, too) learn the languages of our trade — their grammars, dictionaries, editions, *Handbücher*, and so on — that form the foundations (however in need of revision and modification some of them are) of our ability to read the source documents in our fields.

37. On this lengthy and convoluted controversy, see esp. Peter von Moos, *Mittelalterforschung und Ideologiekritik* (Munich: Fink, 1974).

which scholars of the text often colloquially term "Dante," or even scholarship on *Parzival,* since in each an author is named, albeit a two-dimensional one. In each case the *sign* of the father is present, and thus the text is not technically an orphan. Even if the father is only a name, it is after all the name that is important in cases of genealogy; the personality of the long-dead ancestor may or may not be interesting, but is in any case far less significant. For it is the name that fills in the missing link between the revered Tradition and the text, between the supposed creative demiurge and the reader. The creative process is now identified and named and thus, in at least one important patriarchal sense, claimed, controlled, and owned.[38] This identification of the author's name alone may spawn scores of publications: lists of twelfth- and thirteenth-century Wolframs, for instance, not only from all extant Eschenbach*s* but from just about any- and everywhere else. Dante Alighieri is sought in all conceivable forms of documentation throughout the length and breadth of his era for a yield of a handful of meager references, all dwarfed by the literary reputation that exploded within a generation of his death (by which time, alas, the textual tradition of the *Commedia* was already hopelessly complicated).

Thus until the author is named there is a search for the father. If the author cannot be named, the father never identified, other relatives are sought — brothers, mothers, cousins, grandparents, eventually even great-grandparents and their offspring. If the author is unknown and will necessary remain so, then the significance of that gap must obviously be reduced by substituting other genealogical data. In the case of the phallogocentric treatment of medieval texts, this means, among other tasks, that quasi-sources and analogues must be found. And if they cannot actually be found, then their identity and nature must be surmised, must be speculated upon, must be invented, for no branches of the genealogical tree may be left empty if they can possibly be populated.[39]

This is especially problematic if the text-orphan happens to be more highly valued than any other like entity, or even considered the progenitor of oneself — the cultural ancestor, the foundation, or one of the foundation

38. All this without regard to the distinction between author and narrator, and with no thought of the possibility that the name itself may be a fiction, which without question it is, if the name in question is the name of the *narrator,* for instance the allegedly illiterate and non-francophone "Wolfram" of *Parzival,* no matter whether there ever was an actual, historical Wolfram von Eschenbach.

39. There is perhaps no better example of this method in the field of medieval Germanic studies than the scholarship on the *Ackermann aus Böhmen,* which refuses to abandon its invention of a young dead wife for the author, despite all the evidence against the likelihood of this biographical identity with the situation of the text's narrator.

stones of the culture — as the genre of "national epic" is generally conceived by those who concern themselves with such matters. Then the urge is stronger still to find the father. The anonymous *Nibelungenlied,* as German "national epic," has not surprisingly been the subject of myriad publications that have sought this cultural father and patriarch of the national culture and the nation itself.

Such a textual patriarch of the national culture is defective insofar as it provides the point of cultural origin while lacking an identifiable progenitor of its own, and it is thus conceivably illegitimate. It is then no wonder that this patriarchal text is compensatorily viewed, conceived, and constituted by its descendants as necessarily more authoritative, more definitive of the culture, more unitary, more virile, more heroic, than would be the case otherwise. It is then no wonder that in the process of so conceiving this patriarchal text that +*masculine* features are accentuated and −*masculine* features deemphasized if they cannot be eliminated altogether. It is no wonder that the situations, problems and possibilities of two of the four main characters of the *Nibelungenlied* are all but ignored by scholars except insofar as it is recurringly necessary to note and briefly explain why they are not positive figures, not heroic, not representative of the culture in general, but rather simply "typically" weak, unstable, vacillating, childish, destructive criminal females, despite the frequent admission that they are, enigmatically, also the main characters of the national epic. Thus Brünhild and Kriemhild have received a great deal of scholarly attention in the last century and a half, but most of it has focused on the "typicality" of their femaleness, and almost none of it on *their* narrative-social situations, their problems and possibilities for action. It has rather viewed them merely as foils for or caricatures, inversions, or perversions of their male counterparts.[40]

Significantly, a rather different reception-historical (*rezeptionsgeschichtliche*) perspective was displayed by the contemporaries of the *Nibelungenlied* (and those of the immediately succeeding generations), who in their post-texts accepted the possibility that the text was, quite simply, *about* gender relations. The *Nibelungenlied* survives in three manuscript tradi-

---

40. Cf. for example the astute comment by Günther Schweikle: "Kriemhild bildet zwar im Geschehnisablauf eine zentrale Figur, aber in ihrer Eigenschaft als Frau wird sie ganz aus der Perspektive eines männlich-heldischen Ethos betrachtet, in dessen 'ordo' der Frau nur ein nachgeordneter Platz zukommt — wie in der früh- und hochmittelalterlichen sozialen Realität ("Kriemhild is a central figure in the course of the narrative, but in the fact that she is a woman, she is viewed fully from the perspective of a male-heroic *ethos,* in which *ordo* a women was necessarily subordinate — as was also the case in the social reality of the early and high Middle Ages,") Schweikle, "Das 'Nibelungenlied,'" pp. 72–73).

tions, which differ significantly in the texts they present. Recent textual research has finally abandoned the attempt to determine which is the "authentic" *Nibelungenlied* and advocates that, rather than continuing the tradition of publishing more or less conflated texts that could never have existed in the Middle Ages, it be admitted that in essence there exist at least two *Nibelungenlieder*.[41] Compared with both the A- and the B-texts, the C-text is a staunch advocate of the legitimacy of Kriemhild's actions.[42] In addition, *Diu Klage*, probably written within a few decades of the composition of the *Nibelungenlied*, and appended to all significant surviving manuscripts, is single-mindedly polemical in its defense of Kriemhild's motives and actions and its condemnation of Hagen. The evidence of the *Kudrun*, while its ideological argument opposes the *Nibelungenlied* and *Diu Klage*, provides further powerful evidence of precisely the same contemporary interest in the gender issues articulated by the *Nibelungenlied*. If nothing else, the C-text, *Diu Klage*, and the *Kudrun* indicate that gender relations were immediately recognized as one of the most pressing issues treated in the *Nibelungenlied* and that discussion of precisely this type of problem, although not quite in these terms, was most likely widespread among those who engaged in literary discussions of these texts seven centuries ago. The reception of the text by its author's contemporaries, as opaquely visible in the post-texts of the manuscript revisions and ancillary texts, obviously does not constitute the authoritative reading of the *Nibelungenlied*, but it is especially significant given the astounding feats of intellectual sleight of hand performed by modern scholarship in order to ignore the clear evidence that gender issues were relevant for both the author and the initial audience of the *Nibelungenlied*.

For this reason alone, it is time to extend — from a less exclusively masculist perspective than scholarship on the texts has generally offered and in a cultural setting more conducive to such discourse — the thirteenth-century examination of women's roles in the mediated literary form of

41. See especially Helmut Brackert, *Beiträge zur Handschriftenkritik des Nibelungenliedes*, Quellen und Forschungen, n.s. 135 (Berlin: Schmidt, 1963).

42. Despite this fact, or rather ultimately because of it, I base my argument on and cite primarily the edition now considered the "standard," the Bartsch-de Boor-Wisniewski conflation, primarily based on the B-text, since it is the text on which most recent scholarship has based its interpretations, misogynistic and otherwise. And thus it is with that text and scholarly tradition that my thesis must contend. In the end, if my case can be made on the basis if the B-text, then its relevance for the C-text is all but assured. For the sake of comparison, however, corresponding passages from the C-text that parallel, contrast with or seem otherwise particularly significant for the given passage from the B-text under consideration will be cited in the notes.

feudal society as worked out in the *Nibelungenlied,* the almost myopic defense of women's independent actions as argued by *Diu Klage,* and the systematic transmutation of these issues and their relevant fields of application by the *Kudrun.* It is of course not the case that the *Nibelungenlied* has not been viewed as explosively gender-oriented in the centuries since the C-text, *Diu Klage* and the *Kudrun;* nor have direct and immediate feminist responses been lacking, at least in recent years. For the feminist perspective is precisely the one adopted by many first readers — almost automatically — in many university classrooms in which the text is currently discussed, perhaps precisely because these readers are not yet indoctrinated into the specific method of phallogocentrism at the core of professional study of such quintessentially "philological" texts, but certainly also because such a response has in recent decades been granted at least some measure of legitimacy by mainstream literary scholarship.

Some scholars too have already published the fruits of their research on problems of gender in the *Nibelungenlied.* The first and, as a cultural phenomenon, most interesting, were the articles by Berta Lösel-Wieland-Engelmann, then a clerical assistant whose typing of faculty lecture notes brought her into contact with the *Nibelungenlied,* to be followed by reading the text itself and then a (tentative) assertion of the issues in them.[43] This extra-scholarly, rabidly anti-intellectual, and almost apologetically proto-feminist interpretation of the text and her struggle to publish that interpretation make for an interesting and in some senses courageous narrative in itself: as a doubly determined outsider (female and uncredentialed reader/writer), her iconoclastic reading was roundly ignored and mocked (and often still is) by insiders ([mostly] male academics). Her iconoclasm seems perhaps somewhat tame by contemporary standards, as manifested in her general thesis:

> If a person reads one thousand descriptions of the contents of the NL, none will stress what I have stressed, i.e., the wrongs inflicted on the two women. As a rule, those incidents are either treated as minor matters or even as comic interludes. The women's hatred and desire to strike back get treated as abnormal and as some strange and freakish aberrations. As the commentators see it, revenge is a "man's business," and women should suffer in silence whatever is

43. The first article, "Verdanken wir das *Nibelungenlied* einer Niedernburger Nonne?" *Monatshefte* 72 (1980), 5–25, was followed by a second that reported on the ontogeny of the first: "Feminist Repercussions of a Literary Research Project," *Atlantis: A Women's Studies Journal* 6 (1980), 84–90.

being done to them. This type of thinking leads the critics to condemnations of Kriemhild and Brunhild as being "inhuman" monsters.[44]

But tame or not, the general tenor of her interpretation and the perspective from which she views the problem is striking, pertinent, and, in the context of current critical studies, right on the mark. That few are convinced by her argument for female authorship of the *Nibelungenlied* is hardly surprising for several reasons, only the least important of which is that her provocative thesis is supported by little evidence, even of the "soft" kind commonly admitted by humanists. One wonders, however — given the hypothetical case — precisely what kind of evidence it might take to convince the rank and file *Altgermanist* that the author of the *Nibelungenlied* was female. I suspect, at a first reading, that little less would do than a newly discovered and duly authenticated signed autograph manuscript of the author. Even then, I expect it would take decades before this textual paternity/maternity case would be settled, most likely by female scholars and/or dissertation students, for the grand old men would have long since quietly abandoned the sinking ship without ever letting on that it had developed a leak. For to suggest, as Lösel-Wieland-Engelmann did, that a woman and a nun wrote the all but sacred *Nationalepos,* and that this fact had been undiscovered by 150 years of systematic [male] philological research, is tantamount to intellectual castration, and some of Lösel-Wieland-Engelmann's initial readers may have even felt twinges slightly lower down.[45] More threatening still is the circumstance of being told that the long-sought author and thus father of the text is a *mother,* and to be told by a woman who is not a professional academic, but rather a clerical employee of academe. Class prejudice here also raises its ugly head to tower over even gender bias; or does the one merely nod conspiratorily to its long-time cohort?

Ironically (or perhaps not), this first identifiably feminist project in

44. Lösel-Wieland-Engelmann, "Feminist Repercussions," 85–86. But even the problem of the (now) obvious claims of the developing arguments of feminism of only a few years ago is not without interest, for as Sheila Delaney points out: "My aim, therefore, is to problematise the obvious, which always seems less problematical than the obscure, but which — as Roland Barthes showed in *mythologies* and elsewhere — constitutes the ideology-laden language of a culture," in "Women, Nature and Language: Chaucer's *Legend of Good Women,*" p. 150.

45. She comments: "In addition they [scholars] do not cherish the idea that a poem which they always praised and venerated as a national monument could possibly be unveiled as nothing more than a well-disguised feminist manifesto which was intent on exposing men's injustice and meanness, stone-heartedness and greed, solidarity and conspiracies in their dealings with women" ("Feminist Repercussions," p. 90).

the modern reception of the *Nibelungenlied* advanced a thesis that is in *method* anything but revolutionary and feminist, for it still accepts the traditional definition of what constitutes legitimate research on the *Nibelungenlied* — the search for authorial identity — and simply proposes yet another candidate, based on the same kind of circumstantial evidence as all other such research is compelled to employ. Lösel-Wieland-Engelmann's feminist analysis belongs to the category of feminism in which the subject acts/reads almost exclusively through her own experience.[46] In general Lösel-Wieland-Engelmann's articles have been ridiculed in conversation and ignored in print.[47]

If Lösel-Wieland-Engelmann's articles were proto-feminist, then Günther Schweikle's politically-charged interpretation published a decade ago would best be labelled quasi-feminist.[48] Schweikle's essay is, I find, hardly less provocative than Lösel-Wieland-Engelmann's, for his point is to identify gender-relations as a central issue of the text. Viewed culturally, however, the situations of the two writers could hardly be more different, for Professor Schweikle is an insider, a (male) holder of one of the relatively few chairs of medieval German studies in Germany, and his article brings to bear all the tools of traditional scholarship. It appeared in the Festschrift for ### TT#####, #### ##### # ##### ########## ###### #### ####### ## conceived. Despite this external "conformity," his thesis is in context quite radical and as such it was not his first, nor has it been his last.

In the context of a survey of feminist inroads into *Nibelungenlied* scholarship, however, Schweikle's, like Lösel-Wieland-Engelmann's essay may be cited and commended only with caution and qualification. For while Lösel-Wieland-Engelmann emends and then simply continues the traditional scholarly paradigm, Schweikle, despite his topic and approach, makes no overt use of and no reference to the existence of feminism, whether political, literary, critical, or otherwise.[49] It hardly seems possible

46. Jonathan Culler's identification of this type of reading as the first developmental stage of feminist interpretation distorts and devalues important aspects of the entire recent history of feminist scholarship; see *On Deconstruction: Theory and Criticism After Structuralism* (Ithaca, NY: Cornell University Press, 1982), pp. 43–64.

47. Jean Fourquet's recent conference paper is an unfortunate exception: "Un *Nibelungenlied* féministe: la *Lied*fassung," in *La Chanson des Nibelungen hier et aujourd'hui: Actes du Colloque Amiens 12–13 janvier 1991*, ed. Danielle Buschinger and Wolfgang Spiewok (Amiens: Centre d'Études Médiévales Université de Picardie, 1991), pp. 71–79.

48. Günther Schweikle, "Das 'Nibelungenlied'," pp. 59–84.

49. Interestingly, he also does not cite either of Lösel-Wieland-Engelmann's essays, although, since they appeared in 1980 and his article was published in 1981, it is probable that his essay was in press before he could have seen hers.

that he was unaware of the existence of the already significant body of theoretical and practical research by feminist scholars in a dozen fields. Is this simply another example of the age-old male ploy of appropriating, naturalizing, and thus defusing a potentially subversive female act?[50] Even if it is *possible* to write a (quasi-)feminist essay on a given text without citing basic and relevant feminist scholarship, it is certainly not legitimate to do so, in fact no more legitimate than it would be to publish any scholarly article, whether on the *Nibelungenlied* or *King Lear* or the Cambrian on- togeny, without somehow confronting or at the very least acknowledging the existence of previous relevant research. And in fact Schweikle does cite the requisite work in *traditional philological scholarship* on the *Nibelungenlied*. Significantly, had he *not* cited such literature, his essay would not have commanded much respect and would not have been deemed "scholarly" by traditional insiders. By the same token, his ignoring feminist work makes him susceptible to the same charge outside the precincts of the traditionally philological, and in addition severely compromises both the scholarly value of his essay, and its political effectiveness. "Gut-level," "lived," pre-, extra- or simply non-scholarly feminisms obviously and necessarily have their places in the world.[51] The time has passed, however, when naive and uninformed proto-feminist analysis is legitimate in the Western literary-critical *scholarly* forum; perhaps we must admit that it had already passed even twelve years ago.

Or is it just possible that Schweikle — the perennial insider with out- sider's ideas — sacrifices appearances for the sake of *subversive* political effect. The convoluted explication of such a scenario would go something like this: Schweikle as insider realizes that he cannot get a feminist (even a closet-feminist) article on the *Nibelungenlied* published in the mainstream journals, perhaps nowhere in fact except in an unrefereed Festschrift,[52] and not even there if he brings his feminism out of the closet; or, perhaps, even if he could get such an article published, it would have little effect on

50. A ploy that appears not just in the public political arena, but also the realm of literary criticism, as Gayatri Spivak demonstrates, accusing (among others) Terry Eagleton of a masculist annexation of feminism, in his *The Rape of Clarissa* (Minneapolis: University of Minnesota Press, 1982). See her response to the symposium "The Politics of Interpretation." The papers were published under that same title, ed. W. J. T. Mitchell (Chicago: University of Chicago Press, 1983); Spivak's essay: "The Politics of Interpretations," pp. 347–366, here pp. 365–366.

51. In fact they obviously must and do constitute the great majority of feminisms in the world.

52. I realize, of course, that few continental journals of medieval studies are refereed, but my point is not thus denied.

insiders if blatantly feminist. He thus attempts to establish his feminist thesis as if it were part of the traditional mainstream of *Nibelungenlied* scholarship, without reference to feminist scholarship or acknowledgement of its ideological affiliations, and thus subversively to infiltrate the citadel. I must admit that such a scenario is very appealing to my skeptical, cynical, and anti-traditional mind. But my concoction of it might also be read simply as a typically complicit male attempt to exculpate a fellow male whose analysis is *almost* satisfying in/but for his usurpation of a feminist project.

Comprehensive interpretations of the *Nibelungenlied* have almost always been close readings, almost annotated paraphrase, that usually begin with Kriemhild's naive and charming (or alternately: already ominous) "girlishness" in *aventiure* 1 and end with her "devilish" murder of Gunther and Hagen and her own "justified execution" at the end of *aventiure* 39. This albeit unimaginative structuring allows the scholar to build to a crescendo through his (*sic*) readings of the final *aventiuren* to the thunderous climax of engendered moral righteousness in the garish depiction of the final confrontation of the allegedly Medusa-like Kriemhild. One of the problems with this kind of tradition is that after one has read five such *Gesamtinterpretationen,* the *fabula* of the text itself begins to blur, for one has read five tediously detailed and contentious sub-literary critical "translations" of the *Nibelungenlied.*[53]

Since I am here seeking to disentangle not just discrete, individual interpretations but also several of the modern cultural bases of interpretive possibility, I will try to avoid the paraphrase and commentary form ("allegorical" translation). I fear that I will not always be successful, but I will

53. The means, purposes and results of such "translation" as they function ideologically, political, sometimes "unconsciously," and when undetected, insidiously, is perhaps best summarized by Fredric Jameson's designation of them (and much of conventional interpretation in general) as "allegory": . . .

> we will assume that a criticism which asks the questions "What does it mean?" constitutes something like an allegorical operation in which a text is systematically *rewritten* in terms of some fundamental master code or "ultimately determining instance." On this view, then all "interpretation" in the narrower sense demands the forcible or imperceptible transformation of a given text into an allegory of its particular master code or "transcendental signified": the discredit into which interpretation has fallen is thus at one with the disrepute visited on allegory itself. Yet to see interpretation this way is to acquire the instruments by which we can force a given interpretive practice to stand and yield up its name, to blurt out its master code and thereby reveal its metaphysical and ideological underpinnings. (*The Political Unconscious,* p. 58)

nonetheless simply assume that my reader knows the *Nibelungenlied* and the *Kudrun* well enough not to need more of a plot summary than the intentionally contentious single sentence offered at the beginning of this chapter and a similar one for the *Kudrun* at the beginning of Chapter seven. Additionally, to problematize further the tradition of interpreting the characters of Brünhild and Kriemhild by tendentious plot summary, I will generally proceed not *through* the text, whether in forward or reverse direction, but rather thematically.

Philip Anderson has observed that "It would be a mistake to try to reduce the *Nibelungenlied* to a mere parable about the proper roles for medieval women, or to decide that the poet's treatment of Kriemhild is the result of a programmatic fear of strong women" ("Kriemhild's Quest," p. 12). I agree wholeheartedly: while some parables may have significant implications, the parable as a form is by definition a reduction designed for the indoctrination of the (presumed) ignorant. Neither the *Nibelungenlied* nor the *Kudrun* is a parable, and at least the *Nibelungenlied* does not pretend that political, economic, and gender relations are simple. As I noted above, I propose here not that either of these texts is simplistic, but rather that they may both be read as far more complex than has generally been the case in the past, for it seems clear that these thirteenth-century texts enable a reading that radically differs from that proposed by traditional scholarship which, in a sense not unlike that analyzed by Peggy Kamuf in her work on the Abelard-Heloise tradition, has "work[ed] to appropriate and disguise the force of a woman's passion."[54] In one sense then, the present analysis confronts the critics as much as it does the *Nibelungenlied* and the *Kudrun* — as metacommentary, in order better to articulate the issues that arise out of a reading of the texts, based on principles of political economy and feminist analysis. It is a confrontation "not meant to 'restore' an 'original' or even privileged meaning"[55] but to enable a non-traditional critical intervention into the tradition, and — as the following analysis seeks to demonstrate — one that is textually supported. It is thus clearly and unashamedly also a philological project, but one informed I hope by Barbara Johnson's notion

---

54. Peggy Kamuf, *Fictions of Feminine Desire: Disclosures of Heloise* (Lincoln: University of Nebraska Press, 1982), p. xvi. See in this respect also Mieke Bal, *Lethal Loves,* 36: "The real issue of the discussion was not the text but the critics. The practice of criticism as used for the imposition, under the cover of academic authority, of gender-specific interests is what my analysis ultimately was meant to bring to the fore."

55. Bal, *Lethal Loves,* p. 1.

of philology: "What is at stake, then, is clearly the nature of reading; the question is not whether to be or not to be philological but how to read in such a way as to break through preconceived notions of meaning in order to encounter unexpected otherness — in order to learn something one doesn't already know — in order to encounter the other."[56]

56. Barbara Johnson, "Philology: What is at Stake," *What is Philology*, Special Focus Issue of *Comparative Literature Studies* 27 (1990), 27.

3. Women, Property, and Power

In one sense the *Nibelungenlied* is a story of the martial clash of heroic individuals and the catastrophic conflict of kingdoms. Not surprisingly then power and authority, and the material wealth that makes them effective, are among the most important themes. By the same token, since the struggle by Brünhild and Kriemhild to maintain personal independence depends directly on their own power and ability to reward those who perform service for them as dictated by the feudal social formation, and thus on their ownership or control of property, all definitions of gender relations in the tale consist in large part simultaneously of property relations.

Before proceeding to the analysis of the *Nibelungenlied* itself, however, it will be helpful to situate the discussion in a theoretical and a historical context. First, the theoretical articulation of the relationship of power and authority (and their connection to property relations) which has grown out of recent anthropological and sociological research provides a relevant framework for the analysis of the relations among property, power and gender. Secondly, an overview of the social and legal possibilities for women's participation in property relations in the early and high Middle Ages in the Germanic territories of central Europe will suggest legitimate contemporary limits on the kind of female action represented in the *Nibelungenlied*.[1] Finally, the strands are brought together in the detailed examination of these topics in the *Nibelungenlied*.

1. One of the primary obstructions to research in the history of medieval women has been a widespread lack of specification in publications produced in part for a lay reading public. One of the results of such publications, let it be quickly noted, is that a much wider public than ever before — even, obviously, among the scholarly ranks of non-medievalists — is taking an interest in things medieval and becoming aware of problems of gender in the cultures of that period. Another far less fortunate result is a tendency in such popularizing works to make simple, unqualified statements about property rights, marriage customs, women's education, or the literary representation of women in the "Middle Ages." Nowadays few scholars still cling to the analytically rather useless notion of a "Dark Ages" that preceded the Middle Ages proper, so that for the sake of illustration the Middle Ages may be said to comprise the period from the end of what we call late antiquity to the so-called Renaissance, that is, depending on one's criteria of periodization, anywhere from the fifth or the seventh to the thirteenth or the sixteenth centuries, a period of between six hundred and eleven hundred

At the outset let us recall one of the more useful definitions of power as the concept has been employed in recent sociological and anthropological research. In the course of her discussion of "Female Status in the Public Domain," P. G. Sanday has occasion to cite the standard distinction between power and authority, as defined by M. G. Smith: authority is "the right to make a particular decision and to command obedience," while power is "the ability to act effectively on persons or things, or take or secure favourable decisions which are not of right allocated to the individuals or their roles."[2] More concretely and with specific reference to women, Sanday designates four criteria for determining female status in the public domain in a given society:

I. *Female material control.* Females have the ability to act effectively on, to allocate, or to dispose of, things — land, produce, crafts, etc. — beyond the domestic unit.

II. *Demand for female produce.* Female produce has a recognized value either externally — beyond the localized family unit — or in an internal market.

III. *Female political participation.* Females, even if only through a few token representatives, may express opinions in a regular, official procedure and may influence policy affecting people beyond the domestic unit.

IV. *Female solidarity groups devoted to female political or economic interests.* Females group together in some regular way to protect or represent their interests, and are recognized and effectual in this activity.

---

years. Such being the case, we English speakers of the waning twentieth century are about as close in time, speech, and (in some ways) culture to the "medieval" poet of *Piers Plowman* (late fourteenth century) as he was to the "medieval" poet of *Beowulf* (by some accounts eighth century). When someone writes of *the* medieval marriage ceremony, are we to understand that the sixth-century Arian Christian Goths in Spain celebrated marriage in the same way that the contemporary Greek Christians did in Byzantium, or as did the eleventh-century pagan Swedes, or as did *their* contemporaries among the Christians or the Muslims or the Jews in Spain (on this general conceptual problem, see especially Jack Goody, *The Development of the Family and Marriage in Europe* (Cambridge: Cambridge University Press, 1983) p. 8). Certainly in the late twentieth century a pan-European culture is more a reality than it has been at any earlier historical period, but no historian or sociologist of contemporary Europe who wished to be taken seriously would be so lax as to speak of *the* European marriage custom as if it were uniform in Edinburgh and Sarajevo, Helsinki and Montpellier. Thus I will attempt here to be as specific as possible about the periods and cultures to which my remarks, and those of cited scholarship, refer. In general, of course, I attempt to focus on cultures of central Europe during the period 700–1200, but the relatively restricted nature of the data available, as well as the more than occasional cross-cultural relevance of information, make it profitable in some circumstances to admit material from beyond the strict boundaries of the present subject.

2. M. G. Smith, *Government in Zazzau, 1800–1950* (London: Oxford University Press, 1960), pp. 18–19, cited by Peggy Reeves Sanday, "Female Status in the Public Domain," in *Woman, Culture, and Society,* ed. Michelle Zimbalist Rosaldo and Louise Lamphere (Stanford, CA: Stanford University Press, 1974), pp. 190–192.

Despite the fact that the second and fourth criteria, as they appear in the *Nibelungenlied,* are easily characterized, they are no less significant than the first and third. The "female produce" constructed and then desired by the societies of the *Nibelungenlied,* for instance, differs radically from that which Sanday has in mind, certainly, but the social function is ultimately also one in which an indirect economic value resides, albeit one that is ironically the most effective at reducing women's authority. For in a very concrete sense, female "produce" in the ruling class of feudal society consists first of conventional beauty and the conventional honor derived from that beauty, both of which then pertain not to the woman herself, but which rather inhere in the reputation of the man in whose charge she is. Secondly her "produce" is offspring, heirs to the property of her husband. This "produce" is again "hers" only insofar as she is its vehicle, not its owner or controller.

The fourth criterion is even more simply treated, for female solidarity is all but absent from the *Nibelungenlied,* since the culture encourages competition rather than cooperation among represented females, such that they become rivals. In this way the very notion of female solidarity is undermined, if not denied legitimacy, and its very absence indicates a certain restricted female status in that society.

The articulation of the first and third criteria is more complex and requires more attention. As is clear from Sanday's formulation of the third criterion, concerning political status, independent political action by individual women is not assumed, but rather for the most part only their indirect participation via (often male) representatives. The defining presence of this limitation on women's political participation is all but constant in the history of European civilizations, no matter how much the extent of that limitation may vary from one period or culture to another. The consequences of political marginality are more debilitating than the "mere" lack of authority might initially suggest, for in such a political situation, the subject is not only incapable of exercising any direct control on the political process itself, but is also structurally excluded from direct participation. Any breach of this last (not always unwritten) prohibition is judged not just a procedural error, but necessarily an engendered error. As Michelle Zimbalist Rosaldo expresses the problem,

> although women may have neither the right nor the duty to make decisions, they often have a systematic influence on decisions that are made. And although social norms may not acknowledge the positive use of power by

women, they often specify the limits or illegality of such power, treating the powerful or influential woman as disruptive, anomalous, and so on.[3]

J. F. Collier notes similarly that women's quarrels are generally viewed as deriving from personal, individual deficiencies, and thus as manifestations of the propensities of the whole sex, while men's quarrels on the contrary are viewed as deriving from legitimate social and political problems.[4] She counters that even if confined wholly to the domestic sphere, women's actions are social actions and thus necessarily also political.[5] This assertion evokes another of the more commonly found concepts in recent sociological analyses of the cultural and social position of women: that of the public versus the private. Conventionally men are posited as inhabitants of the

3. Michelle Zimbalist Rosaldo, "Women, Culture and Society: A Theoretical Overview," in *Woman, Culture, and Society,* ed. Rosaldo and Lamphere, pp. 21. Whenever women are barred from direct political power, any attempts at participation in the power structure bring the same accusations. The medievalist Barbara Hannawalt notes that women were then viewed as "manipulative and . . . their tools of influence as deceit, intrigue, fickleness, and even witchcraft" (Barbara A. Hannawalt, "Lady Honor Lisle's Networks of Influence," in *Women and Power in the Middle Ages,* ed. Mary Erler and Maryanne Kowalski [Athens: University of Georgia Press, 1988], pp. 188). The fact that such determined political action recurringly draws not just reprimand or punishment for the action itself, but also the accusation of an immorality against contact, that is, action beyond that permitted to females, or as we would term it, a breaching of gender definitions, is one to which we will return later in focusing on the cultural function of the concept of Amazon (see below, chapter 5). Cf. Joan Ferrante's comments on the character of female power in the *Nibelungenlied:* "While the poet clearly thinks that women should be kept out of public affairs, and the only king in the poem who allows them free use of men and money, Etzel, certainly lives to regret it, the story also suggests that if you rob women of the rights and powers they are entitled to, they will find other ways to assert those rights and powers that may be far more harmful to society. . . . [F]or the most part, women in epic are passive victims of power struggles and war, ignored when they attempt to participate openly, forced to maneuver behind the scenes" ("Public Postures and Private Maneuvers: Roles Medieval Women Play," in *Women and Power in the Middle Ages,* ed. Erler and Kowaleski, pp. 215–216).

4. Jane Fishburne Collier. "Women in Politics," in *Woman, Culture, and Society,* ed. Rosaldo and Lamphere, pp. 89–96.

5. See also Marie-Theres Knäpper's comment: " 'Das Persönliche ist politisch,' das ist eine der bekanntesten feministischen Äußerungen" ("the personal is political, that is one of the most widely known feminist observations"), in *Feminismus-Autonomie-Subjektivität: Tendenzen und Widersprüche in der neuen Frauenbewegung* (Bochum: Germinal, 1984), p. 105. Cf. also Fredric Jameson: "The only effective liberation from such constraint begins with the recognition that there is nothing that is not social and historical — indeed, that everything is 'in the last analysis' political" (*The Political Unconscious,* p. 20). And specifically on the *Nibelungenlied,* see Jan Dirk Müller, who, in discussing Siegfried's position as helper/server/servant in gaining Gunther's wife for him: "Schon von der Struktur der Handlung her sind 'private' Interessen und Konflikte immer zugleich 'öffentliche' — wobei diese Formulierung schon eine Trennung voraussetzt, die hier eben noch nicht vollzogen ist" (" 'Even in the plot structure private interests and conflicts are always simultaneously "public" — although this formulation presumes a distinction that has at this point not yet completely developed' "). See Jan-Dirk Müller, "SIVRIT: *künec-man-eigenholt.* Zur sozialen Problematik des Nibelungenliedes," *Amsterdamer Beiträge zur älteren Germanistik* 7 (1974), 113.

public space, that is, most or all of their life activities except the strictly personal and familial take place in a public setting: their work, recreation, friendships, and participation in political life. On the other hand, women's (identical types of) life activities are concentrated in the private space, usually in the (variously defined) family. The concrete consequences are immediately apparent: with very few exceptions, the potential for economic, social, communal, and political activity is severely restricted for women, as compared to men. Such a restriction entails first a reduction in the number of transactions possible, but even more significantly, it imposes conditions that result in a narrower range of possible *types* of activities, and this restriction applies *mutatis mutandis* no matter what class it is to which the women and their men belong.[6]

Gayatri Spivak views the dichotomy between public and private as the necessary antagonist, and thus a prime object of feminist work, for there is

> a certain program at least implicit in all feminist activity; the deconstruction of the opposition between the private and the public. . . . Feminist practice, at least since the European eighteenth century, suggests that each compartment of the public sector also operates emotionally and sexually, that the domestic sphere is not the emotions' only legitimate workplace. In the effectiveness of the women's movement, emphasis is often placed upon a reversal of the public-private hierarchy. . . . The feminist, reversing this hierarchy, must insist that sexuality and the emotions are, in fact, so much more important and threatening that a masculinist sexual politics is obliged, repressively, to sustain all public activity." ("Explanation and Culture: Marginalia," chapter 7 of *In Other Worlds*, pp. 103–117, here p. 103)

As Imray's and Middleton's research (and their compilation of earlier research) indicates, based on a wide range of data from many different cultures and periods in which the valuation of activities of all types is consistently based on the gender of the agents — men (positive value) or women (negative value) — the dichotomy public/private is an ideological construct:

6. Interestingly, the editors of two recent anthologies of essays on the concept of public versus private, Mary Erler and Maryanne Kowaleski and Eva Garminikow and Jane Purvis, caution against the indiscriminate usage of the construct public vs. private, since it may reduce women's roles to a simple bipolarity that does not account for the multiplicity of relevant cultural forces; see Erler and Kowaleski, eds., *Women and Power in the Middle Ages*, "Introduction," pp. 4–5; and Garminikow and Purvis, *The Public and the Private*, ed. Eva Gamarnikow, et al. (London: Heinemann, 1983). On the problems with the model, see Michelle Zimbalist Rosaldo, "The Use and Abuse of Anthropology: Reflections on Feminism and Cross-Cultural Understanding."

Activities in themselves have no absolute and unchanging value, be they
economic, political, cultural. Rather, value accrues to activities by virtue of
who performs them and more importantly who controls their social meaning
and importance. We seek to demonstrate that it is not work *per se* which is
valued and which is part of the public sphere, but rather that it is work done by
men.[7]

Public and private thus take on completely artificial properties, based on
illogical ad hoc principles: "When men act it is defined by them as acting
within the public sphere; when women act men define it as acting within
the private sphere" (p. 26).

Generally scholars who have employed the sociological categories of
public and private have done so in studies of modern European societies.
Those who have had occasion to address this conceptual dichotomy as it
might apply, for instance, to the European Middle Ages, have cautioned
against its uncritical usage or even denied its applicability altogether.[8] There
is good reason for caution, as the identification of but a few of the problems
will illustrate. First, the feudal political formation consists of complex webs
of hierarchical relationships, each one of which is, however, necessarily and
by definition a personal one; the separation of a "private" from a "public"
sphere of action is thus artificial and generally not analytically very useful.
Secondly, the "private" sphere opposite its posited "public" counterpart
would almost have to be, as in the modern context, the family. But David
Herlihy has recently gone a long way toward disabusing classicists and medievalists (among others) of their ahistorical notions of family and kin relations. He argues that Roman society, for instance, may not be analyzed in
terms of "family" since neither the concept nor the fact existed there in the
organization of household and kinship.[9] Classes and categories (rich, poor,
free, slave) differed radically, and there was in *none* of them a *socially* constructed unit of blood descendents corresponding to our "family," which,
according to Herlihy, did not begin to develop in Europe until the early
Middle Ages. But James Schultz imposes further restrictions on the assumption of the presence of the concept: there is for instance no such

7. Linda Imray and Audrey Middleton, "Public and Private: Marking the Boundaries,"
in *The Public and the Private,* ed. Garmarnikow et al., pp. 12–27.

8. Cf., for instance, Judith Bennett, "Public Power and Authority in the Medieval
English Countryside," in *Women and Power in the Middle Ages,* ed. Erlier and Kowaleski,
pp. 18–36.

9. *Medieval Households* (Cambridge, MA: Harvard University Press, 1985), pp. 1–28.
We would do well to keep in mind that *familia,* as Latin pupils worldwide must eventually
learn to respond on examinations, signifies, in the first instance, slaves, that is, the household
personnel of a Roman *pater familias.*

concept and thus no term to express such a concept in Middle High German, and no examples of the "family" as such in Middle High German literature.[10]

If then in the feudal social formation too the "personal is political" by necessity, and there is no "family" to provide a non-public, non-political, private space, what use are the analytical categories public-private? I will suggest two reasons for the retention of this problematic analytical concept for few and specific strategic purposes in the present study. First, there are, not surprisingly, patterns of types of actions performed and performable in the *Nibelungenlied* and *Kudrun* that depend in the first instance on the gender of the performer; the patterning of these types of actions *resembles* (is not identical to) the modern ideological constructions of male public versus female private. For instance, men command feudal allegiances, women do not (at least not unproblematically); men initiate "bridal-quests," women do not initiate "groom-quests"; men decide when and whom to marry, women marry; men rule, women do not (at least not unproblematically, not permanently, not generally); men's political actions are open, direct, and by means of "state institutions" (e.g., the military), women's are often secret, indirect, almost always via a male's access to the "institution" to which the women themselves are denied access; men determine property relations, women do not, even with respect to their own property; powerful men have authority, powerful women are rare and even more rarely and only briefly do they have any political authority; men (even grossly incompetent ones) are empowered to make military decisions, women (even astute strategists) are ridiculed and abused if they offer even momentary, specific advice on such subjects.[11]

There is a clear pattern here, but it is just as clearly not the "public versus private" of, for instance, the (construct of) post-war U.S. capitalist "division" of family labor between the male factory worker and the female "homemaker," nor is it simply some imagined medieval aristocratic reflex thereof. Nonetheless, the distant relationship between this pattern in the

---

10. *The Knowledge of Childhood in the German Middle Ages* (Philadelphia: University of Pennsylvania Press, forthcoming)

11. The recent work of Georges Duby is also of relevance in setting the legitimate boundaries of these terms here: "Aussi faut-il admettre que l'opposition entre vie privée et vie publique est moins affaire de lieu que de pouvoir. Toutefois, le contraste n'est pas entre pouvoir et non-pouvoir, il est entre deux natures de pouvoirs" ("it is also necessary to admit that the opposition between private life and public life is less a matter of place/position than of power. Still the contrast is not between power and non-power, but rather between two types of power"); see Georges Duby, *De l'Europe féodale à la Renaissance*, vol. 2 of *Histoire de la vie privée*, under the direction of Philippe Ariès and Georges Duby (Paris: Éditions du Seuil, 1985), pp. 22–23.

texts under consideration and that which we now often term public versus private seems a useful one to articulate. There are two engendered spheres of activities that signify politically. Male duties and activities are openly, directly, and significantly political, dealing with issues of finances, "state," feudal allegiances (including dynastic marriage), inter-state diplomacy, and war, affecting the lives of acquaintances and strangers alike over broad geographical ranges. Women are generally denied access to those issues and operate in the (ostensibly) smaller and less politically significant sphere of activities that affect fewer (and known) people. Instead of engaging in large-scale political activities, women provide support services to the men who do: the Burgundian king goes abroad to find a mate; his sister sews his travel wardrobe.

In addition to this *literary* pattern, there is a second, restricted, *historically*-based frame of reference in which the general conceptual framework "public/private" is of more than slight significance for some medieval European cultures. One of the prime indicators of its relevance in the various cultures and periods of the European Middle Ages is the social and political function of the clan. During the early Middle Ages in Celtic and Germanic Europe—from Iberian Callaecia (Galicia) to Norway, and Ireland to the lower Danube, rule was generally clan-based.[12] Higher levels of organization certainly existed at various times and places, but they too were often clan-structured and (usually short-lived) superimpositions on the smaller structures. This structure persisted in Europe up to the eleventh century. But already a century earlier, this principle of social organization and the exercise of political power began to change radically, and with that change came the relevance of the distinction between public and private. In this same context McNamara and Wemple too note that early Germanic custom did not distinguish public and private power. They point, however, to the restricted, but undeniable, relevance of that conception in the early medieval gains in women's power through the enhanced power of the household itself, especially as a result of women's access to property rights, which brought power and even authority,[13] for "when a woman inherited her own estate, she inherited the political power that went with it, and frequently exercised it in her own right" (p. 93). From the ninth to the eleventh century one finds women in such diverse roles as "military leaders, judges, castellans, controllers of property" (p. 94). McNamara and Wemple

---

12. See, again, the excellent study by David Herlihy, *Medieval Households*.

13. "The Power of Women Through the Family in Medieval Europe, 500–1100," pp. 84, 90.

mention two of the most famous examples of female authority during this period (pp. 92–94): Mathilda, abbess of Quedlinburg and sister of Emperor Otto II (973–983), who entrusted the regency to her during his absences from the realm;[14] and Eleanor of Acquitaine who took her lands with her into and out of two marriages, ruling them herself after her estrangement from Henry II.[15]

The power to which women—even of the royal class—had access, however, was with very few exceptions based in the household itself and their role in that domestic unit. As Wemple notes concerning the Carolingian period:

> The formalization of wifely duties in the ninth century, while enhancing the wife's influence in aristocratic families, strengthened male dominance in all other spheres and reinforced sexual stereotypes. The wife was occupied in a broad variety of domestic and nurturing roles and remained in the shadow of her husband. Should she try to exercise power in her own right, she met with criticism and was accused of unfeminine behavior.[16]

Thus a woman "could exercise public power only as an extension of her role as wife, mother, and property owner" (p. 106). As the Carolingian reforms of multiple social institutions took hold, women's access to power was restricted even more: "In the more structured Carolingian Empire, women could not exert extensive influence. By enforcing the principle of marital indissolubility, the Carolingians strengthened the position of women in the family, but they also confined women's activities to the private sphere of home and cloister" (p. 123).

Already by the tenth century, however, several complexly interrelated developments that were to restrict the power of women not only in discrete spheres of activity, but more importantly also in profound and pervasive structural transformations of the possibilities of female power, had begun to appear. Although women in the early Middle Ages had never achieved anything approaching tangible political equality, their participation in the body politic had been allowed via their integral role in household and clan life. Now, however, in this changing and changed environment, even that marginal participation was further restricted. Judith Bennett views this situation in terms of power vs. authority: if power is, according to Smith,

---

14. See *Annales Quedlinburgenses, MGH, SS* 3, pp. 75–76.

15. One must also note, however, that Henry then arbitrarily and with impunity imprisoned her.

16. Suzanne Fonay Wemple, *Women in Frankish Society: Marriage and the Cloister, 500 to 900* (Philadelphia: University of Pennsylvania Press, 1981), p. 105.

"the ability to act effectively on persons or things . . . [in ways] not of right allocated to individuals," especially in landholding and legal and social activities, then power was most readily acquired by men, but not denied to women; on the other hand, authority as "recognized and legitimized power," "was strictly reserved for males"; thus women in medieval England (the subject of her study) "were often powerful, but they were never authoritative."[17] As Pauline Stafford points out (p. 195), from the tenth century onward, and especially in the eleventh century, women were less able to inherit property, as the tendency grew to preserve the property of the lineage by allowing only males to inherit.[18] In the aristocratic class, the tendency also became more pronounced as the royal succession became more a matter of the politics of the kingdom and less those of the domestic unit. One of the prime motivations for this transformation arose as a response by aristocratic lineages to feudal territorialization (the extension and consolidation of the territorial powers of the feudal lords over their vassals), for they were then forced to prevent division of the patrimony in order to consolidate their power in the struggle against the resurgent monarchy.[19] That struggle did not abate until recent centuries, but by the twelfth century the monarchy had by means of new institutions already taken over many instances of the exercise of public authority earlier controlled by aristocratic lineages. The aristocracy adjusted to this new political structure, but in so doing all but eliminated women from any significant role: for as charismatic and lineage-based rule disappeared in favor of a rule-governed proto-bureaucracy, the domestic unit and all its appurtenances became a private matter. The consequences, as noted by McNamara and Wemple, were far-reaching:

> But while it was possible for aristocratic men to retain the same power by acting as the administrators of the new institutions, such positions were not

17. Judith M. Bennett, "Public Power and Authority," p. 19, 29.

18. In 1037 Conrad II issued the *Constitutio de feudis,* which excluded women from the inheritance of fiefs, thus attempting to deny women one avenue to property ownership, the primary means to power.

19. An astute observation (in another context) by Stanley Chojnacki suggests a social reason, beyond this directly economic argument, for the patriarchal denial of female property inheritance: "a man was bound to his lineage by an array of legal constraints and economic inducements. A woman, at least a married woman, shared in two lineages and thus was bound tightly to neither except by moral ties which themselves pulled into two directions. In this freer female social space, personal loyalties and sentiments and tangible expressions of them took their place alongside the defined patterns of lineage loyalty and the more adjustable but no less strategically rooted expectations of marriage alliances," in "The Power of Love: Wives and Husbands in Late Medieval Venice," in *Women and Power in the Middle Ages,* ed. Erler and Kowaleski, p. 139.

open to noble women. Their activities were confined to the role of house-keeper, a role whose boundaries were shrinking. With the return of public power and the corresponding loss of domestic power, women were moving back to the conditions that had existed under the Roman Empire. (p. 97)[20]

This phenomenon, already begun by the eleventh century, was the norm by the twelfth. The power of the domestic unit, and thus irregularly of women, was steadily eroded. There was a general decline of personal power as the basis of imperial rule, as institutions came to play a larger role, especially as the power of the aristocracy was consolidated.

The most obvious instances of this social transformation are found in political life, but as J. T. Schulenburg has shown, the same structural change also took place in the Church during this same period.[21] For the half-millennium before 1100, "popular sanctity was essentially predicated on public activities" (p. 105), with the majority of canonized saints to be found in the public sphere: men were kings, emperors, bishops, popes, archbishops, abbots, and monks; women were queens, abbesses, celebrated virgins, nuns; both men and women were hermits and martyrs. One of the most significant aspects of the reforms of the Catholic church, beginning in the Carolingian period and becoming especially important through the Cluniac and Gregorian reforms, was the redefinition of the role of women in the Church. That redefinition entailed, not surprisingly, primarily a restriction of the possible roles women could play: "to limit women's public involvement and their leadership activities in the Church and society through the demarcation of a 'proper' feminine sphere and a delineation of female nature, abilities, rights, and responsibilities" (p. 115). One of the direct results noted by Schulenburg is that a new concept of female sanctity arose in the following period, in which the emphasis was now on domestic activities, whereby those women were deemed pious who performed the duties of household management and motherhood. The church's imposi-

20. See also on this point Pauline Stafford, in *Queens, Concubines, and Dowagers: The King's Wife in the Early Middle Ages* (Athens: University of Georgia Press, 1983), pp. 195–196; and Andrée Lehmann, *Le rôle de la femme dans l'histoire de France au moyen âge* (Paris: Berger-Levrault, 1952), p. 218. Martha C. Howell points out concerning the lack of power and authority among urban women of late medieval Northern Europe, that here individuals rather than lineages ruled, and women whose position did not extend beyond the domestic unit had no access to rule, which was restricted to men: "In northern European cities, a line separating a world exclusive to men from the world that men and women shared was drawn around a small but very significant kind of public activity — the formal, direct exercise of public authority"; see Howell, "Citizenship and Gender: Women's Political Status in Northern Medieval Cities," in *Women and Power in the Middle Ages,* ed. Erler and Kowaleski, p. 37.

21. Jane Tibbetts Schulenburg, "Female Sanctity: Public and Private Roles, ca. 500–1100," in *Women and Power in the Middle Ages,* ed. Erler and Kowaleski, pp. 102–125.

tion of celibacy on its own orders and priesthood and the prohibition of lay investiture further restricted the power of the domestic unit.

Thus there seem to be both engendered dichotomies of action in the *Nibelungenlied* and *Kudrun,* and evidence of historical developments in the construction and definition of gendered activities in several generations on either side of these narratives' composition that enable the theorization of an ideological construction of permissible and non-permissible political action and actants, based on gender (and not just on lineage, wealth, etc.). *That* distinction is regularly constructed by and manifested in the site of normed activity: these sites, male and female, conform more to the modern analytical dichotomy "public/private" than, for instance, to the more general, though no less valid "political/de-politicized." I must acknowledge that my use of the concepts here is a compromise, an approximation, and, for many readers it will be an imprecision. But the fact is simply that this terminological and conceptual dichotomy effectively describes one aspect of these issues in the *Nibelungenlied* and the *Kudrun.*

As is already clear from the remarks of scholars noted above, the fluctuation of women's participation in political life and access to power more than merely runs parallel to their changing access to property ownership. Indeed their control of material wealth is the basis on which political power is directly founded. Thus it remains to address Sanday's first criterion of female participation in the public domain: "the ability to act effectively on, to allocate, or to dispose of, things — land, produce, crafts, etc. — beyond the domestic unit," that is, essentially, property ownership and control of property, both real and movable. The acquisition of property by women was severely restricted during the Middle Ages in northern Europe. When women did gain control of property, it was generally by marriage settlement or inheritance. It is thus impossible to analyze and evaluate accurately the property rights of women in the continental Germanic cultures of the early Middle Ages without also discussing marriage customs, because the two are so closely related, and the distinctions in types of marriage are in large part based on distinctions in property rights.[22] These topics are of especial relevance, as we might note in advance of the discussion, since one of the major elements of controversy in the *Nibelungenlied*

---

22. The otherwise wide-ranging and excellent collection of essays on twelfth-century marriage in various European cultures, edited by Willy van Hoecke and Andries Welkenhuysen, *Love and Marriage in the Twelfth Century* (Leuven: Leuven University Press, 1981), deserves mention here, despite the fact that it includes no studies of the property relations of marriage.

has to do with the ownership of, rights to, and control over Siegfried's hoard of gold after it becomes his bride's *Morgengabe*. While I have above suggested the inadequacy of *literary* analysis of the *Nibelungenlied* on the basis of putative historical sources from the period of the *Völkerwanderung,* the following consideration of the available Germanic legal codes from periods of up to a few centuries prior to the composition of the *Nibelungenlied* does not deal with "imagined historical roots," but rather with concrete historical documents with often quite specific literary refractions.

Scholars of early medieval Germanic societies are fortunate in the relative abundance of relevant legal material that has survived in the Germanic tribal law codes, redacted between the sixth and tenth centuries. The codes are, however, anything but clear, and have been interpreted in radically conflicting ways.[23] In general, early medieval household structure among the Germanic tribes was such that the father held a kind of guardianship over his dependents that resembled in some ways the Roman concept of *manus,* called *munt* or *munduburdium* in Frankish law. Upon reaching maturity, sons, but not daughters, became *sui iuris*. There were generally two forms of marriage, roughly corresponding to the Roman *in manu/cum manu* and *sine manu,* formal and informal marriage, subject to or free from the *munt* of a male guardian, conventionally called *munt-* or *mundium*-marriage and *Friedelehe*.[24] The formal, *munt*-marriage proceeded in three stages: contractual betrothal (*desponsatio/sponsalis*), payment by the groom of the brideprice (*pretium nuptiale, wittimon, meta*), and delivery of the bride to the *mundium/manus* of the groom (*frô*) by the *Muntwalt/ mundoaldus* (conventionally designated *traditio puellae*), followed by consummation (*nuptiae*) and celebration.[25] Among the primarily agricultural Germanic tribes, the brideprice was, according to Wemple (p. 13) a compensation to the bride's relations for the loss of a farm laborer (obviously then such a characterization does not apply to the nobility, with which we

23. A particularly helpful summary of the information relevant to the present topic is presented by Herlihy, *Medieval Households,* pp. 48–111 passim.

24. Diane Owen Hughes, "From Brideprice to Dowry in Medieval Europe," *Journal of Family History* 3 (1978), 268, points out that some theories argue for a variety of marriage types among early Indo-European societies, from which the two Germanic types might be descendants. Thomas Grenzler inexplicably claims that the terms and analytical concepts, *munt* and *Friedelehe,* are modern scholarly constructs (which they are not), before going on to imply that such modern analytical models are inappropriate to the study of medieval culture (in *Erotisierte Politik — Politisierte Erotik,* see particularly his conclusion, pp. 531–637). Such a proscription would of course disallow *all* methods of cultural study currently practiced, not just those to which Grenzler apparently objects.

25. See particularly Gunther Grimm's excellent summary: "Die Eheschließung in der Kudrun. Zur Frage der Verlobten-oder Gattentreue Kudruns," *ZfdPh* 90 (1971), 48–70.

are here primarily concerned). At the same time, it "created a new network of kinship" and was thus also ideally a profitable exchange. The practical function of the brideprice was, however, as the purchase price paid by the husband for the woman's *mundium* to the kinsman in whose guardianship she was at that time, whereby the husband acquired control over her, her body, and her legal rights and obligations. According to Hughes (pp. 266–267), the Germanic tribes seem to have given up brideprice payments relatively soon after they made contact with Roman culture (which knew no such custom), so that by the time the early Germanic law codes were recorded, it is not mentioned, unless the token payment among the Franks to the bride's relations is a vestigial relic thereof. But among those tribes whose migration took place late and was of longer duration, and which also recorded their laws late, there are more than merely vestigial remains.[26] By the period when the *Nibelungenlied* was composed, however, a second type of marriage settlement, designated in Middle High German the *morgangabe* (*pretium pulchritudinis* or *pretium virginitatis*), given to the bride by the groom after the consummation of the marriage, had become the norm.[27] Although the codes express the *Morgengabe* in terms of money, in actuality, as deeds indicate, already by the seventh century it was often the husband did not revert to his relations. As Wemple summarizes this development:

> Direct ownership of land received as *dos*[28] and *Morgengabe* represented an important step toward the economic independence of women. Although a

26. As a representative selection of the law codes' treatment of this topic, see, for instance, *Leges Burgundiorum* 66.1–3; 69.1–2; 86.2, *MGH Legum sectio* I,ii,i, pp. 94–95, 108; *Leges Langobardorum*, 2nd ed., *edictum Rotharii*, 178; on Salic and Ripuarian law, see *MGH Legum sectio I*, 5/1, 131 & *sectio* I, 3/2, 90; *Leges Vis.* 3.1.6 (*MGH Legum sectio I*, 1, 130); *Pactus legis Sal.* 101.2, *MGH Legum sectio I*, 4/1, 256–257; *Lex Alam.* 54.1–2, *MGH Legum sectio I*, 5/1, 112–113; *Lex Bai.* 15.8, *MGH Legum sectio I*, 5/2, 427]; *Lex Rib.* 41 (37).2, *MGH Legum sectio I*, 3/2, 95; *Lex Saxonum* 40; in *Leges Saxonum und Lex Thuringorum, MGH Fontes iuris germanici antiqui in usum scholarum* 4, pp. 27–28.

27. This is also the type of settlement made by Siegfried in his marriage to Kriemhild. The precise distinctions between bride-price and *Morgengabe* and their social functions are thus of great importance and have become the subject of a vast body of research in medieval legal and social history. The best brief analyses are those by Diane Owen Hughes, "From Brideprice to Dowry," pp. 262–296 (esp. 266–270 for the points at issue here), and Wemple, *Women in Frankish Society*, esp. pp. 32–49.

28. The dowry in the Roman sense of *dos*, that is, a gift from the bride's relations to the groom's, disappears from early medieval texts, where the term comes to signify the reverse gift from the groom to the bride (cf. Herlihy, *Medieval Households*, p. 73). This is what Jack Goody calls "indirect dowry." From the migration period to the twelfth century, this reverse dowry was the rule. Statistically marriage partners during this period of time also seem to have been about the same age, in their mid- to late twenties (cf. Herlihy, p. 77).

husband had the right to manage his wife's property, he could not alienate it
without her consent. If the alliance was dissolved or the husband died, the
woman could assume full ownership. Even though she could not freely dispose
of her property if she had children, she could exercise economic power. This
was an important development that undermined the old Germanic prejudice
against women holding and inheriting real property.

Under the influence of Roman law, which recognized the right of women to
hold land and allowed daughters to claim an equal share with their brothers in
the paternal inheritance, Germanic inheritance laws gradually became less
restrictive. But the old prejudices were never completely eliminated, and
marriage remained the principal means by which women came to possess land
and the concomitant economic power.[29]

Generally, as Hughes notes (p. 270), a childless widow received the
entire *Morgengabe,* while a widow with children had the usufruct until her
death, when it passed to her sons. The bride's control tended to increase as
the decades and centuries passed, such that she came to control the full
Morgengabe. According to Alemannic law, a childless widow and a woman
divorced through no fault of her own "could assume full control of her *dos*
and *Morgengabe.*"[30] The Burgundian code stipulates that as long as a widow
did not remarry, she could usually also claim as her dower the usufruct of
part (usually one third) of her husband's land.[31] As the right of women to
own land generally became recognized, they lost the right to claim the
dower unless they had received no land from their parents or husband; even
then the woman could claim, depending on the tribe, one third or more of
the land accrued to her husband during the marriage. As Wemple points
out (p. 49), generally "as a widow, particularly if she had no living sons, she
could exercise considerable power in transmitting and alienating praedial
and other kinds of property."[32] While life became more concentrated in

29. On the developing tendency toward permitting women to inherit real property (but
especially on the growing ability to retain control of their own praedial property) in the early
Middle Ages among the continental Germanic tribes, see also Karl von Amira, *Germanisches
Recht,* 4th ed. by Karl August Eckhardt, Grundriß der germanischen Philologie 5/1–2 (Berlin:
de Gruyter, 1960/1967), II, 76. On the function of the *Morgengabe* as provision for the widow
in the case that her husband died, see the sociological and legal evidence marshaled by Solveig
Widén, "Morgengåvan som grund för änkeförsörjning," in *Förändringar i kvinnors villkor under
medeltiden: Uppsatser framlagda vid ett kvinnohistoriskt symposium i Skálholt, Ísland, 22.–25.
juni 1981,* ed. Silja Aðalsteinsdóttir and Helgi Þorláksson (Reykjavík: Sagnfræðistofunun
Háskóla Íslands, 1983), pp. 71–81.

30. Wemple, *Women in Frankish Society* p. 48; *Lex Alam.* 54, MGH *Legum sectio I,* 5/1,
112.

31. *Leges Burg.* 74.1, MGH *Legum sectio I,* 2/1, 98.

32. A brief overview of inheritance laws is given by Peter Ketsch, *Frauen im Mittelalter,*
ed. Annette Kuhn, vol. 2: *Frauenbild und Frauenrechte in Kirche und Gesellschaft, Quellen und
Materialien* (Düsseldorf: Schwann, 1984), esp. pp. 157–165.

private spaces, and women lost access to some kinds of power, they gained in some rights to inherit property under some conditions, although restrictions to obstruct the division of the patrimony hindered this development. Thus there is no linear development in medieval women's property rights, which is rather a complex web of relations.

The formal marriage differed from the informal *Friedelehe*, in which the partners were in some senses treated as equals, in that no *mundium* was transferred and no brideprice paid.[33] In such cases the *Morgengabe* itself was the sign of actual marriage (distinguishing it from concubinage).[34] Herlihy characterizes it as "a kind of abduction, to which the bride consented. She was more than a concubine, for the union was public and recognized, and she also received a morning gift" (p. 50). The church assumed a more significant role in marriage and tried to outlaw such unions through the rule that without a dowry no marriage existed. The Trier synod of 1227 forbade marriage without ecclesiastical participation, and began to champion the concept of consensual marriage according to the Paris school's *solus consensus facit nuptias,* as against the school of Bologna's *copula carnalis* as constitutive of marriage. But ecclesiastical marriage was still actually only a confirmation of marriage, not the legal act itself (which had by that point already been performed by the legally responsible portion); generally the

33. On *Friedelehe* in literary documents of the eleventh and twelfth centuries (e.g. *Ruodlieb* and *Rother*), both before and after the twelfth-century reform of canon civil law (cf. H. Conrad's *Deutsche Rechtsgeschichte*), see Christian Gellinek, "Marriage by Consent in Literary Sources of Medieval Germany," *Studia Gratiana* 12 (1967), 555–579. Gellinek views the development of *Friedelehe* as an indicator of "self-assertion of women." According to the *Schwabenspiegel,* during the twelfth century women could at age twelve gain control of their property and could contract marriage even against the wishes of their guardians; if they were younger than twenty-five when they did so, however, they forfeited their inheritance rights in their own lineage; see also Ketsch, *Frauen im Mittelalter,* p. 162. Hughes notes (p. 268) Herbert Meyer's now generally discounted theory ("Friedelehe und Mutterrecht," *Zeitschrift der Savigny-Stiftung für Rechtsgeschichte,* Germ. Abt. 47 (1927), 198–286) that *Friedelehe* is an indication of matriarchy, while *mundium*-marriage is patriarchal.

34. On concubinage, see especially Pauline Stafford, *Queens, Concubines, and Dowagers,* pp. 62–71, esp. 62–65. It seems to have had a quasi-legitimate status at various times and places. According to von Amira, *Kebsehe* was one of several types of recognized legal union (*Germanisches Recht,* II, 75). According to Gunter Grimm, *Friedelehe* was viewed by the church like any other non-church union, that is, as concubinage ("Die Eheschließungen," p. 50). Concubinage was such a common practice at times that in some of its conventions it overlapped with other marriage types, and it is with some difficulty at some times and places that it is distinguished from marriage proper, since the offspring of both inherit in some cases (although wives and their offspring did so more commonly). Even among Carolingian royalty concubinage was not uncommon, and the term *kebse* was not an uncommon insult during that period, since it questioned the status if not the legitimacy of the union. Thus for Kriemhild to call Brünhild *kebse* would have been in the ninth century not a moral or even political insult, but rather only a personal one, but for the audience of the *Nibelungenlied,* which no longer knew concubinage as a legal status, it was more likely a threefold insult.

church's involvement did not occur immediately after the legally binding act (*desponsatio*) but the execution of that contract (*nuptiae*). Ecclesiastical marriage consisted of three acts: consensual discussion, the joining (*copulatio*) of the couple by a priest, *benedictio* and *nuptiae*. In the course of the thirteenth century, ecclesiastical marriage became common in the noble ranks, while in the *Nibelungenlied* and the *Kudrun* it is still an addenda to the legal lay marriage performed.[35]

The demographical pattern of marriage also changed, reverting in essence almost to the extremely patriarchal Roman pattern: the bride was generally younger (sometimes far younger) than twenty, while the groom was generally in his late twenties. Such arrangements obviously made it all but impossible for a marriage to be a partnership of equals in any sense; the hierarchy of authority was established from the outset. Financial arrangements also evolved — that is, they were altered — to the detriment of women. In the course of the tenth and eleventh centuries, the bridegift, given by the husband, came to be replaced by the *dos* in the Roman sense. The bridegift, as we saw in its earlier form, whether given as usufruct, which had to be passed on to the children after the wife's death, or as property, which the wife owned outright and could alienate or leave to whomever she wished, was turned over to her on her wedding day and usually represented a specific tract of land. But in the tenth and eleventh centuries, fewer deeds gave the wife outright ownership, and even the usufruct was generally restricted to the use of the husband and wife jointly, not to the wife exclusively.[36] Instead of specifying a given piece of property, some deeds spoke only of a fraction of the income derived from the husband's patrimony. On the other hand, the dowry itself was given to the bride by her father or brother, and as a consequence neither she nor her offspring could thereafter advance any claims on the patrimony. In the event of her husband's death, the woman was thus provided for by the remnants of the bridegift, but her economic independence during his lifetime, and, to some extent, after his death, had vanished (pp. 96–97).[37]

35. See particularly Gunter Grimm, "Die Eheschließungen," pp. 50–56.

36. In England the dowry, which had before been and remained the woman's property, now became her husband's property after marriage, to which she had only usufruct — not ownership rights — after his death. See Herlihy, *Medieval Households,* on similar laws elsewhere (p. 100).

37. See here also Roger Bataille, *Le droit des filles dans la succession de leurs parents en Normandie* (Paris, 1927), noted by McNamara and Wemple. See also, however, Jack Goody's cautious skepticism about the validity of such generalizations based on incomplete data and on the complexity of such practices in the whole context of social relations, in *The Development of the Family and Marriage in Europe,* Appendix 2: "From Brideprice to Dowry?" pp. 240–261.

The foregoing discussion of the multiple forms of marriage settlements and their changes through time functions to provide a schema of historical situations and their regulation, which form part of the historical basis mediated by the *Nibelungenlied;* it provides a context in which to read the several types of male-female relationships in the *Nibelungenlied,* as well as the property relations dependent on them. A second inevitable result of such a protracted (though summary) discussion is, however, that the accents have been misplaced, and essential social and political issues—especially gender—deemphasized, almost obscured: for in all marriage types noted, however the settlement was arranged, it was arranged by men, primarily for the sake and benefit of men. The women were the objects of exchange, a reified commodity which the men traded among themselves. This system of the marital exchange of women by men necessarily empowers men to act on and through women, while women become the mere vehicles of male power. As Gayle Rubin notes, this male power illustrates the Lacanian sense of the "phallus," for the power merely passes through women without inhering in them. Thus it may lead to "penis envy," again in the symbolic (not anatomical) Lacanian sense, which, according to Gayle Rubin, "acquires a rich meaning of the disquietude of women in a phallic culture."[38] This disquietude foments rebellion, and it is rebellion that Brünhild and Kriemhild perpetrate in their rejection of their assigned role as commodity.

In moving from a consideration of the legal and historical foundations of marriage and property relations in the early and high Middle Ages in central Europe to an analysis of related issues in the *Nibelungenlied,* three things become immediately apparent: first, property ownership seems the most obvious and important means of access to political power and authority, and is so recognized by the characters of the *Nibelungenlied;* second, the models of marriage available to the society are here exemplified and, via personal relationships, examined; finally, these two issues are combined, in that the control of property becomes a central issue in the articulation

38. Rubin, "The Traffic in Women," p. 192. On the necessarily political nature of feudal marriage see also Friedrich Engels, "Für den Ritter oder Baron wie für den Landesfürsten selbst ist die Verheiratung ein politischer Akt, eine Gelegenheit der Machtvergrößerung durch neue Bündnisse; das Interesse des *Hauses* hat zu entscheiden, nicht das Belieben des einzelnen" ("For the knight or baron as for the prince himself marriage was a political act, an opportunity for the increase in ones' power through new alliances; the interest of the dynastic house was decisive, not the desires of the individual"); in *Der Ursprung der Familie, des Privateigentums und des Staats,* in Karl Marx und Friedrich Engels, *Ausgewählte Schriften in zwei Bänden* (Berlin: Dietz, 1989), II, 197–347, here p. 250.

of male-female relationships. The public-private dichotomy in the highly qualified sense articulated above obtains and, through its assumption by the male characters, offers an opportunity for the imposition of a typically patriarchal double standard. Political action of any kind on the part of a woman is considered by men to be an intrusion of the private into the public space inhabited by males and one that must be prevented at all costs. The political and public implications of allegedly private actions are thus already recognized by male characters, but they seek nonetheless to maintain the fictional dichotomy, since it continues to serve their purposes.[39]

Several issues arising from the gender-based perspective here emphasized must be addressed in the course of the discussion. Considering the immediate sociological context of the *Nibelungenlied* in the late twelfth-century continuation of the erosion of women's public authority, legal rights to inherit property and generally participate in the body politic, it seems likely that the *Nibelungenlied* takes as one of its central topics this issue of gender relations,[40] especially as that issue is determined by property relations. If so, then the greedy obsession with treasure that scholars have long imputed to Kriemhild must also be reexamined.[41] For if she takes a great interest in material wealth, then surely not more so than her male counterparts, who take their own control over treasure for granted and do all within their power to deprive women of such independent control. In the end it seems that if women's attention to property control must be labelled an obsession, then it is one caused by the corresponding male obsession with depriving women of property. They are obsessed only because they are not allowed to *possess*.

Let us first address the issue of marriage types. Depending on the system of classification used, there are either two or three types of marriage represented in the *Nibelungenlied*: the two historical, early German types, or the three types based more closely on the power relationships of the spouses. The first two marriages of the *Nibelungenlied* — Kriemhild's to Siegfried and Brünhild's to Gunther — represent patriarchal marriage in all respects. They also represent respectively both *munt*-marriage and abduc-

<hr>

39. Claudia Becker equates the Inside with the private and the Outside with the public (without using these terms) and thus concludes: "A life in an outside area is almost impossible for a woman," in "Spatial, Societal, and Personal Distance Among the Protagonists in the *Nibelungenlied*," unpublished ms. (1988), p. 15.

40. And perhaps also the struggle between the monarchy and the aristocracy as manifested in the characters of Hagen and perhaps also Rüdiger in conflict with their kings.

41. Cf., for example, Karl Heinz Ihlenburg, *Das Nibelungenlied* and Weber, *Das Nibelungenlied*, pp. 7–8 on Kriemhild as power and money hungry; cf. also Schweikle "Das 'Nibelungenlied,'" (p. 62) for a refutation of such arguments.

tion/rape. Kriemhild, along with (the offer of) a substantial dowry, is bartered to Siegfried and placed under his absolute authority by her brothers as "payment" (*lôn,* as specified by Siegfried, 333, 4) for his service to Gunther in deceiving and physically assaulting and subduing Brünhild.[42] For Brünhild's marriage differs in no significant respect from forced marriage: she goes to Worms as Gunther's bride only after decisive defeat in single combat, where she is sexually assaulted by Siegfried and Gunther. Some few aspects, however, also point toward the *Friedelehe* model. Ostensibly she stands under no one's *munt* and marries without transfer of dowry or *munt;* the marriage also conforms to the model suggested by Herlihy (see above) of "abduction with consent," if we concede that Brünhild's faithful keeping of her bargain (to marry Gunther if she is defeated in the contests) implies consent.[43] The blending of the model of *Friedelehe* and rape serves a clear purpose in seeking to disguise the brutality and humiliation of this particular example of patriarchal marriage while at the same time making unmistakably clear the consequences of women's attempts to maintain and satisfy their own desires in opposition to, and at the expense of male desire.

The third marital model occurs in Kriemhild's marriage to Etzel, which differs in important respects to Brünhild's and other marriages. In that Kriemhild, now a widow and no longer altogether under the legal protection (*munt*) of any male,[44] has some small measure of independence even within the traditional system. That this independent tendency continues later allows for the condemnation of Kriemhild and the implied and expressed censure of Etzel by characters in and scholars of the *Nibelungenlied.*[45]

It is necessary to bear in mind the severe restrictions on any notion of

---

42. Cf. also Hugo Bekker: "it is more accurate to say that she is bartered to Siegfried" (p. 60, n. 24); and: "women are the mute objects of gifts and barter, in the eyes not only of brothers, but also of lovers" *The Nibelungenlied: A Literary Analysis* (Toronto: University of Toronto Press, 1971), p. 108.

43. Should the conventional view of Brünhild's position at this point in the narrative — as independent of male control and freely consenting to the marriage with Gunther — seem too much in conflict with my view here, I refer the reader to the detailed treatment of this marriage in Chapter five below.

44. Although in fact her brothers seek to exercise this authority, and Rüdiger also pretends to have assumed it in proxy while in transit to Hunland.

45. McConnell, for instance, claims that "Kriemhild's marriage to Attila [*sic*] is a sham" since its purpose is not "harmony and productivity" for the Huns or "inner peace" for Kriemhild, "but solely for the purpose of obtaining another power base" ("Marriage in the *Nibelungenlied* and *Kudrun*," p. 20). That is, it is a political marriage, which is apparently normal for men, but inconceivable for women, except as they are given and received by men for male purposes.

female independence here: for while Kriemhild is allowed some latitude in deciding whether to marry Etzel that she was not permitted in her first marriage,[46] it is, for instance, Etzel, not Kriemhild, who initially decides on this marriage. It is not the case that Kriemhild independently decides to marry and is empowered to seek out a husband of her choice. Furthermore, the arrangement of the marriage *per se* is in the hands of men — as proxy-suitors, pseudo-guardians, escorts, etc. Nonetheless, despite the men's belief that the decision was theirs, it is in fact Kriemhild who makes the decision to marry Etzel for her own private *and* political reasons.[47] As a result of Kriemhild's motivation, the traditional associations with the notion of *Friedelehe* — mutual affection and a bond of equals — seem only vaguely relevant, for Kriemhild's role is necessarily a much more active one than would normally be assigned to the woman even in *Friedelehe*. This aspect of her second marriage becomes one of the cruces of the scholarly evaluation of her character: she has clearly overstepped the bounds of the traditionally permissible, for despite the fact that as a widow she is permitted more independence in the arrangement of marriage, she decides to marry not for either of the reasons deemed permissible by modern patriarchy — "love" or male political purposes — but rather for *her own* political purposes.

Turning specifically to property relations, one remarks that the *attitudes* of male characters toward female ownership of property are as interesting in some ways as the *facts* of women's potential relations to property. Such attitudes are obviously intimately related to issues of gender and power; they are complex and, like all social relations, overdetermined. Men consistently and immediately take action to deprive women of their legal property through their own appropriation of it, through both legitimate and illegitimate distribution of it to other men, and through arbitrary repudiation of the woman's claim to it. In other words, despite the woman's legally recognized ownership of property, men recurringly assume the right to dispose of it, even against the express wishes of the woman, and they do so in most cases openly, in some cases mockingly and in such a way as to

---

46. Despite Gunther's pretense of asking for her consent — long after he had already promised Siegfried her hand and long after he had already worked out the brideprice, as it were — Siegfried's aid in defrauding Brünhild.

47. Theodore Andersson suggests that Kriemhild is caught in a conflict of the two models of marriage — the old aristocratic *munt*-model in which marriages were arranged for the political purposes of the families, and the ecclesiastical model, more closely related to traditional *Friedelehe,* based on the indissolubility of marriage and the devotion to one's spouse (*Preface,* p. 93).

increase their own reputations (among men) for political acuity, male cameraderie, and feudal generosity.[48] There are three primary instances of this mode of behavior in the *Nibelungenlied* to be reviewed here.

The most complex and significant such scene occurs as Siegfried and Kriemhild prepare to depart from Burgundy for Xanten after their marriage.[49] Kriemhild remarks on the obvious fact that she must still receive her share of the dynasty's allodial lands before leaving: *mir suln ê mîne brüeder teilen mit diu lant* ("my brothers must first divide our lands with me" 691,3). Siegfried's reaction is initially utterly incomprehensible: *leit was ez Sîfride do erz an Kriemhilt ervant* ("Siegfried was annoyed/grief-stricken when he discovered this about Kriemhild" 691,4). While perhaps not as stupendously rich as Siegfried, due to his possession of the Nibelungenlied hoard, the Burgundians are nonetheless quite wealthy. Kriemhild's share of the lands and vassals would be a substantial addition even to Siegfried's holdings. Furthermore, as soon as the wedding festival had ended, the Burgundian princes themselves introduced the topic without prompting by Kriemhild, and they are immediately ready to make the division (693).

Why, then, would Siegfried be troubled by such a matter of fact busi ness transaction? Assuming many possible answers, three seem most relevant, especially as property rights in general and women's property rights in particular are treated in the *Nibelungenlied*. As discussed above, in the century before the composition of the *Nibelungenlied* the abilities of women to acquire and control property and exercise authority had undergone radical modification. Already in this early scene of the *Nibelungenlied,* both that particular social development and the more general tendency to avoid the division of the patrimony and the alienation of a part of it from the dynasty may be topicalized. In this case, the lands would have been permanently alienated from the Burgundian crown.

Secondly, in any highly stratified society in which goods are generally transferred from the higher to the lower levels in exchange for services rendered, as was the case in feudal societies in medieval Europe, the person who accepts a gift incurs in its receipt an obligation, a debt, as it were, to the

---

48. Significantly, this type of male behavior has been documented by recent sociological and psychological research as a commonplace of spousal abuse: the systematic deprivation of all economic independence comprises one recurring component of such abuse; see Lenore E. Walker, *The Battered Woman* (New York: Harper and Row, 1979), pp. 127–144.

49. The explosive significance of the scene is well captured in Seitter's ironic understatement: "die nächste Aventiure beginnt mit einem kleinen — wie es scheint — Dissens," in *Das politische Wissen im Nibelungenlied*, p. 174.

donor; in the case that more is given than can be reciprocated, the recipient is in some sense humiliated, or at least given concrete evidence of social subordination, while the donor gains political power through that same act.[50] This is the classic *do ut des* system. Gift-giving is thus a problematic kind of behavior in medieval European literature (and history too, of course). Generally it is service that the subordinate offers to the superior, the vassal to the lord, while transfers in the opposite direction consist of material rewards, gifts, and usufruct of property (fiefs).[51] Thus a material gift immediately *implies* that the recipient is the subordinate, which then has important implications for the further relationship of the parties. Secondly, as noted above, the recipient incurs an obligation to the donor simply by accepting the gift, due to the conventional code governing the transfer of goods.

At the same time, however, largesse is a vital aspect of the feudal system, for it functions to distribute goods, to allow for profitable administration of feudal territory, and to create and cement hierarchical relations. The generous lord is a cliché of feudal literature. The acceptance of a gift, or even of a share of inherited land or vassals, participates however tangentially in the economy of such a ubiquitous and pervasive system of order. Thus for Siegfried to accept property and vassals from the Burgundians, even as Kriemhild's legal share of the inheritance, would in this very important sense bind him to an obligation. The distinctions involved here are subtle, as is obvious in the seeming contradiction that since his arrival in Burgundy Siegfried has time and again performed service of almost menial nature: as field marshal against the Saxons and Danes, travel guide to Iceland, stuntman cum gladiator, captain of the Nibelungen guards, and messenger. The difference is that those tasks were performed both without material reward[52] and without expectation of such, except insofar as Kriemhild as bride is treated as a material reward, for these services were performed in prospect of acquiring her as a bride. Whether or not this service

50. See especially Gayle Rubin, "The Traffic in Women," pp. 171–172, and her analysis of Marcel Mauss's "Essai sur le don: Forme et raison de l'exchange dans les sociétés archaïques," *L'Année Sociologique* 25. 1 (1923–24); rpt. in Mauss, *Sociologie et anthropologie* (Paris: Quadrige 1950), pp. 143–279.

51. Certainly there was also a transfer of basic material goods — food, cloth, wood, quarried stone, etc. — from the lowest levels, the serfs, to all higher levels, but that transfer was in general of a wholly different kind, since the lord always *owned* the produce of the land, which was then manufactured and/or (re)distributed under his auspices.

52. At least there was none from the Burgundian kings; Kriemhild offered a reward to Siegfried for his messenger service, and he gladly accepted it without incurring any obligation, which demonstrates here already that gifts by females to males signify in a completely different manner from corresponding exchanges between males.

need be called *Minnedienst*, as earlier critical generations deemed appropriate, it can at least be considered in materialist terms as service performed with a direct view to payment by the transfer of a female *to* the control of the male performing the service and *by* the male who has received it. To this special kind of quasi employee-employer relationship no stigma attaches, while to that of a direct material gift, no stigma perhaps, but certainly an implied obligation and more than merely a hint of subordination.

A third problem is also apparent in this proposed transfer of property, and one that recurs throughout the *Nibelungenlied*. This particular instance of male-female interaction prompts Hugo Bekker to remark: "The poet does not say why, but there are several indications in the *Nibelungenlied* that marriage is a doubtful venture for a woman, and that she may do well to take with her whatever worldly goods she can."[53] As Bekker further notes, Siegfried fears that an independently wealthy wife "might be less tractable" than one not so endowed. If Kriemhild were to enter the marriage with Siegfried as a landed princess with a third of the Burgundian feudal ranks as her vassals — for Gunther offers her one thousand of the three thousand Burgundian vassals (697,3) — then she would have a feudal status and concrete power far beyond that adhering to her status as the consort of the king (*regis uxor*) of the Netherlands, even if the Burgundian holdings were administered either jointly by Siegfried and Kriemhild, or by Siegfried alone, either of which courses would have been both legal and customary.[54] For the lands could ultimately still have been Kriemhild's, just as the vassals were directly attached to her without either mediation through her husband or obligation to him except as ordered by her. Kriemhild in other words would not have been just Siegfried's wife, defined by her lineage, renowned beauty and attachment to her husband, but would have also remained in a more concrete sense apart from that relationship a princess or perhaps even *regens regina* with holdings in land and vassals of monarchical dimensions. She would have been a potential political rival of some consequence, especially when one reckoned with her powerful Burgundian allies.

For at least these reasons Siegfried categorically refuses to accept the

53. Bekker, *The Nibelungenlied*, p. 64. A double standard is implicit here too in the notion that the woman's "need" to retain possession of her property arises from a *specific* threat, and thus that female ownership may not be a simple matter of fact. Or to put it the other way around, by contrast it would be ridiculous even to suggest that the reason *men* do not give up *their* property when they marry is because matrimony is such a risky business.

54. Cf. above, on actual historical practice with respect to joint governance. And here: "*der sult ir teil vil guoten   mit samt Kriemhilde hân*" ("of them [their extensive realms] you shall have your share to hold jointly with Kriemhild" 693,4).

Burgundian offer, countering with the claim that becomes the standard cliché offered by men in the *Nibelungenlied* to justify the despoiling of women — that in his kingdom Kriemhild will wear a crown and be richer than anyone alive (694–695); it will, however, be the crown of the *regis uxor* and the wealth of her husband, whereby she will be stripped of all independent power. Thus while the Burgundians acknowledge by mentioning her name that Kriemhild must at least have some share in the administration of the holdings offered, their offer is made directly to Siegfried, who is obviously empowered, or perhaps simply assumes the authority, to decide not just whether an offer is equitable, but also whether to renounce any and all offers of and claims to her inheritance. Kriemhild's participation thus far has been restricted strictly to the private sphere — in remarking to Siegfried that a settlement must be reached. Males alone make the public decisions in this matter of Kriemhild's property — how much land and how many vassals, if any, are to be transferred — even though, strictly speaking, none of them has any legal ownership interest in her property.

It is in fact only in the case that Kriemhild were disinherited that any of the males might profit, and then all of them would do so, albeit in various ways: Siegfried would maintain his independent status without obligation to the Burgundians and without potential political rivalry with his disinherited, penniless and thus powerless bride, whose future wealth and power would consist solely of that granted to her by him, based exclusively on her status as his wife. The Burgundians would also profit quite concretely by not having to divide their wealth and realms with Kriemhild. One notices that her brothers utter not a single word of protest as they graciously accept Siegfried's renunciation of Kriemhild's inheritance.

As a result of the direction taken by these negotiations, Kriemhild is forced to take part in the otherwise strictly male transaction, if she is to prevent the complete loss of her property. She immediately proposes a compromise: *habt ir der erbe rât, / um Burgonden degene   sô lîht'ez niht enstât* ("'even if you renounce my land-inheritance,[55] one may not be so flippant when it comes to Burgundian knights'" 696,1–2). From the men's perspective this utterance can only be seen as an intrusion by a woman into men's business. It matters little that it is *her* property under discussion. This distinction also illustrates the classic case defined by Imray and Middleton above, in which identical acts (discussion of property settlement) by men

---

55. So Lexer: *Grundeigentum* as opposed to movable goods and feudal grants.

and women are perceived (by men) as public acts by men and private acts by women.

A. T. Hatto's influential translation of this sentence differs so dramatically from my own and in a way relevant to my argument that it might be profitable to do more than merely note the difference in passing.[56] His rendering is: "'You may well renounce my inheritance,' said Lady Kriemhild, 'but it will not be so easy where knights of Burgundy are concerned'" (p. 96). The syntax of the sentence is somewhat convoluted, but not much more than is common in Middle High German rhymed and accented verse. The first clause begins with the finite verb, but is neither a question nor an imperative, as this position otherwise commonly indicates. Rather the verb-initial position here indicates another common syntactic usage: a conditional clause with implied, quasi-deleted *ob* "if" and inverted word-order. Thus Kriemhild's initial words do not by any means accept and acknowledge Siegfried's renunciation of the whole of her inheritance — as Hatto's "you may well . . ." implies — but rather protest it first by turning that renunciation into the protasis of a conditional sentence, and then by labelling that renunciation careless and flippant (*lîht*) and thirdly by indicating that she will not give up her right in Burgundian vassals. She then momentarily bows to the vanity of her husband by noting that Burgundian knights would look good in any king's triumphal procession, but then drives home her point succinctly and unmistakeably: *jâ sol si mit mir teilen   mîner lieben bruoder hant* ("my brothers must indeed / shall divide them with me" 696,4).[57] Her comment redirects the entire conversation of the men, effectively eliminates Siegfried's further participation, and prompts Gunther to offer her a free hand in choosing her third of the vassals.[58]

In the end she takes along only five hundred, that is, only half of the number agreed upon (and thirty-two maidens, 700,3). No reason is given by the text for this discrepancy, and it is hardly in the spirit of the preceding stanzas to impute the reduction either to Kriemhild or to her brothers, both

56. The difference was called to my attention by undergraduate students in a class on the *Nibelungenlied* in translation, who, on the basis of Hatto's translation, took exception to my interpretation of the Middle High German passage.

57. Hatto's rendering weakens the force of the modal: "I request my dear brothers to make division of them with me."

58. Her attempt to take Hagen demonstrates less her naïveté in realpolitical terms, as some critics have claimed, than it indicates that even at this early stage she is well aware of Hagen's potential value as an ally and danger as an enemy. His refusal to submit to this feudal transfer of his service from one of his superiors to another is merely the first instance of Hagen's disobedience of his feudal superiors.

of which parties, one would assume, would accept the larger number—Gunther *expressis uerbis,* Kriemhild on principle. The most likely alternative is to attribute this reduction in number to Siegfried, as a final offstage attempt on his part to reduce both his obligation to Burgundy and the independence of his wife. But again, the text is silent on this point, and Siegfried may only be suspected, not accused. At any rate, it is only by first forcing the issue on Siegfried and then by direct intervention in the patriarchal process of inheritance distribution that Kriemhild manages to salvage anything of her patrimony. Otherwise, she would have gone to Xanten with nothing more than her personal effects, and perhaps the requisite female retinue. As it is, she enters her marriage with slightly more than a tenth of the female and exactly a quarter of the male retinue that had accompanied Brünhild from Iceland.

And it is to Brünhild that we must now turn, for hers is in fact the first property struggle in the work, and the first instance of this paradigmatic scene of despoiling and consequent disempowerment. After the initial Burgundian defrauding of Brünhild in Iceland and during the preparations for the departure to Worms, Brünhild asks for a volunteer vassal to perform the service of distributing her largesse to her guests, as a concrete demonstration of the generosity necessary for the reputation characteristic of feudal aristocracy, and also concomitantly to bind the recipients to her, reward them for past and obligate them to future service. The Burgundian vassal Dancwart volunteers, and his largesse is initially described in the terms of feudal generosity that are so well known from a variety of the medieval literatures of Europe, that they are simply clichés of the courtly and *comitatus*-literatures: *sô manige gâbe rîche bôt des helden hant* ("the hero offered so many magnificent gifts" 515).[59] But the picture is immediately skewed by his lack of proportion and moderation:

> swer einer marke gerte,   dem wart sô vil gegeben,
> daz die armen alle   muosen vrœlîche leben.
> Wol bî hundert pfunden   gap er âne zal.

(Whoever wanted a mark, he gave him so much, that all the poor could live happily on it. Time without number he gave away portions of a hundred pounds [of gold] each) (515,3–516,1)

---

59. Cf. also Bekker, *The Nibelungenlied* (pp. 101–103) on Siegfried's generosity as a requisite characteristic of kingship.

Just as she had promised when she asked for assistance in distribution (*ich wold' im wesen holt, / der geteilen kunde   mîn silber unt mîn golt* "I would be grateful to anyone who could distribute my silver and gold" 513,1–2), now Brünhild employs the same formula to elicit aid in halting the squandering of her treasury (*der iz noch understüende,   dem wold ich immer wesen holt* "I would be eternally grateful to anyone who would put a stop to it" 517,4).[60] The poet twice uses the stock term designating feudal generosity: *milte*, but in each instance the usage is open to ironic interpretation: *daz er milte wære,   daz tet er græzlichen schîn* ("he gave plain evidence that he was generous / he made a great show of being generous" 514,4) and *sô milten kamerære   gewan noch küneginne nie* ("no queen had ever had such a generous treasurer" 518,4).

In response to her request that Dancwart stop, or rather that he be stopped, another Burgundian vassal, his brother Hagen, takes this opportunity to justify the despoiling of this woman by making use of the cliché soon to be employed by Siegfried in Burgundy: Hagen replies that the Burgundian royal treasury has so much gold and so many fine garments that Brünhild has no need to take any of her property along (519). The communicative context has thus been shifted drastically. Brünhild had not addressed the issue of the amount of treasure to be transported to Worms, but rather the fact that it was now being squandered. Hagen's reply ignores the request that that action cease, and offers instead an indirect justification for its continuation: since Gunther is immensely wealthy, she will have no need of her own treasure, and thus they apparently intend to empty the Icelandic royal treasury altogether as a sign of *their own* generosity.

To this insubordination on the part of her new vassals and the concomitant unwillingness or inability of their king, her espoused husband, to prevent it, Brünhild responds not verbally — which had already failed to produce any tangible result — but rather physically as has been her practice in the past, by redirecting the flow of treasure into trunks to be distributed as largesse in Worms (520) rather than through Dancwart's brief and

---

60. Seitter's remarks concerning Brünhild's reactions seem on the one hand cleverly pertinent: her reaction is "ein ökonomischer Ohnmachtsanfall" ("an economic fainting spell," *Versprechen*, p. 25); on the other hand, conventionally excessive: her reaction is "sehr heftig, sagen wir hysterisch" ("very vigorous, let us say, hysterical," *Das politische Wissen*, p. 129; cf. also p. 105). The C-manuscript makes no mention of a struggle between Brünhild and Dancwart/Hagen as despoilers. Rather, she simply distributes treasure to *vremden* and *chvnden* (526) in Iceland as she wishes and then packs up twenty trunks of treasure to take along to Burgundy, that is, the same amount with which she leaves Iceland in the B-text against the will of the men. Thus the C-text need not exaggerate Brünhild's wealth, but rather only allow her independent action and control of her property, in order to empower her.

would-be final custody in Isenstein. This act, and the fact that it is carried out by her own vassals and not Gunther's (e.g., Dancwart), prompts her counterparts, Gunther and Hagen, to mocking laughter (521,4). Nelly Dürrenmatt's comment (p. 224), that the poet "inserted" this scene in order to show that Brünhild lacked the cardinal feudal virtue, *milte* "generosity," seems inaccurate, since in fact it was Brünhild who initiated this distribution of goods, and who now acts to retain some of her property, *so that* she might distribute it later. There is no evidence for stinginess on Brünhild's part, but ample evidence of her understanding of the political implications of *who* gives gifts to whom. This distribution of largesse is, as suggested above, necessarily a political act. Were Dancwart distributing Brünhild's treasure according to her will, he would increase primarily her reputation, although his own would also profit indirectly. By squandering it against her will, he usurps the act itself by eliminating her from participation and responsibility. The fact that she finally acts to save a portion for herself to give away in Worms may seem ironic, but in fact is again a clearly political calculation of which all are aware: Brünhild's distribution of *her own* treasure in Worms will create allegiances and obligations directly to her, not first mediated by feudal obligations through her husband.[61]

Gunther shows not the slightest interest in what would seem the primary order of business for a king, to guarantee the continuance of government in the absence of Iceland's ruler. When Brünhild courteously asks him, as her espoused husband and lord, about a regent, his response could be interpreted in two rather different ways: *nû heizet her gân, / der iu dar zuo gevalle;   den sul wir voget wesen lân* ("summon whomever you please; we shall appoint him governor" 522,3–4). One might say that he defers to her sovereignty, but it seems just as likely, as Mowatt and Sacker point out and Gunther's complete disinterest in Iceland hereafter suggests, that he has little interest in Brünhild at all except as his wife and appurtenance.[62] The fact that she is the sovereign of a realm and thus is not just of

---

61. Hildegard Bartels notes the correspondence of wasting Brünhild's wealth and the theft of Kriemhild's hoard as a diminution of power. With the squandering of her wealth begins "der Prozeß des zunehmenden Verlustes von Brünhildes 'epischer Selbständigkeit' und ihre Anpassung an die Rolle einer Königin im das 'Patriarchat' konsequent verteidigenden Burgund" ("The process of Brünhild's increasing loss of 'epic independence' and her accommodation to the role of a queen in a Burgundy that consistently defends patriarchy"). Herewith she loses her heroic individuality; see *Epos — die Gattung in der Geschichte: Eine Begriffsbestimmung vor dem Hintergrund der Hegelschen "Ästhetik" anhand von "Nibelungenlied" und "Chanson de Roland"* [Heidelberg: Winter, 1982], pp. 254–255.

62. Cf. Mowatt and Sacker, *The Nibelungenlied: An Interpretive Commentary* (Toronto: University of Toronto Press, 1967), p. 66: "The brutal indifference of the Burgundians to any

his class, but his hierarchical equal,[63] is a fact to be denied if possible, to be ignored at all times, and all evidence of that fact is to be systematically eliminated before it can appear and be acknowledged in Worms. The Burgundians wish to return to Worms with the king of Burgundy and his bride, not with the king of Burgundy and the queen of Iceland. As the poet notes upon their departure: *sî rûmte ir eigen lant* ("she left her own/sovereign land," 526,1). In doing so, Brünhild also takes along as her retinue two thousand of her vassals (524,1), eighty-six ladies and two hundred maidens (525,1–2).[64]

The cause of the men's fear of independent female largesse in each case thus far — Brünhild's in Iceland and Kriemhild's in Worms — becomes clear years later, when Kriemhild herself distributes her *Morgengabe* generously, legally, and, as inevitable whether performed by male or female, with political purpose. The earlier scenes resonate clearly here. Despite the fact that this treasure is not her inheritance, it is acknowledged by all concerned to be her rightful property. Both the narrator (1116,4) and Alberich (1118,4) acknowledge Kriemhild's right to the hoard as her *Morgengabe*,[65] and thus Alberich, as *kamerære* (1120,4), immediately performs his duty by yielding the treasure to its lawful owner. In this, by now, third such episode of despoiling, the established pattern is followed, and Hagen (with the approval of the Burgundian kings) again deprives her of the treasure and thus of access to power. The consequences of this theft, however, have repercussions for the entire remaining history of the Burgundian monarchy. In this case there is so much treasure that when Kriemhild manages to save only a minuscule portion of it, that fraction is still considered so significant that a second theft is later perpetrated, again by Hagen and the Burgundian kings. Attempts to determine the amount of treasure are doomed to failure, for it is described in the vague terms necessary to emphasize its indescrib-

---

emotion that Brünnhilde might experience is made extraordinarily clear here. She has, after all, ruled very effectively on her own for some time, her riches are considerable, and her beauty is internationally renowned. Having surrendered all this, she is entitled to expect the winner to take some interest in the prize. Instead, he wants to leave as soon as possible, appoints a governor at her request in a decidedly off-hand manner, allows his underlings to jeer at her wealth, making it as clear as he can that her achievements up to now are expendable. The Burgundian attitude seems all the more obnoxious, when one realises how little they have done to deserve the prize anyway. No wonder they are unable to appreciate it."

63. Not to mention his physical and, in view of his means of winning the contests, his ethical superior.

64. C-manuscript: 1000 vassals, 86 ladies and 100 maidens (532–533).

65. Also C-manuscript 1129–1131.

able immensity. It seems nonetheless that it can be transported by 144 *kanzwägene*.[66]

The theft of the hoard is obviously of great significance to the development of the narrative, and there has been a great deal of critical attention to this motif. The interpretations by Friedrich Maurer and W. Schröder may be taken as representative. Maurer deftly incorporates this topic into his thesis concerning *leit* as the prime motivation of action in the text. The loss of the hoard is a further *leit* ("insult") to be avenged, while the emphasis on the hoard toward the end of the *Nibelungenlied* does not, he argues, indicate greed on Kriemhild's part, but rather her attempt to regain that which has caused her *leit,* to recoup honor from him who had deprived her of it.[67] According to Maurer, the hoard signifies honor. In his attempt to refute Maurer's entire thesis concerning *leit,* W. Schröder counters that while the hoard serves as a means to power (*Machtmittel*), and its loss diminishes Kriemhild's honor, its significance to her is strictly limited to its symbolic value in representing Siegfried, insofar as it is her *Morgengabe* from him: "im Hort lebt für sie der tote Geliebte fort" ("her dead lover lives on for her in the hoard," p. 75). It seems, according to Schröder, that Kriemhild is incapable of any acts except those motivated by love: "aus unstillbarem *Herzeleide* um ihren *holden Vriedel,* letztes Endes aus Liebe" ("from unquenchable heartache for her true love, in the final analysis, for love," p. 76).[68] This point represents a single aspect of Schröder's larger argument, in which he attempts to reduce Kriemhild from a knowledgable participant in political action to a wronged subject, from a political actant to an private sufferer, from a (momentarily) triumphant politician and warrior queen to a grieving widow, incapable of rationality. Thus she returns to Worms because of *Heimweh* ("homesickness" p. 69); her part in the beginning of the argument with Brünhild is merely a "proud outcry" that has "no political aspiration," but is rather "unconsidered," a "harmless, impulsive remark." According to Schröder, women are emotional, thoughtless, impulsive and by nature apolitical creatures.

Since in Schröder's views political interpretations of the *Nibelungenlied*

---

66. Twelve wagons carrying three loads per day for four days (1122); cf. C-manuscript: *hundert chantz wægene* (92), but also in the passage corresponding to the present stanza: twelve wagons carrying *nine* loads per day for four days (1135).

67. Friedrich Maurer, *Leid: Studien zur Bedeutungs- und Problemgeschichte besonders in den großen Epen der staufischen Zeit* (Bern/München: Francke, 1951), pp. 21–22.

68. Werner Schröder, "Die Tragödie Kriemhilts im Nibelungenlied," pp. 66–67.

are a matter of momentary fashion ("Neuerdings ist es Mode geworden, mittelalterlichen Dichtern ausgeprägt politisches Denken zu unterstellen" ["Recently it has become fashionable to impute blatantly political ideas to medieval poets" p. 67]), he argues that Kriemhild's actions are utterly apolitical: "Daß ihre Entscheidungen, die ablehnende wie die zustimmende, zu irgendeinem Zeitpunkt von einem heimlichen Willen zur Macht diktiert worden wären, wird kein unvoreingenommener Beurteiler behaupten wollen" ("No unbiased judge would maintain that her decisions, whether those of rejection or consent, were dictated at any point by a secret will to power," p. 126). In this view there seems no alternative to the bipolar opposites of motivation — either purely emotional or "Wille zur Macht." As Andersson (p. 150) notes, in general both Werner and W. J. Schröder seek a kind of rehabilitation of Kriemhild. But it is a rehabilitation based on a reduction of her from political to purely emotional being.

The only significations of Kriemhild's treasure suggested by these critics is as a subversive threat, an abstract "honor," or a symbol of her long-dead and beloved husband. In each case a strictly idealist interpretation is offered for a blatantly materialist issue. As indicated above, however, Hildgard Bartels has at least noted the significance of wealth as power in both the wooing of Brünhild's treasure and the theft of Kriemhild's hoard. Likewise the argument that Kriemhild's treasure is taken from her in order to prevent her threatening the realm further by means of her increasing number of vassals, as McConnell among others notes,[69] is at best only partially valid. For in fact at the first mention of the treasure in this context (*aventiure* 19), Hagen's purpose is, to the extent possible, to appropriate the hoard for the Burgundian treasury:

> *Dô sprach der helt von Tronege:*   *"möht ir daz tragen an,*
> *daz ir iuwer swester   ze vriunde möhtet hân,*
> *sô kæme ze disen landen   daz Nibelunges golt.*
> *des möht ir vil gewinnen,   würd' uns diu küneginne holt."*

(Then the warrior from Tronege said: "if you could bring it about that your sister were friendly to you, then Nibelung's gold would come to

---

69. McConnell argues quite accurately, I think, that the hoard is a threat to Hagen, especially since Kriemhild uses it as a "power basis" to " 'deal' with Hagen," for which reason, the "removal of the treasure is, from Hagen's point of view, the only solution" (*The Nibelungenlied*, p. 19).

this country. If the queen were well-disposed to us, you could gain possession of much of it.") (1107)[70]

Gunther is immediately willing: *wir sulnz versuochen* ("let's try it" 1108), and in three stages the plan is executed: Kriemhild is convinced to reconcile with her brothers (1109–1115); the treasure is brought to Worms (1116–1125); and it is stolen by Hagen and sunk in the Rhine with the intent of later recovery and use (1130–1137).

In Worms Kriemhild took possession of the entire treasure (*diu küneginne alles underwant* 1125,2), after which her behavior was simultaneously praiseworthy and seriously threatening:

> *Dô sie den hort nu hête,   dô brâhtes' in daz lant*
> *vil unkunder recken.   jâ gap der vrouwen hant,*
> *daz man sô grôzer milte   mêre nie gesach.*
> *si pflac vil guoter tugende,   des man der küneginne jach.*

(When she then had possession of the hoard, at that time she brought many foreign warriors into the country. Indeed the lady's hand gave such gifts, that no one has ever seen such generosity since. She cultivated many fine virtues, which were recognized and acknowledged.) (1127)

Here Kriemhild simply performs the role of treasurer on her own behalf, and, according to the narrator, she does so in the context of practicing virtuous behavior. There is nothing in this stanza that indicates any wrongdoing. Instead, Kriemhild simply engages in the behavior typical of feudal royalty: she distributes the realm's possessions in order to secure strong and loyal allies and vassals. In this case the knights are not Burgundians, since the latter already have committed loyalties and feudal bonds, specifically to her mortal enemies. They are instead "unknown" warriors, i.e. warriors from outside the court. Such behavior is, however, also legitimate, even praiseworthy, in rulers, for thus they attract strong vassals and allies from beyond the borders of the realm, establish alliances that may prove useful later, and extend the throne's reputation for munificence.

Kriemhild's behavior in this regard has nonetheless generally been

---

70. Hagen's desire for the hoard is noted by the narrator: *jane het es âne schulde   niht gar Hagen gegert* ("indeed Hagen did not desire it without good reason" 1123,4).

interpreted as provocative, threatening, foolhardy, and inviting outside intervention. The first reason for such an interpretation derives obviously from the fact that Kriemhild is assembling a military force inside Burgundy that owes loyalty solely to her. The negative interpretation of this potential threat may be seen, for instance, in the modern scholarly glosses of *brâhtes* ("she brought [sc. many foreign warriors]") most commonly by a word with negative connotations: for example, by de Boor as "sie lockte" and A. T. Hatto as "she lured." Hagen also attaches a negative interpretation (1128) to the use of the wealth to increase the military — and thus political — strength of his feudal superior, who is also his victim's widow. A second potential problem in this stanza, not remarked by critics as far as I have noticed, is that if Kriemhild's distribution of treasure is reckoned less as largesse to the general populace than as politically and militarily purposeful — and I think we have to agree with de Boor, Hatto, and Hagen that it is — then the fact that she does not discriminate between rich and poor recipients (*Den armen unt den rîchen begonde si nu geben* "now she began to give to the poor and the rich" 1128,1) is also significant, for she is thus not only recruiting a quasi-paramilitary force in the royal city, but *may* be doing ⸓⸓ ⸓⸓⸓ ⸓⸓⸓ ⸓⸓⸓⸓ ⸓⸓ ⸓⸓⸓ ⸓⸓⸓ ⸓⸓⸓⸓⸓⸓⸓⸓ ⸓⸓⸓⸓⸓⸓ ⸓⸓⸓⸓ ⸓ ⸓⸓⸓⸓ ⸓⸓⸓⸓ ⸓⸓⸓ ⸓⸓ ⸓⸓⸓⸓ ⸓⸓⸓⸓ ⸓⸓ ⸓⸓⸓⸓⸓⸓⸓⸓⸓ ⸓⸓⸓⸓⸓⸓ ⸓⸓ ⸓⸓⸓ ⸓⸓⸓⸓⸓⸓⸓⸓⸓⸓ ⸓⸓ ⸓⸓ duties. On the other hand, she may simply be rewarding and raising members of the knightly class that was dispossessed, masterless, and thus on the roam. At any rate, such actions as Kriemhild here performs, without discrimination on the basis of wealth and class, are by definition considered politically subversive by those concerned with the preservation of the status quo. She may be fomenting class friction here and undermining the strict hierarchy of the feudal class structure.

Hagen's recognition of the threat is typically astute politically. In the report of this recognition and in preparation for gaining support from the Burgundian kings for his response (as the context of the following stanzas makes clear), Hagen utters a phrase of astounding significance: she will cause trouble for the Burgundians, if she continues to recruit so many men, but only *ob si solde leben / noch deheine wîle* ("if she were to live for a while longer" 1128,2–3). To be inferred is that, according to Hagen, the most prudent political course would be to kill Kriemhild, as an immediate consequence of which the treasure would devolve on Gunther, he presumes, which has, after all, already been established several stanzas earlier as Hagen's ultimate goal in this episode. While the implications of Hagen's conditional *ob*-clause are clear, it must be noted that there are several layers of qualification that render the suggestion less shocking and less demanding of reply. First, the idea is expressed in a subordinate, not a main clause; second the clause is conditional, and the verb is modal *and* subjunctive of unreal condition; finally, the entire utterance is reported by the narrator in indirect speech.[71] Thus Hagen's suggestion to the Burgundian king that the Burgundian princess [and nominally still Nibelungen queen] be murdered for the dual purpose of fending off her military threat and appropriating her property for the Burgundian realm, is somewhat distanced if not defused for both Gunther and the reader. The suggestion has, however, been concretely made, the advice offered, and Hagen in typical fashion may simply proceed with his plan to steal Kriemhild's property, though without eliminating Kriemhild.

In typical fashion, however, Gunther, who rarely understands the political import of direct statements, manages either to miss this imposed condition or to ignore it. Gunther's reply is, as usual, doubly curious, for it is hardly to the [indirectly expressed] point of Hagen's suggestion, in that it merely acknowledges that Kriemhild has control over herself and her property (*ir ist lîp und guot* 1129,1–2), whether legally as a widow, or simply because he, the king, so pronounces.[72] Hagen is relentless, however, in his purpose, and that purpose is well-served by his deep-seated misogyny: *es solde ein frumer man / deheinem einem wîbe niht des hordes lân* ("no real man would leave any of the treasure to a woman" 1130,1–2). Gunther gives a twofold reply: he has sworn an oath not to cause her further pain, and she is his sister (1131,1–3), but he does not forbid Hagen's execution of his plan.

As the scene progresses from this point, and the theft itself and the reactions to it are described, numerous incongruities and ambiguities of responsibility arise. Hagen suggests that he alone do the deed (1131,4). The narrator reports that the oaths of "some of them" (*ir sumelîcher*) were

71. Or so it would seem, depending on whether Hagen's words are understood as reported *thoughts* (which mode does occur, though infrequently in the *Nibelungenlied*) or as words spoken to himself, or whether they are part of an overt conversation. The choice depends on the interpretation of the word *in* (1128,4). The word is unambiguously the dative, third-person plural personal pronoun "to or for them," as predicate object of the verb *ergan,* which governs the dative case. Whether Hagen's words are thoughts or private speech, the *in* most logically refers to the Burgundian brothers; if it is direct speech to Gunther, who, according to the context established in the following stanza *may* already be Hagen's interlocutor, then Hagen's *in* could only refer to some (plural) others not including Gunther. For to include Gunther would require the second-person plural dative, probably in the polite form typically used by Hagen: *iuch.*

72. The extent to which Kriemhild's *munt* is nonetheless still assumed by Hagen and the Burgundian kings becomes clear when Etzel's marriage embassy arrives in *aventiure* 20.

broken, when they (*si*) took the treasure from Kriemhild (1132,1–2). Gêrnôt responds to the theft with anger (*zurnde*), Gîselher with a claim that were Hagen not a relative, he would pay for this deed with his life (1133). Gêrnôt suggests sinking the treasure in the Rhine (1134,1–3). After he returns with his brothers from their planned alibi-trip, during which Hagen carries out Gêrnôt's suggestion (1137), Gîselher agrees to be Kriemhild's protector (1135–1136). After their return Hagen avoids the brothers until their anger cools. Their direct response is limited to: *er hât übele getân* ("he has done wrong" 1139,1), although they had in fact already sworn conspiratorily that the treasure be hidden (*dô heten siz gevestent   mit eiden alsô starc / daz er verholn wære* ("then they had sealed a pact with strong oaths that it be hidden" 1140,2–3).

Although this scene is generally the only one mentioned in discussions of the theft of the hoard, there are in fact *two* further thefts of Kriemhild's treasure. The motivations for use (by the woman) and deprivation (by the men) of the property are identical here to those governing the earlier episodes of despoiling Brünhild and Kriemhild. In *aventiure* 28, as she prepares for the journey to Hunland, Kriemhild intends to take the remains of the hoard with her in order to distribute it as largesse to the Huns (much as Brünhild had planned to do with her treasure in Worms), the remains of the hoard originally carried by 144 wagons still amount to more than a hundred packhorses could carry (*daz ez wol hundert mære   ninder kunden tragen* 1271,3).[73] Hagen prevents her from taking the treasure, apparently by preventing her from bringing together the horses necessary to carry it. The Burgundian kings wish to countermand Hagen's action (*si woltenz gerne wenden* 1274,3), but — without further specification by the narrator — do not do so. Rüdiger is pleased by this loss of treasure, because, as he proudly proclaims, reenacting here the already typical patriarchal and patronizing renunciation of female property, Etzel will give her more treasure than she could ever *squander* (*er gît iu alsô vil, / daz irz verwendet nimmer* 1275,3–4). Gêrnôt takes the matter in hand, by taking the key [from Hagen?] and giving thirty thousand marks to "the guests" (*die geste* 1277,4) — not to Kriemhild — which greatly pleased Gunther — but *not* Kriemhild. Rüdiger then declines *all* of Kriemhild's treasure, perhaps even the minuscule fraction that has survived the initial theft, the second appropriation by Hagen, and the restricted withdrawal by Gêrnôt. And he does so *authoritatively: sîn solde lützel rüeren   mîn oder der küneginne hant. / Nu*

---

73. C-manuscript: 600 packhorses (1294).

heizet ez behalten, wand' ich es niht enwil ("neither my hand nor the queen's shall even touch it. Now order [plural imperative] it to be kept/saved/protected. I do not wish to have it" 1278,4–1279,1). Traveling costs are to be paid from his own funds (and apparently not Etzel's: *des mînen* 1279,2). Even after this, Kriemhild's ladies manage to extract a thousand marks as an offering for Siegfried's soul, and enough gold to fill twelve trunks, which in fact make it onto the road with them (1281,2–4). In addition to the fractional part of her gold retrieved,[74] Kriemhild also manages to leave Burgundy with the standard second type of feudal equipage: vassals. Eckewart volunteers and brings five hundred knights (1283–1284); in addition, Kriemhild takes one hundred maidens (1286).[75]

This scene is one of the more problematic in the whole text, whether one deals only with narrative logic or whether issues of economics and gender are also addressed. The legal owner of the property in question is Kriemhild, as both the characters (Gunther *expressis uerbis,* and Hagen too by implication) and modern scholars agree. Nonetheless it is the men who decide, allow, prevent, countermand, overrule, distribute, and receive the distributed money. The woman's actions are initially limited to those of a passive spectator: she is prevented, dispossessed, and promised future access to a squandering allowance, as it were. Perhaps most problematic is the lack of narrative logic (or is it political logic?) in the scene: how does one reconcile the brothers' intent to prevent their vassal Hagen from blocking Kriemhild's access to the remains of her material property with his unexplained and unqualified success in doing precisely that despite their intentions, unless one finally acknowledges that they are his puppets? For he does not actually commit a theft of the treasure this time, in the sense that he does not furtively abscond with it. Rather, in this case, his action is simply a direct and open blockage of Kriemhild's access to and control and use of the property, which in effect is then technically not theft but robbery. Significantly, this time the treasure is not sunk or hidden, but merely remains under lock and key, in Burgundy and under direct Burgundian control.

But since this type of extraordinary behavior on Hagen's part has occurred before and will occur again, such that it becomes one of his

---

74. Although it is unclear whether the treasure to which Kriemhild refers in 1282,4, as the funding for horses and clothing for her retinue, is taken from the extracted and packed gold or from the remainder of the treasure.

75. Or, according to st. 1294, one hundred and four maidens. We might note here, that she takes to Hunland the same number of vassals that she took to Xanten after her first marriage (and approximately three times as many maidens).

identifying features, this problem seems in the end far less enigmatic than the strictly economic matter at hand: the disposal of personal property by its acknowledged owner, Kriemhild. Yet she makes no effective decisions concerning the property here, despite her intent to do so and her initiation of action to that end. Instead, the focus of the scene, and of modern comment, is shifted away from Kriemhild altogether. This primary issue of property disposal is obscured by the imposition of a secondary issue — by the all-male cast of characters surrounding Kriemhild's initial intent to take her property along to Hunland. That issue does not concern her *legal* right to dispose of her property, which no one openly disputes, but rather simply the *necessity* of her taking direct possession of it and ultimately the actuality of doing it; that is, despite the fact that no one denies her right, and Rüdiger recognizes it in attempting to persuade her of its superfluity, the men quite simply act to prevent its occurrence, or in the case of Gêrnôt's forcible withdrawal, to enable it in only a severely restricted way, defined and executed strictly according to their own terms. In the face of his kings' express wishes to the contrary, Hagen prohibits Kriemhild's access to the property; Rüdiger prohibits even touching it during the journey; the Burgundian kings prohibit these prohibitions, which are in turn overruled without comment. The sorted issue is thus no justified and endless liminality. For whether Kriemhild is to take her property has now been decided several times: by Hagen, by Rüdiger, and by the Burgundian kings. Hagen's and Rüdiger's decisions that she will not take it do not stand unqualified, for in fact she does take twelve trunks full; Gêrnôt's decision that thirty thousand marks be given to *die geste,* does not stand, for it is apparently undone and the gold returned to the vault; finally the decision of her brothers is also without full authority, for she only takes twelve trunks full. The twelve trunks are themselves, however, salvaged only because Kriemhild's maids acting on her behalf furtively packed them while the men argued. Here let us recall that the minuscule portion of Brünhild's property was also salvaged by her own women's packing it into (twenty) trunks — by female deeds, not male pronouncements.

The point here is that the disposition of Kriemhild's property is *considered* by all the men to be within the purview of their authority. And on this principle they debate and act, not only without consulting Kriemhild's interests or will, but also ultimately without any legal authority. For the brothers no longer have the complete and unambiguous legal *mundium* of their widowed and propertied sister, despite a textual bow in that direction when Kriemhild more or less accepts Gîselher as her protector (*aventiure*

18). Nor does Rüdiger even as Etzel's proxy have such extensive authority over his charge.[76] Nor certainly does Hagen have any recognized legal authority in the case at all. Yet they do clearly win the point, so that Kriemhild comes away with a fragment (twelve chests) of a fragment (thirty thousand marks) of a fragment (the cargo of one hundred pack-horses) of the treasure (144 transport wagons).

In this case also, Hagen is not the sole culprit, for it is only in the context of an unrestricted patriarchal system that a Hagen can rampage. Here all males present in effect participate in a cumulative decision that brings about the ultimate outcome: if Gêrnôt could withdraw thirty thousand marks without Hagen's obstruction, then why not forty thousand, or the whole, unless he agreed that Kriemhild should not have all of her property? Why does the king not order his vassal out of the way? And how is Rüdiger's behavior to be explained? He has just sworn a monumental oath that he and his men would avenge all wrongs done Kriemhild (1257–1258) and would do all her bidding, both in Burgundy and Hunland, provided it was not shameful (1266), and he did so fully cognizant of her personal history, including the facts of Siegfried's murder and the circumstances of Hagen's prior theft of her treasure.

The oath and the conflict into which Rüdiger falls during the final confrontation in Hunland as a result of it have evoked inordinate attention on the part of modern commentators, while this first opportunity for vindication of wrongs done to his soon-to-be queen is generally ignored. This discrepancy presents no enigma, however, for in each instance the case is viewed simply as a matter of male honor. In the first instance the men contend with one another about who has the authority over the woman and her possessions—the present male guardians or the proxy of the future male guardian; in the second instance the man struggles with his own sense of honor. In neither case is the oath viewed from any other than Rüdiger's perspective, for if it were he would be condemned immediately and outright, without hand-wringing or moralizing, for in each case his personal oath and feudal loyalty is to his queen. His first opportunity to fulfill his oath by righting a wrong done to Kriemhild is clearly in the scene of despoiling, for as we know, and as he cannot help but see and hear from her

76. Cf. also Rüdiger's remark to Kriemhild at her meeting with Etzel and his vassals in Hunland, identifying for her the legitimate recipients of her kiss of greeting, as if he were, as de Boor claims, in possession of her *mundium* (1348); and also the narrator's remark that Rüdiger did not wish to allow Etzel to *heinlîche pflegen* Kriemhild during the ceremonies of greeting (1358).

direct explanation of the situation past and present (1276), this property is of the utmost significance to her. Its loss occupies her mind to the extent that it is invariably the topic mentioned at critical moments later in the poem (for example, on Hagen's arrival in Hunland and at his final capture). Yet Rüdiger not only does not act to carry out his lady's will and fulfill his oath, he actively controverts it, and even reverses her fortunes once Gêrnôt has salvaged something of the treasure. Even her duly sworn protector is thus a despoiler in his engendered blindness.

This overriding drive on the part of the patriarchal system to strip females of the control of property in order to render them powerless clearly suffices to motivate both Kriemhild and Brünhild to do all within their power to maintain some measure of financial independence, such that they can maintain some control of their lives and have access to the power structure that obtains in the societies of the *Nibelungenlied,* instead of having only indirect power via dynastic or marital ties. We need not see a cause-effect relationship here. Rather, the women already know that the male despoiling of women is the norm, and act to counter it even from the beginning.

The further history of Kriemhild's use of treasure and largesse in general is typically courtly in a fascinating way — and fruitful to look at historical and literary sense. Her uncle, the bishop of Passau advises her to follow the model of Etzel's first queen, and win honor through largesse. Nowhere is the naked financial basis of the feudal system more candidly described. His actual words are: ... *er ir ... riet, / daz si ir êre koufte, als Helche het getân* ("he advised her to buy her honor, as Helche had done" 1330,2–3). In fact it becomes almost a cliché that Kriemhild's virtues are compared point by point with Helche's, the epitome of the perfect courtly wife, especially in courtly generosity: beauty (1351); general "quality of life" they effect (1379); power (1383); virtues (*tugende* 1389). Kriemhild is not initially said to be generous to excess, but rather only more generous than Helche, which in feudal terms signifies: more virtuous, more honored, more beloved by the Huns. Even with the minute portion (relatively speaking) of her property with which she escapes Burgundy, she astutely manages to build a feudal following of international significance, including twelve kings. Eventually, however, the positive valuation of her generosity is called into question in Hunland too, here again not by the narrator, but by Kriemhild's male counterparts (and their scholarly advocates).

In her first meeting with Hunnish knights in Hunland, she demonstrates her generosity so plainly that she wins their praise (1333). In the course of the opening festivities, the function of her own wealth becomes readily apparent, and is susceptible to both strictly political and diplomatico-charitable interpretations: in successive stanzas, we are told that Kriemhild won more vassals than she had controlled as Siegfried's wife, and that by means of gifts she established new relationships with many who had hitherto been strangers (1365–1366). An ancillary result is of course the establishment of her reputation as a generous queen, wealthy in her own right, as the reported comment of "many a" new acquaintance indicates. For not only was Kriemhild not poor, as had been thought, but indeed her generosity was so great as to be considered miraculous (*nu ist hie mit ir gâbe   vil manic wundêr getân* 1366,4). The fact that she participates in what is the typical festival generosity of medieval European epic, without being made an example of excess, is also of great significance here. Yet Kriemhild is not alone in her generosity. Mentioned too are Etzel, members of Kriemhild's retinue; Etzel's vassals (1368–1370); Dietrich, who is said to squander (*verswant*) what Etzel had given to him; Rüdiger, who, like Kriemhild, is said to have worked wonders by his generosity (*ouch begie dâ michel wunder   des milten Rüedegêres hant* "generous Rüdiger also worked many wonders there" 1372,4); and Blœdelîn, who empties many a *leitschrîn* (1373,2).

Despite the fact that the tale is hardly finished, this aventiure ends with a generalizing summary of the future continuation of the situation as depicted, more or less in the sense of — "and they lived happily ever after," as if a major demarcation were being made, which in fact turns out to be the case. The final leg of Kriemhild's journey to Etzel's court from the point of the initial festival to the capital moves in fits and starts through the final three stanzas of the *aventiure,* as three intricately related topics of interest are addressed, albeit significantly in parataxis, as it were, without causal connectors, but making reference to Burgundy and Hunland and to what she has left behind, what she has brought along, and what she finds here: Kriemhild received new loyal vassals; she gave away all of her treasure (1384); all of Etzel's vassals and household are made subject to her, so that Kriemhild had more power than Helche ever had (1385); as a result of Etzel's affection and Kriemhild's however diminished wealth, the court and the kingdom enjoyed such honor that everyone lived according to his/her own pleasure and will (1386). Etzel's benevolence and Kriemhild's wealth and generosity together *seem* to have created an ideal realm, of harmonious political and even ethnic, religious, and racial diversity,[77] free from want and coercion, filled with harmony, good will, and freedom of thought and action.[78] This spirit continues until the arrival of Hagen and the Burgundian kings.

Through her unexcelled generosity and just rule in Hunland, Kriemhild's reputation became known at home and abroad (1390). It is these qualities, displayed during her thirteen year co-rule in Hunland, that result in her having twelve kings as vassals and that give her the unqualified authority over them, *despite* the fact that technically she is queen only insofar as she is the king's consort (*regis uxor*) and not a ruling queen (*regens regina*) as Brünhild had been in Iceland. Her power base is nonetheless solid and she recognizes clearly the basis of her strength, which, whatever the conventional powers of her beauty, actually resides in the power derived from her wealth: *ich bin sô rîche   unt hân sô grôze habe, / daz ich mînen vînden gefüege noch ein leit* ("I am so noble / powerful and have such wealth that I may yet do my enemies some harm" 1396,2–3). Paratactically appended to her thoughts of revenge is a reiteration of the affection of *alle 'sküneges man,* here called *die Kriemhilde recken,* for her, a situation approved by the narrator (*daz was vil wol getân*). Again without relational connective follows in the same phrase the statement that Eckewart was her treasurer and won her friends thereby, followed by yet another paratactic statement that no one could stand against her will.[79] Hereafter the connection between her wealth

77. While the religious tolerance of the *Nibelungenlied* is apparently uncompromised, the epithet *die wilden Petschenære* is at least potentially derogatory as a cultural designation. Even so, there is no blatant racism as, for instance, is present in *Kudrun,* where Siegfried must be de-Moored before he can marry a christian; or in *Parzival,* where the condescension toward Islam and the mocking racism in the depiction of the literally particolored Feirifeiz due to his mixed parentage is blatant and repugnant (1664,2; ed. Lachmann). That Wolfram is all but completely ignorant of Islam and Arabic culture only explains one aspect of his bigotry, but does not justify it. The *Nibelungenlied*-poet makes as much an issue of the pagan religion of his fictional Huns as is necessary in order to convince his audience both that his characters are pious enough to be concerned about it and that the issue itself is for further narrative purposes insignificant — Etzel may or may not convert (1262); the distinctions in outward manifestations of the religion may be reduced to their different ways of singing the mass (*si sungen ungelîche* 1851,1). While this is certainly a culturally biased and ethnocentric construct of the Other, in that it trivializes the differences and attempts to reduce them to identities, it is at the same time not judgmental.

78. That is, as long as one ignores the essential exploitative nature of the operative feudal system, that enables the depicted ruling class to live in luxury.

79. *Ze liebe si dô hêten   alle 'sküneges man,*
die Kriemhilde recken; daz was vil wol getân.
der kamern der pflac Eckewart,   dâ von er friunt gewan.
den Kriemhild willen   kunde niemen understân (1398)

All the king's vassals there, Kriemhild's warriors, had great affection for her; and

and power and the execution of her plan for revenge is more clearly made. As it is announced to her that the Burgundians approach, she thinks (or says): *swer nemen welle golt, / der gedenke mîner leide,   und wil im immer wesen holt* ("whoever wishes to take gold, let him remember my sorrow, and I will always be obliged to him" 1717,3–4).[80]

The importance of the stolen property to Kriemhild is again emphasized upon the arrival of the Burgundians at Etzel's court. For with their arrival, property again gains a double significance that derives from Kriemhild's present position as queen of Hunland *and* her past position as queen of the Netherlands. After Kriemhild greets Gîselher, she confronts Hagen and asks directly whether he has brought her treasure. His double reply is revealing:

> des ist vil manec tac,
> *daz ich hort der Nibelunge*   niene gepflac.
> *den hiezen mîne herren*   senken in den Rîn (1742,1–3)

(It has been many a day since I had charge of the Nibelungen hoard. My lords ordered it sunk in the Rhine.)

Hagen thus assumes without qualification that at one time the hoard was not just briefly in his possession but indeed under his authority. In addition he gives evidence that the Burgundian kings are a collective, in that he implicates the Burgundian kings in the plot, despite the fact that only Gêrnôt suggested it.

From this point on, the narrative tends toward both a negative evaluation of the typically material basis of the characteristic feudal relationship and an emphasis on Kriemhild's dependence on the more direct and simple exchange of reward for service, since she lacks that characteristic necessary for the charismatic command of (authority over) a *comitatus*: male gender. A variety of types of actions performed for and around Kriemhild are de-

---

rightly so. Eckewart was the treasurer; he won friends thereby. No one could withstand Kriemhild's will.

Cf. the C-manuscript corresponding to 1398,4: *den Chriemhilt willen. mohte niemen verstan* (1426). David Herlihy points out ("Land, Family, and Women," pp. 24–25) that according to Hincmar of Rheims's 882 treatise *de ordine palatii* written for King Carloman (which incorporates an earlier treatise of Adalhard of Corbie for Charlemagne), the royal treasurer, *camerarius,* is directly subordinate to the queen who is in charge of distributing annual gifts to knights; he also notes eleventh-century examples of similar practices in Spain and Italy.

80. Lacking in C, but cf. 1755–1757.

picted in terms of their relation to this kind of exchange, such that the latter part of the poem, after the Burgundian arrival in Hunland, is in one sense presented via a narrative strategy of feudal economics, in which public, political action in the name of the ruler is performed for, conceived in terms of, and even metonymically expressed as monetary gifts. A few examples may suffice to illustrate the range of such usage. On the simplest level, Kriemhild promises a reward for killing Hagen (1765,1). Ultimately the Hunnish knights refuse to fight against Volker and Hagen "for gold" (1794,3; 1795,2). Hildebrand refuses to fight the Burgundians *durch deheines schatzes liebe* ("for the love of any treasure"/"for the sake of any material reward" 1900,3), since they are invincible. Unlike them, however—and the distinction is an important one not just for the sake of their general characterization but also for the determination of their feudal relations—Dietrich refuses also, because the feud is not his (*mir habent dîne mâge   der leide niht getân* "'your relatives have done me no harm'" 1901,3), although he does recognize the legitimacy of the motivation and even phrases his refusal in terms of the legally open-ended case: *Sîfrit ist ungerochen   von der Dietrîches hant* ("'Siegfried is not to be avenged by Dietrich's hand'" 1902,3). Finally in order to initiate action, Kriemhild does find a willing champion, but by now she has in fact run through the heroes, as it were, and found them unwilling. Thus it is not until she has been forced by the dysfunction of the feudal system of obligation to descend to the level of the incompetent and cowardly Blœdelîn that her offer is both accepted and acted upon. To him she offers silver, gold, lands and a bride (1905,3; 1906–1907), for which he in turn manages only to slaughter the weaponless squires.

Military action becomes almost synonymous with the transfer of treasure. Kriemhild counsels Etzel to offer gold by the shieldful to his warriors to spur them to fight (2021,3). She openly offers gold, castles, and land to the one who would kill Hagen (2025), and when no one steps forward, Volker can taunt Etzel's vassals both with cowardice for their present inaction, and with ingratitude and dishonesty for not doing their warrior duty in return for past gifts and upkeep. The results of such inaction in the face of feudal obligations are *lasterlîch* "disgraceful," *zagelîch* "cowardly," and the knights *müezens immer schande hân* ("will always be disgraced because of it" 2027). Another usage shimmers through in a few instances. Volker comments for instance that the Danes buy/pay for Kriemhild's gifts with their lives (*mit dem tôde* 2075,4). The irony is blatant here, since they should be earning the gifts via the deaths *of others*. This is after Irinc's dying words specify that since they cannot beat Hagen, they are not to accept the queen's gold. Here the phrase has come to signify no more than: they are not to fight (2068). Thus in the end, "accepting gifts/gold" comes metonymically to be substitutable for fighting, as is clear from another of Volker's comments on the attacking Huns as "those who have accepted the king's gold," which is not a negative valuation, but rather merely an epithet signifying "the warriors," since accepting the king's gold and fighting is what warriors do (2131).

In contrast to this state of affairs, one might note the identified motivations of the Burgundian vassals. Hagen fights for the Burgundian kings, it seems, as Dietrich does for Etzel: for the sake of a romanticized almost mythicized heroic "duty" as much as for feudal bonds.[81] Volker, who is of a slightly lower feudal rank, is said to earn Gunther's silver and gold through his fighting. This relationship is, however, viewed in a positive light, and the phrase carries the laudatory connotation: not that Volker is venal, but rather that he earns his pay. That is, he does his job and performs his feudal duty. With reference to those fighting against Kriemhild, then, it is simply assumed that warriors fight for reward, and there is nothing either unusual or unworthy of praise in it (2006,2). But the lack of constant reminders that Volker, Dancwart, Rumold and Hildebrand necessarily also receive regular and adequate compensation from their lords does not deny that such is the case. Perhaps the best illustration of this principle is found in the case of Rüdiger, especially as the function of feudal largesse is demonstrated in *aventiure* 36.[82] For here the underlying, assumed, and thus usually un-

81. Hagen does admit to being the vassal of the Burgundian kings — *die heizent mine herren,   und bin ich ir man* ("they are called my lords, and I am their vassal" 1788,3), but does so at a moment when his insubordination against the feudal system is at its most blatant, in his refusal to honor a queen, his own lords' sister and his present hostess. Dietrich also recognizes him as such, at least formally, when he offers Gunther the opportunity to surrender himself and his *man* (2337,1).

82. In the following discussion I by no means intend to imply that Rüdiger's famous dilemma consists entirely of problems of property distribution. I do, however, think the moral and ethical problems associated with his decision to fight against the Burgundians have been greatly exaggerated by modern scholars who have sought moral depth (in a dissociative romantic sense) where it is simply not to be found. The poem itself gives ample evidence of the inappropriateness of Rüdiger's own evaluation of the import of his decision. When he claims that he as the guide of the guests may not fight them, he imposes a condition of honor of *his own* choosing; when he claims that he will lose his soul if he fights, he merely indicates to the thirteenth-century audience that he is either basking in bathos or embarrassingly ignorant even of practical lay theology. His is a personal catastrophe, but it is one ultimately deriving from his involvement in a political system that generally does not admit the modern distinction between personal and political. He is unable to manage his own affairs within that system. In betrothing his daughter to the enemies — as he must have known — of his queen and thus of his king and feudal lord, he is at one and the same time attempting to establish a further

discussed premise of the feudal system and thus each and every feudal relationship, is laid bare. Here there is no promise of gold by the shieldful, of fiefs to be granted, or women to be bartered. Rather, since Rüdiger is already Etzel's most important landed vassal, those lands themselves are at issue. His feudal land holdings, granted by Etzel, are mentioned at four key moments in this dramatic enactment of the feudal relationship as ritual death. The first instance occurs as a transition to his direct involvement in the feud, when a Hunnish bystander comments on Rüdiger's obligation to Etzel and his inappropriate inactivity in the present state of emergency, expressed strictly in terms of Rüdiger's enjoyment of his lord's largesse in lands, castles, and subjects (2139). Rüdiger too views his feudal obligations as based on his holding of fiefs, and in a desperate attempt to free himself from his duty to fight his king's enemies, he attempts to renounce his feudal holdings (2157). Etzel responds with an equally extraordinary offer—to transform these holdings from feudal fiefs into outright property gifts to Rüdiger, thus at a stroke making of his vassal a king—not in degree, but certainly in kind—on a par with himself, again with the proviso, that Rüdiger in reciprocation fight the Burgundians (2158). Rüdiger then prophesies as it were the inevitability of the next transfer of these properties, as they will, after his own impending death at the hand of the Burgundians, revert to Etzel.

The function of gifts is a recurring theme in the remainder of the Rüdiger episode, for the Burgundians remind him that as a result of his gifts to them, their fighting each other would be grossly inappropriate (2180–2181). Hagen manages to elicit another gift (a shield) from Rüdiger and pledges not to fight him in return (2201). Gêrnôt then kills Rüdiger with the sword given him in Pöchlarn (2220). The interpretive grid through which the entire episode is here viewed seems also to be operative for the characters themselves, as is clear from Volker's comments noted above, and also from Kriemhild's reaction to the silence following Rüdiger's death. She suspects his betrayal of their cause and expresses this doubt in terms of his inappropriate feudal service (*dirre dienste*) and his not having returned adequate service for having been granted all that he wished (2228–2229).

---

political tie between the two realms, and thus fulfilling the role of king's vassal, but also exposing himself to more than merely potential catastrophe, should a conflict then arise between his lord and his new "relations." Thus his contradictory position allows that as ward of the western mark he also becomes protector and guarantor of the safety of aliens, who, however provoked, make war on his king and queen. On the one hand, his construction of potentially conflicting feudal relations is his own business and his own concern, should a conflict arise; on the other hand, the fact that he allows such a conflict to arise is ultimately a flaw in the performance of his feudal duties.

The conclusion of the poem includes numerous elaborate plays on the notion of payments received, payments for services due and done. Kriemhild thanks Dietrich for capturing and binding Hagen with the words, *du hâst mich wol ergetzet   aller mîner nôt* ("you have well compensated me for all my distress" 2354,3), and in the following stanza, Dietrich reverses the phrase and adds another to it, in asking her mercy for the bound Hagen, complicating still further the notion of payment: if Hagen is allowed to live: *wie wol er iuch ergetzet,   daz er iu hât getân! / er ensol des niht engelten,*

daz ir in seht gebunden stân ("how well he will compensate you, for whatever he has done to you. He must not be made to pay for the fact that you see him in bonds before you" 2355,3–4).

Even *in extremis,* as Kriemhild holds him prisoner, Hagen is incapable of interacting with her as a significant interlocutor. She offers him one last chance to return her property — *welt ir mir geben widere,   daz ir mir habt genomen, / sô muget ir noch wol lebende   heim zen Burgonden komen* ("if you will return to me what you have taken from me, you may still return home to Burgundy alive" 2369,3–4). Nowhere does the text present any evidence that Kriemhild has reneged on any pact before, and there is no reason to suspect that she would now. Hagen nonetheless refuses even here to treat her as an equal partner in negotiations, even when they have to do with matters of (his own) life and death. He replies not yes or no, but again indirectly, again lying, and lying with the purpose of now finally having his king killed. One might object that he neither performs the act nor orders it done. But his carefully concocted lie about the oath of secrecy concerning the treasure (2368) is calculated to elicit Kriemhild's ordering the death of Gunther. Is Hagen then less guilty than Kriemhild simply because his "order" is an additional step removed from the act than her subsequent order, simply because his "order" is less unambiguous than her (offstage) imperative must have been? If so, then he is still not quite as innocent, for instance, as Gunther (as *râðbani*) is of Siegfried's death.

Hagen's final refusal to reveal the whereabouts of the treasure elicits Kriemhild final words, also, appropriately, couched in terms of payment: *so habt ir übele   geltes mich gewert* ("thus you have paid me in base coin" 2372,1). If nothing else, Hagen finally, but uncomprehendingly, gives voice to the *movens* of the entire tale: *du hâst iz nâch dînem willen   z'einem ende brâht* ("you have now brought it to an end according to your will" 2370,3). Kriemhild's will, her desire, has been thwarted throughout, sometimes subtly and almost imperceptibly, at other times openly and brutally. It is only in this single moment that it can be satisfied, in its triumph over the systematic refusal by a patriarchal society to allow her will and her desire, since female, to achieve satisfaction except as that satisfaction is secondary to, dependent on, governed by, and ultimately fully appropriated by males. The denial not only of the legitimacy of female will and desire but of its existence except as processed by patriarchy has here resulted not in a feminist triumph over the patriarchy, nor in the patriarchal squelching of a feminist uprising. Rather the society itself has — by means of its male representatives — destroyed itself from the ground up. In the absence of the authority to exert her will in the specific case at hand, circumstances offer Kriemhild no choice but to apply power on a broader front. It would be of little import to call her the winner, and of course not just because she is immediately murdered by Hildebrand — one must note that hers is the most graphically described and brutal murder among the approximately 40,000 deaths that occur. But Hagen too, the champion simultaneously of his own egotistical cause, of the cause of Burgundy, of heroic society, and thus ultimately of the patriarchal system, clearly and unequivocally loses and is killed by his enemy.

Thus while Kriemhild as an outsider to the system must constantly impoverish and ultimately humiliate herself by begging and buying (as her opponents and occasionally the narrator claim) insiders (that is, male warriors) to champion her cause, those same opponents are themselves on the inside of the system, buying and being bought to defend it. While she remains on the outside opposing the patriarchal system, her opponents are the flower of warrior society. By contrast, her champions are second-rate at best, except, finally, for Dietrich, who, however, fights ultimately not for *her,* but only because his own feudal status has been all but destroyed by the loss of his entire vassalage except for Hildebrand. His is now an army consisting of a general and a field marshal but no soldiers. He fights then perhaps for the sake of honor, perhaps because of obligations to Etzel, but in no sense does he fight for the sake of Kriemhild's cause. And finally, even with this champion, she must finish the job herself if Hagen is finally to be punished for his crimes, since Dietrich in he end refuses to do so, just as he has all along.

Ultimately there is an unmistakable double standard at work in the granting and establishment of authority, and it operates quite concretely insofar as material wealth as power base is concerned. The possession, control and distribution to subordinates of property by men results in honor, power, and authority; its possession, control, and distribution by women results in honor and power, but no authority, and such honor and power are limited in ways that men's are not. Gifts by a male to subordinate males are the social norm and constitute one of the integral elements of the feudal economic formation. Female gifts to male subordinates, on the other hand, are in all but a few specific types of situations abnormal or at least extraordinary, and as such they are always defined far more specifically. A man grants a fief to another man and in exchange receives his support both in a very general and a very concrete way (e.g. a supply of a specific number of equipped cavalry and foot soldiers for a specific number of days per year). By contrast a woman's gift seems to have far more restricted and even more specific, almost ad hoc, application. It may be given as a reward for a specific act already performed (Kriemhild's gift to Siegfried when he performs messenger service); or may function to induce a specific act (the promise of land and bride to Blœdelîn, leading to his misguided depredations). But female gifts do not seem capable of binding men to a general kind of loyal service of long duration to women.

Just as women's participation in property inheritance becomes restricted to the "private" bounds of marital settlement without power of alienation or further inheritance, so too does a woman's distribution of property function and signify on a more personal, private level than do identical acts by men. On receipt of property (from a man) a knight may become the "man" of Gunther or Siegfried or Etzel, for instance, for that exchange is an act of public, political import. On receipt of (an identical gift of) property from a woman the same knight may (be expected to) perform only a single, specified task with no further obligations or repercussions, for a woman's gift is personal, private and without long-range political signification. This kind of exclusion from the public sphere and from the possibility of political participation will concern us in the next chapter as well, where the concrete limitations placed on female participation in property and power relations are simultaneously mirrored, enacted, and undermined in that most personal (but at the same time dynastically, and thus politically, significant) site to which women are relegated: the marriage bed.

4. Pillow Talk: Intimate Conversations — Political Strategies

There are a number of scenes in the *Nibelungenlied* in which women carry on conversations with men, ultimately for the sake of exercising political power. These recurring and volatile scenes and the roles and behavior of the male and female participants in them are parallel in structure, almost in the same sense that Kriemhild's dreams are: in their structure, motivation, and imaginative and argumentative flexibility. Thus the variations in these quite similar scenes are then themselves significant for other scenes and the larger issues involved. Additionally, there seem to be paradigms of behavior informing the scenes and controlling possibilities for action. The conversations themselves are more often than not instigated by the women for the purpose of requesting information or action or influencing behavior that would tend to bring about the actions the women desire. The intimate nature of these conversations stems ultimately from conventional restrictions on political action by women. And thus they represent the women's recurring attempts to exercise political power by ostensibly individual, indirect means.

As was analyzed in some depth in the last chapter, the implications of property ownership for power relations are manifold. Recent sociological research has addressed related issues of power that illuminate two aspects of these scenes in the *Nibelungenlied*. In an article entitled "Power as Ideology,"[1] Jane S. Jaquette addresses the questions: "Is there an 'ideology' of power? In other words, does the way we define power affect the way it is used and who can use it?" Her article answers in the affirmative. She argues that, since *power* cannot be used as verb, it "inevitably takes on properties of a substance 'possessed' or 'used' by individuals even though it is in fact clearly relational." Thus any definition must indicate the conditions of possession and use. In general, Jaquette observes, definitions of power

---

1. Jane S. Jaquette, "Power as Ideology: A Feminist Analysis," in *Women's Views of the Political World of Men,* ed. Judith Hicks Stiehm (New York: Transnational, 1984), pp. 7–29; here pp. 9, 18.

"define women out of the universe of political power holders and thus, in a very real way, out of politics itself." Traditionally female power has been viewed as consisting only of "influence" and "manipulation," both of which are exercised necessarily only in the private sphere. Thus it takes place in what is conventionally the female space, but even there females lack all "authority or a credible threat of force" and thus resort to influence and manipulation not because it is "a typically 'female' form of power 'by nature,' as is often asserted," but as "a direct result of their powerlessness." At any rate, Jaquette observes, since these particular types of power are negatively valued, "all female exercise of power, even in the private sphere, is thus denied legitimacy." Similarly, in her analysis of a case from medieval England, Barbara Hannawalt notes that since women were officially barred from "direct lines of political influence, historians have often described their role in the power structure as manipulative and have characterized their tools of influence as deceit, intrigue, fickleness, and even witchcraft. When an undeniably outstanding woman did appear on the historical stage, she was described as acting with 'manly virtue.'"[2]

A logical corollary of a society's denial of power to women is a radical inequality in the society's valuation of women, as compared to men. The low value placed on women tends to reify (and commodify) them, so that they are routinely subject to debasing, dehumanizing treatment by both men and other women. Some manifestations of that kind of treatment were dealt with in the last chapter. In the present chapter's attention to intimate, primarily marital, episodes of male-female communication and confrontation, we turn to scenes that in their hidden and personal nature are potentially far more likely to lead to physical confrontation and not just fiscal exploitation. Due to the radical differences in the traditional definitions of their power — male = physical strength, female = manipulative cunning — attention must be given here to the consequences of such confrontations that are imbued with an underlying sense of the physical that often is revealed in sexual power, violence, and rape.

Peggy Reeves Sanday, in her article, "Rape and the Silencing of the Feminine," also addresses the notion of the traditional powerlessness of women and observes that this issue correlates with the socio-cultural preconditions for the existence (or non-existence) of rape in a society: "Rape is an expression of a social ideology of male dominance. Female power and authority is lower in rape-prone societies; women do not partici-

2. Barbara A. Hannawalt, "Lady Honor Lisle's Networks of Influence," p. 188.

pate in public decision-making and males express contempt for women as decision-makers. The correlates of rape that I present suggest that rape is the playing out of a socio-cultural script in which the expression of person-hood for males is directed by interpersonal violence and an ideology of toughness."[3] The life-controlling tentacles of such an ideology reach far and deep, as Lenore Walker elucidates: "Cultural conditions, marriage laws, economic realities, physical inferiority—all these teach women that they have no direct control over the circumstances of their lives. . . . They are subjected to both parental and institutional conditioning that restricts their alternatives and shelters them from the consequences of any disapproved alternatives."[4] Unlike men's, women's power resides in those attributes that enslave them to the ideological cycle in the first place: "Women are system-atically taught that their personal worth, survival, and autonomy do not depend on effective and creative responses to life situations, but rather on their physical beauty and appeal to men" (Walker, p. 51).

One of the recurringly common consequences of such an ideology of male dominance and disproportionate power relations is violence in the form of physical abuse of wives, often including sexual abuse, marital rape, sometimes ultimately culminating in murder. Irene Frieze has noted that marital rape is typically associated with battering, and may be one of the most serious forms of battering."[5] Despite the conventional denial of the possibility of rape in marriage, Angela Browne's simple and commonsensi-cal definition of rape, in her in-depth analysis of battering, indicates how that convention too is a social construct: "a mutual act is being carried out against one person's will."[6] In one study cited by Browne, twice as many women report being raped by husbands as by strangers (p. 100), despite the fact that since our society still does not generally accept the use of the term rape for any sexual relations of married partners no matter what the circumstances of consent or violence, women are less likely to describe such attacks by their husbands as rape.[7]

3. "Rape and the Silencing of the Feminine," in *Rape: An Historical and Social Enquiry,* ed. Tomaselli and Porter, p. 85; see also her "The Socio-Cultural Context of Rape," *Journal of Social Issues* 37 (1981), 5–27.

4. Lenore E. Walker, *The Battered Woman,* p. 52. Walker writes of the lives of women in the late twentieth century in the United States. How much more circumscribed and restricted were the possibilities of personal freedom and individual development available to women (even of the ruling class) of the thirteenth century in central Europe?

5. Irene H. Frieze, "Investigating the Causes and Consequences of Marital Rape," *Signs: Journal of Women in Culture and Society* 8/3 (1983), 552.

6. Angela Browne, *When Battered Women Kill* (New York: Free Press/Macmillan, 1987), p. 95.

7. She also points out that "the same system that failed to protect them from their

As will become clear in the present chapter, Jaquette's and Sanday's, Browne's and Walker's observations on twentieth-century behavior are very relevant indeed to the situation of women in central Europe during the thirteenth century and especially so to the behaviors and situation of the female characters of the *Nibelungenlied,* where "influence" and "manipulation" are the primary means of conventionally female power and where "the social ideology of male toughness," spousal abuse, and rape are the order of the day.[8] An important caveat concerning research on rape and its representations is Hazel Carby's comment: "Rape itself should not be regarded as a transhistorical mechanism of women's oppression but as one that acquires specific political or economic meanings at different moments in history."[9]

Before turning to the text of the *Nibelungenlied,* however, two preliminary tasks are necessary: first to problematize the insistence of my position that literary rape is culturally significant and necessarily and legitimately to be discussed in the context of the society's historical construction and construal of rape; and secondly, it will be then necessary to establish at least a general legal and historical context of rape in the high Middle Ages, for as the historian of medieval canon law, James Brundage, points out: "the offence of rape, as it is currently conceived and defined in European and American law, has only gradually become what it now is and the definition of this offence presently in use would have been unrecognizable to European courts in the early middle ages."[10]

As Kathryn Gravdal incisively comments, literary studies have been slow in coming to acknowledge the necessary link between the literary representation of sexual violence and "actual" rape.[11] This still lingering tardiness is to a great extent the residue of the profoundly political New Critical conception of a literary work as a self-referential artifact having no addressable connection to its contemporary social reality but only to the social "reality" depicted. Recently it has been remarked that this tenet of European literary criticism has arisen as part of one of the last schools of

---

partner's violence immediately arrested and prosecuted them when they responded in their own defense" (p. 159).

8. Browne also notes (p. 96) that among the more common types of current marital sexual abuse is "forced sex with others," a remark not without significance in Siegfried's and Gunther's dual sexual assault on Brünhild.

9. *Reconstructing Womanhood: The Emergence of the Afro-American Woman Novelist* (Oxford: Oxford University Press, 1987), p. 18.

10. James Brundage, "Rape and Marriage in the Medieval Canon Law," *Études offertes à Jean Gaudemet = Revue du Droit Canonique* 28 (1978), 62. He also offers a very brief orientation in the Roman, Justinian and Germanic laws on rape.

11. Kathryn Gravdal, "Chrétien de Troyes, Gratian, and the Medieval Romance of Sexual Violence," *Signs: Journal of Women in Culture and Society* 17 (1992), esp. p. 559.

literary theory that was exclusively male- and masculist-conceived, and that this disavowal of the importance of the author and 'his' voice, intention and personal life experience came just as the authorial ranks were beginning to become less univocal due to the growing number of publications by those who are not elite white males.[12] Gravdal observes that this distinction between rape and literary representations of rape is drawn on the basis of a differential valuation on various discursive fields: the aesthetic, literary, imaginative, is trivialized as "unreal" and deemed incomparable to "real" rape.[13] She further remarks, however, that as attention to any rape trial graphically demonstrates, "real" rape is also always a matter of representation ("specifically, conflicting representations of force, resistance, and consent"), and, one might add, also of presentation. In any case, the connection between represented and actual sexual violence, whether causal (as some sociological positions hold) or not, seems similar (and thus tentatively subject to comparative analysis) in its "eroticization of dominance and submission."[14]

In Roman law *raptus* might refer both to the abduction of a woman (and not necessarily to her sexual ravishment) and to the theft of property, since both were conceived of as crimes against the man who had legal power over the property or the woman as property.[15] Roman law prescribed as penalties for rape death and confiscation of the rapist's property.[16]

12. This has been one of the subtexts of much of Gayatri Spivak's work; see esp. the collection of reprinted essays, *In Other Worlds: Essays in Cultural Politics,* which brings together a sampling of that important work. A sharper focus on this particular problem is found in the revised and reprinted versions of Nancy Miller's essays, "Arachnologies: The Woman, the Text, and the Critic," pp. 77–101 and "Changing the Subject: Authorship, Writing and the Reader," pp. 102–121, in *Subject to Change: Reading Feminist Writing* (New York: Columbia University Press, 1988).

13. Cf. the title of Susan Estrich's excellent work, *Real Rape* (Cambridge, MA: Harvard University Press, 1987).

14. Catherine Mackinnon, "Feminism, Marxism, Method, and the State: Toward Feminist Jurisprudence," *Signs: Journal of Women in Culture and Society* 8 (1983), 650.

15. Pomeroy, *Goddesses, Whores, Wives, and Slaves: Women in Classical Antiquity* (New York: Schocken, 1975), pp. 160–161. Some aspects of this older concept of rape still linger in our society, even as official "definitions": see, for the sake of its ubiquity, *Webster's Ninth New Collegiate Dictionary* (Springfield, MA: Merriam-Webster, 1983), which offers three significations for the verb *rape:* (1) "to seize and take away by force"; (2) "despoil"; (3) "to commit rape on." Thus this standard dictionary gives no explicit indication that the verb may have any *direct* signification of sexual violence, although that is its most common signification in contemporary English. To follow the lexicographical circle, we may then pretend ignorance of the noun form as used in the third signification above, and look at the next entry for the noun *rape.* Here we again find three significations, only one of which indicates rape as sexual violence, which again perpetuates the usage (noted in the verb entry as "archaic"): "an act or instance of robbing or despoiling or carrying away a person by force."

16. *Codex Theodosianus* 9.13.1, 4,5; 1.3.53 (54), 3–4.

The Roman legal codes, which treated *raptus* as a serious offense, prevailed in the context of secular law during the early Middle Ages, but medieval secular law offered the possibility of substitute penalties, such as castration coupled with fines.

In the codification of canon law around 1140 in Gratian's *Decretum* and in the subsequent refinements by canonists, rape law was generally made more lenient on the perpetrator, for the sake of christian love, as the code expressed it.[17] Capital punishment was not prescribed, and a layman might now in fact avoid physical punishment altogether and "only" suffer excommunication. Rape was defined as consisting of four elements: violence, abduction, coitus, and lack of consent on the part of one of the participants.[18] It was commonly thought that only moderate force was necessary to satisfy the requirement of violence, and certainly there was no need for the rape victim to prove mortal danger. Nor was physical resistance necessary; a cry of protest sufficed to demonstrate lack of consent. Canon law understood *raptus* solely in the sense of the marriage via abduction of a woman without consent or even knowledge of the bride's relations. Thus in general the legal question had little to do with a crime against the raped woman, and not with a crime at all, unless the act could not be subsumed under marriage law. But on the subject of sexual violence committed outside the context of an abduction, canon law has nothing to say, and thus a statistically most significant (perhaps the most numerous) category of sexual violence was simply ignored legally: such actions were considered sins by the church, but not criminal actions. Ecclesiastical courts avoided sentences involving mutilation and instead imposed "excommunication, public penance, imprisonment, whipping, fines, and possibly even enslavement, or some combination of these, depending on the circumstances of the case."[19] Thus it was to the rapist's benefit to be tried by an ecclesiastical court, and he could bring that about by fleeing to an ecclesiastical sanctuary for trial.

Not surprisingly, however, according to Brundage's research, this superficially rather progressive status of one type of rape law merely masks a deeper social problem, for during a ten-year period in the early fourteenth century examined by Brundage rape constituted only one percent of all sexual offenses tried in the court of Cérisy in Normandy. Rape cases were,

17. *Decretum magistri Gratiani,* in *Corpus iuris canonici* ed. Emil Friedberg, 2 vols. (1879–1881; repr. Graz: Akademische Druck- und Verlagsanstalt, 1955).

18. C. 36 q. 1 d.p.c. 2 pr. See also Brundage, p. 67.

19. Brundage, "Rape and Marriage," p. 73; C. 27 q. 2 c.33–34; C. 36 q. 2 c. 2,5.

then as now, rarely reported and even more rarely brought to trial. The rapist often avoided all punishment merely by consenting to marriage. Finally, it should be noted that although Roman law recognized the possibility of marital rape, and prescribed the usual penalties for it,[20] canon law did not, even if the woman was taken from her home and force was employed.

Although the issue of rape is present in only two of the male-female private confrontations in the *Nibelungenlied,* a general pattern of behavior is nonetheless discernible, which signifies in the social system of women's sexual oppression in which rape is a primary component. The briefest example of a private conversation between a man and woman is also the first to occur in the poem. Following the Saxon war, Kriemhild secretly (*das gescach vil tougen* "that was done very secretly," 224) summons a messenger to private audience in order to learn of the conduct and outcome of the war. She must act indirectly and privately in order to get information about public and strictly male activities even though the outcome of the Saxon invasion obviously also has direct, political importance for women's lives. In each example of this type of scene in the *Nibelungenlied* the information or request has both a public and a private, personal aspect. Thus when the woman requests the order or commission of the man for the public action, she does so *in order that* the private action may take place. The two are related in this, but in no other respect, since they have quite different purposes and ends. The women attempt to achieve their ends indirectly in two senses: via another action related only metonymically to the desired action, and by the only means available — their men. And thus here too the women's actions are susceptible to the label of scheming and conniving, both by other characters and by modern scholars.

In four instances the scenes are even more highly charged and susceptible to more overtly patriarchal interpretation, since the participants are engaged in circumcoital conversation; in three of those cases the participants are married couples; in the fourth a proxy assumes the role of husband. This marital connection is not accidental. The depiction of the relationship of the royal husband and wife is otherwise almost wholly public and thus necessarily openly political. An unofficial, personal matter, a private request, can hardly be dealt with before the court, especially if it is a delicate matter anyway — that is, politically significant *despite* its private nature. A primary opportunity for the woman/wife/subject to approach

---

20. *Codex Theodosianus* 9.13.1.1 (b).

the man/husband/king about a private matter is in or around bed, where this culture has given her some measure of direct power, although little authority, over the king, via the conditions she may impose in exchange for sexual compliance.[21] Here she may take advantage of the king's ease and relaxed mood, his satiated, post-coital disposition, or perhaps better his pre-coital pliability.

In the twelfth *aventiure* comes the first of the royal invitations and the first of the *amicable* private conversations by a married couple. Power is the motivating agent. The instigating factor, clearly indicated in the first stanzas of the *aventiure,* is Brünhild's wish to receive the feudal service due the Burgundian realm from its supposed vassal Siegfried, which may best be acknowledged and rendered by the vassal in person. Since Siegfried and Kriemhild have been absent for a decade, there seems to be no overt political compulsion for their return, and thus if Brünhild's wish for service due (and even for clarification of what is clearly an ambiguous situation) is to be satisfied, then *she* must act, but she may do so only privately and indirectly, via the king: *Si versuochtez an dem künige* (726).[22] As Lexer (III 259) suggests (among other possibilities), she "tries it out" on the king, and she does so in a particular setting: *si reitez heinlîche, des si dâ hete muot* ("she spoke *heinlîche* concerning her desire/wish/will/plan/decision" 726). De Boor glosses *heinlîche* in st. 726 as "vertraulich." Thus she chooses an intimate, private setting, where they can shed at least their public roles and be "simply" wife and husband, queen and king, sister-in-law and brother of Kriemhild. Gunther thinks little of the plan and tries to dissuade Brünhild with specious general arguments: it is impossible to bring them; they live too far away; he dare not order them to come. This last excuse prompts Brünhild again to give Gunther the opportunity to explain (though not to undo) his initial deception of her by admitting that Siegfried is not his vassal. Instead, after she notes that he can in fact order a vassal to do his bidding, Gunther merely smiles in reply.[23] This facial gesture apparently suffices as Gunther's second conversational turn, and Brünhild changes tack and notes that this request is a matter of her desire/will (*durch den willen*

21. The economy of this relationship resembles typical feudal relationships insofar as it participates in the relational structure *do ut des,* and especially insofar as the woman's "produce," as defined in light of Sanday's criteria in chapter two, consists of her beauty which may be enjoyed by her husband both through sexual relations and through the honor that accrues to him as a result of his possession of a beautiful object.

22. Cf. C-manuscript: *si versvchtez manigen ende. ob kunde daz geschehn* (733).

23. Cf. Siegfried's sincerely amused and condescending non-response to Kriemhild's warning of impending danger, just before he leaves for the hunt and his own murder (925).

mîn, 729) and then requests his aid (*sô hilf mir*) in its satisfaction. We must here again remember the intimate context, now further charged by Brünhild's identification of her entreaty as one deriving from a desire that the king can satisfy.

Old troublesome memories, or rather suggestive references to them, are then evoked: Kriemhild's courtliness, how Brünhild and Gunther sat together on their wedding day. No reference is made to their wretched wedding night, but her final reported remark enigmatically comments on that topic as well: *si* (sc. Kriemhild) *mac mit êren minnen   des küenen Sîfrides lîp* ("she may love/make love to bold Siegfried/Siegfried's body[24] honorably/victoriously/authoritatively") (730; lacking C 737). This last connotation derives from Lexer's gloss (I 624): "gewalt des gebieters," which describes exactly Brünhild's conception of the relationship between the Burgundian princess Kriemhild and Siegfried, the allegedly unfree vassal of the Burgundian realm. Brünhild hereby suggests that the relationship between Kriemhild and Siegfried is improper. Her reasons might include her suspicion that the partners are of unequal rank, since she considers Kriemhild the superior and thus, based on her own experience, worthy of command.

No further argument for or against inviting Siegfried and Kriemhild, or rather none is reported. Instead, the poet merely notes that *si gertes alsô lange,   unz daz der künic sprach.* . . . ("she desired it so long, until the king spoke. . . ." 730). That is, again, the queen's *desire* is strong, enduring, and ultimately the factor that sways the king and establishes state policy, forcing the king to issue an official invitation to a neighboring monarch and relative-by-marriage, whose visit he perhaps already fears may lead to trouble. Immediately after Gunther's concession, Brünhild again assumes the ostentatiously subordinate role, requesting that she be informed by his majesty when and for what dates the invitation might be issued. In response Gunther, either playfully or, more likely, characteristically oblivious to the substantive implications of events around him, takes her cue and assumes the external aspects of his assigned role by shifting into the register of royal pronouncement. The scene seems typical of those constructed according to the tenets of a mascu-

24. The widespread notion that *lîp* with genitive of person signifies no more than the person in question, is at least in part a result of a prudish age of scholarship that sought metaphor wherever denotation was uncomfortable. Cf. Czerwinski, "*Das Nibelungenlied:* Widersprüche höfischer Gewaltreglementierung," pp. 67–68.

list ideology, in which whatever power women are granted consists in their quasi-deceptive manipulation of men to their own ends.

As a bridge to other instances of circumcoital, marital conversation, let us return to the term *versuochen,* noted above. Among its semantic possibilities, those having to do with "attempting" and "tempting" figure prominently. In this context they also make sense: Brünhild "tries it (out) on" or "tries it with" the king, or "tempts" the king or "leads the king into temptation," all of which are commonly attested significations of the word. But to interpret *versuochen* in this way would perhaps be too daring even in the present context of the marital bedroom and recurringly emphasized female desire, except for the use of *heinlîche* in the next sentence, where it specifies her method: *si reitez heinlîche, des si dâ hete muot* ("she spoke *heinlîche* concerning her desire/wish/will/plan/decision" 726). This word, in this and similar contexts in the *Nibelungenlied,* emphasizes the private, personal nature of an interaction and also resonates with the potential connotations of *versuochen.*

Lexer offers several related significations of *heinlîche* (I 1217–1218):

(heim-, hein-)lîche *adv. vertraulich; heimlich. — stf. heimat; vertraulichkeit; euphem. für eheliche beiwohnung; heimlichkeit, geheimnis, vertrauliches schreiben; ort zu dem nur die vertrauten zugang haben, kabinett.*[25] ("adverb: intimately; secretly. — strong feminine noun: home(land); intimacy; euphemism for marital intercourse; secrecy; secret; intimate letter; place to which only intimates have access; small chamber.")

The word appears four other times in the *Nibelungenlied,* in each case in another key scene of male-female conversation and female persuasion in a private context. The usage of the word is uniform enough that it may cast some light both on these scenes and on the possibilities of female action.

The first instance occurs in the tenth *aventiure,* during Siegfried's and Gunther's sexual assault of Brünhild. The narrator recurringly assures us only that Gunther, in his state of restricted perception (hearing only), convinced himself that Siegfried did not have sexual contact with Brünhild: *Gunther wol hôrte (swie er sîn niht ensach), / daz heimlîcher dinge von in dâ niht geschach* ("although he could not see him at all, Gunther heard clearly that they engaged in no *heimlîchiu dinc*" 667,3), where *heimlîchiu dinc* is glossed by de Boor as "Vertraulichkeiten. Ständiger Ausdruck für den Liebes-

---

25. *(heim)lîchkeit* is *mutatis mutandis* provided with similar significations.

genuß" ("Intimacies. Standard expression for lovemaking"). When Gunther enters the bed, however, after Brünhild has been subdued, the performance of the act is explicitly noted, again using the same term, now as a substantive:

> *Er pflac ir minneclîchen,   als im daz gezam,*
> *dô muoste si verkiesen   ir zorn unt ouch ir scham.*
> *von sîner heimlîche   si wart ein lützel bleich.*
> *hey waz ir von der minne   ir grôzen krefte entweich!* (681)

(He took care of her/used her lovingly/sexually, as was his due; at that time she had to give up her anger and also her shame/genitals. From his *heimlîche* she became a bit pale. As a result of love/intercourse — Zowee! — she lost her great strength.)

Here as well de Boor attributes the same significance to the nominal *heimlîche:* "Vertraulichkeit, Beischlaf" ("Intimacy. Sexual intercourse"). As demanded by the context, my translation differs in several instances here from the standard renderings. The phrase *er pflac ir minneclîchen* is a cliché of the courtly lit-eral, signifying the general practice of courtly love as well as any of the specific aspects of that practice, including the sexual act, which despite traditionalist scholarly misrepresentations to the contrary, quite often plays a role in the tradition of courtly love literature, especially in Middle High German. This same phrase is, for instance, used only a few dozen stanzas earlier to describe Siegfried's "treatment" of Kriemhild on their wedding night:

> *Dô der herre Sîfrit   bî Kriemhilde lac,*
> *unt er sô minneclîche   der juncvrouwen pflac*
> *mit sînen edelen minnen,   si wart im sô sîn lîp.*
> *er næme für si eine   niht tûsent anderiu wîp.* (629)[26]

(As lord Siegfried lay with Kriemhild and so lovingly/sexually took care of/used/treated her with his noble love/intercourse, they became as one/she became for him as his own body. He would not have taken a thousand other women for her alone.)

---

26. Cf. C 634, corresponding to B 629,4: *daz chvnde ovch si verdienen. als ein tvgende riche wip.*

Whether one reads these metaphors as signifying romantic love or more specifically the physical act of sexual intercourse does not alter the fact that the phrases whose subject is male are transitive or have female verbal complements; the female subject has an intransitive verb with a governing agentive complement, for whose sake the action of the intransitive verb is performed: the man *acts on* the woman; she *is enacted* for the sake of the man. It is in, by means of, and at the moment of (*dô*) the sexual act that the woman is transformed and appropriated, physically and politically: just as *minne* annihilates Brünhild's individual and independent strength, *minne* annihilates Kriemhild's possession of her own body, which becomes Siegfried's. The relationship is expressed in terms of possession: he prefers the appropriation of her to that of a thousand other women. The only other outcome of the marriage of Siegfried and Kriemhild is that he was well entertained (*Sîfrides kurzewîle   diu wart vil græzlîche guot* 628). That *minne* may signify an emotional or intellectual attachment even in these passages is not to be denied, but the physical connotations of the term certainly dominate here.

To return to the culmination of the assault on Brünhild in stanza 681: the text remarks that she gives up her anger and her shame. On the one hand, one might interpret this enigmatic statement as signifying her loss of independence, since she gives up two of the strongest personal emotions. Additionally, however, there may be another resonance in the term *scham*, for in both Middle High German and modern German the term itself and compounds of *Scham-* also signify the (usually) female pubic area (e.g., *Schamhaare* "pubic hair," *Schamlippen* "vaginal lips").[27] Thus for Brünhild to yield up her "shame" is to offer / renounce / abandon her genitals and her possession and control of them.

The *hey* of the stanza's final line is often ignored in translations and commentary, but since it indicates not just a metrical, but also a semantic, emphasis, it must be accounted for. Generally the term is an expletive expressing joy, grief, or wonder.[28] Here it might well be interpreted in all three ways, although such a polysemous combination requires constant adjustments in ideological point of view: rejoicing at the final consummation of the royal marriage, at the belated sexual satisfaction of the beleaguered king, and at the long-expected taming of the "shrew"; wonder at transformation itself; grief at Brünhild's loss of strength and independence.

27. Not so extraordinary, apparently, since a similar polysemous usage (for both sexes) is found in Latin *pudenda* and Greek αἰδοῖα.

28. Cf. Lexer, I 1209: "zum ausdruck der freude, trauer, verwunderung."

The third instance of the use of the term *heinlîche* occurs in the fourteenth *aventiure* during the queens' argument and after Kriemhild has accused Brünhild of concubinage, when she further states that *getriuwer heinlîche   sol ich dir wesen umbereit* (842); de Boor stiffly glosses: "Ich bin nicht mehr zu aufrichtiger Vertraulichkeit dir gegenüber bereit, d.h. ich bin nicht länger bereit, dein schimpfliches Geheimnis zu hüten" ("I am no longer willing to be loyally discreet with respect to you, i.e. I am no longer prepared to protect your dishonorable secret"). While the term may well denote a more general *Vertraulichkeit,* the object of that secret trust, according to Kriemhild, is *heinlîch* in just the sense that *kebse* "concubine" is, the insult that she throws in Brünhild's teeth. In this case the usually implicit sexual connotation is made explicit.

Finally the word appears in Rüdiger's culminating and successful attempt to woo Kriemhild to become Etzel's wife: *Niht half, daz si gebâten, unz Rüedegêr / gesprach in heimlîche die küneginne hêr* ("Their entreaties came to nothing until Rüdiger spoke to the noble queen *heimlîche*" 1255). Here de Boor offers less for more: "unter vier Augen" ["tête-à-tête"]. Here the sexual act is not imposed or performed, but rather prepared for and deferred. Rüdiger as Etzel's fully empowered marriage ambassador is in fact suing for Kriemhild's hand, and his position as proxy is merely a material, not—with some very specific physical restrictions—a functional, distinction: in accepting the proposal, Kriemhild commits herself bodily to Etzel, and in lieu of the king until such time as he may himself take possession of her, Rüdiger not unproblematically[29] assumes that possession in a taking control of her *mundium,* as we see clearly when he later takes over the administration of Kriemhild's relations with strangers. While the term here clearly does not signify the sexual act and may illustrate the far more general denotation 'privately' (as it also denotes in each of the cases discussed above), it nonetheless establishes the conditions necessary for the legal performance of the act at a later time by the same (unproxied) functional participants.

As was noted at the outset of the present chapter, and as the analysis of the keyword *heinlîche* has further demonstrated, sexuality is of primary importance in the discussion of communicative possibilities between men and women. In a society that denies women significant forms of communication such as participation in financial affairs and verbal participation

---

29. Since Kriemhild is a propertied widow.

in public events,[30] women's communicative possibilities are forced to be played out behind closed doors, or at least beyond the overtly political sphere, with those intimates who are permitted access to such quarters. Thus the emphasis on the physical and the enhanced sexual atmosphere of such forms of communication are not surprising.

30. Cf. Siegfried's remarks to Gunther on how women should hold their tongues (862). One might recall here as well the conventional refusal of men in the *Nibelungenlied* (and other medieval literary texts) to acknowledge the significance of that most overdetermined form of communication—the dream, if it comes from a woman. Particularly pertinent here is Kriemhild's narration of her two dreams, warning Siegfried of impending catastrophe, which he rather brusquely ignores before rushing out to his death (921–924). In *aventiure* 25, Uote's narrated dream is more rudely rejected by Hagen and set in the context of engendered behavior:

> Dô sprach zuo z'ir kinden   diu edel Uote:
> "ir soldet hie belîben   helde guote.
> mir ist getroumet hinte   von angestlîcher nôt.
> wie allez daz gefügele   in disem lande wære tôt."

> "Swer sich an troume wendet,"   sprach dô Hagene,
> "der enweiz der rehten mære   niht ze sagene,
> wenn'ez im ze êren   volleclîchen stê.
> ich wil, daz mîn herre   ze hove nâch urloube gê.

> Wir suln gerne rîten   in Etzelen lant.
> dâ mac wol dienen künegen   guoter helde hant,
> dâ wir dâ schouwen müezen   Kriemhilde hôhgezît." (1509–1510)

(Then noble Uote said to her children: "you should stay here, good warriors. Last night I dreamt of a frightful catastrophe: how all the birds of this country were dead." "Nobody who puts stock in dreams," said Hagen, "has the least idea of the real requirements of honor. I wish my lords to ask leave to depart. We must ride to Etzel's country, where worthy warriors may serve their kings well, since we must there attend Kriemhild's festival.")

The Queen Mother of Burgundy thus reports an ominous dream to her sons just before they set out on a journey whose potentially catastrophic consequences they had themselves already discussed at court and which will end in their own deaths among the corpses of thousands of others. The dream nonetheless receives no explicit interpretation, whether because its specific symbolism was immediately clear enough, or whether, as seems more likely, Hagen's condescending and sexist grandstanding merely assumes that this is another attempt by someone besides himself to influence the Burgundian kings, here in fact a female attempt to influence male behavior, which he characteristically and immediately interrupts with a scoffing challenge to the machismo of any who might wish to hear more about the dream. Uote's sons, on the other hand, who are kings and her direct addressees, make no reply, prevented by Hagen's trivialization of this entire attempt at overdetermined communication. Here, as in the example of Kriemhild's attempt to warn Siegfried, death is the result. On the similar (non-dream) attempt at warning and its similar rejection, followed by similar catastrophe at the siege of Kassiane in *Kudrun*, see below, Chapter seven. On dreams in the *Nibelungenlied*, see Jerold C. Frakes, "Kriemhild's Three Dreams: A Structural Analysis," *Zeitschrift für deutsches Altertum* 113 (1984), 173–187 (with bibliography) and D. G. Mowatt, "A Note on Kriemhild's Three Dreams," *Seminar* 7 (1971), 114–122.

One of the scenes mentioned above is that of the cosummation of Brünhild's and Gunther's marriage, which involves several instances of intimate communication over the course of a thirty-six-hour period at the palace in Worms. The tenth *aventiure* has received the manuscript subtitle: *Wie Prünhilt ze Wormez empfangen wart* ["How Brünhild was received in Worms"].[31] If we momentarily (mis)construe this subtitle as a question, then we might answer that the former ruling queen of Iceland and present queen of Burgundy is received with the continued contempt and treachery of her husband and his trusted accomplice, with yet another instance of deception that signifies on the personal as well as political level, with one attempted but unsuccessful rape, and finally with a successful (gang-) rape.[32] By dealing with this episode as rape and by identifying it as such from the outset, I am obviously predetermining the course of my investigation of the scene. But I do so for reasons similar to Gravdal's in reading Chrétien's scenes of sexual violence:

> Because Chrétien tends to veer away from the literal violence of rape, embedding it in situations that are moral and sentimental, and because Chrétien scholars have avoided the question of violence, focusing on topics such as courtly love, chivalry, irony, and romance composition, I want to read against the text, press the pile of weave of Chrétien's romances in the "wrong" direction, in order to push toward the repressed violence in romantic love. I also stubbornly commit the critical crime of taking episodes "out of context." I do so because as long as the rape scenes remain "in context" they will continue to be obscured by the harmonious whole, by the overall design of the romances' composition (on the subject of which a significant body of critical

31. The C-manuscript has a different title: *wie der kunec Gunter ze Wormze mit frov prvnhilt prvtte* ("how King Gunther consummates marriage/breeds with Lady Brünhild in Worms").

32. Mary Fleet may have been the first scholar to have used the word *rape* to identify and name these actions: Fleet, "Siegfried as Gunther's Vassal," *Oxford German Studies* 14 (1983), 1–7. She does so three times: Siegfried "having overcome her [Brünhild], he keeps his word and leaves it to Gunther to deflower her, although rape would probably be the better word" (p. 5); "until she was raped by Gunther"; and "the rape of Brünhild by Gunther" (p. 6). The article's title is misleading, however, and except for this veritable breakthrough in terminological accuracy and frankness, the article itself accomplishes little, for its main scholarly authority seems to be Hatto's *translation,* and its subject is far less Siegfried as vassal than simply a pointed re-narration of key scenes of realpolitical deception. In recent years quite a number of scholars have used the term *rape/Vergewaltigung* to designate the events of this scene; see, for instance, Barbara Siebert: "Was Siegfried in der Hochzeitsnacht leistet, ist nicht mehr und nicht weniger als Beihilfe zur Vergewaltigung" ("what Siegfried does in the wedding night is no more and no less than aiding in rape") in *Rezeption und Produktion.* p. 102; cf. also Otfrid Ehrismann, who designates the action a "malicious rape," in "Disapproval, Kitsch, and the Process of Justification: Brünhild's Wedding Nights," *Waz sider da geschach: German-American Studies on the Nibelungenlied Text and Reception,* ed. Werner Wunderlich and Ulrich Müller (Göppingen: Kümmerle, 1992), p. 167.

work exists already); it is that aesthetico-moral harmony and unity that have kept the representation of sexual violence invisible for so long. (p. 570)[33]

There are in fact three private conversations in this *aventiure,* all of which involve Brünhild and her actual or proxy husband. The first such conversation occurs at, and in stark contrast to, the [hyper-]courtly wedding banquet (i.e. not behind closed doors, although apparently still at least semi-privately). The parodic potential of the courtliness of the episode

33. Here Gravdal also refers to an interesting observation by the late John H. Winkler on the ideological implications of the critical dictum that nothing beyond the author's intended meaning should be the scholar's goal: "If our critical faculties are placed solely in the service of elucidating an author's meaning, then we have already committed ourselves to the premises and protocols of the past—past structures of cultural violence and their descendants in the bedrooms and mean streets and school curricula of the present. This above all we will not do" ("The Education of Chloe," in *Rape and Representation,* ed. Lynn Higgins and Brenda Silver [New York: Columbia University Press, 1991]), p. 30. One of the more striking peculiarities of the tradition of *Nibelungenlied* scholarship is the occasional construction of the rape scene as comedy, about which Otfrid Ehrismann has recently offered the shrewd comment: "Der Dichter, der sich nicht wie andere Kollegen vom Gaudi der nächtlichen Ereignisse mitreißen läßt, entfaltet ein resigniertes Geschichtsbild und erzählt von der verbrecherischen und intriganten Zerstörung der Frau, ihrer politischen und menschlichen Würde" ("The poet, who unlike other colleagues, does not let himself be carried away by the 'fun' of the nocturnal events, displays a resigned view of history and tells of the criminal and scheming destruction of the woman, her political and human dignity" p. 135). The most comprehensive version of this argument appeared two decades ago, but may be briefly exhumed here for the sake of illustration. Stephen L. Wailes identifies the scene's tone as 'burlesque,' understood as an unexpected narrative attitude or tone inappropriate to content ("Bedroom Comedy in the *Nibelungenlied," Modern Language Quarterly* 32 [1971], 365–376); he comments on Brünhild's complaint that Siegfried has rumpled her shift: "her response and the ensuing events are out of all proportion to the offense. This is a touch of the mock-heroic—the rumpling of the shift, the rape of the lock." But here it is in fact not a Popean lock, but rather the queen who is about to be raped, and the rumpled shift and her complaint about it are not innocent, not without context, but rather simultaneously a reference to Gunther's sexual assault on her the previous night and a warning about any further attempt at rape, such as the one that this "rumpling" suggests is impending. Wailes calls the rape "entertaining in incident as well as in structure," "humorous," and no more than a "wrestling match"; in Siegfried's reflections on the effect of his defeat on the behavior of wives, Wailes sees an indication that "the poet discards any last semblance of serious involvement in this donnybrook between hero and heroine and asks us to regard it as the paradigm of marital conflict" (p. 371). But since Siegfried and Brünhild are not married to each other they cannot, by definition, engage in "marital conflict"; moreover, their "donnybrook" consists of a struggle in which disguise and deception are essential, and which will end *only* in the death of the one or the murder or rape of the other, the last of which in fact occurs. Wailes claims further that "By withholding her love, Brünhild is nothing more or less than a disobedient wife" (p. 372). Actually she is both more and less than a wife, for she is not yet technically married and she is still the queen of Iceland; additionally, Brünhild is hardly withholding "love," but rather sex, for no such post-Romantic mental-emotional-social construct as "love" existed for Brünhild or the audience of the *Nibelungenlied.* To this point in the *Nibelungenlied* not even "affection" has been an issue with Brünhild and Gunther, and in neither this nor the ensuing scenes does it become one. Theirs is a relationship of necessity (in several senses) and of dynastic and political import, but sentiment has little to do with it now or later.

has been well-prepared through the lavish descriptions of the clothes, feasting, jousting, and guests. The second royal marriage (Kriemhild to Siegfried) and the one that is secondary to Gunther's and Brünhild's, since dependent on it, has also been presented as executed with courtly aplomb. The only blemish on the entire festival has been Brünhild's weeping in response to Kriemhild's marriage to Gunther's *eigenholden,* which was an expression of her desire, in general, to break the betrothal and renounce the marriage to Gunther, and specifically to refuse consummation of the marriage, if no satisfactory explanation of this incongruous situation were forthcoming:

> *wess' ich, war ich möhte,   ich hete gerne fluht,*
> *daz ich iu nimmer wolde   geligen nâhen bî,*
> *ir'n saget mir, wâ von Kriemhilt   diu wine Sîfrides sî.* (622)

(If I only knew where I could go, I would flee, so that I'd never have sex with you, unless you tell me why Kriemhild is the lover/spouse of Siegfried.)

Gunther initially defers explanation until after Brünhild makes explicit her wish to renounce the marriage. Then he offers a true and straightforward, but incomplete account: Siegfried is as royal and landed as Gunther himself. But he does not repudiate the explicit claim of vassalage made by Siegfried in Iceland and implicitly accepted by Gunther and everyone else (except Kriemhild) since then[34]; and thus Gunther also does not renounce Brünhild's present claims on Siegfried's vassalage. That Brünhild is dissatisfied with the explanation lies not in any malevolence on her part, but rather stems from a threefold cause. First, while this information does not actually contradict the earlier pretense of Siegfried's vassalage,[35] it would, nonetheless, describe a radically different relationship from the one that she had been led to accept, and one to which she would need time to become

---

34. The most explicit gesture of vassalage, Siegfried's holding Gunther's stirrup while the Burgundian king mounted his horse, hardly constitutes evidence that Siegfried was Gunther's *eigenhold,* however, for a recent (for the audience of the *Nibelungenlied*) historical event of some significance clearly resonates in this act: in 1154 Emperor Frederick Barbarossa rebelled at performing a like service for the pope at Sutri, since it would have signified his subordination to the pope, but in no way could it have been thought to constitute evidence of his being *eigenhold.*

35. Lesser kings are often vassals of greater kings, in both feudal literature and feudal history. For example, in the course of expanding his territory, Philip Augustus of France (1180–1223) technically became the vassal of other lords; in the mid-thirteenth century the king of England was again technically the vassal of the king of France for Gascony.

accustomed. Secondly, a contradiction does arise insofar as Siegfried was said to be Gunther's *man,* if that term is interpreted to mean *eigenman,* an unfree vassal, as Brünhild interprets, for no *eigenman* can at the same time be a king. Feudal allegiance is one thing; the distinction between free and non-free is another. Finally, Gunther's explanation, accurate so far as it goes, is simply incomplete: he does not clarify *his* relationship to Siegfried, but rather simply indicates Siegfried's extra-Burgundian status, at best a matter of irrelevance, at worst of unnecessary complication and confusion for Brünhild at the moment, who has just seen her new husband's sister married to — for all intents and purposes — a military serf.

No further comment indicates whether Brünhild has accepted this truncated explanation as sufficient until the second private conversation explodes during the wedding night. Initially Gunther's experience with Brünhild on this night is described in contrast to his premarital experience: *er hete dicke sampfter   bî andern wîben gelegen* ("he had often had better sex / lain more peacefully with other women" 630).[36] The images proper to a royal wedding night, and parallel to the apparently courtly and affection-ate consummation of the marriage of Kriemhild and Siegfried just de-scribed, are assembled: the groom's libidinous expectations, the withdrawal of the servants from the chamber and its closing, the white shift of the virgin bride, the extinguishing of the candles by the groom. Gunther even thinks: *nu hân ichz allez hie, des ich ie dâ gerte   in allen mînen tagen* ("Now I have everything here that I have ever desired in all my life" 632). One of the "things," however, is another human being, who has a will and desires of her own, which sharply diverge from his.

Brünhild states clearly and unequivocally her desire to remain a vir-gin, her reason for that desire, and the condition necessary for her volun-tary modification of that resolve.[37] Gunther responds immediately and di-rectly — with violent assault: *dô rang er nâch ir minne   unt zer fuort' ir diu kleit* ("Then he fought for her love / attempted to rape her and ripped off her

36. And thus *legen bî* does not exclusively signify sexual intercourse (although in the context that is its primary denotation), because none occurred in this night between Gunther and Brünhild.

37. Schweikle suggests that Brünhild acknowledges Gunther's *Vormundschaft* in Iceland after the contests (466 and esp. 510), which "steht dann allerdings ihr Verhalten in der Hochzeitsnacht in Gegensatz" ("certainly contradicts her behavior on the wedding night," p. 71). Schweikle thus disallows the possibility of independent female action within the system of *munt*-marriage (if indeed that is the type found here, which is not altogether clear); on the other hand Brünhild's character is thus reduced to a mechanism that must automatically switch from independence to blind obedience at a moment's notice. Neither notion seems par-ticularly compelling.

gown" 636).[38] But his strength, as both she and the reader know, is negligible, and his attack lasts only one line of the text, for she immediately subdues, binds, and hangs him up, after she had caused him *grôzer leide genuoc* ("a great deal of pain"); his sexual assault had almost caused his death: *von ir krefte   vil nâch gewunnen den tôt* ("very nearly died from her strength" 636–637). Gunther responds with pleas, acknowledgement of his subordinate status, and a promise *harte selten* (litotes: "very rarely" = "never again") to lie so close to her (638). As a result of this wedding night, Gunther's negligible strength is acknowledged by the narrator, perhaps in suggesting that the circumstances in which he passed the night further reduced it. By contrast, the result of the second night is to reduce Brünhild's significant powers to negligible levels. The male's lack of strength is demonstrated, if not reduced, by enforced lack of consummation; the female's is annihilated by its forcible completion.

Gunther's succinct report to Siegfried of the night's activities (but not of Brünhild's condition for consummation) prompts a premonitory confusion of identities on the part of Siegfried. One after the other he promises his service in the coming night, smugly notes his own "success," and predicts the inevitability of Brünhild's consummation of the marriage in the coming night. As is customary for Siegfried, he in turn so immediately complicates the entire matter by bringing up issues better left unmentioned: in describing his plan, he verbally identifies his action as *dienen* "service," promises *sô twinge ich dir dîn wîp, / daz du si hînte minnest* ("'I will force your wife for you, so that you will have intercourse with her tonight'"), or will die in the attempt (654). Thus he again clouds the issue of feudal service, is prepared to risk his life in the struggle, and promises to "force" Gunther's wife *for* him: This last phrase is exceptionally strange, for its syntactic inconcinnity adds to the ambiguity: syntactic possibilities are multiple: A can force (*twengen*) B for someone else's sake, or A can force B *to do* something, but in terms of syntactic logic A can hardly force B that C does something. Thus there is a combination of syntactic constructions: Siegfried promises to force Brünhild in any and all senses of the word and simultaneously promises to force her to submit to intercourse (*minnen*) with Gunther. Gunther understands the ambiguity and immediately imposes the condition on Siegfried *âne daz du iht triutest,* glossed by de Boor as "'[nicht daß du] ihr in irgendeiner Weise zu nahe trittst'" (["without your] approaching her too closely in any way"). Actually, however, this phrase is commonly used in Middle High German to make specific refer-

---

38. In place of the last phrase, the C-manuscript has: *daz was der frowen leit* (641).

ence to the sexual act, and it appears elsewhere in the *Nibelungenlied* in precisely this sense (1400). And Siegfried, in accepting the conditions, employs the other common term for love and intercourse in a courtly context: *minne*. The present context—a virile man forcing a nubile woman to submit to sexual intercourse—certainly allows the interpretation of *triuten* as "have intercourse with."

This is the only condition set by Gunther on the nature of Siegfried's physical assault on the queen, and he *expressis uerbis* condones the use of any degree of force deemed necessary by Siegfried, even to the point that he may kill Brünhild with impunity (655). She is, after all, according to Gunther, *ein vreislíchez wîp* "'a terrifying/fearsome/destructive woman'"; this is after he had already called her *den übeln tiuvel* "'the evil devil'" in his initial complaint to Siegfried about his wedding night. Gunther stops short of permitting Siegfried sexual relations with Brünhild, however, for that would constitute adultery, which would be not just personally humiliating for Gunther (as the whole affair already is), but would have legal and political implications as well.[39]

Siegfried's modus operandi in this scene is identical to that employed in Iceland: by the agency of his magic cape, he again assumes the proxy role of Gunther. Here only he and Gunther are party to the deception, thus further obscuring the distinction between them. In each case, Gunther's achievements are unexpected and improbable, but there is no sensory evidence that Gunther is not the winner, either in the Icelandic contests, where "seeing is believing" or in Worms, where the evidence is aural only. In general the use of the senses is foregrounded in the bedroom scene by their very suppression. The sensuality of the scene has far less to do with the fact that it depicts a rape, which recent sociological research has shown is a matter of a demonstration of power more than sexual desire,[40] than it does with the economy of violence and physical power. Since all three

39. A capital offense only for the woman, not the man, according to Germanic law (von Amira, II, 73). In this case, of course, Brünhild, if raped, could hardly be *legitimately* charged with adultery. But then there is little about such a case that may be termed legitimate anyway.

40. See the recent summary of this position, which first gained wide acceptance through Susan Brownmiller's *Against Our Will: Men, Women, and Rape* (New York: Simon and Schuster, 1975), in the article by David Lisak, "Sexual Aggression, Masculinity, and Fathers," *Signs: Journal of Women in Culture and Society* 16 (1991), esp. p. 244: "More recently it [sc. rape] is usually defined as an act of violence in which sexuality is only the vehicle for the expression of anger and dominance. . . . [W]hile there is considerable evidence that sexuality is not a prominent factor in the motivation of most rapists, there is considerable evidence that gender is." Gradually this position is replacing the traditional patriarchal conception of rape as the "natural" (albeit, as usually conceded, overzealous) sexual exuberance of young males to reproduce the species, an exuberance beyond their control due to hormones, that is, the once common "boys will be boys" justification of rape.

characters are deprived of sight, the characters' aural and tactile senses seem heightened, for certainly those types of sensory data are more specifically reported by the narrator. At the same time, however, all sensory data necessary for the identification of the individual participants is lacking. The narrator recurringly maintains that Gunther heard that Siegfried was not transgressing the sexual limits agreed upon but takes no responsibility for the accuracy of Gunther's hearing. Nor does he make any authoritative pronouncement of his own about Siegfried's conduct in this regard. Instead, the narrator merely reiterates: *Gunther wol horte*. . . . Gunther is thus merely an ear-witness, whose only evidence is, ironically, *ex silentio* in a crash- and groan-filled encounter that is anything but easily interpretable on the basis of aural evidence.

In fact all participants are sensory-deprived. Gunther is reduced to a silent, nontactile, immobile auditory witness: the king unbound but powerless in his own castle, unable to control, influence or even understand what takes place in his own bed although he is right next to it. Here for the first time Siegfried too is restricted. In Iceland he retained all his sensory powers, while his cape rendered him invisible to others; now he too is blind in the darkened room; he must also remain silent and is rendered doubly invisible by his magic cape and the darkness. Brünhild is initially unrestricted in the *use* of her senses (except for sight), but must cope unknowingly with deprivation of available sensory data: Gunther's removal from the active sensory field (and reduction to a passive aural sensor), Siegfried's mistaken identity due to the "disguise" of his assuming Gunther's place, his (double) invisibility and his silence. Later she is also deprived permanently of her strength, independence, and therewith in essence also her distinct identity, since she is thus reduced to an appurtenance of Gunther.

From Brünhild's perspective, of course, her opponent, both in Iceland and in the first *two* nights in the Burgundian royal bedroom actually is Gunther. The reader knows better. Moreover from the reader's perspective, all significant activity thus far reported concerning the relationship of Gunther and Brünhild has been a result of the teamwork of Gunther and Siegfried. Gunther's relationship with Brünhild does not simply *include* Siegfried, but rather Siegfried's participation has, even from the moment of Gunther's incipient infatuation with Brünhild's reputation, been a necessary precondition of the existence of that relationship.[41] This necessary

41. Kriemhild, the only one to make an *open* issue of the episode, in her confrontation with Brünhild in *aventiure* fourteen, is also the only participant not present at the event, which

association of Gunther and Siegfried may provide some insight into the problems of the various relationships here, for obviously identity is one of the primary problems in this scene of disguise and deception. One might indeed ask whether Siegfried as a quasi-Gunther is aware of his identity as distinct from Gunther's. But the problem is more complex, for Siegfried assumes not just Gunther's place and role, but in the face of impending defeat in battle at the hands of a woman, he also assumes the more elemental role of man defending male ideology against a potential female usurper (673). I am not suggesting that Siegfried's personal identity merges with Gunther's, but rather that his functional identity, as it were, the identity of the *actant* as perceived by others, does so, and Siegfried himself seems to act within the expanded limits of his role. This interpretation is made available to the reader by means of the constellation of details that disguise, confuse, or merge identities in this scene: sensory deprivation, double invisibility, role exchange at two critical moments (Siegfried and Gunther), and gender-role reversal (Brünhild and Siegfried, see below).

The status of the evidence and even the conditions of knowledge about the events of this scene are quite ambiguous. The known facts of the case are: (1) Gunther, Siegfried, and Brünhild were present in the Burgundian royal bedroom in total darkness; (2) as prearranged by Gunther and Siegfried, Siegfried assaulted and brutally beat Brünhild, (3) who was then raped;[42] (4) Siegfried broke contact with Brünhild, stole her ring and belt, and left the bedroom; (5) Gunther entered and consummated his marriage with Brünhild. There obviously remains a trace of ambiguity even in the recounting of these few facts, for in my ordering of items three and four, I have begged the question. Reversing them would, however, absolve Siegfried of only a negligible portion of his responsibility for the rape and transfer primary responsibility for the sexual act to Gunther.

The age-old question of whether Siegfried "actually" had intercourse with Brünhild or not has traditionally been confused by the inevitable

---

also makes her the only one completely deprived of immediate sensory evidence. But she must have received her information from Siegfried, that is, she has received the interpretation of an aural and tactile witness. The quality of Siegfried's testimony is, however, subject to a number of radically different evaluations, for he may have lied to Kriemhild about some part, or the whole, of this escapade. Kriemhild herself, who has a personal and political stake in the outcome of the encounter with Brünhild, may be lying; one or both may have told or be telling the truth. We know that Siegfried casually practices violent deception even to the point of defrauding royalty. It may be another instance of Siegfried's machismo, blindly intended either to impress his bride with his sexual prowess or humiliate her by such outrageous behavior and thus further subordinate her to his control.

42. I contend that submission to sexual intercourse in order to prevent one's own murder hardly constitutes consent.

philological adduction of Norse and even Wagnerian analogues. The Middle High German poet is deemed moral for his modification if not avoidance of the adultery motif, while Siegfried himself is commonly absolved of guilt. Even ignoring external (pseudo-)evidence, however, the case is complex, and here too it seems a complexity that is not due to faulty piecing together of "sources." Did Siegfried sexually penetrate Brünhild? Kriemhild, who was not there, says yes; Gunther, who more or less was, *hears* no. No one else in the text comments on the matter — nor does the narrator — for when Siegfried is summoned to the juridical ring ten years later to clear himself by oath, he is to swear only that he did not tell Kriemhild of such a deed (*ichs ir niht gesaget hân* 858,4), not that he did not perform it. This transformation of his crime from alleged deed to word, from act to speech, from rape to locker-room boast,[43] proceeds in several stages and represents another instance of the effective appropriation, redirection, and final erasure by men both of women's public action *and,* in this case, of their own private actions.

Kriemhild's initial accusation is that Brünhild was Siegfried's *kebse* (839,4), which, three or four centuries earlier would have been at least a bigamous insult — "informal wife" — coming from the man's "formal" wife, but perhaps even then there would have had a sharper sting. In the late twelfth century, when *Kebsehe* as a recognized legitimate institution is long dead, to be *verkebset* (840,1), as Brünhild reformulates the charge in her response, is to be called concubine, bed-companion, adulteress. Kriemhild's next formulation of the deed is:

> den dinen schœnen líp
> den minnet' êrste Sîfrit,   der min vil lieber man.
> jane was ez niht min bruoder, der dir den magetuom an gewan (840,2–4)

(Siegfried, my very dear husband, it was, who first had intercourse with your lovely body. It was not at all my brother who took your maidenhood.)

This reformulation is more specific than the first, describing the action with the recurring, polysemous *minnen* (repeated in 841,2), which here clearly tends toward an explicit sexual connotation; adding the concrete, descriptive, if not sensual, detail of Brünhild's beautiful body, and emphasizing that this action deprived Brünhild of her virginity both by specifying that

---

43. Or rather bedroom boast, for the bragging allegedly was done to his wife!

Siegfried was the first (*êrste*) and then by explicitly naming the act of rupturing the hymen (*den magetuom an gewan*).

Kriemhild's next formulation is the explosively multivalent *jâ wart mîn Sîfrit dîn man* ("'my Siegfried did become your husband/your vassal/did have sex with you'" 849,4), which has interesting and ironic associations with Brünhild's beliefs concerning Siegfried's feudal status,[44] while also maintaining the semantic association to marriage and quasi-marriage that *kebse* probably still evoked. Here too Brünhild's response merely reverses the perspective of Kriemhild's terms[45]: *ich sî Sîfrides wîp* (851,4). The formulation of the official charge, as it were, is left to Brünhild, however, for she delivers it to Gunther, the king, who will take whatever action is to be taken. Her formulation is: *si giht, mich habe gekebset   Sîfrit ir man* ("'she said that her husband had sex with me/made me his *kebse*'" 853,3).[46]

This is the point at which the matter is transferred from the female to the male sphere. The fact that Kriemhild's accusation was delivered before witnesses necessarily makes it a political act, but that potentially political nature of the case is not opened up until the politically responsible, male parties become involved. Thus Gunther's initial response is of paramount importance, and significantly it is not anger toward the alleged perpetrator of the crime, but rather an immediate verdict passed on the one who has reported it, Kriemhild: *sô hetes' übele getân* ("'If so, then she has done wrong'" 853,4). When he does turn to the matter of the accusation and the accused, he radically reformulates the case: no longer is Siegfried charged with *kebsen*, but rather with *sichs rüemen* ("boasting of it" 855,2). When Siegfried actually appears to hear the charge, however, Gunther takes the transformation one step further and claims now that it was a charge of boasting that Kriemhild advanced and that Brünhild has now reported to him.

> *mir hât mîn vrouwe Prünhilt   ein mære hie geseit,*
> *du habes dich des gerüemet,   daz du ir schœnen lîp*
> *allerêrst habes geminnet,   daz sagt Kriemhilt dîn wîp.* (857,1–3)

(My wife has told a tale/reported to me, that you boasted that you were the first have sex with her, that is said by Kriemhild, your wife.)

44. Which, as Kriemhild points out in 841,1–2, are undermined by Brünhild's alleged stooping to have sex with her vassal; that is, mirroring the charge Brünhild makes concerning Kriemhild's marriage to a vassal.

45. Cf. above: *mannes kebse — [mich] hâstu hie verkebset.*

46. Cf. Lexer, I 1533, sub *kebesen* "fornicari."

Siegfried responds in exactly the same form as had Gunther: first with a threat of punishment for the wrong-doing of the *reporter* of the crime, then by proposing an oath *daz ichs ir niht gesaget hân* (" 'that I did not say it to her' " 858,4). In the end, however, even this oath is not necessary, since Gunther claims to trust in Siegfried's innocence (*iuwer grôz unschulde* 860,3).[47] It is more likely, however, that Gunther simply cannot afford to have Siegfried swear any such oath in public. As a tag to the preemption of the oath, Gunther then adds absolution of the *original charge* made by the women (*des iuch mîn swester zîet* " 'of which my sister accuses you' " 860,4), although that charge has not been addressed and its existence not even acknowledged since the affair passed into the realm of male, public action.

If we then attempt to extrapolate from this "trial" the evidence about the events of the night in question, we must admit that there is none. It is not even clear if in their suppression of the entire matter Siegfried and Gunther here again demonstrate their ability to disarm female threats and render them ostensibly harmless, or if they are in fact far more concerned with the word than the deed, with Siegfried's alleged tattling, his inability to keep "state secrets." At any rate, it seems that here is a clear case of what Gravdal has observed in Chrétien's treatment of sexual violence: his "eli sion . . . of rape leads the audience to ignore . . . its literal consequences for the female victim and to focus instead on the ideology of chivalry" ("Medieval Romance," p. 569).

In general I see no reason to attempt to build an argument in favor of Siegfried's actual intercourse with Brünhild, for there is neither concrete evidence for it, nor any argumentative benefit to be gained. For two reasons, however, the topic is significant in the context of my articulation of a pervasive patriarchal system. First is the fact that in the matter of what actually happened in the royal bedroom, the text introduces a host of ambiguities and emphasizes them at every turn. On the one hand such ambiguity reinforces that functional identity, suggested above, of Gunther and Siegfried. In the larger context of this team's recurring and identical method — Siegfried performs, while Gunther stands by — their consistent deception of Brünhild both in Iceland and Worms, and their team rape of Brünhild here, it matters little whether Siegfried actually penetrated Brünhild, for he is the means to [Gunther's] penetration of her. From Brünhild's perspective of course, sex with Gunther is at this moment as abhorrent as,

---

47. That there was no oath sworn is not the only possible interpretation, of course. The scene is clearly ambiguous here too. See Otfrid Ehrismann's tally of opinions for and against the existence of an actual oath here; *Nibelungenlied: Epoche — Werk — Wirkung*, p. 146.

we must imagine, it would be with Siegfried, if she were to know that it was he who was in bed with her. The fact that she is betrothed to Gunther clearly plays no role in her desire or lack thereof. She who had conceived, conducted, and, in all but the last instance, won the contests to maintain her independence in Iceland certainly now recognizes these events in the Burgundian bedroom for what they are—a power struggle.

Whatever the "actualities" of Siegfried's specifically sexual encounter with Brünhild in the *Nibelungenlied,* a significant encounter occurs on the metaphorical level. For there seem to be such a number of puns in this scene that a purposive pattern *almost* takes shape—a pattern that *metaphorically* signifies a Siegfried-Brünhild rape, just as it is denied literally by the text. But, note the qualifications in the previous sentence. Puns are as difficult to "prove" outside the performative context as is irony. Often, I fear, when one begins to look for puns (especially in a seven-hundred-year-old text), they suddenly appear everywhere, which is an interesting phenomenon in itself but not particularly compelling as scholarly evidence. Nonetheless, I offer the following observations about possible puns as suggestive of a narrative/metaphorical potential in the text.

Just as the clichés of the cracked jar of the milkmaid or the speeding train entering a tunnel were clear signs of sex in the less sexually explicit recent past in painting and film, the rumpled nightgown, the bride's cracked member (*lit*), the stolen ring and girdle are no less suggestive here. There is even a sudden and profuse flowing of blood from the body of the (momentarily) vanquished one, i.e., rather unexpectedly, Siegfried. The expected flowing of blood conventionally associated with the sexual initiation (if via heterosexual intercourse) of the human female is thus inverted, but the fact that the male, not the female, bleeds and is on the point of defeat does not refute but rather—yet again—complicates and renders ambiguous this interpretation. For the entire context is replete with indicators of role reversal, thus foregrounding the paramount significance of gender roles and the individual and gender identities in these scenes. Brünhild has already pinned, bound, and hung up her bridegroom and thus proven herself the stronger, the more "virile" in the conventional terms of female naturalization, while Gunther undergoes this humiliation and superficial emasculation. On the second night, Brünhild's vigorous activity with her current bed-partner (Siegfried) includes first tossing him from her bed to a bench and then banging his head on her *schamel* "footstool" or perhaps *scham-el* "dear little crotch" (668,3–4); she claims that she will "get it into him" (670,4 *innen bringen,* usually "make aware of") not to rip her clothes;

she squeezes him in her embrace (671,1); she wishes to tie him up (or down), so that she may have some peace/a piece in bed (671,2–3 *gemach* "peace" ~ *gemaht* "testicles/genitals")[48]; she overcomes him physically (672,2); she *druht' in ungefuoge   zwischen die want und ein schrîn* (672,4) "pushes him improperly between the wall and a trunk"/"rams him obscenely between her gown and her box"[49] (672,3–4); she bears down on him until the blood spurts (675,2–3); she takes off her girdle, intending to tie him down.

On the other hand, Siegfried embraces Brünhild (668,2); he wishes to force her (*er sie wolde twingen* 669,3); he rips off her gown (670,2 & 671,4); he wants to make an example of her to "uppity" women (673)[50]; he tries it out on her (674,4); he will force her (675,1); he forces her to renounce her improper/obscene will (675,4–676,1); he presses her onto the bed (673,3); he cracks her *lît* "member/joint" (with the common elision of initial prefix *ge-*, the word *gelit*) or "bed" (a loan word from Old French) and her whole body (677,3). It is at the moment that her member is cracked that the struggle ceases, the narrator informs the reader, and Brünhild simultaneously becomes Gunther's wife. *Gunther's* wife? How so? He does not enter the bed until later.

In the end, we might agree that some or all of these alleged puns are figments of a runaway twentieth-century imagination. But, if nothing else, in teasing out their possibilities, the already complex construction of conventional gender roles on which the scene is based has gained more depth, for it now seems clear that on one level at least the interaction of Siegfried and Brünhild has a great deal to do with the trading back and forth of those *ad hoc* gender constructions. There is no need to tally instances of Brünhild's and Siegfried's male versus female metaphors in order to decide which role each plays here (or whether there need only be two roles available). What is clear is that the roles are traded back and forth, resulting not in a confused

48. Depending on speed, clarity and intent of recitation, the two words might have been phonetically indistinguishable in *this* context: . . . *gemach. daz* . . . [gemaχ, das / gemaχtas].

49. The definite article *die* would agree with both feminine singular *want* "wall" and neuter plural *(ge)want* "article of clothing." The colloquial semantic association of *schrîn* and the female genitalia is attested in Middle High German (Lexer, II 800) and suggests the possibility of word play here.

50. The narrative thus shifts the focus of the scene from the rape in progress to a matter of knightly honor, from the specific to the abstract, from a matter of immediate female concern to a general reflection on male privilege. Similarly Gravdal notes that in Chrétien's interruption of the rape scene in *Lancelot* 1096–1107, 1112–1115, the reader's focus is shifted from the "sense of danger and the immediacy of the violence of the scene. At the very moment in which the audience might see rape in all its horror, interest is shifted to a moral meditation on chivalric honor" (p. 577).

narrative, but in ambiguity; not in nonsense, but in a profession that they are in fact conventional, constructed roles whose legitimacy may bear investigation. Brünhild mounts an aggressive defense whose narration may make use of multiple sexual puns, underscoring the fact that the event being described in the scene is a rape. But rape is a typically male act and weapon. In thus imputing to Brünhild the images and actions of the rapist in the first part of the scene, while reversing them in the conclusion of the struggle, the thirteenth-century text already seems to presage the twentieth-century recognition of rape as defined primarily by power and violence, not by sex.

At the same time, however, this representation of Brünhild's rape is significantly defused textually precisely by that which has gone on before: as Gravdal observes about Chrétien:

> Rather than allowing the audience to be too dismayed (or too stimulated) by the representation of erotic violence, Chrétien consistently diverts audience attention to the male character in the sequence. He both creates sympathy for the masculine position and justifies the audience's interest in rape by making it a vehicle for the intellectual analysis of a moral dilemma. (p. 569)

In the very fact that Brünhild refuses to consummate her marriage with the king, she challenges the entirety of male ideology and thus becomes by definition the aggressor. Since the conventional system only allows for one active role, Brünhild, in her independence and action for the sake of her own desire, in her defiant *clitorality*—as Gayatri Spivak and recent French feminisms designate independent female action—political, sexual, and otherwise—for the woman's own purposes and desires,[51] has by default assumed the active role (leaving only the passive role for Gunther and/or Siegfried), forcing her own will on the other party. In this case the matter is sex or rather the subordination that coerced sex subsumes. Thus the vocabulary of rape seems only appropriate for Brünhild's forceful refusal of sex. The double cut of this irony is powerful, but ultimately also deceptive, for Brünhild is finally not the rapist, but the raped.

Perhaps the scene's most graphic metaphor is also one that had venerable age and widespread use: the ring and girdle stolen from Brünhild by Siegfried at the moment of truth.[52] Significantly, in the *Nibelungenlied* the

51. Spivak uses the word *clitoris* "as a name (close to a metonym) for women in excess of coupling-mothering. When this excess is in competition in the public domain, it is suppressed in one way or another" in "Feminism and Critical Theory," reprinted in Gayatri Spivak, *In Other Worlds*, p. 280, n. 32. Her use of the term has often been misconstrued as an example of an essentialist argument; I wish to partake here of her anti-essentialist use of this trope.

52. This metaphor calls to mind one of the most obvious parallels between the Greek

first mention of the belt is not Brünhild's loosening it for a lover's access, nor in the rapist's assault, but rather when she binds Gunther the would-be rapist with it on the previous night. Gunther has in some very real sense become bound to Brünhild, sexually and otherwise; he is in thrall to the physical and potential sexual prowess of this quintessentially clitoral female. What better metaphor than the girdle, both as belt and as conventional symbol of the vagina, with which to bind the weak and treacherous would-be husband? Even in the scene of Siegfried's theft, she is again the one who first attempts to use the girdle, to bind this night's rapist also. This time, however, her strength is insufficient to bind Siegfried whether physically or sexually, and he steals ring and belt.

There is a multitude of significations and resonances for the modern reader in the ring as a token of a bond, perhaps of marriage, or at any rate as a symbol of loyalty and faith, and in some cases also of wealth, possession, ostentation. The girdle or sash too is a private gift, a lady's token, a remembrance of shared intimacy. As alluded to above, for the reader familiar with the pan-Germanic Nibelungen traditions, the scene resonates with Sigurðr's encounter with the shield maiden in the *Sigrdrifomál,* and ultimately also with the pseudo hyper Germanic and vibrantly romantic~~ Wagner's~~ ~~Siegfried and Brünhild and their equally roman~~ tic and heroic troth. Additionally the circular ring and girdle are clichés of

---

legend of the Amazon and this Teutonic tale. (The significance of the invention of the Amazon as it relates to the *Nibelungenlied* forms the subject of the next chapter.) Apollodorus, the late compiler of Greek mythological tales in his ἡ βιβλιοθηκὴ (*The Library*) II v 9, recounts the ninth labor of Herakles, to bring the belt of Hippolyte to Eurystheus. The belt itself is actually, according to Apollodorus, τὸν Ἄρεος ζωτῆρα and symbolizes Hippolyte's general preëminence and also of course her martial superiority among the Amazons. Her murder by Herakles results from a seemingly perfidious attack by the Amazons, motivated by the machinations of Hera, so that Hippolyte, who was voluntarily giving the belt to Herakles, was killed and the belt taken. Apollodorus's summary is succinct in the extreme, but his expression of the climax of the sexually charged scene is overdetermined: ὡς δὲ εἶδεν αὐτὰς καθωπλισμένας Ἡρακλῆς, νομίσας ἐκ δόλου τοῦτο γενέσθαι, τὴν μέν Ἱππολύτην κτείνας τὸν ζωτῆρα αφαιρεῖται ("And when Herakles saw them [the Amazons] armed, thinking that this was due to treachery, he killed Hipolyte and took her belt"). According to the ideology operative here, armed women automatically and necessarily signify treachery. William Tyrrell notes that the girdle functions both as a symbol of a female girdle and as the word "belt." He also notes the "synonymity of *zôstér,* the word used for Hippolyte's girdle, and the common word for a woman's girdle, *zoné.* For a woman to loose her *zoné* for a man was both a prelude to and a metaphor for her sexual submission. When Heracles takes the *zôstér* by force, he symbolically rapes Hippolyte. Rape, the violent use of the male genitalia, becomes the means to humiliate and aggregate the Amazon's female aspect" (pp. 90–91). Froma Zeitlin comments: "They [Amazons] may excite men's desire to conquer them in a more equal combat between male and female, and like the ambivalence of the Amazon's girdle, a cross between a warrior's belt and a maiden's cincture, the encounter releases the ambivalence of masculine sexuality that may more safely conjoin the sword with the phallus" (136).

Freudian mythoscopy as symbols of the female genitalia.[53] Some of these significations were probably accessible to the medieval audience as well.[54] But the associations and expectations of the reader coming from Norse literature or Wagnerian music drama are disappointed in the *Nibelungenlied,* where there is no relationship between Siegfried and Brünhild prior to the Burgundian bridal-quest, no love, pledge, intimacy, romance, gift, or betrothal. The *structural* similarities are nonetheless maintained, for the man receives (1) from the woman (2) the ring and belt (3) after physical intimacy (4) in bed. But the readerly expectations are triggered by these apparently familiar fragments that appear in a scene in which no love, no redemption, no pledge is enacted. In the *Nibelungenlied* it is rather simply a sexual assault. The irony is bitter. Siegfried the proxy rapist merely steals the ring and belt after brutally subduing Brünhild. Just as Gunther literally appropriates Brünhild's genitals several stanzas later (681,2), here Siegfried takes symbolic possession of them in stealing the belt and ring. It is in precisely this sense and to this end that Kriemhild presents this "evidence" a decade later: to prove that Siegfried had taken Brünhild's virginity.[55] In this appropriation and aggregation, not only is Brünhild the former *regens regina* of Iceland deprived of her virginity; also her will and desire are mocked, trampled, and destroyed. Her independence and strength, as represented by and for a patriarchal society (her clitorality) is destroyed in this rupture of the hymen.

To return to the question of the significance of the metaphors. The principles operative here are literary, and they partake indirectly of legal, historical, social, ethical, and sexual principles, but are not bound by any of

53. That a ring and belt may be symbols of the female genitalia and thus of heterosexual intimacy is not an isolated occurrence in Apollodorus or the *Nibelungenlied;* another of the more famous occurrences is equally unambiguous: the implications of the green sash given to Gawain under similarly sexually charged circumstances in *Sir Gawain and the Green Knight.* Closer to home, however, in *Kudrun,* Horant, as Hagen's proxy suitor, receives Hilde's ring and belt when she consents to marry his lord (398, 3–400,2). One might question, however, whether such tokens in *Kudrun* are not simply borrowings from the quite influential *Nibelungenlied* tradition rather than from a stock set of symbols.

54. Hans Naumann ("Brünhilds Gürtel," *Zeilschrift für deutsches Altertum und deutsche Literatur* 70 [1933], p. 47) comments: "Kriemhild kann . . . die Wegnahme des Gürtels gar nicht anders deuten, als sie sie deutet" ("Kriemhild can interpret the appropriation of the girdle in no other way than she in fact does interpret it" p. 47). Orilus in *Parzival* interprets similarly when Jeschute has her jewelry stolen by Parzival; see *Parzival* 133–34, ed. Karl Lachmann, 6th ed. (Berlin: de Gruyter, 1926), p. 72.

55. Heinz Rupp suggests that Siegfried's taking Brünhild's ring and girdle is a *private* affair until Kriemhild makes it *public,* at which time it inevitably becomes a political problem. Herewith she insults the *honos imperii* ("Das 'Nibelungenlied' — eine politische Dichtung," 169).

them. For, to state the obvious, literature conventionally operates rather differently from non-literary experience. Did Siegfried commit adultery? Ultimately the technical question is moot, for Siegfried, the literary fiction, is subject to neither trial nor conviction. In this case, nonetheless, at least a shadow of a doubt remains, in fact much more than a mere shadow: that is precisely what makes the situation so significant for the issue of gender, and so interesting for the reader, and also apparently for the fictive participants. Gunther seems fully convinced of Siegfried's innocence during and after the fact, and indicates no concern with the matter until it is forced on his attention years later by the distraught Brünhild.

Finally it is necessary to recognize the implications of the immediate narrative context for the interpretation of the scene as rape. That Brünhild has in Iceland consented to marriage and after the assault by Siegfried consented to intercourse — in each case consent by means of coercion — inscribes this scene of sexual violence into what the medievalist recognizes from the *Spielmannsepik* and the courtly romance as a courtship sequence. Coerced sex, sexual assault, rape, has become "decriminalized," as it were; it has been naturalized, it has become an integral part of romance, marriage, and marital sexual relations; and most importantly in the present context, it has become a naturalized element in this type of narrative. Brünhild's refusal of marriage until she is militarily defeated and her refusal of sex until beaten almost to death are erased by her "consent" and by the fact that she then *does* have intercourse with her "conqueror." That is, she consummates the marriage. Rape is recuperated by, is inscribed into, and disappears underneath courtship and marriage. What might have been criminal has become an element of a strictly controlled legal institution. As Gravdal so splendidly expresses it: "Rape, from a woman's point of view, is not prohibited, *it is regulated*" (p. 583).

The final instance of a marital tête-à-tête in the *Nibelungenlied* contrasts sharply with the Burgundian scene of Brünhild's subjugation: it occurs in the bedroom of Kriemhild and Etzel. The constellation of the participants' power relationships in this scene also differs radically from those of the earlier parallel scenes. Kriemhild is here a foreign bride of the king, as Brünhild also was in Burgundy, but Kriemhild's status in Hunnic society is quite different. Her power and reputation surpass even that which Helche, the former Hunnish queen, had enjoyed; she has twelve kings as vassals; her vassals (thus far) unquestioningly do her bidding (1389–1391). She apparently controls the treasury and has delegated it to her vassal Eckewart, whom she brought from Burgundy and through whose generosity supporters are won for her. It is in this larger context that she reflects on the wrongs done her, which prompts her to think of actually taking revenge. She thinks of inviting the Burgundians and then simultaneously of seeing her beloved brothers and taking vengeance on the villains (st. 1397). Both are objects of her desire.

From this position of strength, she approaches Etzel with a plan for inviting the Burgundians. In stanza 1399 both Kriemhild (in direct speech) and the narrator (in indirect speech) express this plan in terms of a request by the queen of the king: "'ich wil den künec bîten,' daz er ir des gunde . . ." ("'I wish to ask the king,' that he would grant it to her (that) . . ."). The plan is executed in the privacy of the royal chamber:

> Dô si eines nahtes bî dem künige lac,
> (mit armen umbevangen   het er si, als er pflac
> die edeln vrouwen triuten: si was im als sîn lip),
> dô gedâhte ir finde   daz vil hêrlîch wîp. (1400)

(One night while she was having sex/lying with the king (he had his arms around her, as was his custom[56]), the glorious woman was thinking of her enemies.)

In the specificity of its sexual reference, the setting of this scene is much less ambiguous than is that of Brünhild's request of Gunther to issue an invitation to Kriemhild and Siegfried. Key terms from the previous scenes recur here: pflegen "treat/use/customarily do," or minnecliche pflegen "make love/have intercourse"; si was im als sîn lip "she was to him as his own body/as dear to him as life itself." Apparently during the act itself Kriemhild thinks neither of her partner's nor her own immediate desires, physical or otherwise. Her fantasy during the sexual act is not restricted to sex at all, but rather focuses on another kind of desire, a passion of a different but still comprehensible order. She thinks of other men (plural!) during the conjugal act and does so with vengeance (not affection or lust) in mind. We might recall here some of the experiences that determined the course of such a fantasy life (having one's husband murdered by one's brothers and their trusted servant). Often sexual identity and sexual fantasy are tied up with issues of power and domination as those issues intersect with the bounds of the body, especially for individuals who have experienced rela-

---

56. Or, if the common usage of minnecliche pflegen in the sense of intercourse resonates in the pflac here, then we might also translate: "during the act."

tions with others, sexual and non-sexual, primarily as hierarchies of power. In a feudal system such as the one underlying the literary society of the *Nibelungenlied,* the hierarchies are in place and are rigid to the degree that they disallow even horizontal displacements.[57] Certainly Kriemhild's relations with men have been exclusively hierarchical and susceptible to power analysis.

Kriemhild begins the post- (or intra-?) coital conversation with a (hyper-polite, multi-qualified) question, intended to prepare for her request, as to whether Etzel has any regard for her kinsmen. His response — that they are the best friends he had ever gained *von wibes minne* — ironically refers to one of the most common uses of marriage in the European feudal, as well as other, ages: the male exchange of women for the sake of dynastic ties or alliances and as tokens of treaties or peace bonds. In affirming his good will, Etzel manages inadvertently to indicate another cause of the reification of Kriemhild, who simply ignores this comment and continues with the execution of her plan to elicit Etzel's invitation of the Burgundians. Her argument drips with irony: since her brothers (and Hagen) — her worst enemies in the world — do not visit her in Hunland, where she is held in the highest honor of any queen in the world, she is considered friendless. Etzel then volunteers to invite the Burgundians whom an expert requests from Kriemhild. Like Gunther, he too mentions the distance, but as a matter of concern to the invited guests, not to himself.

Kriemhild rejoices in her *ervinden* "learning," or perhaps more appropriately "inventing," the king's will, and then takes over the further plan, designing the conversation so that Etzel can at least pretend to be the granter of boons: she instructs him to send messengers, so that the Burgundians can know *her* will (*muot* 1405). He practically asks her permission to choose the messengers (1407), and then after they receive their instructions from the king — *ich sage iu, wie ir tuot* ("'I'll tell you what you are to do'" 1410) — on the external aspects of their mission, they are summoned secretly (*tougenliche* 1413) to the queen's private chamber to receive even more explicit instructions on specific and clandestine details of their task, hinging directly on their serving her will/desire: *nu dienet michel guot, / daz ir minen willen   vil güetlichen tuot* (1414).

As a postscript to this scene, at the end of *aventiure* 24, Kriemhild approaches Etzel to ask his reaction to the Burgundian's acceptance of their invitation. She expresses the questions as follows: *Wie gevallent iu diu*

---

57. For example, two ruling kings from different realms to coexist in the same place without rearranging the vertical relationships (as Gunther and Siegfried).

mære,   lieber herre mîn? / des ie mîn wille gerte,   daz sol nû verendet sîn.
("How do you like the news, my dear lord, that that which I have long
desired is now about to be accomplished'" 1503,3–4). Etzel replies in kind:
Dîn wille deist mîn vreude ("'Your desire is my delight'" 1504,1). Thus the
primacy of Kriemhild's will/desire is again emphasized as the deciding
factor in the royal state action. This king not only grants Kriemhild's desire
and makes it state policy, but here claims it to be identical to his own
pleasure. Nonetheless this is achieved only by means of Kriemhild's intimate, private action that then prompts the male to public, political action.

A final indicator that the pattern of gender and power relationships in
the *Nibelungenlied* is presented in such scenes of private female attempts to
communicate with and make requests of males, is found in the incongruous
scene of Hagen's request of information from Kriemhild about Siegfried's
vulnerability [891–905], which seems almost an inverted example of the
quasi-type scene of the marital tête-à-tête. Here the traditional roles are
quite reversed. The woman is approached in private by the subordinate
man, who has a need that only the woman can fulfil. In this case too it is
information that is sought. Since that information concerns a sensitive
topic, however, Hagen may not request it directly, but must dissimulate
and invent a ruse to elicit it without arousing the suspicions of the other
party. That is, he must plan and direct the conversation and, in this case,
even invent the external circumstances that make the information necessary
(the feigned war). If he were female, the scholarly terms used to describe
his actions would certainly be pejorative, as they conventionally have described the actions of Brünhild and Kriemhild in the invitation scenes
discussed above.

Hagen initiates the audience by going to ask permission to leave (*bat
im geben urloup,* 891), which he need not do, and which is not at all his
purpose. Ultimately permission for him to leave court is not ostensibly
given, but rather he transitively takes it at the termination of the interview
(*urloup nam dô Hagene,   dô gie er vrælîche dan* 905), which in the mean-
time has filled fifteen stanzas. Hagen's ostensive purpose is thus deferred by
his actual purpose. For instead of giving permission for him to leave the
country, Kriemhild praises Siegfried's ability to defend Burgundy, claims
her good will to Hagen, and expresses her repentance for annoying Brünhild. Hagen on the other hand elicits the desired information from her by
promising to protect Siegfried, and she conjures him to swear fealty and
protection. And finally, he also gets both the necessary information and
Kriemhild's concrete, direct assistance, in that she will sew an indicator of

the vulnerable spot on Siegfried's clothing. Contrary to the established pattern of the private male-female conversation, there is no sex, implied or deferred, in this scene, although there is a preparation for violence, which has already been established as a common concomitant to sex in the *Nibelungenlied*. The scene is nonetheless one of the most explosively emotional in the work, for the passions which are unleashed as a direct result of this tête-à-tête are the most long-lived and powerful of the entire tale. Hagen here begins to enact his deepest desires to kill Siegfried, while Kriemhild displays several types of emotional needs and desires: she refers to her still firmly-held belief in kin loyalty, professes her affection for Siegfried, and, perhaps most significantly, reveals that she is, in contemporary terms, a battered wife [893–894].

This last revelation imbeds into one private male-female audience another, rather different kind of male-female confrontation. The framing scene between Kriemhild and Hagen is not constructed around marriage partners, but rather between a vassal and his former feudal superior, who will become — as a result of the actions consequent on this scene — the two most bitterly antagonistic characters in the work. The framed scene (Kriemhild and Siegfried), on the other hand, does conform to the type of ⟨…⟩ ⟨…⟩ ⟨…⟩. This scene, however, is not actually presented, depicted, or described, but rather its main event only named: Siegfried's assault on his wife as punishment for her confrontation with Brünhild. Thus in the one scene the two kinspeople and future enemies cozily plan the protection of their mutual lover/ally, which results in his murder; while in the other, the myth of the marital bliss of the model couple is exploded in the violence typical of exploitative and authoritarian marriage traditions.

In an interpretative context that admits gender as an important issue — such as, for instance, the thirteenth century of the *Nibelungenlied*, especially the C-text and *Diu Klage*, or the late twentieth century — this revelation, around which the scene of Hagen's first betrayal of Kriemhild is set, presents evidence that allows a radically different interpretation of many of Kriemhild's later actions. In the course of the conversation with Hagen, she refers to the episode in which she had accused Brünhild of having been sexually initiated by Siegfried, and remarks:

> "Daz hât mich sît gerouwen,"   sprach daz edel wîp.
> "ouch hât er sô zerblouwen   dar umbe mînen lîp;
> daz ich iz ie geredete,   daz beswârte ir den muot,
> daz hât vil wol errochen   der helt küene unde guot." (894)

("I have since repented," said the noble lady. "And in addition he has thus beaten my body black and blue; that ever my words caused her annoyance, that bold and good hero has avenged quite well.")

That Siegfried is a batterer and has physically attacked his wife comes as no surprise; after all he has already—as proxy husband—battered another bride and participated in her rape. And at the time of the incident that served Siegfried as sufficient cause for assaulting his wife, he already intimates that some such action is to be expected:

"*und hât si daz geseit,* / *ê daz ich erwinde,*   *ez sol ir werden leit*"
    (858)

("If she has said that, she will regret it before I'm done with her.")

"*Man sol sô vrouwen ziehen,*"   *sprach Sîfrit der degen,*
"*daz si üppiclîche sprüche*   *lâzen under wegen.*
verbiut ez dînem wîbe,   *der mînen tuon ich sam.*
ir grôzen ungefüege   *ich mich wærlîche scham.*" (862)

(Siegfried the warrior said: "one should train women to avoid idle chatter/not to speak except when necessary. Forbid it to your wife, and I shall do the same to mine. Her great impropriety shames me truly.")

Hagen replies to Kriemhild's admission that Siegfried has attacked her with the response typical of masculist institutions to claims of battering: *ir wert versüenet*   *wol nâch disen tagen* ("You'll patch it up, just give it some time").[58] De Boor and Hatto (transl. p. 121) both construe *ir* as referring

---

58. Cf. Walker, *Battered Woman*, pp. 15–16:

From the beginning of my research, it seemed to me that these women were physically and psychologically abused by men and then kept in their place by a society that was indifferent to their plight. Thus, they were both beaten and then blamed for not ending their beatings. Told they have the freedom to leave a violent situation, they are blamed for the destruction of their family life. Free to live alone, they cannot expect to earn equal pay for equal work. Encouraged to express their feelings, they are beaten when they express anger. They have the same inalienable right to the pursuit of individual happiness as men do, but they must make sure their men's and children's rights are met first. They are blamed for not seeking help, yet when they do, they are advised to go home and stop the inappropriate behavior which causes their men to hurt them. Not only are they responsible for their own beatings, they also must assume responsibility for their batterer's mental health. If they were only better persons, the litany goes, they would find a way to prevent their own victimization.

to Kriemhild and Brünhild, although one might as easily construe it as referring to Kriemhild and Siegfried, especially since he is the subject of the final line of the previous stanza and thus grammatically the more logical antecedent, although here again the ambiguity perhaps need not be denied.

The fact that no one (including Kriemhild) seemed particularly alarmed about this instance of battering indicates both that this behavior has been legitimized by patriarchal society,[59] and that Kriemhild had accepted that legitimacy, which ultimately simply further strengthens an identification of the event as battering. For, as Lenore Walker points out, it is commonly true in cases of battering that the women "did or said things to make the batterer angry," but those acts by the women were ultimately unnecessary to provoke the assaults, since in each case the woman "had accepted his right to discipline her through violence"; and in the final analysis, the society itself had "socialized her into believing she had no choice but to be such a victim" (p. 14). Kriemhild's narration of the event and Hagen's response conform exactly to this modern pattern.

Extrapolating from this situation, then, perhaps different accents should be placed on the false problem of why Kriemhild does not return to Xanten with Siegmund. She went there because she had been battered to Siegfried in a trade and had not any active reason. With Siegfried now dead, why should she return there? Even if it were conceded that she "loved" Siegfried (in some vaguely modern sense), that personal affection would not constitute a tie to Xanten. It might be maintained that the natural (or merely sensible) means to revenge would be by means of the forces that Siegmund and his kin could muster in Xanten, but the text immediately indicates the military ineffectiveness of Siegmund in his blustering and clearly suicidal preparations for attacking the Burgundians in Worms.[60] The fact that he has only a small force there does not mean it is only a token force, and at any rate he and it embody the strength of Xanten, which,

---

59. Otfrid Ehrismann points out that in beating Kriemhild, Siegfried was—from the medieval perspective—merely fulfilling his "Pflicht und Recht" ("duty and right," p. 147).

60. Schweikle suggests that Kriemhild refuses to seek revenge both by not returning to Xanten, where she could have enlisted a champion to take vengeance for Siegfried's murder (p. 62), and by remaining inactive in Worms, where the material means to vengeance (Siegfried's treasure) were in her power (p. 71). But after the elimination of Siegfried the Burgundians were the greatest warriors known; in the event they were finally defeated after the loss of tens of thousands of lives and were survived by only two opponents. It is thus difficult to imagine that a suitable Netherlandic champion might have existed. Secondly, Kriemhild was hardly inactive while in possession of the treasure in Worms. It was in fact precisely her conscious and effective political use of the treasure directly to the end of vengeance that brought about its theft by Hagen.

without Siegfried, is hardly a threat to the Burgundians, now or later. Without Siegfried Xanten is a third-rate province, while in a world from which Siegfried has been eliminated, Burgundy is one of the ranking powers.

Moreover, is there any concrete evidence that Kriemhild's relationship with Siegfried and Xanten has been the perfect union (especially as a contrast to the marriage of Gunther and Brünhild) that decades of romanticizing scholarship have assumed? Reading "love" in any remotely romanticized modern sense into this arrangement is a *petitio principii* and an exercise in self-deception. The thirteenth century certainly knew of personal affection in marriage, but the notion of star-struck, gut-wrenching love[61] that has developed in the last several centuries in Europe and (some of) its colonies is nowhere documented, certainly not in the literature of courtly love, in which such business is the stuff of elaborate rituals and games, but of hardly more than assumed "emotions."[62] On a very concrete level, except for Kriemhild's initial adolescent infatuation with the dashing hero at the time of her marriage, what more do we know of their relationship? Before her return to Worms for the festival (and Siegfried's murder), she had been offstage for a decade, about which we know nothing more concerning her relationship with Siegfried than that she has provided him with an heir, which fulfilled his dynastic duties (715, 3–4). Only two instances of their interaction are presented after their return to Worms. One is the final dream scene in which Siegfried treats Kriemhild like a child intruding into an adult matter. She accepts this treatment in a resigned manner so practiced that it seems she is accustomed to it. The reporting of his physical attack on and brutalizing of Kriemhild is the other. Why indeed should she return to Xanten, now that she has escaped a forced relationship that took her so far from home that she returned only once a decade, that so alienated her relations that they killed her husband, and that at least once erupted into physical abuse. Now she can cut her ties to the site of that relationship, and she immediately does so.

Based on this analysis of the phenomenon of male-female communication in the *Nibelungenlied,* perhaps a response to the remarks by Karl Heinz Ihlenburg in his astute political analysis of the *Nibelungenlied* might serve as

61. Examples of which are found in Greek antiquity, where they are perceived as destructive madness in tragedy but as common, often slightly ridiculous, sometimes almost commendable in the ancient Greek novel.

62. See especially Joachim Bumke, "Liebe und Ehebruch in der höfischen Gesellschaft," in *Liebe als Literatur: Aufsätze zur erotischen Dichtung in Deutschland,* ed. Rüdiger Krohn (München: Beck, 1983), pp. 39–40.

a conclusion (*Das Nibelungenlied: Problem und Gehalt*). Ihlenburg discusses Kriemhild's invitation of her brothers to the Hunnic court in an almost indignant tone, in terms of her lies to and deception and betrayal of both Etzel and her brothers, since her actual goals are different from those that she openly acknowledges (p. 84). One could hardly deem Ihlenberg's interpretation inaccurate simply because of his couching it in such terminology. But it is quite interesting that his evaluation of this scene differs so radically from that of the parallel scene of Brünhild's convincing Gunther to invite Kriemhild and Siegfried (pp. 64–65). His argumentative strategy here is one of the more common among critics of the *Nibelungenlied:* he tacitly assumes that guilt writ large necessarily inheres in a female character, and thus that the critical problem is to determine which woman is (the more) guilty. As is customary, he has chosen one of the women as rather less criminal than the other(s) and then tried to rehabilitate her slightly, while damning the other to the degree possible. Nonetheless, even this tendency does not preclude the general similarity of his treatment of the two scenes in question. The essential commonalities of his interpretations are themselves not surprising. In each case, Ihlenburg implies that the marriage bed is a site in which all deception is abhorrent. In the context of the present discussion, we need only recall, for the sake of some perspective, exactly what has in previous nights gone on in the sacred precincts of the marriage bed of Brünhild and Gunther. Ihlenburg makes only a single brief reference to those events in the course of his book, and then only to Gunther's "humiliation" on the wedding night, but not to the proxy-assault and team-rape of Brünhild, and not to the socio-political implications of those acts. Brünhild, he claims, wishes to convince Gunther to invite Siegfried and Kriemhild for the "wrong" reasons, that is, for reasons of her own, not for those of Gunther or of state (employing such terms as "unehrlich" and "Täuschung"). He contrasts inner with external happiness: "nach außen lebt sie als glückliche Gattin Gunthers, dem sie sogar einen Sohn gebiert" (Brünhild, p. 64); "nach außen ist ihr Glück so vollkommen, daß sie Etzel sogar einen Sohn gebiert" (Kriemhild). But (not just) in the Middle Ages a queen's bearing a son *for* the king would reveal little about the *queen's* "happiness," except as defined by a masculist ideology. In European feudal society as mediated by the *Nibelungenlied,* a wife (especially a queen) bore sons because that was her single specified and unavoidable duty; a duty so important, that if she did not bear a son then the fault would automatically be attributed to her, with the result that her marriage could be annulled. If the fact that in the course of a decade of "marital bliss" Kriemhild and

Brünhild have each born a son must be over-interpreted, then I might alternately suggest that since only one son had been born in so many years, then things might not have been going well with the king and queen. Perhaps the women (who else?) were not performing their marital duties. But in fact there is no need to overinterpret. The queens have each born a son; the kings have heirs. The simple and straightforward signification of these lines is: dynastic necessities have been satisfied. Personal needs, desires, and satisfaction are, quite simply, not addressed from such a narrative perspective. To claim that Kriemhild and Brünhild lead happy lives because they have born sons is to read an inappropriately modern form of patriarchal psychologism into the text.

Finally, it may be relevant to comment on one of the more mundane aspects of the invitation scenes. Let us momentarily leave aside the fact that both of the women have ulterior motives and merely consider that in each of the two conversations, a woman asks her husband to invite her/their long-absent relatives to visit. On the surface there is nothing remotely unusual about such conversations. Even if we remark that such conversations may only take place in relationships and societies that conventionally disallow women all but the most trivial and illusory aspects of power, these exchanges are not in themselves extraordinary. How then can women so functioning in such a society be criticized for their behavior, with or without ulterior motives, since they have no other choices for political action. They may not themselves invite state guests, and thus when they want to do so (for whatever reasons) they *must* make behind-the-scenes arrangements, for the system gives them no other option. Were the actions of men at issue, such negative valuations would not be considered, for in the realm of male political activity there are positive technical terms for such *diplomatic negotiations*. The women, however, patriarchy has traditionally assumed, are merely conniving cheats who extort acquiescence to their schemes during, before, or after intimate moments in bed with their husbands, thus identifying both woman and wife generally as *kebse*.

But the women also outsmart their men, as even their critics must admit. Even by means of such ridiculously restricted avenues to power, then, these women are able to shake entire kingdoms, not exactly *despite* the wishes of their men, but rather precisely by understanding the male ploys of power politics and macho-mentality so very well, that they simply push the requisite male ego buttons. The political implications are legion for the limitations on feminine action, reduced to sexual extortion, although the women in each case are more efficient in carrying out their political projects than the men. And in each case, the men are utterly unaware of the possible consequences, although they are ostensibly the political creatures, those empowered to act and to recognize and deal with political situations. They are however, unable to take women, even their own wives, seriously as political beings, and thus they are incapable of recognizing the implications even of their own actions. Such impenetrable barriers to communication obviously also preclude any understanding of the male construct of the Other's character. If in this, as in other, human societies, interaction is nonetheless necessary, then gross misunderstanding of even basic personality and character traits, and of motivations and purposes is inevitable. Thus the self-willed and independent woman comes to be viewed not as a determined, courageous individual, as such male characters in epic are generally viewed, but rather as a deviant, operating outside acceptable role-definition, that is, a "monster," an identification to which we must now turn.

5. Teuton as Amazon: The Devil's Bride and the She-Devil

In an essay on the *Nibelungenlied* aptly entitled "Aufstand der Frauen," Lore Toman inadvertently but inevitably finds herself grappling with the terminology of gender roles and ultimately arguing against herself.[1] She makes the essentialist claim for instance that Kriemhild employs "male methods" to achieve her ends, although "sie ist völlig Frau hinter der Maske männlicher Rache, und doch menschlich genug, um, wie sonst nur Männer, an die tödlichen Auswirkungen ihrer Tat keinen Gedanken zu verschwenden."[2] Ultimately, however, Toman claims, Kriemhild finds that male methods of achieving one's ends are unsuccessful, even when employed by women (p. 32). The transgression against traditional lines of gender specificity that Toman notes in which the woman becomes a pseudo-male, motivates much of the plot of the *Nibelungenlied* as males react to the woman's behavior.

The underlying assumptions on which Toman's interpretation is based are of particular interest here, for, like it or not, she has uncritically accepted the essentialist and masculist notion that equates non-conformist female with pseudo-male. The specific character of this masculist construct of gender "transgression" is of course not unique to the *Nibelungenlied,* but is rather a cliché of the literature of Western cultures. In the course of the

---

1. Lore Toman, "Der Aufstand der Frauen: Ein strukturalistischer Blick auf die Brünhild-Sage," *Literatur und Kritik* 14 (1979), 25–32. Toman's theoretically naive feminism represents one widespread (but certainly not dominant) type of German scholarly feminist work. Having said as much, however, I must immediately add that there obviously exist in German feminisms numerous schools that are not French, not American, and not theoretically naive. Thus I would very much like to dissociate myself from the view of Martha C. Howell, who upbraids German medievalists for neither reading U.S. scholarship nor imitating it; see Martha C. Howell, with Suzanne Wemple and Denise Kaiser, "A Documented Presence: Medieval Women in Germanic Historiography," in ed., *Women in Medieval History and Historiography* ed. Susan M. Stuard (Philadelphia: University of Pennsylvania Press, 1986), pp. 101–131.

2. "Behind the mask of masculine vengeance she is completely woman, although still human enough not to waste a single thought on the lethal results of her deed, as otherwise only a man could do" (p. 29). Hugo Bekker also sets up the contrasting categories *person* and *woman* (*The Nibelungenlied*, p. 72).

millennia its most famous articulation was in the literature of ancient Greece, where it acquired a quasi-historicized fictional and metaphorical representative with a mythological pedigree: the Amazon. Since the characters of both Brünhild and Kriemhild bear strong resemblance to the mythic Amazon *and* especially since conventional and even feminist critics have responded to them as such, then examining the workings of that myth (via one of its Greek reflexes) and similar constructions in the *Nibelungenlied* provides a new means of feminist analysis of Brünhild and Kriemhild. By articulating several salient types of transgression against gender definition found in the cultural problems subsumed under the invented category of the Amazon, this chapter addresses some essential aspects of the basic conflicts and impossibilities of gender conflict resolution in the *Nibelungenlied*.

Let it be made clear at the outset: I doubt that it would be of much value to determine whether the poet of the *Nibelungenlied* knew the legend of Amazons, or (were that provable) which particular version of that legend might have been available or how it was adapted.[3] My interest here on the contrary is in developing the ideological, not philological or historical, similarities inherent in the literary and cultural invention of both the Amazons by Greek culture and Brünhild and Kriemhild as quasi Amazons by the poet of the *Nibelungenlied*.[4]

A second caveat is also necessary in advance. I am aware that in developing an articulation of Brünhild and Kriemhild as Amazons I come dangerously close to continuing the masculist ploy that originally led to the

3. The image of the poet of the *Nibelungenlied* as the noble bard of a heroic yet semi-barbaric tribe of Teutons has finally paled, but there is now no reason to posit in its place that of a twelfth-century *savant* acquainted with Amazons "in the original." That century did see the beginnings of the recovery of access to Greek language and philosophy as had no other Western culture for half a millennium, but that access did not yet extend far into Plato, and not yet at all to Homer or the Attic dramatists. Thus the *Greek* legend of the Amazons was still utterly inaccessible, and indeed quite unnecessary, for ancient and medieval Latin adaptation (e.g., the *Historia de preliis*; Quintus Curtius Rufus's *Historiae Alexandri Magni*; or the later adaptations in Paulus Orosius's *Historiae aduersum paganos* and Adam of Bremen's history) would have provided ample grist for such mills. See, most recently, on treatments of this legend by post-*Nibelungenlied* medieval German poetry, Helmut Brackert's analysis of Rudolf von Ems's *Alexander*: "Androgyne Idealität: Zum Amazonenbild in Rudolfs von Ems 'Alexander,'" in *Philologie als Kulturwissenschaft: Studien zur Literatur und Geschichte des Mittelalters, Festschrift für Karl Stackmann zum 65. Geburtstag,* ed. Ludger Grenzmann, Hubert Herkommer, and Dieter Wutke (Göttingen: Vandenhoeck & Ruprecht, 1987), pp. 164–178.

4. For none of the earlier texts develops this aspect of Brünhild's character to the extent that is found in the *Nibelungenlied*. Certainly the Icelandic *Sigrdrifomál* depicts a warrior-maiden Sigrdrifa, who in many ways resembles the functional character of Brünhild in the *Nibelungenlied,* and who is associated with, if not obscurely identified with, the image of valkyries, who, however, as *servants* of Óðinn only superficially resemble the Amazons of Greek legend.

male invention of the Amazon as simultaneously female scapegoat and pseudo-male. The blind dualistic reduction of gender (and character) possibilities to those of conventional male or conventional female render nonconformist characters necessarily gender-based anomalies, such that the cowardly male was deemed effeminate, while the independently active female emasculates in her pseudo-maleness. No provision seems to have been made for other possibilities. Thus I tread a thin line here in attempting to analyze without propagating the myth by repeating and extending it.

Examples of the phenomenon are common in Greco-Roman antiquity. As Sarah Pomeroy points out, Antigone's problems in Sophocles's play are viewed as deriving primarily from her usurpation of masculine characteristics and behavior.[5] Pomeroy also notes that in Rome Fulvia was described as "female in body only"; her "'masculinity' consisted in entering spheres reserved for men. Her political manipulations in behalf of her various husbands were of benefit to them, but Fulvia's ambitions provoked hatred of her," and also of her husbands, allowing other men (competitors or rivals) to exploit the misogynistic tendencies already present to depict her as a monster (p. 185). Marie-Luise Portmann notes the developing use of the Latin term *virago* in ancient Roman and patristic literature in a positive sense for the "masculine" woman.[6] The usage, however, remains characteristic of masculist inventions, since it too circumscribes female behavior and defines the only possibility of independent female action as quasi-*vir*. In a slightly later period, and one more closely related culturally to that which produced the *Nibelungenlied*, Janet Nelson indicates an identical Merovingian usage, by which two queens regent, Brünhild and Balthild, were said to have ruled *viriliter*, whereby they nonetheless earned the hardly praiseworthy epithet "Jezebel."[7]

Bridenthal and Koontz note that this phenomenon is one not just of historical, but also of historiographical import, for women who somehow, somewhere had political power

> are "exceptional" women, who managed to survive and flourish in a male world. Historians have been fascinated by these women because of their

5. Sarah B. Pomeroy, *Goddesses, Whores, Wives, and Slaves: Women in Classical Antiquity* (New York: Schocken, 1975), p. 99.

6. Marie-Louise Portmann, *Die Darstellung der Frau in der Geschichtschreibung des früheren Mittelalters,* Basler Beiträge zur Geschichtswissenschaft 69 (Basel and Stuttgart: Helbing & Lichtenhahn, 1958), pp. 19–24.

7. Janet L. Nelson, "Queens as Jezebels: The Careers of Brunhild and Balthild in Merovingian History," in *Medieval Women,* ed. Derek Baker (Oxford: Blackwell, 1978), esp. pp. 73–77.

pseudo-maleness. Thus, they attract special scrutiny for being unnatural: men in women's bodies at best, monsters at worst. In no case are they considered representative of women generically. This is a realist assessment. The "exceptional" women viewed themselves as atypical; frequently they rejected or ignored contemporaneous efforts to advance women's status. Their lives remain exceptions that prove the rule and do not help us to understand the common experience of women in politics.[8]

Obviously this problem is not simply one of sexism in historical societies or in ancient or medieval literature, but one that pervades modern Western culture so thoroughly that it conventionally even blocks some women's perceptions of the possibilities for their own development. And thus we return to the similar image of the Amazon.

The scholarly literature on the multi-stranded and multi-valanced Greek legend of Amazons is vast, primarily philological and generally beyond the bounds of my present interests, which focus on *patterns* of engendered character *construction* instead of instances thereof. Generally Amazons were viewed by ancient (*sc.* male) Greek civilization as polar opposites of the ideal Greek (male). According to Sarah Pomeroy:

> Greeks tended to view the non-Greek world as topsy-turvy and opposite from the Greek world. In most of the Greek world women were in a subordinate position. Hence evolved the symmetrical view that male/female relationships would be the opposite among the barbarians. Herodotus (e.g. IV 26), indeed, reported that among some barbarians women actually held equal power with men. The notion of an Amazon society then would be the *reductio ad absurdum* of the distorted Greek view of the non-Greek world.[9]

There is a double essence and a self-contradiction in the definition of the Amazon in Greek legend: the Amazon is at once both opposite *and* identical to the Greek, for "the Greek," according to the terms of such a definition, is male, while the Amazon is female, but in other *essential* aspects, the two are all but identical. The Amazon is a Greek (male) as female, or rather a female as (if) Greek, which is of course not at all to say, a Greek female.[10] Since in a patriarchal system all unqualified positive traits are male, the

8. Renate Bridenthal and Claudia Koontz, eds., *Becoming Visible: Women in European History* (Boston: Houghton Mifflin, 1977), "Introduction," p. 3.

9. Sarah Pomeroy, "A Classical Scholar's Perspective on Matriarchy," in *Liberating Women's History: Theoretical and Critical Essays,* ed. Berenice A. Carroll (Urbana: University of Illinois Press, 1976), 217–223.

10. On whose life situations, see the classic study by Pomeroy, *Goddesses, Whores, Wives, and Slaves,* esp. chapters II–VI, on which, in the ensuing decade-and-a-half, a burgeoning literature has built.

Amazon — as all other (men and) women — can only be evaluated in terms of male attributes. Thus, as William Tyrrell notes concerning the Greek notion that language too is the province of the male, Aeschylus's chorus "compliments Clytemnestra by saying, 'You speak sensibly like a prudent man.'"[11]

Amazons embody a human antipode of Greek civilization: they live on the margins of the known world; they are renowned warriors, hunters, and rulers, and thus they inhabit the space outside, not inside the home, in the conventionally public, not private sphere; and most importantly they mirror the Greek gender-based stratification of society, for they capture and keep men only for the purposes of reproduction, since otherwise they prefer their own company. The men are then cast off or enslaved; sons born are exposed to die, for only daughters are valued. Thus as Froma Zeitlin comments, "by their identity as females they challenge the cultural conception of a docile femininity contrasted with a naturally dominant masculinity."[12] They in fact turn the gender roles upside down, as if the masculist (Greek) social model had simply switched the positions of the genders.

According to Tyrrell, the Greek myth of the culture of the Amazons "is a product of the Greek view of the human condition as civilized, mortal, Greek, and, most of all, male" (p. 63). The Athenian male thus forms by definition the norm, and as Page duBois argues: "The sum of these polarities yields the norm, the Greek male human being, and the others, on the opposite side of the series of polarities, are grouped together by analogy. Barbarian is like female is like animal."[13] The position of women in general becomes problematic, for "the position of women was gradually revealed as contradictory, since women were the objects of the culture-founding act of exchange. They were excluded from the city yet necessary for its reproduction. They came to represent a potentially dangerous, even poisonous force which was both within the city and outside it" (duBois, p. 5).

But the conception of the Amazon goes far beyond this marginalization of the Athenian woman, for as Zeitlin points out, Amazons do precisely that which is forbidden them: "Women may not reject men nor exhibit an independent sexuality. They may not reverse roles by using men for reproductive purposes, discarding sons to keep daughters, and they may

---

11. Wm. Blake Tyrrell, *Amazons: A Study in Athenian Mythmaking* (Baltimore: Johns Hopkins University Press, 1984), p. 37.

12. Froma Zeitlin, "Configurations of Rape in Greek Myth," in *Rape: An Historical and Social Enquiry*, ed. Sylvana Tomaselli and Roy Porter (Oxford: Blackwell, 1986), p. 135.

13. Page duBois, *Centaurs and Amazons: Women and the Prehistory of the Great Chain of Being* (Ann Arbor: University of Michigan Press, 1982), p. 4.

not claim equivalent status with men by refusing domestic life in favour of the military exploit. Above all, they may not, in exercising their dominance subjugate or destroy men" (136). In fact, however, the accents would seem more accurately set were we to reverse the mode of expression here, for the Amazons do — not the opposite of what Greek females do (for that would impute a significant role to the historical ancient Greek female in public culture, which she did not have) — but rather precisely what the Greek *male* does.

The essential aspect of the definition of each — Greek male and Amazon — is the independence of desire and will. Tyrrell notes the conventional limitations placed on female desire by Greek society:

> Physicality cast negatively becomes seductive, self-gratifying sexuality, while the negative mental element is characterized as boldness and daring. The negative side of the construct Woman, the female pole, represents in fact no more than the capacity of women to act on their own for their own pleasure and purposes. That potential, defined by Greek polar thinking as destructive to men, is contained by patriarchal marriage; in other words, the bestiality of women's condition is civilized by marriage, which thus becomes in the myth-making a structure of male order. (p. xvi)

This female "bestiality," this female desire and will, is, as we have noted already, what Gayatri Spivak terms "clitoral": the independent action — political, sexual, and otherwise — of the female for her own purposes and desires.[14]

Beyond this reversal of the conventional Greek gender roles, and despite the extraordinary (by heroic Greek male standards) strength and courage of the Amazons, however, an essential aspect of the Amazon is that she is a sexually attractive female (also and especially to Greek males[15]), which is necessarily a conventional, ideological construct. Thus the Amazon possesses the most outstanding (by Greek male standards) characteristics of both genders, but since she is constructed as quintessentially Other, both her "masculinity" and "femininity" are necessarily dangerous. Such doubled features in a single person cause the erasure of gender boundaries, and thus here too Amazons inhabit the margin, partaking of both sides.

---

14. "Feminism and Critical Theory," repr. in Spivak, *In Other Worlds*, p. 280, n. 32. It should be kept in mind here, however, that the use of "clitoral" in such an argument is strategic and metaphorical; it should not be turned round into evidence for an essentialist argument, in either Spivak's usage or my adaptation.

15. Who are, after all, the inventors and consumers of both the myth and the standard of beauty.

According to Tyrrell then, "they share in the strengths of both sexes and so are stronger than either. Mightier than ordinary men, they challenge even the hero, limited as he is by a single-sexed nature. They are hybrids, androgynous monsters, neither male nor female. . . . It is therefore not surprising that fear of the Amazons, as well as their formidability as foes, is attributed to their androgyny" (p. 89).[16]

The fact that the Amazons are warriors, are initially direct and powerful threats to patriarchal society, and are also women, the "natural" prey of hegemonic patriarchy, predisposes the plot of the legend to military conflict. Since the Amazons are women, however, they are not, when defeated, simply massacred, sold as slaves, or subjected to tribute, as would happen to men conquered in a conventional war, with the victor "punishing" the specific excess of the defeated opponent. In addition the Amazon is generally raped and taken to Greece as a slave-concubine, thus also adding to the conventional punishment of the defeated enemy's excess a reaction to her specific supplemental (gender-based) excess: the abandonment of her female role (coupling-mothering) and usurpation of the male role. Her clitoral behavior is recompensed by male aggregation of her (sexual organs) through rape.

Perhaps in each case the notion of punishment could best be supplemented by the concept of active recategorization: the formerly strong male military enemy becomes weak and demilitarized as a result of defeat, thus leaving him now only as "enemy"; all characteristics of the first two attributes must then be eliminated: the enemy is disarmed, despoiled, enslaved, and/or killed. The anti-Greek–women are forced to become sub–Greek-women, the anti-wives to become sub-wives, the independent warriors to become enslaved weavers, the outlanders to become alien residents of Athens, the inhabitors of the margin to become marginalized inhabitants. Their "anti-model of Greek marriage," as Zeitlin terms it (p. 135), is destroyed, and their androgyny is in effect disallowed by the victorious Greek male, to whom military defeat signifies emasculation. Thus the Amazons are "emasculated" and Hellenized in defeat—they are reduced to merely sexually enticing females. As Tyrrell comments: "this explains, moreover, why through death in combat or death by rape they are reduced

16. In the concept of androgyny, whether in ancient descriptions or in modern analyses of the phenomenon of the Amazon, a basic essentialism again appears: non-conformist females are constructed as "fake men," as if only the two rigidly defined categories of gender construction/identification—women and men—existed. But then, as we must constantly be aware, Amazons are after all always "Amazons," the literary political inventions of patriarchy and its cultural producers.

in the myths to either nubile girls or mothers. . . . The masculine side of the Amazon androgyne is cut away, and the feminine side is ravished into submission. The daughter must marry" (pp. 89, 93).

It is perhaps this single aspect of their being that is most abhorrent to the Greco-patriarchal mentality—the nubile (that is, of marriageable age) female, who refuses to marry,[17] for it is not just their virginity that signifies their repudiation of "civilization," for virginity was valued under certain specific circumstances also by the Greeks (and other patriarchal cultures), but rather it was the Amazon's repudiation of marriage as an institution that was the crime to be punished and eradicated, for it simply and effectively denies patriarchy, since without traditional (Greek) marriage, the foundation of male dominance disappears.[18] As duBois notes, the Amazons' "very society denied the necessity of marriage. Men were used by them for reproduction, but their domestic life was predicated on exclusion" (p. 40). Most significantly, *with* the Greek-male-like sexual independence exercised by the Amazons, patriarchal society was not just denied but travestied.

The Amazons ultimately outdid the Greeks in their independence, in their courage, daring, and achievement. And it is this courageous *action* that denies the traditional female role assigned them and contributes to the Greeks' inability to tolerate them. For as Tyrrell notes on the Amazons (and Clytemnestra and Deianira), they

> are all impassioned for power or dominance. They dare to act against the male and marriage. . . . Theirs are deeds heinous in outcome, but to confuse outcome with daring is to be hoodwinked by Aeschylus's mythmaking. They are deeds censured speciously for their result but actually because they are done by a woman on her own initiative. Daring is a quality admirable only in men. Although it is no more than the capacity to act on one's will in order to achieve goals, daring is what it means to be a person—that is, manly. (pp. 102–103).

Thus the Amazons are "outside the Athenian patriarchy's definition of woman and marriage as a structure of order between the sexes" (p. 104).

Yet they ultimately are abducted into the dominant male society and

17. Ovid, perhaps the favorite ancient (secular) author during the twelfth and thirteenth centuries in northern Europe, had learned this essential lesson of Greek mythology thoroughly and transmitted it no less so in his *Metamorphoses,* where nubile females who refuse the "natural" transformation into wives and mothers are recurringly forced to undergo more radical transformations.

18. Cf. Sarah Westphal-Wihl, *"The Ladies' Tournament:* Marriage, Sex, and Honor in Thirteenth-Century Germany," *Signs: Journal of Women in Culture and Society* 14 (1989), 380: "The marriageable woman who is not married emerges as a complex anomaly who challenges her society's deeply embedded assumptions about her gender role."

their power is usurped by its representatives. One of the most powerful images of this disempowerment in the Amazon legends is the recurring motif of rape. As duBois notes, the versions vary greatly in narrative detail: Herakles sometimes ventures to Amazon territory alone, sometimes accompanied by Theseus, sometimes by an army; the Amazons variously inhabit territory on the eastern or northern shores of the Black Sea; Herakles sometimes fights Hippolyta, sometimes Melanippe. Despite this variation, however, the legends relate the tale of a male hero, renowned for his strength, who in the course of combat with an Amazon takes her girdle as a prize.[19]

The Amazonian legend in general seems then to say much about the Greek construct of female gender as well as, obviously, much about its male constructers. For it provides what seems almost a blueprint of the province of both male and female. The Amazon as clitoral woman is banished by the very act of inventing the legend, to the (geographical and ideological) margins of civilization, where she lives in an "alien" society that, from a conventional patriarchal perspective, is turned on its head: women are warriors; they rule and rule well; they act for their own desire and will; they refuse any sexual relationship that subordinates them (marriage); they fight to preserve their independence; they make sexual use of men according to their own desire; ultimately, however, they are defeated in battle, disempowered, despoiled, raped, abducted, and incorporated into the patriarchal system.

Such a summary treatment of the Amazon legend has rounded a few edges, of course, in focussing on the aspects important to the present topic, but without misrepresenting its tradition, for in fact nowhere in Greek literature is the whole of the story told as a single narrative. Rather only fragments of the whole are incorporated into other narratives.[20] This distillation of the relevant issues of gender politics all but demands comparison with the role especially of Brünhild but also of Kriemhild in the *Nibelungenlied;* and to that we now turn.

Not surprisingly the term Amazon occurs relatively frequently in the

19. One of the clearest examples of the significance of this symbol is found in Apollodorus' version of Herakles's murder of Hippolyta and theft of her girdle, noted in Chapter four.

20. This fragmentation itself may be of some significance, for it presupposes a well-known tradition of the integral legend, perhaps in variant forms, but in any case unneedful of summary elaboration in the fragments themselves. Likewise the fragmentation scatters the effect of the Amazonian experience, just as it disperses and dif- and defuses its ultimate significance for the culture.

scholarly literature on the *Nibelungenlied* as a designation of Brünhild. And even when the term itself is lacking, its ideology dominates.[21] At the same time, however, even when the term does appear, it is, as far as I have seen, used only in a non-specific sense, with no attempt to articulate the ideological implications of such an identification. The immediate narrative similarities of Kriemhild and Brünhild to the construct of the Amazon are obvious: they both reject marriage (Kriemhild as an adolescent, Brünhild until she is compelled to marry); they both at various times inhabit the margin of "civilization": Brünhild in Iceland, Kriemhild (after her marriage to Siegfried) in Xanten, and again later in her newly built palace after Siegfried's death (at the "center" of the civilized world, but effectively isolated from it), and finally and most clearly in her withdrawal to Hunland and marriage to Etzel, where she is on the margin of the known world.[22] Both Brünhild and Kriemhild bear sons, who are then utterly ignored and

21. A number of scholars have discussed Kriemhild and especially Brünhild in terms of the "Amazon." Cf., for instance, Winder McConnell, who astutely comments: "The wooing of Brünhild might be regarded by some as an attempt on the part of a male-dominated society to force the individualistic female who lives by her own rules into conformity with that society. Intentional disregard for the plight of the female protagonists in the *Nibelungenlied* constitutes one of the basic reasons for the catastrophe which ensues" *Nibelungenlied*, p. 7). Unfortunately, he never ... ... "Amazon" in the remainder of the paragraph. His construction of the non-conforming female as demon is clear from the outset; he suggests that "Brünhild's Amazon-like existence on Isenstein may be regarded as symptomatic of a particular type of self-exaltation and hubris" and that her living in an " 'Amazon-like' state" may be the cause of Siegfried's considering her a threat to society. He finds "intriguing" Brünhild's "position as a supernaturally strong queen who appears to have established herself as a formidable counterpart to an otherwise male-dominated world." In addition, her "self-assertion has a dark side," and her killing suitors is "inherently demonic" (p. 45). Also Amazon-like is Brünhild's state after marriage, for when she is "deprived of her dignity, power, and any possibility of happiness, she is destined to live out a weary existence as queen of Burgundy, a life to which even her son, Siegfried, is incapable of restoring a sense of productivity" (p. 48). Often associated with the analysis of the phenomenon of the Amazon is the construction of primitive matriarchy. See particularly in recent years Hildegard Bartels's discussion of Brünhild as a representative of primitive matriarchy (*Epos — Die Gattung in der Geschichte*, p. 46). See also Albrecht Classen's recent foray into similar territory; he simply identifies strong female characters as representatives of matriarchy, despite all evidence to the contrary ("The Defeat of the Matriarch Brünhild in the *Nibelungenlied*, with Some Thoughts on Matriarchy as Evinced in Literary Texts," in *Waz sider da geschach: German-American Studies on the Nibelungenlied Text and Reception*, ed. Werner Wunderlich and Ulrich Müller [Göppingen: Kümmerle, 1992], pp. 89–110). In addition to the ubiquitous skepticism of historiography, sociology, and anthropology about the patriarchal myth of primitive matriarchy, cf. also Sheila Rowbotham's biting political critique: "Even the myths of tribes and races of strong women, the golden age of matriarchy, are the creations of male culture. The only means we have of even fantasizing free women is through the projection of male fears" (in "Through the Looking Glass," from *Women's Consciousness, Man's World*, anthologized in Roger S. Gottlieb, ed., *An Anthology of Western Marxism: From Lukacs and Gramsci to Socialist Feminism* [Oxford: Oxford University Press, 1989], 279–295, here p. 286).

22. Exactly like the Amazons, and, from the Northern European perspective, geographically not all that far from their legendary home, relatively speaking.

abandoned, by both their fathers and mothers — or perhaps rather, only by the narrator, since after it has been acknowledged that heirs have been born, the children have no further role to play.[23] An articulation of the relationships herewith implied would need to address in some depth such issues as marginalization as it opposes or as it is consequent on marriage, and the ideology of beauty vs. demonism.

As discussed in chapter three, there are three types of marriage represented in the *Nibelungenlied*. The two that occur in the first half of the text — Kriemhild's to Siegfried and Brünhild's to Gunther — represent patriarchal marriage in all respects. Kriemhild's marriage to Etzel in part two differs in important respects deriving specifically from the degree of female independence allowed Kriemhild: that is, with the woman's role in deciding *whether* to marry, and if so, under what conditions. The concrete conditions of Brünhild's marriage may in general be characterized as *Brautraub* or even rape. Kriemhild's marriage, on the other hand, represents a second type, in which she is used by her brothers to pay a debt, as bartered goods, for in her first marriage Siegfried receives her, as he specifies, as "payment" (*lôn* 333,4), for his service to Gunther in defeating and defrauding Brünhild. As far as the reader is informed, Kriemhild seems to find Siegfried a suitable partner. Despite this inclination, however, as her own response to Gunther's question about her willingness to marry Siegfried indicates, she either has little if any actual choice in the matter, or that "choice" is merely of a formal nature, as in the female "consent" to marry: *jâ wil ich immer sîn, / swie ir mir gebietet,   daz sol sîn getân* ("indeed I wish always to be, whatever you order me, that shall be done" 613, 2–3).[24] As Günther Schweikle notes, the fact that a woman's wishes are taken into account in such situations does nothing to better her legal status as subordinate to a male guardian; nor, as Gayle Rubin points out in another context,

23. Except in the case of Kriemhild's son by Etzel, whose murder by Hagen serves as a catalyst to the impending crisis in Hunland. The B-manuscript tradition imputes to Kriemhild the responsibility for having her son brought to the banquet and thus makes *possible* the interpretation that she does so in order to sacrifice the son by provoking Hagen to kill him, thus initiating the battle (st. 1912), although this hypothesis is unlikely despite its uncritical repetition now by generations of scholars; by contrast, in manuscript C, the boy is brought to the hall not on her orders or with her complicity. Cf. Werner Hoffmann, "Die Fassung *C des Nibelungenliedes und die 'Klage,'" p. 128, and also Otfrid Ehrismann, *Epoche — Werk — Wirkung*, pp. 178–179.

24. I see no reason here not to construe the middle clause with both the preceding and following clauses (cf. also de Boor's comment): "whatever you [Gunther] order me to be, I will always wish for myself" (your order is my will); and "whatever you order shall be done." Bekker notes: "In fact, it could be argued that it is a piece of sheer luck for Kriemhild that she is bartered to a man of her liking" (p. 72).

does it change the practical exploitation of the situation itself, for she is still an object of exchange, a passive *lôn* paid by men to men, not an active subject.[25]

In both the legend of the Amazons and in (especially the first half of) the *Nibelungenlied,* marriage plays an integral role in disempowering, dispossessing, and generally marginalizing women made wives. The personal attribute of most importance in the articulation of female character in the *Nibelungenlied* (and the Greek ideology of Amazons) is the ubiquitously emphasized beauty. In addition both Brünhild and Kriemhild are defeated "militarily" by men.[26] Brünhild is also openly taken from her homeland and incorporated into patriarchal society, where, having been dispossessed, raped, and deprived of her strength, and thus deprived of further capability of independent action, she apparently masters her new role as "courtly lady" quickly and effectively. Gail Newman has analyzed this transformation of Brünhild contra Bekker and generally in terms of Jan Dirk Müller's "Künec—man—eigenholt" constellation of charismatic versus traditional leadership roles, according to which Brünhild is charismatic as independent queen in Iceland, but becomes traditional after her abduction to Worms, ⸱⸱⸱[27] ⸱⸱⸱ "she would appear to the Burgundian court, and to the poet's courtly audience as well, as a monster, outside the bounds of accepted female behavior. Even Siegfried's charismatic behavior is more acceptable than Brünhild's, because he is a man" (p. 76). An untransformed Brünhild would have been "an alien element, threatening the very foundations of feudal-courtly order" (p. 78).

Kriemhild is less obviously abducted from her own space outside of the patriarchal system and incorporated into that system, since she is from the beginning a part of that system. Instead, her movement is in part the reverse of Brünhild's, in that she moves from the (displaced) center (since she is female) to the margin, from patriarchy to independence, from arranged marriage to a marriage of personal-political value to *her.* It seems at

---

25. Schweikle, "Das Nibelungenlied," p. 71; Rubin, "The Traffic in Women," p. 174.

26. Brünhild by Siegfried (twice) and Kriemhild ultimately by Hildebrand.

27. Gail Newman, "The Two Brunhilds?" *Amsterdamer Beiträge zur älteren Germanistik* 16 (1981), 69–78; Jan Dirk Müller, "SIVRIT: *künec-man-eigenholt.* Zur sozialen Problematik des Nibelungenliedes." Generally against the notion that Brünhild becomes courtly in Worms, cf. Nelly Dürrenmatt (*Das Nibelungenlied im Kreis der höfischen Dichtung* [Bern: Lang, 1945], p. 298).

first glance then that Kriemhild's movement is toward independence. Even so, I would argue that there is an element of patriarchal abduction at work in Kriemhild's "biography." Her murder by Hildebrand fully tames, silences, and incorporates her into the interpretive scheme of patriarchal society: she becomes the defeated demon, the subdued wife, the punished criminal. From the very beginning, however, Kriemhild seems to oppose the social strictures placed on her; her "abduction" as it were is all the more insidious, since it occurs *within* the society. One of Kriemhild's first acts in the *Nibelungenlied* — when she categorically rejects her mother's interpretation of her falcon dream and its implications of her training a falcon as marrying a warrior — is to declare her independence from the patriarchal claims on her as a marriageable commodity.[28] She, like Brünhild, is forced into marriage, but unlike Brünhild, the method of coercion is indoctrination (a courtly upbringing), not defeat in combat and rape.

Even more clearly is the patriarchal abduction executed by the scholarly reception. For in recuperating Kriemhild's role *in* the patriarchal system by means of her "execution" by Hildebrand, Kriemhild is moved by the male (scholarly world) from outside to inside, from independent *agens* to dependent, subordinate, disposable chattel, from (in some restricted sense) *regina regens* on the Hunnic margin of civilization to a sub-plot of the larger Dietrich-Hildebrand cycle of tales, central to canonical Middle High German literature. The most significant aspect of this naturalization process is of course the scholarly interpretation *qua* appropriation of Kriemhild's murder at Hildebrand's hands as a legitimate execution of a criminal.[29]

Both Brünhild and Kriemhild are, at the time of their most spectacular transgressions against the patriarchal order, ruling queens,[30] residing at the (opposite) margins of the known world: Brünhild in the far North / West (?), Kriemhild in the far South-East. The journeys to each place undertaken by the Burgundians for the sake of the women are depicted as extremely dangerous, necessitating an experienced guide: Siegfried to Iceland and Hagen to Hunland. On these margins, however, unlike those of the Amazons, the societies are not completely inverted. Rather, in the case of these

---

28. See particularly my essay "Kriemhild's Three Dreams: A Structural Analysis," *Zeitschrift für deutsches Altertum* 113 (1984), 173–187.

29. See below, Chapter six.

30. That is, *regina regens,* and not merely *regis uxor,* although for Kriemhild in Hunland this is a practical, not a formal, status. On historical ruling queens in the Middle Ages, see the useful orientations in Lehmann's chapter: "La femme segneur de fief," pp. 213–218, and Janet L. Nelson, "Queens as Jezebels," esp. pp. 73–77.

Teutonic Amazons, the queen alone is the locus of this reversal, which does not affect any other women in the kingdoms.[31] In each case the queen acts for her own desire and will.

Kriemhild initially (*aventiure* 1) rejects marriage, and later, after her first husband, Siegfried, has been murdered, she repudiates all further association with the marriage and her husband's kingdom. Instead, she remains in the household of her own relations and only accepts the generally subordinating institution of marriage (with Etzel) after she realizes that in this case, if she wishes, the institution can be an avenue to what on the surface seems all but independent control of one of the most powerful kingdoms on earth. It is then, after circumstances and societal expectations have forced marriage on her (twice), that she acts among, with, and against men (in Hunland) as her main syntagonists. Thus even in marriage, by means of which her political aims may also be achieved, she in some Amazonian sense refuses a sexual relationship that would subordinate her and retains and even augments her independence of will and desire.

In Brünhild's case, however, this Amazonian attribute is far more obvious, for she apparently acts with all but complete independence: she refuses marriage as long as possible, and after being militarily forced to accept it against her will, she must only seek the confirmation of her be-trothal from her *vassals* (not the *permission* of *guardians*). She in fact refuses marriage altogether unless it is literally impossible to avoid it, that is, unless she is physically unable to ward off the suitor. Before the arrival of Siegfried and Gunther she had already repelled numerous such assaults. In order to get at Brünhild's *modus operandi* it is necessary to expand on the discussion of rape offered above from a different perspective. Let us here note that two of the customary components of the historical definition of rape are present here: sexual intercourse forced on an unwilling partner, usually a woman, by a man; and forcible seizure and abduction by a man of a woman. In each case, an act — usually violent — is perpetrated by a man on a woman against her will, with the purpose of depriving her of her own will and independence and of subordinating her to his own control for the further purposes of his own choice, sexual, social, or marital. Brünhild's is then a classic

---

31. Of whom few are mentioned: none in Iceland, only Siglint in Xanten and Uote in Burgundy, only Gotelind and her unnamed daughter in Pöchlarn, and only Herrat (who does not appear), niece of Helche and betrothed of Dietrich, and the deceased Helche in Hunland. In any case, all females in these realms except Brünhild and Kriemhild seem to follow the prescribed patriarchal conventions of behavior.

example of doubly multiple rape, in that her abduction and the sexual assault on her are plural acts, perpetrated in each case by a double assailant.

Theodore Andersson has recently commented astutely on the abduction of Brünhild in the context of the ubiquitous twelfth-century literary convention of the "bridal quest" (*A Preface,* esp. pp. 81–92). In the minstrel epic (*Spielmannsepos*) the bridal quest is of prime importance. It conventionally includes the motifs of contests (real and feigned), and of deceptions practiced on the bride and her guardians and realm by suitors and proxy-suitors who assume fictitious identities. The contemporaneous audience of the *Nibelungenlied* would thus have recognized such motifs as conventional, and, as Andersson notes, "would have appreciated . . . the parody of underlying literary forms" (p. 87).[32] The use of these conventions in the *Nibelungenlied* obviously goes far beyond parody, of course, for the text ultimately requires the reader to question the innocence or perhaps only the pardonability of such actions. As such, it is one of the first literary attempts in German to question the social legitimacy of such masculist machinations. The quasi-fairy-tale world of the *Spielmannsepos* permits more freedom in the use of such motifs perhaps, without incurring social responsibilities or liabilities. The qualified "realism" of the *Nibelungenlied,* however, renders such usage impossible, unless it is made the object of irony, is criticized, undermined, or somehow socio-politically marked. As Andersson notes: "Disguise was the secret of success in the minstrel epic, but it becomes the mainspring of disaster in the *Nibelungenlied*" (p. 88). A second pertinent distinction between the function of shared motifs in the *Spielmannsepos* and the *Nibelungenlied* is that the latter unlike the former does not *end* with marriage(s) in which the striving of the characters culminates and which portends a blissful future. Instead the initial marriages in the *Nibelungenlied* occur quite early in the course of the action, while the marriage of part two also takes place near its beginning. Andersson notes that these marriages are "not joyous finales but harbingers of doom" (p. 90) and that in general part one of the *Nibelungenlied* and especially *aventiure* 16 (the hunt) show "that traditional optimism of bridal romance is a delusion."[33] In general, marriage in the *Nibelungenlied* fails to fulfil its traditional role of cementing

32. Lynn Thelen also notes that the bridal-quests of Gunther and Siegfried are structurally parallel and so characterize and contrast the two figures, such that, for instance, Siegfried's strengths and Gunther's weaknesses are shown in highlight, in "The Internal Source and Function of King Gunther's Bridal Quest," *Monatshefte* 76 (1984), 143–155.

33. The marriage of Kriemhild to Etzel and the betrothal of Giselher to Rüdiger's daughter also participate in this same mode.

clan relationships (the undermining of which, one must of course note, is also a common motif in early Germanic literature). Rather, as Andersson comments:

> All the marriages are undermined by fraud, not just the rectifiable misunderstandings of Hartmann's [von Aue] couples but intentional deceit. The very foundations of marriage are flawed. . . . The story is a fabric of domestic lies, and when the truth comes out, the domestic structures crumble. . . . One of the most palpable themes binding the poem together is treachery, specifically domestic treachery. . . . [The *Nibelungenlied*] analyzes the mechanisms of family disintegration, how Kriemhild is married in the family interest of acquiring a formidable vassal, how she is pitilessly widowed when the vassal becomes more of a liability than a support, how she is then deprived of the means to reassert herself (Siegfried's treasure), and how she is finally married off again in the hope of removing her from the scene and limiting her capacity for creating dissension. Family politics are consistently the determining factor in this sequence of events. (p. 90)

This concern with quasi-familial (household) relations is inextricably tied up with marital relations and their inevitable collapse under the present conditions as opposed to those predicted at the end of the minstrel epic and romance. One of the reasons for this failure of marriage may lie in the definition and function of "love." As soon as we agree for the sake of argument to extract the male-female relationships of the *Nibelungenlied* from the contemporal literary context of the idealized fiction of "courtly love," and view them as representative of the relation Greek-Amazon, then the question of love demands radical reformulation. The "love stories," as it were, or the *minne*-tales of the *Nibelungenlied* are in a cultural sense necessarily unidirectional: Siegfried *pfliget minnecliche* his bride, Kriemhild, as Gunther does Brünhild. But not the other way around. Nowhere does the text intimate that either of the women "loved" their husbands. If used of women, the customary idiom — *pfliget minnecliche* — is incongruous (and no other is made available by the language), for it would give Kriemhild an active role (and her male partner a passive role) in the personal, sexual, romantic, and institutional relationship. And that she may not have. On the other hand, does *minnecliche pflegen* indicate that Gunther and Siegfried "loved" their brides, or, since the phrase is actually used to indicate the consummation of the marriages, is it not rather, as discussed in chapter three, merely a euphemism for sexual intercourse, in which activity, the male, by patriarchal social convention, is the active, the female, the passive, participant? Does Kriemhild "love" Siegfried? Does Brünhild "love" Gunther? Do such questions make any sense? Is it a matter of "love" in any remotely twentieth-century sense? Joachim Bumke answers:

In einer Gesellschaft, in der die Beziehungen zwischen Männern und Frauen einerseits durch politisch-dynastische Erwägungen und andererseits durch die gewaltsamen Formen männlicher Lustbefriedigung bestimmt wurden, war kein Platz für Liebe. Liebe gab es nur als Literatur und als höfisches Gesellschaftsspiel. . . . Alles, was die Wirklichkeit der feudalen Liebes- und Ehepraxis ihnen vorenthielt, war hier zu finden: zwischengeschlechtliche Beziehungen, die nicht durch die physische Überlegenheit des Mannes oder durch seine rechtliche Position als Ehemann bestimmt wurden, sondern durch die Qualität der höfisch-ritterlichen Gesinnung; statt Gewalt und Hemmungslosigkeit eine höfische Etikette, die es vorschrieb, den Frauen mit besonderer Höflichkeit zu begegnen; statt der üblichen Benachteiligung und Ausnutzung der Frau ein Rollenspiel, das der Dame den Part der Herrin und Richterin in Liebesfragen zuwies; statt einer Sexualität, die nur auf körperliche Befriedigung aus war, eine erotische Gesellschaftskultur, die auch ein persönliches Liebesverhältnis nicht ausschloß."[34]

Kahn Blumstein's critique of the *literary* construction of *minne* is equally rigorous and takes a feminist step beyond Bumke's sociological clarity:

There are elements of the *overt* misogynistic tradition present in the romance, all the obfuscating talk of chivalry, idealization and women on pedestals

34.
 There was no place for love in a society in which relationships between men and women were determined on the one hand by political-dynastic considerations and on the other by the violent forms of the satisfaction of male desire. Love only existed as literature and as a courtly parlor game. . . . Everything that the realities of feudal society's practice of love and marriage denied [women] was to be found here: heterosexual relationships that were not defined by the superiority of male strength or his legal position as husband, but rather by the quality of his courtly-knightly character: instead of violence and lack of inhibitions, courtly etiquette that prescribes treating women with special courtesy; instead of the usual discrimination against and exploitation of women, a play in which the lady was assigned the role of superior and judge in questions of love; instead of a sexuality that was directed solely to the satisfaction of corporeal desire, an erotic social culture that did not exclude the possibility of a personal love relationship. ("Liebe und Ehebruch in der höfischen Gesellschaft," in *Liebe als Literatur: Aufsätze zur erotischen Dichtung in Deutschland,* ed. Rüdiger Krohn [Munchen. Beck, 1983], pp. 25–45, here pp. 39, 40).

On the incongruities of forcing a modern notion of love on the twelfth century, see the terminology employed by Peter Czerwinski, "*Das Nibelungenlied:* Widersprüche höfischer Gewaltreglementierung," *passim,* and specifically his comment: "Wenn aber 'Liebe' eine Kategorie bürgerlicher Gesellschaftlichkeit ist, muß *minne* etwas anderes sein; das Wort kann also auf keinen Fall mit 'Liebe' übersetzt werden" ("However, if *Liebe* is a category of bourgeois society, then *minne* must be something else; the word may not by any means be translated by *Liebe,*" p. 67).

notwithstanding; and, secondly, that the "courtly code" of love and most especially the idealization of women in the romance are in many respects a *covert* form of misogyny; chivalry is but one more method by which what has been called the "great patriarchal conspiracy" is perpetrated and perpetuated in our culture.[35]

Brünhild's repudiation of patriarchal marriage leads inevitably to violence, as men arrive to force marriage on her, for whenever a suitor arrives in Iceland, it is as a kidnapper-rapist, who has set himself the task of forcing marriage on a woman who has made it quite clear that she does not wish it, and is willing to fight (in military contests) to avoid it. Brünhild has, we are informed, already defeated numerous suitors in combat(-like contests) and killed them.[36] Thus for the man it is literally a matter of life and death; and, as Gunther later instructs Siegfried on his tasks and the limitations on his actions in the Burgundian bedroom, the struggle may at any time ultimately take on lethal implications for the woman too, for Siegfried is given permission by Brünhild's husband to kill her if she cannot be otherwise subdued. In any case, even if the woman survives she will have been raped, kidnapped, and despoiled. In the end then, Brünhild marries Gun-

ther and because of "love," or minne, or compatibility, or her political

35. Andrée Kahn Blumstein, *Misogyny and Idealization in the Courtly Romance,* Studien zur Germanistik, Anglistik und Komparatistik 41 (Bonn: Bouvier, 1977), p. 2. In his construction of all situations as epiphenomena in an inevitable dialectical progression of history, Ihlenburg claims that *minne* represents an advancement of women's rights (*Das Nibelungenlied,* pp. 93, 173, n. 128).

36. Seitter acknowledges the nature of Brünhild's "contests": "Die Werbung um Brunhild war tatsächlich — fast — ein Krieg" (*Das politische Wissen,* p. 34). The conventional scholarly evaluation is represented by Bekker's interpretation of the events in Iceland as a courting ritual, and of Brünhild as a would-be bride, waiting for a *suitable* husband. He argues that if Brünhild had really wished to remain unmarried, she could have simply refused to marry. Instead, however, he maintains, she has a "rational and pragmatic" approach, so that she can lure a partner stronger than she is, who can "thus do justice to her status": "It is part of Brunhild's philosophy of kingship that she must be taken by force, as it is Siegfried's philosophy . . . to take a wife or crown by force" (p. 74). A woman taken by force means, quite simply, raped. Bekker then not surprisingly attributes to Brünhild the responsibility for all that happens to her: her uniting of the concepts of marriage and kingship has "contradictions" and is "charged with potentially ironic consequences, of which she herself ultimately becomes the victim." He then reduces Siegfried's crimes to his *not* raping Brünhild (which is an unendurable insult "to her status as queen"), and reduces Gunther's to a moment of alleged naughty sensuality (in spilling wine). The villainies of the male actants are completely effaced and trivial pseudo-crimes invented to replace them, which then enables the construction of female culpability. For in marrying the unkingly Gunther, Brünhild has "become guilty of violating the code by which kings must live." Thus the deceptions, rape, and theft are trivialized, depersonalized and reinscribed into a masculist reading of a royal behavioral code that is, unfortunately, never explained, and which Jan Dirk Müller points out is not a rule of behavior either in theory or practice in the year 1200 ("SIVRIT," p. 114).

advantage, or rape wish, but rather only because she cannot kill him and his accomplice.

At any rate, when the Burgundian gang of four arrives in Iceland, Brünhild does not promise to *love* the winner of the contests, but rather to kill them all if she can, and in any case to resist and remain unmarried and independent unless she be defeated by a suitor whose strength suffices to take her by force. Her situation is commonly treated as extraordinary, but it seems so at most only in degree, not kind, for it differs little from the common motif of *Brautraub* "bride-theft," a form of marriage common to patriarchal societies in which the groom-to-be forcibly abducts the woman from her male guardians, if he is strong enough to do so; if not, they kill him or drive him away. This is the course of action that recurs in *Kudrun*, and is in fact what Siegfried himself proposes to his father as the means of winning Kriemhild, and perhaps obliquely hints at in his enigmatic bluster-ing upon arrival in Worms in *aventiure* 3. Here the difference is that Brünhild defends herself without reliance on male guardians. And it is only under the conditions of defeat and life-threatening danger that she "con-sents" to marry.

The third type of marriage occurring in the *Nibelungenlied* is repre-sented by Kriemhild's union with Etzel. Its arrangement and its later execution allow for a great measure of independence for Kriemhild. It is precisely this aspect of the marriage that also allows for the condemnation of Kriemhild and implied and expressed censure of Etzel by characters in and scholars of the *Nibelungenlied*. For entering into such a marriage for reasons other than rape, male trafficking in women, or "love," Kriemhild has been roundly castigated — not just by her male co-characters, but also by modern scholars — as heartless, cold, manipulative, and deceitful.[37] She knows Etzel only by reputation, it is noted, and thus can have no affection for him, while she is additionally ill-disposed to his paganism. But she appreciates his wealth and power, and especially the pledge of one of his most powerful vassals, Rüdiger, to avenge any wrong done her (1257–1258). In other words, lacking all affection for Etzel, she marries him for

37. Cf., for instance, Ihlenburg (*Das Nibelungenlied* p. 83), who seems to have forgotten both Gunther's transference of Kriemhild as commodity to Siegfried in exchange for Brünhild, and the conditions of Gunther's "courtship" of Brünhild, when he claims that, in marrying Etzel, Kriemhild "wirft über ihr weiteres Leben den Schatten von Lüge, Täuschung und Heuchelei" ("she casts a shadow of lies, deceit and hypocrisy over the remainder of her life"). Cf., however, also Philip Anderson, who claims that "Kriemhild also fails as a wife" via an alleged betrayal of both her husbands ("Kriemhild's Quest," *Euphorion* 79 [1985], p. 8).

"ulterior motives": not for unselfish and self-less reasons of "love," but for the sake of her own desire. In short, Kriemhild marries for the same reason that motivates Gunther, Siegfried, and Etzel, who upon deciding to marry, "knew" and "loved" their prospective spouses in exactly the same way that she "knew" and "loved" Etzel: in addition to propagating the dynasty, they want, and for the sake of their social position, need, suitable (beautiful and noble) wives as co-indicators of status, wealth, and power along with their other "possessions." No role is played by love, affection, sentimentality, or anything of the kind. For Gunther, Siegfried, and Etzel, marriage is a matter of business, or more properly, of power. For Kriemhild, apparently, it may not be so, unless she is prepared to answer the outraged charges of her (male) critics both fictional and scholarly.

Perhaps the starkest illustration of the problematic of independent female action vs. its male perception is found in the text's terminological contrasts, especially in descriptive terms such as the epithets applied to Brünhild and Kriemhild. Since practically the only women to appear and to be spoken of in the polite literature of the time are aristocratic, courtly ladies, and since only such paragons of courtliness and "womanly virtue" are to be represented and emulated, it is simply assumed unless otherwise marked that females are by nature such creatures. The analysis in the previous chapter of Kriemhild's first appearance (in *aventiure* 1), demonstrated that she is the epitome of courtliness, breeding, grace, and especially beauty. With few exceptions the perception of her remains so until after Siegfried's death, and with some modulation, until the Burgundian arrival in Hunland (and even in the narrator's usage until the moment of her murder). Then the terms of male address vacillate from those typical of courtly usage to designations of her as monstrous and devilish.

As suggested above, much about the relationship of the characters of Kriemhild and Brünhild is chiastic in structure. So is it in this case as well, for the character of Brünhild is initially ambiguous or even negative in male perception, only later to conform consistently to courtly standards. The inconsistencies of the early usage regarding Brünhild and the late usage regarding Kriemhild are especially revealing about the functions of masculist ideologies in the text.

The epithets used to designate Brünhild in *aventiure* seven, when she is introduced to the tale, are astonishing in their characterization of her, for they differ radically from the characterization conventionally constructed of her by scholars, ostensibly based almost exclusively on her *actions,* to a far lesser degree on her words, and almost not at all on the epithets assigned to her. In the men's conversation concerning the proposed expedition in *aventiure* six, and in Iceland itself in *aventiure* seven, the terms used to designate, describe and characterize Brünhild are on the one hand: *beautiful, noble, good, praiseworthy, worthy of minne, maiden, lady, queen, virgin;* and on the other, as *strong, hostile, angry, terrible, proud.* It might be better for the moment to eliminate the term *küneginne* "queen" from the count, since it is not yet clear whether this recurring designation (twelve times in these stanzas) is positive or negative; the same may at this point also be true of references to Brünhild's strength (seven times), although it plays a role in her later condemnation. While statistics may not signify much in such cases and with such a small sample, perhaps they still indicate an important tendency. There is a total of seventeen positive terms, occurring all told seventy-five times, mixed and combined in a total of forty-seven phrases, while the total number of negative terms is only seven in six phrases.[38] Brünhild is thus designated here over twelve times more often by positive terms than negative.

The positive terms of evaluation in the text of the *Nibelungenlied* are the narrator's as well as the male characters'. Of the negative terms, however, only *zornec* and *Prünhilde nît* occur in the narrator's comments. The first occurs twice in describing Brünhild's reaction to the outcome of each of the contest events. The second term designates what Siegfried and Gunther are said to fear from Brünhild during the contests. Neither of these terms then seems to be inappropriate in context: if not an antagonistic attitude (*nît*), what is to be expected from one's antagonist, and if not anger (*zorn*) what would be a suitable response from the defeated combatant? On the other hand, both uses of *vreislîch* "horrifying / horrible" issue from Siegfried, and he and Hagen each use the term *übermuot* "uppity / high-handed attitude" once, while it is Hagen who calls her *des tiuveles wîp* "the devil's bride." Actually, of course, she is no one's *bride,* and that is after all the crux of the problem: a nubile female who refuses to marry, "reasons" patriarchal ideol-

---

38. In *aventiure* seven: *diu wolgetâne* (2x), *diu schœne/scœn* (5x), *daz schœne magedîn* (2x), *daz vil schœne magedîn, schœne meit, diu maget schœne unde guot, guot, schœn' unde hêr, diu maget* (2x), *diu maget edele* (3x), *diu vil hêrliche meit, diu hêrliche meit, diu edel maget guot, diu maget wol getân, diu maget lobelîch, diu vil wætlichen wîp, gezieret was ir lîp, schœner lîp, minneclîch, diu vil minneclîche meit, daz minneclîche wîp, diu künegîn/küneginne* (8x), *küneginne rîch, küneginne hêr, diu vrouwe* (2x), *diu starke vrouwe, diu Prünhild sterke, krefteclîche* (2x), *mit ir kreften* (2x), *Prünhilde nît, in zorn zornec, des tiuveles wîp;* in *aventiure* six, while the men are deciding whether to make a wooing expedition, the following terms are used of her: *küneginne* (2x), *unmâzen scœn, vil michel was ir kraft, frouwe wol geborn, juncfrouwe, daz scœne wîp, vreislîch* (2x), *daz minneclîche wîp, daz vil hêrliche wîp, ir übermuot, diu hêrliche meit, minneclîch, scœn; minne* is associated with her four times in the first stanzas that concern this venture.

ogy, must have illicit relations elsewhere, thus perhaps with the devil, for her simple independence cannot be accepted at face value.[39]

The narrator of the *Nibelungenlied* says that it was the devil who prompted Kriemhild to break her truce with Gunther (1394; lacking C 1421); Dietrich, however, calls Kriemhild herself a devil (1748; C 1789: *vahen dinne*), as does Hagen (2371); in each case the term used is *vâlant/vâlandinne*. Hagen and Gunther call Brünhild *tiuvels brut, tiuvels wîp* or associate her with the devil in Isenstein (438 [C447: *des valandes wip*], 442, 450), and Gunther calls her *tiuvel* after his wedding night (649). Dürrenmatt (p. 223) claims that this terminological usage indicates that the poet has an "Abneigung gegen die männische Frau." But in fact it is neither the unknown and inaccessible "poet," nor even the narrator, but rather Siegfried, Hagen, and Dietrich — hardly objective participants — who employ these terms.

There may also be a second field of semantic association here, for in the second half of the *Nibelungenlied* regular use is made of the word *tiuvel* in a variety of idioms, generally, however, having to do with battle and a formidable warrior.[40] When asked whether he had brought Kriemhild's stolen property with him to Hunland, Hagen replied: *Jâ bringe ich in dem tiuvel* ("Truly I've brought you the devil'") (1744; lacking C 1784) only immediately to list his combat gear as if gift *and* devil. Dietrich uses the word similarly in reply to the aggressive and challenging boasts of his vassal Wolfhart: *"nu swîget," sprach her Dietrich: "ir habet den tiuvel getân"* ("'Silence now!' said lord Dietrich, 'you've done the devil'" 1993,4; also C 2046). On this enigmatic usage, De Boor refers here to the previous use, on which he offers only the gloss, "den Teufel, d.h. nichts." Certainly this sense

---

39. Otfrid Ehrismann notes the connection between a woman associated with the devil and the designation "witch" (*Epoche — Werk — Wirkung*, p. 175); in general, both the Inquisition and New World witch hunts have also participated in this tradition of demonizing independent unmarried women.

40. Cf. also below on the designation of Kriemhild by *valantinne* and, in *Kudrun*, this use of the term for Hagen in a positive sense (*valant aller künige* 168,2 and 196,4) and for female characters, especially Gerlind (ms. Gottelint), in a negative sense (*die alte Vallentinne* 629,4). See especially Ian R. Campbell, *Kudrun: A Critical Appreciation* (Cambridge: Cambridge University Press, 1978), p. 71, who identifies three areas of association with *vâlant* in *Tristan* and *Biterolf und Dietleib*: "(i) the devil himself as arch-schemer and plotter of malice, together with persons who scheme in similar fashion, (ii) demonic giants and dragons that harass civilized communities, and (iii) civilized knights who are feared as devils or demons because of their gigantic proportions and extraordinary strength." According to Campbell, it is this last category into which Hagen falls, while the first two are appropriate for Kriemhild and Gerlint, who are in his view actual she-devils, since they turn order into chaos, the courtly world into wilderness, life into death (see also pp. 131–132).

of *Teufel tun* has become idiomatic in twentieth-century German, but that in itself provides little evidence for an identical medieval usage. At the end of that same scene, after leaving the hall under safe conduct, Etzel comments on the horrifying martial prowess of Volker and then concludes: *ich dankes mînem heile,   daz ich dem tiuvel entran* (2001,4; C 2054 *valande* for *tiuvel*). It hardly seems likely, but perhaps there is nothing more here than a naturalized Christian metaphor, in which "to escape the devil" is simply to avoid death. Before being wounded by Irinc, Hagen later makes reference to a personified, but possibly still highly metaphorical, devil: *dich envride der übel tiuvel, dune kanst niht genesen* ("'unless the evil devil protects you, you are about to die'" 2051,2). After running away from Hagen, Hildebrand reports to Dietrich: *mit dem mînem lebene   ich dem tiuvel kûme entran* ("'I scarcely escaped from the devil with my life'" 2311,4; C 2370 *dem selben valande entran*).[41] If Brünhild is the female companion of, or female reflex of this metaphorical (*not* personified or mythological) "battle demon" or "devil's warrior," then the designation of her as *tiuveles wîp* seems in the context of the contests in Iceland only appropriate, as long as we recognize that *wîp* will be an eternal interpretive crux.

Especially important here is the initial designation of Brünhild as beautiful twenty times through direct usage of the terms *scœn* and *wœtlich*. Scholars have generally been less than willing to believe the text on this subject than on her demonic nature. Hugo Bekker claims: "Though she is said to be beautiful, we may gather that her appearance lacks something which Kriemhild is thought to possess by those experienced in such matters" (p. 72). He attempts to support this interpretation with stanza 593, which, however, merely states that Brünhild is beautiful and Kriemhild is more so, *not* that Brünhild lacks anything. The point of Bekker's claim becomes clearer only as his ideological mask slips in succeeding statements, when he claims, for instance, (p. 73) that "Brunhild may be dazzling, but she is queen before she is woman"; and that "perhaps we are intended to consider hers a beauty with a gloss of regality subduing the pure femininity that is Kriemhilde's." His is merely a slight variation on the typically patriarchal ideology that prescribes an opposition between nature and culture, so that an opposition obtains between strength and intelligence in men, and beauty and both intelligence and strength in women. According

41. De Boor comments: "Übermaß an Kraft und Tat hebt den Gegner ins Dämonische" ("An excess of strength and ability raises the opponent to the level of the demonic").

to Bekker, it seems, Brünhild can hardly be both beautiful and strong, or both *truly* beautiful *and* a queen.[42] Gottfried Weber also vulgarizes Brünhild's beauty as described by the text: "von etwas grobschlächtiger Schönheit" ("of somewhat coarse good looks," Weber, *Das Nibelungenlied*, p. 35). For some scholarly medievalists, as for the medieval literary hero, Brünhild's beauty is permitted to be real only when it is reduced, vulgarized or otherwise demeaned, for it can only be viewed in such valuative terms.

On the other hand, Franz Bäuml's reservations concerning the semantic weight of the epithets are more telling.[43] The development from oral to written literature has, he argues, left its traces in the text. In saying of Brünhild, for instance, *sprach das minnecliche wîp*, the conventional oral formula is used and signifies no more than "the woman said," and has nothing to do with whether Brünhild is actually "lovable." According to Bäuml's thesis then this usage is ironic for the *reader*, whose eye can dwell on the words, while the aural audience only notes a standard phrase. While Bäuml's argument is sound, I nonetheless think the sheer concentration of the epithets in *aventiures* six and seven, along with the specifics of the distribution of positive and negative epithets among narrator and various male characters is in fact significant for the characterization of Brünhild and her male antagonists (and perhaps also for that of the narrator)

If the narrator and also generally the male characters view Brünhild as a magnificent example of the courtly lady — beautiful, noble, worthy of *minne* — what is it that also allows them almost simultaneously to designate her high-handed, horrifying, and the devil's bride? In his study of the evil woman motif, Franz Brietzmann specifies a tenet of medieval masculist ideologies: that the devil's influence causes women to disobey God's commandment that women submit to their husbands.[44] Such a notion is interesting for several reasons in the present context. If the responsibility were simply the devil's, then any and every such woman would ostensibly be innocent of wrongdoing. But Christian theology actually assigns the re-

42. For Mowatt and Sacker, on the other hand, Brünhild's "bellicosity" is part of her attractiveness. and the motivation for the fact that she is called *minneclich* (in st. 425) derives directly from her Amazonian characteristics (*Nibelungenlied*, pp. 62–63). Cf. the similarity of the notion, noted above, that the Amazon of Greek legend is attractive precisely *because* of her strength.

43. Franz H. Bäuml, "Transformations of the Heroine: From Epic Heard to Epic Read," in *The Role of Women in the Middle Ages*, ed. Rosmarie Thee Morewedge, Papers of the Sixth Annual Conference of the Center for Medieval and Early Renaissance Studies, SUNY Binghamton, 6–7 May 1972 (Albany: SUNY Press, 1975), pp. 23–40.

44. Franz Brietzmann, "Die böse Frau in der deutschen Literatur des Mittelalters," *Palaestra* 42 (1912) (rpt. New York: 1967), 120–122.

sponsibility for (dis)obedience only to human beings, diabolical influences notwithstanding. Thus this construct of woman is not innocent, but again merely a reiteration, a reenactment of Eve, the arch-female, and, in christian patriarchal rewritings of *Genesis,* archsinner, who succumbed to this same devil's influence.[45] A wife's disobedience of her husband, a woman's clitorality, simply reenacts the innate sinfulness imputed to her by this ideology. As Eve was the serpent's dupe, so the witch, the shrew, and the Teutonic Amazon, it is implied, are merely the devil's brides.

The seeming inconsistency in the intermittently lavish praise of Brünhild's beauty and the brutal designation of her as bride of the devil is the nexus of several ideological planes. My designation of the two types of epithets used of Brünhild as positive and negative already partakes indirectly of the feudal, quasi-courtly ideology that assigns beauty, wealth and nobility of blood to the requirements of female courtliness, and the identical attributes, substituting only the male *specificum* (physical strength) for the female (beauty), to those of males. The valuation placed on these attributes contributes directly to the larger problematic at issue here: the construct of acceptable female behavior, as evaluated in the context of the courtly ideology just noted, for it is obviously a manifestation of historical patriarchy. As long as female attributes and behavior conform to or approximate the norms constructed by/through the dominant social formations, then all is well: a beautiful, noble, wealthy maiden, e.g. Kriemhild, is so designated and is assigned a specific role and function in the system: as barterable sister or daughter, as available status augmentation via marriage. That a female is beautiful, noble, and wealthy is simultaneously both assumed and strongly marked by the system. If the female does not conform to or approximate the norms, then other reactions are automatic — no more or less rational than the straitjacketing of the woman as courtly commodity, but in the patriarchal context more striking.

The most obvious non-conformity is also all but invisible in medieval belles-lettres: the very existence of the quintessentially nonconformist female, the non-aristocratic woman, is denied.[46] Those females who fulfill

---

45. See esp. Mieke Bal, *Lethal Love: Feminist Literary Readings of Biblical Love Stories* (Bloomington: Indiana University Press, 1987), esp. "Sexuality, Sin and Sorrow: The Emergence of Female Character," pp. 104–130, on the notion of "original" sin and the role of Eve in the creation narration of the Hebrew Bible and in the Pauline rescripting of it. We might, however, also note that this notion is strictly a christian construction: the Jewish tradition knows no such concept and certainly has never stigmatized Eve as the culprit.

46. As is of course also that of her counterpart, the male serf. Cf. Chrétien's bigoted portrayal of the herdsman in *Yvain* and Hartmann's preservation of the scene in his adaptation, both examples of the (rare) portrayal of commoners in contemporaneous belles-lettres.

one or more of the requirements, may find a reduced ad hoc functional role in the society of the literature (for instance, the noble, but not beautiful, Cundrie in *Parzival* or Dame Ragnell in the Middle English romance).[47] But an essential problem arises when a female possesses attributes other than the accepted ones, for if those supplemental characteristics become either so numerous or so dominant that they begin to determine the character definition itself, then that character can no longer be accounted for within the strictures of the ideological system. Such deviant behavior is then designated by terms that deny the conventional characteristics: not good, receptive, and complacent, but horrifying, not *minneclich* for a human husband, but bride of the devil. Mowatt and Sacker (p. 109) aptly comment: "For them [sc. Gunther and Hagen], apparently, hell is peopled with women they do not understand, or cannot manage."

The most visible problem in Brünhild's case is her specific non-conformity: her strength. But, to voice the obvious here: her strength only becomes a problem when she uses it. As such her strength represents the same concept and actuality of independence found among the Amazons. For until it is used, men can simply ignore female strength, or at most note its existence and then ignore it, all the while gushing forth conventional courtly epithets concerning beauty and nobility. Such is certainly the case when the Burgundian expedition ventures to Iceland to challenge Brünhild. The larger context of combat is clear from the beginning, as Siegfried makes clear in his descriptions and in his designation of Brünhild as *vreislich*. Thereafter, the men ignore this character deviation and pretend that Brünhild is what they wish her to be, despite evidence to the contrary. This attempt to deny her character, to usurp her right to self-definition, to impose with their words and terminological system their own will and ideology on her actions, seems to be successful in Iceland.

It is only when Brünhild is conceived of as amenable to the male plans for her use that she is designated by positive terms. It is not simply that one aspect of her character is made to signify the whole, but rather, her existence as such is subsumed under or summed up by these epithets. When she does not conform to them, the male inventors of the terms do not revise their inaccurate descriptions of the reified Brünhild, such that their designations better describe this "object," but rather simply vilify her character for non-conformity to their expectations. In fact, however, Brünhild's character has not changed at all; nor have her social and political role and function. The

47. In each case, however, appearance is a significant cipher of the conventional relation of beauty to morality, and thus yet another instance of the patriarchal differentiation of beauty and sexuality from moral value.

only difference is that the intruders into her realm have arrived with a rather bulky heap of ideological baggage that they attempt simply to impose on her, not on the basis of her character, but rather *despite* it, and in spite of all evidence that would deny the relevance of their conception. Even in their terminological usage then, they attempt to abduct and transform Brünhild's character, to reduce her independence to (courtly) subordination.[48]

Like Brünhild, Kriemhild is designated by a term of devilry — *vâlan-dinne* — also by male opponents who have journeyed far from home to the margins of civilization to find her: Dietrich in his exile from "Bern,"[49] and Hagen after the laborious journey from Burgundy. It is a journey, obviously, that she too has had to make, and its recounting conveys something of the tendency toward constructing an exotic and fabulous "Orient." The beginning stanzas of *aventiure* 22 describes the external circumstances of Kriemhild's initial intrusion into the culture of the East, after she has already crossed numerous borders, political as well as metaphorical, leaving behind her home country and crossing into the Bavarian wilderness, as the poet seems to jibe: she first visits, receives advice from, and leaves behind her last relative, who at the same time is the last official institutional vestige of the church."[50] She then briefly stops at Pöchlarn, seemingly the last outpost of the courtly civilization of the "home" culture, although it is already a part of Etzel's kingdom and therefore oriented toward the East, and thus the final border or margin. Finally she enters Hunland and, as they press farther east, sees Etzel's multinational hordes ride out to meet them and join the column — Russians, Greeks, Poles, Pechenegs, soldiers of Walachia and Kiev.

This is the narrative mode of new beginnings in unknown places. But the last stanzas of the previous *aventiure* seem to be winding down. They display all the characteristics of closure.[51] This sharp disjunction appropri-

---

48. As has been argued in the previous chapter, the situation of Kriemhild's initial characterization by her male counterparts is similar. She is conceived as the ideal courtly princess, i.e. beautiful and compliant and therefore a valuable commodity for her lineages of both birth and marriage.

49. The literary reflex of Verona, which itself is a displacement from the actual residence in Ravenna of the historical Gothic king, Theodoric, who had vaguely to do with some aspects of the construction of Dietrich's legendary character.

50. Mass is celebrated in Hunland for the Christians, but there is little indication that the Catholic Church has any other significant presence.

51. This disjuncture may be the concrete result of the practicalities of the *Nibelungenlied*'s pre-history as part of an oral tradition. Specifically, this could conceivably be a stopping point for an evening's recitation, which might require some kind of summary devices of quasi-closure. But, on the other hand, the *Nibelungenlied* is itself a written work, a text, and is susceptible to textual analysis, obviously, and this particular possibility of its pre-history need not take precedence.

ately marks a border between two worlds. Just to the other side Kriemhild runs into the Eastern hordes of Slavs and nomads and, strangest of all, Greeks. She has entered the realm of the constructed Other, and her progressive isolation from her previous life continues as she makes a place for herself in Hunland.

Once oriented toward Hunland, however, she is the outsider, and she must ultimately endure the fate of almost all outsiders who have somehow found space on the inside: they are rarely accepted by insiders as authentic.[52] Thus as the final crisis comes, and Kriemhild must call in her feudal vouchers as it were, and ask her Hunnic warriors to kill Hagen, they repeatedly refuse, renege after consenting, or are killed in combat, always without success. In the end, then she has become utterly marginalized even on the margin: she is quite literally alone, for (only) apparently all males in Hunland are dead except Etzel, Hildebrand, Dietrich and Hagen. When feudal service is finally effectively performed for her, by Dietrich, and Hagen is delivered to her bound, she must execute him herself, since Dietrich, Hildebrand and Etzel have not and will not.

And like Brünhild it is in that outside, alien space that Kriemhild's own independent development can reach its logical end. Consequently it is also in that alien realm where she is isolated from known society and marginalized from dominant culture that she undergoes final marginalization. As Brünhild began, so ends Kriemhild. It is in Hunland that she is first called a devil and treated like one by her male opponents.

The terminological usage is complex, as are the variations in the manuscript traditions. In an attempt to naturalize the use of the term *vâlandinne*, Hans Kuhn reads far too much significance into the scene in which Kriemhild and Gunther kiss and superficially reconcile (*aventiure* 19). Kuhn calls the result of this kiss a "sacred peace." Batts (p. 233) views it as evidence of Kriemhild's gullibility. I would on the other hand interpret this staged reconciliation as a politically astute move on Kriemhild's part, cementing her stable position in Worms. After all, it was her brothers who had asked for a reconciliation, not Kriemhild. What would she gain by refusing, besides suspicion, of which she certainly had no need. Kuhn suggests that in breaking her pact of reconciliation with Gunther and then actually carrying out her vengeance, Kriemhild becomes not just the devil's dupe, but a devil herself. This development, he claims, is represented in the early use of the empty (even when applied to Brünhild, st. 438) epithet *tiuvel* and the later

---

52. This situation is of course particularly common for females subject to dynastic marriage, or in fact of any females marrying beyond the larger borders of the clan.

use of the highly charged *vâlant* (B1394) by the poet about Kriemhild and the feminine *vâlandinne* (B1748, 2371) in direct address by characters to her ("Der Teufel im Nibelungenlied" pp. 280–306). This not altogether logical difference in signification is not explained, but rather conveniently attributed by Kuhn to pre-*Nibelungenlied Sagengeschichte.*[53]

In any case, Dietrich is the first to use the epithet *vâlandinne* of Kriemhild (1748,4), in response to her exclamation of anger as she recognizes that the Burgundians have been warned (*und wesse ich, wer daz tæte,   er müese kiesen den tôt* " 'if I knew who had done that, he would certainly die for it' " 1747,4). Dietrich, who has in fact warned them twenty stanzas earlier, explodes (*mit zurne*) with his admission of having done so and taunts her: *nu zuo, vâlandinne, du solt michs niht geniezen lân* (" 'now come on, she-devil, you mustn't let me go unpunished' " 1748). The semantic value of *vâlandinne* is partially lost in the translation "she-devil," which conveys the concrete denotation, but lacks the emotive connotation of contempt, condescending sexism, and perhaps even still some hint of religious curse.

Immediately following this challenge and Kriemhild's powerlessness to act on her threat,[54] Dietrich and Hagen take part in what contemporary popular psychology would call a male bonding scene:

> *Bî henden sich dô viengen*   *zwêne degene:*
> *daz eine was her Dietrîch,*   *daz ander Hagene.*

53. Kuhn's conclusions about the issue of distinctions in terminological usage among the manuscripts (*Kriemhild's Hort und Rache* p. 297) also seem ill-founded. Where, for instance, manuscripts AB use *tiuvel,* C has *vâlant* (=B2001, 2311). Kuhn then suggests that in C *vâlant* is used only in a trivial sense, for C has *vâlant* in 1748 & 2371 where it refers to Kriemhild, and thus must be meaningless, since C otherwise tries to defend Kriemhild's innocence. The *tiuvel* of B2230 corresponds to *vreislîch* in C, and thus Kuhn suggests that *tiuvel* was a pejorative term in C, while *vâlant* was not. The "reconciliation scene" (B1113–1115, C1124–1128), is *longer* in C, which also lacks the kiss of Kriemhild and Gunther that plays such an important role in Kuhn's condemnation of Kriemhild and prompts him to absolve Hildebrand of all wrongdoing in his butchering of her. Nor does C designate Kriemhild *vâlant* in C1421 = B1394. In C1488 (=B1460), however, the kiss is mentioned, but Kuhn here denies its significance by claiming that it is here merely a remnant of a previous source and thus meaningless. The C manuscript does invoke the participation of the devil far more often *and* as a far more significant player than does AB. In C822 it is the *tiuvel* who causes Brünhild to start the argument with Kriemhild. In C2143 the *tiuvel* causes Kriemhild not to restrict her revenge to Hagen. In this way, she is in one sense freed of the responsibility for the death of Gunther by the C-poet. On the other hand, her status as a free agent, as a freely responsible human being is again paradigmatically denied, and she once again becomes merely a reiteration of Eve and the devil's dupe. At the same time, however, this usage does in fact place the "devilry" one remove from Kriemhild, for it is not she, but the devil who is here so identified. Perhaps this compromise is the best the C-poet could manage under the circumstances.

54. Despite all Kriemhild's power, wealth, and vassals, she has no vassal who can match Dietrich in combat.

dô sprach gezogenlîche   der recke vil gemeit:
'daz iuwer komen zen Hiunen   daz ist mir wærlîch leit,

Durch daz diu küneginne   alsô gesprochen hât.'
dô sprach von Tronege Hagene: 'es wirt wol alles rât.
sus redeten mit ein ander   die zwêne küene man. (1750,1–1751,3)

(The two warriors then took each other by the hand, the one lord Dietrich, the other Hagen. Then the bold warrior spoke courteously: "Because of what the Queen has said, I am truly sorry that you have come to the Huns." Hagen of Tronege replied: "Things will turn out all right." Thus the two bold men spoke to one another.)

Hagen's enemy is female, and thus Dietrich's sympathies are, according to the patriarchal values of this heroic society, with Hagen, even though his duty would specify that he protect the interests of Kriemhild, the queen of his own protector.[55] His warning of his only peer in the warrior caste is in a broad sense a betrayal of his allegiance to his protector, since it countervents the plans of the queen. And thus Dietrich and Hagen share the same enemy, and according to the threat made against the betrayor of her secret plans, they also share the same punishment intended by Kriemhild: death. Dietrich's danger is of course negligible. The only important consideration is, however, that they as warriors have a common enemy, who is of the royal, not warrior caste, but who presumes to usurp the role of a warrior; finally, she is also female, the quintessential Other. For all these reasons she is, from their perspective, beneath contempt, unworthy of human dignity, no more than a devil.

De Boor suggests that the term *vâlandinne* is inappropriate both at this particular point in the narrative and in Dietrich's mouth, and thus he plays the recurring trump of *Nibelungen*-scholarship: this *faux pas* is merely a *Stilfehler des jüngsten Dichters* "a stylistic error by the most recent poet," that is, not original, and thus not significant; additionally it is only a problem in style, not content. On the contrary, I would argue, the term is appropriate to the context both in style and meaning, for whether or not Dietrich is here (or at any later point in the text) the positive model of Christian, courtly,

---

55. Dietrich's general view of women may also be gathered not just from his treatment of Kriemhild and his interaction with Hagen, but also from his reprimand of Hildebrand for reminding Hagen of his cowardice in the fight against Walther: *daz enzimt niht helde lîp, / daz si suln schelten   sam diu alten wîp* ("it is unseemly for warriors to insult each other like old women" 2345,1–2).

heroic or any other *valued* behavior (as scholars have frequently maintained),[56] since he in some respects embodies the values of the entire feudal
cultural amalgamation depicted in the work, he is also the prime example of
their dysfunction. Thus it seems only appropriate that he open this semantic pandora's box in the presence of Hagen and Kriemhild at the beginning
of the Burgundian visit in Hunland, for the same three (plus Hildebrand)
will also be present at the final use of the term. After Gunther's death and
when Hagen knows that he is the only Burgundian left alive, he says to
Kriemhild: *den schaz den weiz nu niemen   wan got unde mîn: / der sol dich,
vâlandinne,   immer wol verholn sîn.* ("'Now no one knows the whereabouts of the treasure but God and I; it will be hidden from you forever,
you she-devil'" 2371,3–4).[57] That Dietrich is present at both the first and
last confrontation between Hagen and Kriemhild in Hunland, that he
survives, and that his vassal, Hildebrand, chops up the alleged *vâlandinne,*
does not make him the spokesman for ideal (or "the poet's") values.
Instead, it implicates Dietrich in the entire catastrophic affair.[58] Simultaneously it renders Dietrich, as the embodiment of heroico-courtly society,
utterly superfluous, since that culture has now, at least momentarily, and
perhaps (despite the post-textual claims of the *Klage* to the contrary) in this
fictional realm forever vanished, for in the course of the tale, the splendour
of all major courts in the known world (that is, those with powerful heroes
and beautiful women) have successively been essentially diminished or
utterly destroyed: the Nibelungs have been deprived of their rulers and
financial means, Isenstein of its queen and finest knights and ladies, the
Netherlands of its king, Saxony and Denmark of their honor, Burgundy of
its ruling house and its entire knightly class, the Hunnic realm and its
dozens of vassal realms of their entire knightly class.[59] Where are Dietrich

56. De Boor, for instance (*ad* 1993,1) remarks that with his perfect combination of *Kraft*
and *mâze* Dietrich is an example of "männlicher Vollkommenheit" ("male perfection"); cf.
also Ehrismann, *Epoche — Werk — Wirkung,* p. 206: "Dietrich repräsentiert zeitlos höfische
Ideale" ("Dietrich represents timeless courtly ideals").

57. Significantly, De Boor comments at this point: "Das Wort darf nicht verblaßt
genommen werden. Kriemhild hat nicht nur die Grenzen des Höfischen, sondern des Menschlichen überschritten, sie ist dämonisch verzerrt" ("The term should not be understood in a
weakened sense. Kriemhild has not only exceeded the limits of courtliness but also of human-
ity; she is demonically distorted").

58. Just as Rüdiger is also implicated: had he fulfilled his duty to King and Queen, and
his vow to the Queen, he would have attacked Hagen at the beginning of the conflict, without
all the irrelevant hand-wringing about honor, duty, the damnation of his soul, and also
without pledging, before his belated entrance into the fray, to the Burgundians *not* to fight
Hagen, Kriemhild's *only* opponent.

59. Cf. Ehrismann, *Epoche — Werk — Wirkung,* p. 196: Dietrich "hat nichts mehr, kein
Reich, keine Krieger, er ist ganz auf Etzel zurückgeworfen" ("has nothing more, no kingdom,

and Hildebrand and Etzel to be courtly and heroic now? Over whom are they to be kings? Who will prepare their sumptuous clothes and meals, and who will praise them, serve them and humbly accept their largesse? Is Dietrich not rather a pitiful and perhaps even morbidly comical figure at the end? A representative of a class that has lived beyond its time, and a conception of gender that is, sooner or later, doomed?

Despite the fact that Kriemhild is despoiled by the Burgundians (and Rüdiger) of Siegfried's hoard, she does not submit to the ideology of male dominance. Whatever hints of the typical motifs of the legend of the subdued Amazon — kidnapping, rape, subjugation — are present in her first marriage, she seems to escape from the excesses of male ideology when she decides in favor of the second marriage, thus volunteering to go beyond the margins of civilization, where she enjoys the enormous power of a *regens regina*. Thus her fate seems on the one hand quite unlike that of the Amazons of Greek legend, and even that of Brünhild as Teutonic Amazon. In the end, however, it becomes clear that the chiasm that describes Brünhild's rape and disempowerment in Burgundy and Kriemhild's empowerment in Hunland breaks down, for while Kriemhild has temporarily postponed the confrontation with the forces that seek to eradicate her clitorality, that conflict is ultimately her wish (especially since she accomplishes it in order to take vengeance on Hagen). In the end her invitation of the Burgundians brings it about, and the fragility of her *power without authority* becomes apparent. For despite the fact that she has power and wealth and vassals and beauty and class and rank, she has no authority, as is clear finally and incontrovertibly in Hunland, when her vassals — the vassals of, apparently, the greatest realm on earth — refuse to fight Hagen or are outfought and killed by the Burgundians. In the end she must act herself, by and for herself. And since she is a women, she dies for it. For her nonconformity, for her "pseudo-maleness," for her "unnatural unwomanliness," she, like Hippolyte before her, is put to the sword by a patriarchal hero. Afterward she, unlike Hippolyte, is then further chopped into pieces by that same hero.

---

no warriors; he is again made fully dependent on Etzel"). He goes too far, I think, when he bathetically claims: "Das Schlußbild ist einprägsam: neben dem gebrochenen, weinenden König und dem zornigen Vasallen steht der weinende Held, ohne Reich, ohne Krieger, ohne politische Bindungen. Es ist ein Bild unendlicher Trauer" ("'the final scene is impressive: beside the broken, weeping king and the angry vassal stands the weeping hero, without kingdom, without warriors, without political bonds. It is a scene of eternal grief," p. 206). But then this attitude is the necessary corollary to the conventional notion that "Dietrich repräsentiert zeitlos höfische Ideale." Had they in fact been "timeless," they would not have been so utterly destroyed at the end of the *Nibelungenlied*, where the ideal, as well as the (literary) fact of feudal chivalry is dead.

Male ideology — or rather, what is left of it in the three surviving males — has, it seems, triumphed over the Teutonic, just as it had over the Greek Amazon. Interestingly, in the Greek myth the Amazons lose and the Greeks win, which for reasons discussed above serves to recuperate and reinforce conventional gender roles. In the *Nibelungenlied,* on the other hand, not only Brünhild and Kriemhild, but also their male opponents lose, and while the women are recuperated for the patriarchal system, it is only at the cost of the destruction of almost all extant representatives of that system. There is more than merely a hint of subversion here.

6. Inconclusive Intermezzo: The Monsters, the Critics, *Diu Klage*

In comprehensive studies of the *Nibelungenlied,* there have generally been three tropes of emplotment that form the basis of concluding sections or concluding chapters[1]: the *Nibelungenlied* as tragedy, as monster tale, or — rarely — as, for lack of a better designation, a complexly ambiguous aporia. Most often, when the *Nibelungenlied* is called a tragedy (normally in scholars' requisite lament of the deaths of Burgundian and Hunnic knighthood) it is in a vague, lay sense that nowadays can apply as well to the death of a beloved cat as to the tearing of a quarterback's ligaments. Schweikle rather uncharacteristically even offers the hybrid designation: "heroisch-tragischer Liebesroman" ("heroic-tragic love-romance").[2] On the other hand, of course since twelfth-century northern Europe did not know Aristotle's *Poetics* or the works of any ancient Attic tragedian, there is no need to pretend that an Aristotelian or a modified (modern) Aristotelian paradigm or definition of tragedy is relevant to a discussion of the *Nibelungenlied,* and so we need not necessarily disallow other definitions of tragedy.[3] Karl Heinz Ihlenburg's attempt at redefinition is perhaps the most interesting, because the best grounded in the text; by means of a discussion of marxist definitions of tragedy, he situates the *Nibelungenlied* somewhat more concretely in this genre. The *Leitmotiv* of his study is that the *Nibelungenlied* expresses the "Desillusionierung der höfischen Welt" (*Das Nibelungenlied* p. 51). This concept has a direct connection both to his view that the motivating historical impulse of the narrative is the weakening of the mon-

1. On the (now common) analysis of *scholarly* texts by means of rhetorical and narratological categories, see the groundbreaking work by Hayden White, *Tropics of Discourse: Essays in Cultural Criticism* (Baltimore: Johns Hopkins University Press, 1978).
2. Günther Schweikle, "Das 'Nibelungenlied,'" pp. 59–84; cf. also, for instance, M. S. Batts, "Die Tragik des *Nibelungenliedes*," *Doitsu Bungaku* 16 (1960), 42–48; Werner Schröder, "Die Tragödie Kriemhilts im Nibelungenlied," *Zeitschrift für deutsches Altertum und deutsche Literatur* 90 (1960–61), 41–80, 123–160.
3. See Paul Zumthor, *Parler du Moyen Age* (Paris: Éditions de Minuit, 1980), on the illegitimacy of the common, tacit assumption that ancient and modern generic categories are relevant in discussions of medieval European literatures.

archy and growing strength of the vassalage around the year 1200 (pp. 166–167, n. 113) and to his understanding of "tragedy" in this context:

> Während in bürgerlicher Auffassung echte Tragik nur dann vorliegt, wenn das menschliche Individuum an überweltlichen Mächten zerbricht, so geht die marxistische Literaturauffassung davon aus, daß der tragische Held histori-schen Notwendigkeiten unterliegt. Man unterscheidet zwei Grundmöglich-keiten echter historischer Tragik: Entweder findet der tragische Held den Tod, weil er in falscher Einschätzung des historisch Möglichen über die erreichte gesellschaftliche Entwicklungsstufe hinausstrebt, oder er geht unter, weil er in historisch zwangsläufiger Bindung an das Alte von der geschichtlichen Ent-wicklung überholt wird.
>
> While in the bourgeois conception, actual tragedy exists only when an individ-ual human being is destroyed by supernatural powers, the marxist conception of literature assumes that the tragic hero is defeated by historical forces/inevitabilities. Two basic possibilities of actual historical tragedy may be distin-guished: either the tragic hero dies, because, in misjudging what actions are possible, in historically developmental terms, he strives beyond the current developmental state of society; or he is destroyed, because, as a result of an inevitable historical connection to the past, he is overtaken by historical development. (p. 140)

Thus the Burgundians suffer a "tragic" end because they live according to norms that had been valid for centuries, but which by the period of the composition of the *Nibelungenlied* were being called into question (pp. 141–142).[4] The "tragedy" of the *Nibelungenlied* results then from the destruction of the obsolescent class structure of the Burgundians by a newly rising one, in this case manifested in the appearance in late twelfth-century Germany of an essential conflict between a strong vassalage and a weak king (pp. 140–144).

While the strict orthodoxy of Ihlenburg's model of literary structure as reflection of its socio-historical basis is far too restrictive, on a higher level of generalization, his definition of tragedy is of some relevance to the present argument: "Der tragische Konflikt beruht also . . . darauf, daß ein Individuum mit dem historisch Gesetzmäßigen kollidiert" ("The tragic conflict is thus based on the fact that an individual collides with historical

---

4. He also suggests that Hagen and Dietrich represent the two tendencies: Hagen, the old, heroic, autonomous power-politics oriented action versus Dietrich's "versöhnungswillige Friedensbereitschaft, seine maßvolle Beherrschtheit und humane Denkungsart" ("conciliatory readiness for peace, his measured self-control and humane mode of thought") of the future. In the seven centuries since the work's composition *that* future has not yet arrived; cf. Ekkehart Krippendorff's *Staat und Krieg: Die historische Logik der politischen Unvernunft* (Frankfurt: Suhrkamp, 1985).

legitimacy"). His schema then might well point to a different conclusion altogether from the one he draws. For it seems that the "tragedies" of Kriemhild and Brünhild are of the first type discussed by Ihlenburg: they are individual representatives of a social group (powerful, independent women) that is not yet acceptable to the traditional social formations and their component gender constructions, and thus these women are systematically prohibited participation in public action and authority by those formations. In attempting to circumvent such restrictions, they are forced by the countering moves of patriarchy into ever more transgressive actions until ultimately they are forced into (self-) destruction. For both that means capitulation to patriarchy or death; for Brünhild, capitulation in Iceland and later in Worms; for Kriemhild, death in Hunland. Ihlenburg describes the tragic hero thus: "Hierher gehört u.a. der Untergang des geschichtlich zu früh gekommenen Revolutionärs, der sein auf das Wohl der Menschheit gerichtetes Wollen für etwas einsetzt, was in der gegebenen Zeit noch nicht zu verwirklichen ist. Er wird von der Macht der bestehenden Gesellschaftsordnung tragisch vernichtet" ("This is the case for, among other things, the revolutionary who is before his time, and who commits his humanitarian will to a cause that cannot yet be realized. He is tragically destroyed by the power of the existing social order," p. 140). Were we to change the gender of his generic male revolutionary, this description would define rather well the situations of both Kriemhild and Brünhild in the *Nibelungenlied*.

But this tragic reading is not the most common concluding trope in *Nibelungenlied* studies. Instead rather a different goal by means of rather a different method is generally sought. And here we find that with very few exceptions, the innumerable and often antagonistic schools of *Nibelungenlied* scholarship during the last two centuries are drawn into solidarity on at least one issue of great significance in this context: their condemnation of Kriemhild's revenge and their designation of her as an inhuman monster to be slaughtered by Hildebrand in his role as the instrument of divine justice. The fact that almost before Hagen's head has hit the floor, Kriemhild is chopped into pieces (*zu stücken . . . gehouwen* 2377,2) by an outraged Hildebrand, has evoked shrieks of self-righteous ecstasy from generations of *Nibelungenlied* scholars, whose remarks often assume the — for the *Nibelungenlied* — inappropriate tone of *biblical* retribution, as they remind us that divine justice is necessary and necessarily swift and pure, in punishing the immoral, ungodly, demonic. Mergell, Weber, and Rupp, for instance, call Kriemhild a "demon," while Northcott claims that she is simply "possessed by a demon," and Nagel maintains that her deeds are "ultimately the work of the devil"; Weber, Bekker, Hans Kuhn, and Werner Schröder claim that she literally becomes inhuman; for Ihlenburg she is "fury of vengeance," for Wahl Armstrong a "devil of vengeance"; R. M. Meyer deems her a Gorgon and claims that her execution "frees the world of a monster, and liberates her from life."[5]

In order to understand this recurring and rather unscholarly emotional litany, we need only consider the larger ideological context. Here too, William Tyrrell provides an interesting and relevant insight in the course of his analysis of the Amazon phenomenon in Greek culture, in his remarks on the killing of Agamemnon by Clytemnestra:

> Both Agamemnon and Clytemnestra choose a victim who has an avenger. Their acts transform ritualized slaughter into murder, thus introducing violence into the family and community. The difference between them is that Agamemnon's act is an iniquitous extreme of a father's mastery, something we can overlook without condoning because it is done in support of the system of male rule. Clytemnestra's act confounds the distinction between human sacrificer and animal victim, thereby eliminating the distinction between men and animals, overthrowing male rule, and opening up an unbreachable gap between men and their gods. (*Amazons,* p. 38)

Similarly, Hagen kills Siegfried "in support of the system of male rule," for which there might be several kinds of explanations in realpolitical terms: perhaps to avenge a wrong done to a possessed woman (Brünhild) by besmirching her honor and thus devaluing a marital commodity in the

---

5. Mergell, "Nibelungenlied und höfischer Roman," *Euphorion* 45 (1950), p. 15; Weber, *Nibelungenlied: Problem und Idee,* pp. 11–12; Nagel, *Das Nibelungenlied: Stoff — Form — Ethos,* p. 255; Ihlenburg, *Das Nibelungenlied: Problem und Gehalt,* pp. 10, 51; Marianne Wahl Armstrong, *Rolle und Charakter: Studien zur Menschendarstellung im Nibelungenlied* (Göppingen: Kummerle, 1979), pp. 129, 291; Bekker, *Nibelungenlied,* p. 29; Hans Kuhn, "Der Teufel im Nibelungenlied: Zu Gunthers und Kriemhilds Tod," *ZfdA* 94 (1965), p. 294; Werner Schröder, "Zum Problem der Hortfrage im *Nibelungenlied," Nibelungenlied-Studien* (Stuttgart: Metzler, 1968), p. 177; Ursula Schulze, "Nibelungen und Kudrun," in *Epische Stoffe des Mittelalters,* ed. Volker Mertens and Ulrich Müller (Stuttgart: Alfred Dröner, 1984), p. 125; Rupp, "Das Nibelungenlied," p. 174; Batts, "The *Nibelungenlied,"* p. 233; Meyer, in *Die deutsche Literatur bus zum Beginn des neunzehnten Jahrhunderts,* ed. O. Pniower, Volksausgabe (Berlin 1916), cited by Otfrid Ehrismann, *Das Nibelungenlied in Deutschland,* pp. 155–156. Ehrismann turns the scholarly claims that Kriemhild is a monster back on the scholars themselves: "Die Begriffe für Kriemhild sind starke Worte, die ein Zeugnis ablegen von der Unruhe der Interpreten" ("the designations of Kriemhild are strong terms that testify to the anxiety of the interpreters," *Das Nibelungenlied: Epoche,* p. 202). Even so, he immediately reverts to the same ploy himself, for he still finds her worthy of the designations *Teufelin* and *Hexe,* insofar as she broke the rules of "Gastrecht, handelte arglistig, nahm den Tod tausender unschuldiger Männer in Kauf" ("hospitality, acts with cunning, and was willing to accept the deaths of thousands of innocent men").

possession of the king; perhaps simply so that Hagen can eliminate the only other (pseudo-)vassal at the Burgundian court who might compete with him; perhaps to eliminate a potential threat to the Burgundian realm. On the other hand, despite the fact that Hagen admits to Siegfried's murder and the natural world corroborates that admission (the bleeding of the wounds at Hagen's approach to the bier), despite the text's recurring evidence that Kriemhild seeks *only* Hagen's death (which is consistently prevented by the codes of heroism, honor, and male solidarity, that is, the feudal-patriarchal system),[6] Kriemhild obviously kills Hagen *outside* of, and in direct opposition to, such a system, and thus she is perceived by that system as the guilty party. And since she acts not just outside the only operative system of human justice — the male system — but also in opposition to it, she is judged not just guilty (as a male transgressor would also have been) but inhuman. The scholarly howls of righteous delight at her murder give rather embarrassingly clear evidence of the unrelenting and adamant scholarly defense, tacit and not so tacit, of patriarchy.

As with most norms, however, here too there is a range of exceptions to this condemnation of Kriemhild's vengeance. Beyschlag argues, for instance, that Kriemhild's act of vengeance, not just as initially conceived soon after Siegfried's death, but also as executed over two decades later in Hunland, is legitimate, based on a single act of Hagen's: when Hagen plays the insubordinate vassal and refuses the hoard to his superior (Kriemhild) upon arrival in Hunland, he gives her free hand to execute him: "Hagen schlägt durch die kompromißlose Verweigerung des Hortes Dietrich jene Bedingung aus der Hand, und Kriemhild erhält Freiheit zum Vollzug der persönlichen Rache" ("By his uncompromising refusal to give up the hoard, Hagen denies Dietrich this condition, and gives Kriemhild license to execute her personal vengeance," Beyschlag, "Das Nl. als aktuelle Dichtung," p. 228). Czerwinski carries this type of argument still further in analyzing the larger conception of legality in such a society, but again without attempting to discuss the gender-based political implications of such a conception:

6. See especially C. 1882, Kriemhild's explicit instructions before the battle begins in Hunland: *daz ir da slahet niemen. wan den einen man. den vngetriwen Hagenen. die andern svlt ir leben lan* ("that you kill no one here except the one man — disloyal Hagen; the others you ought to let live"); lacking in B; and C 2142 (the entire stanza is lacking in B): *Sine het der grozen slahte. also niht gedaht. si het ez inir ahte. vil gerne dar zvo brahte. daz niwan Hagene aleine. den lip da hete lan. do geschvof der vbel tivfel. deiz vber si alle mvose ergan* ("she had not planned on the great slaughter; she had in mind rather to bring it about that Hagen alone would lose his life there. It was the devil's doing that this had to happen to them all").

Es geht nicht um Sühne für die Verletzung einer abstrakten Sittlichkeit, sondern um die Wiedergutmachung eines konkreten Schadens, des Schadens, der der Sippe durch den Tod eines ihrer Mitglieder, Kriemhild und der Landesherrschaft durch den Tod des überragenden Herrn entsteht. Dieser Schaden muß ausgeglichen werden, darin steckt nichts Moralisches. In der Hinsicht ist Rache keine Eigenmächtigkeit gegen eine allgemeine Gesetzlichkeit, die Unrecht zu beseitigen monopolisiert ist, sondern selbst Recht, Durchsetzung personaler Ansprüche in einem noch nicht institutionell verselbständigten Zusammenhang. Statt einer allgemeinen, aber abstrakten Rechtsform herrscht hier also eine partikuläre, aber konkrete und Rache ist eine durchaus legitime Reaktion auf *leit*. (*Das Nibelungenlied,* p. 77)

(The issue is not atonement for a violation against an abstract morality, but rather reparation for a particular instance of injury, specifically that which comes about for the clan as the result of the death of one of its members, and for Kriemhild and the governance of the land as the result of the death of the lord and master. For this injury there must be compensation; it is not a matter of morals. In this respect, revenge is not an arbitrary act against a general legality, which has a monopoly on the elimination of illegality, but rather it is itself the law, the realization of one's individual claims in a situation that has not yet become institutionally independent. Thus instead of a general, abstract legal form a more particular, concrete one obtains here, and vengeance is an altogether legitimate reaction to *leit*.)

This last term hints at the direction which his argument is to take from this point: he condemns Kriemhild not because she took (legitimate) vengeance, but rather for the *Modalitäten* of that revenge, which transgresses against *entwickeltere Rechtsformen* in Worms and at the Hunnic court, for her betrayal of the kiss of peace bestowed upon her brother, and for her betrayal of Etzel's *triuwe*. These crimes suffice, in Czerwinski's view, to make possible their expression only by means of the metaphor that imputes their ultimate source to the devil: *ich wæne der übel vâlant   Kriemhild daz geriet* (1394,1, quoted by Czerwinski; lacking C 1421). There is, however, no evidence that there existed either in Worms or in Hunland any "more advanced legal forms," especially since the only "case" presented at either court is Kriemhild's, in which the evidence is in fact all against such a claim for their progressive legal systems. In Burgundy the kings as instances of justice are themselves complicit in the murder; they commit perjury, willfully obstruct "justice," and refuse to punish the acknowledged and confessed murderer. In Hunland the only two characters actively interested in the case are Rüdiger and Dietrich. The latter refuses to have anything to do with its settlement (1904), while Rüdiger who has already pledged his support, initially only waffles and blusters about the fate of his soul, when faced with Kriemhild's calling in that pledge, and then refuses to fight her single designated enemy.

Schweikle also views Kriemhild's killing Hagen as lawful vengeance, while he calls the legitimacy of her murder by Hildebrand into question (p. 74), thus posing the larger question that forces the issue of gender relations. Ehrismann sees the issue even more clearly in terms of just action:

> Rache ist Recht, und mit ihrer Rache vollzog Kriemhild auch das Recht, das ihr — gegen das Recht — Gunther verweigerte. Die Könige deckten den Mörder, den die Bahrprobe entlarvt hatte. Dies in einer Welt, in der das Recht alles galt. Als sie Gunther töten ließ, Hagen selbst tötete, stellt die Entrechtete das Recht wieder her. Es war eine Restitution des Rechts im Rechtsbruch. Dies könnte sie noch einmal mit Judith verbinden, die ihr Volk durch die Tötung des Holofernes rettete. (p. 202)

> (Vengeance is the law, and through her vengeance, Kreimhild executes the legality that was illegally denied her by Gunther. The kings protected the murderer that the 'test of the bier' had revealed. This in a world in which legality was paramount. When she has Gunther killed, when she kills Hagen herself, the one who has been denied her rights restores legality. It was a restitution of the law in the act of breaking the law. This could link her again to Judith, who saved her people by killing Holofernes.)

He errs in his zeal (or his irony is overly subtle) perhaps too far in the direction opposite the scholarly norm here, when he calls the sword-bearing Kriemhild "ein Bild der richtenden Göttin" ("a representation of the goddess of justice"). Nevertheless it is significant, as he notes, that even as Hildebrand hacks her to pieces, the poet calls Kriemhild *daz edele wîp* (2377), which demonstrates "seine Distanz zum Geschehen, auch zum Männerverhalten" ("his distance to the event, and also to the actions of the men," p. 203).[7] Thus, according to Ehrismann, the poet "zeichnet Kriemhild als diejenige, die ihr Recht sucht in einer Gesellschaft, die es ihr verweigert" ("depicts Kriemhild as one who seeks her rights in a society that denies them to her," pp. 204–205). Schweikle also notes the ambiguity of the poet's representation, which clearly concerns itself with issues of female disempowerment and exploitation, but does so without so much as questioning the heroic-masculist perspective from which the whole narrative is conceived and related.[8]

---

7. Ehrismann also suggests that the surviving men do not lament Hagen's death, but rather simply the manner of it — that he was killed by a woman (p. 203).

8. Cf. Schweikle, "Im Schlußgeschehen wird vollends deutlich, was schon in den vorhergehenden 'âventiuren' angelegt ist: Kriemhild bildet zwar im Geschehnisablauf eine

The *Nibelungenlied* is a text that consciously confronts the problems of gender which were generated by the social changes of the eleventh and twelfth centuries and which were highlighted in the developing "courtly" literature of the period. It is obvious that among the most significant conflicts in the narrative, those that underlie the individual male duels, are those that occur between men and women (for example, Siegfried and Gunther versus Brünhild, Hagen versus Kriemhild). It seems just as obvious that the overwhelming tendency in modern scholarship has been to attack both Brünhild and Kriemhild, their actions, motives and achievements, all as part of a larger ideological project, conscious or not, to recuperate the hegemony which the poem's foregrounded inability — or refusal — to resolve gender conflicts calls into question.

As I have noted at various points in the argument, however, in the C-text of the *Nibelungenlied* there was already a thirteenth-century revisionist view of many of the problems addressed in the present study.[9] Perhaps even more blatantly, *Diu Klage* problematizes many of these same issues. In his study of the *Klage*'s generic affiliations, Hans Szklenar suggests that the text is not a *lament* (*Totenklage*), a sequel to the *Nibelungenlied* or a commentary on it, but rather a mixed genre (*Mischgattung*), consisting in part of all three, the point being: "'diu mære' so zu erzählen, daß der in ihnen verborgene Sinn deutlich hervortrete" ("to tell the tale such that the meaning hidden in it is revealed"), that is, in some sense as a corrective to the tradition of which *Nibelungenlied* was the prime contemporary representative.[10]

The primary contributions of the *Klage* to this thirteenth-century debate that are relevant to the issues of the present study are, to put

---

zentrale Figur, aber in ihrer Eigenschaft als Frau wird sie ganz aus der Perspektive eines männlich-heldischen Ethos betrachtet, in dessen 'ordo' der Frau nur ein nachgeordneter Platz zukommt — wie in der früh- und hochmittelalterlichen sozialen Realität" ("In the concluding events, that which was sketched out in previous *aventiuren* finally becomes clear: Kriemhild is in fact a central figure in the plot, but insofar as she is a woman, she is nonetheless viewed solely from the perspective of the male-heroic ethos, in which a woman can only have a subordinate role — as was also the case in the social reality of the early and high Middle Ages," "Das 'Nibelungenlied,'" pp. 72–73).

9. See also the defense of Kriemhild in the Latin sermon by Bertold von Regensburg (Leipzig Hs. 496, fol. 57e), cited by Wilhelm Grimm, *Die deutsche Heldensage,* 3rd ed. by R. Steig (Gütersloh: Bertelsmann, 1889), p. 181.

10. Hans Szklenar, "Die literarische Gattung der *Nibelungenklage,*" p. 57. G. T. Gillespie similarly suggests that "it seems appropriate to use the Kl[age] as a commentary, not only on the text which we have, but also on the story of the Nibelungen which was told and discussed among the circle of poets, listeners, and readers: the Kl analyses and explains in detail problems presented by the NL"; opinion differed on the interpretation of this "leading protagonist in the NL" (i.e., Kriemhild) and commentary was necessary; in "'Die Klage' as a Commentary on 'Das Nibelungenlied,'" in *Probleme mittelhochdeutscher Erzählformen. Marburger Colloquium 1969,* ed. P. F. Ganz and W. Schröder (Berlin: Schmidt, 1972), pp. 157–158

it bluntly (and the *Klage* does): Hagen is guilty of all the destruction that occurs in the narrative (625–627, 651), as a result of his *übermuot* ("pride" 2015).[11] Kriemhild, on the other hand, is innocent of wrong-doing, acted solely out of *triuwe* ("loyalty")[12] to her dead husband Siegfried (79, 415), sought vengeance only on Hagen (118–120, 131), and only *ordered* Hagen's death and did not kill him herself (1969). Thus her soul was taken to heaven at her death (286–288). The Burgundians died as a direct result of divine justice (635–641). Kriemhild's surviving foes in the *Nibelungenlied* regret their own wronging of Kriemhild: Hildebrand (1249–1254), whom the narrator claims killed Kriemhild *mit unsinne* ("senselessly" 366) and *ane not* ("without reason" 376); Dietrich grieves for Kriemhild and praises her *triuwe* (386ff.); Brünhild regrets having angered Kriemhild and thus having motivated events that led to Siegfried's death (1987–1991).

But despite the fact that the *Klage* gives greater emphasis to many of the fissures in the anti-Kriemhild case of the male characters of the *Nibelungenlied* and masculist scholarship, one must be cautious about construct-ing it as a feminist manifesto that opposes the *Nibelungenlied*'s position on a wide range of gender issues. These are, after all, thirteenth-century texts and do not contradict very many of the basic assumptions concerning gender held by their contemporaries. The narrator does recognize the strictly engendered code of vengeance: *ob si möhte sîn ein man, ir schaden, als ich mich verstân, / errochen manege stunde. geschehen ez niene kunde: wan si hæte vrowen lîp* ("had she been a man, she could have avenged herself many times, as I understand it; but it could not happen, because she had a female body / was a woman" 65–67), but assumes many of the same misogynistic notions inscribed in the *Nibelungenlied* and its modern reception. Amid its re-habilitation of Kriemhild and condemnation of Hagen, the *Klage* notes, for instance, that Blœdelîn's massacre of the unarmed squires was *durch eines wîbes lêre* ("by a woman's instruction" 168), and the entire catastrophe was due to *eines wîbes zorne* ("a woman's rage" 160). In a condescending move to spare Rüdiger's wife and daughter sorrow over the death of Rüdiger, Dietrich forbids the messengers sent to Worms to inform anyone at Pöch-larn about the catastrophe at court (1331 ff.).[13] Despite his heroic prowess,

---

11. He is also the only character in the *Klage* designated *vâlant* (625, C 1315) and *tievel* (658). On Hagen's pride in the *Klage*, see esp. Werner Hoffmann, *Das Nibelungenlied*, p. 118. *Diu Klage* is cited according to Karl Lachmann's edition.

12. See Francis G. Gentry, Triuwe *and* vriunt *in the* Nibelungenlied (Amsterdam: Rodopi, 1975) on the complexities of this semantic field.

13. Dietrich's wish to break the news himself, as he specifies, does not lessen the condescension of this withholding of what is hardly indifferent information. Gotelind actually does die soon after hearing the news (2115).

Hagen was slain by a woman, which, it is more than implied, serves him right, for it is the ultimate disgrace for a hero (370). Rüdiger, who is one of the more insidiously masculist figures in the *Nibelungenlied,* is here *vater aller tugende* ("father of all virtues" 1067). And after all, Kriemhild acted, according to the *Klage, solely* for the sake of *triuwe* to Siegfried, which then recuperates all her putatively independent, gender-defying action for the patriarchal code.

Despite these necessary qualifications, however, the *Klage* demonstrates—as does the C-text of the *Nibelungenlied*[14]—what the thirteenth century knew about the *Nibelungenlied,* and most nineteenth- and twentieth-century readers have forgotten, misunderstood, refused to believe, or have been prohibited from considering seriously: that the narrative is, to a significant extent if not primarily, about the social construction and imposition of gender roles and the inevitability of conflict arising out of this particular construction of them (whether we side with the *Klage*'s myopic condemnation of Hagen or not), and it is replete with undecidable ambiguities on almost all major issues, as the disagreements between the *Klage* and the various traditions of the *Nibelungenlied* on such issues indicate. Enforced simplification and resolution more often than not lead to the suppression of issues and to sterile dogma; open ambiguity often allows for pluralistic discussion without subscribing to the positivistic fiction of a single, final, and correct interpretation. Scholarship on the *Nibelungenlied* might well profit from the recent tendency toward accepting the undecidability of many of its prime issues.

Perhaps I might best conclude this consideration of the *Nibelungenlied* by returning to the narrative's initial scene of male deception of a woman (before the games in Iceland) and then spinning out some speculations in that illegitimate scholarly realm of what happened while they were "living happily ever after," which, in this case, means after the death of almost the entire cast.

> *Si sprach: "ist er dîn herre   unt bistu sîn man,*
> *diu spil, diu ich im teile,   getar er diu bestân,*
> *behabt er des die meisterschaft,   sô wird'ich sîn wîp,*
> *unt ist, daz ich gewinne,   ez gêt iu allen an den lîp."* (423)[15]

14. Here one might also note Theodore Andersson's comment that not just the *Klage* and C-text of the *Nibelungenlied* are revisionist of Kriemhild's reputation and character, but in fact so is the entire *Nibelungenlied* tradition, for there her actions are already narratively *motivated:* by the betrayal by Hagen and her brothers, 4½ years of isolation in Worms, and the loss of her "bridal price" (Andersson, *Preface,* p. 166).

15. C 432 is even more blunt: . . . *maisterschaft   so minne ich sinen lip   anders mvz er*

(She said: "If he is your lord, and you are his vassal, if he dares take part in the games that I will impose on him, and if he wins them, then I will become his wife; if, on the other hand, I win, it will cost all of you your lives.")

And in fact Siegfried is *not* Gunther's man, Gunther himself does *not* win the games, and all the men involved *do* die as a result of their lies to, deception and robbery of, and contempt for women. After the slaughter in Hunland, however, Brünhild, the initial victim of their misogyny, queen in Burgundy, queen mother of the young prince Siegfried (son of Gunther), and still ruling queen of Iceland *in absentia,* is safe at home in Worms. The Titan of the age, Siegfried, has long ago been eliminated, and now the entire clan of sometimes courageous, sometimes cowardly, lying and conniving, albeit wealthy and thus powerful, Burgundians, as well as their only political and military rivals, the Huns, lie dead in Hunland. In Worms, as the *Klage* informs us, Brünhild weeps for the dead.[16] As Seitter notes, there may be two sources of Brünhild's tears — grief, but also a desire expressed long before and now finally realized: "jetzt ist sie alle los. Sie wollte sich ja unverändlich alle Männer vom Leib halten. Diejenigen, die das nicht wahr haben wollten, hatten mit dem Leben bezahlt ('Now she is rid of them all. For originally she wanted to keep all men at a distance / away from her body. Those who refused to accept that have now paid with their lives," *Versprechen,* p. 53; cf. also p. 55). Seitter also reminds us that when Gunther journeyed east to his death, he did not leave Brünhild in charge, but rather delegated that power to the *Küchenmeister* (*Versprechen,* p. 47). Nonetheless, when the news of the Burgundians' annihilation arrives from Hunland, Brünhild in fact immediately assumes the throne and continues as regent even as her son's eventual claim on the throne is recognized.[17]

Heroic *action* as traditionally defined has been undermined by Brünhild's actions in part one and by Kriemhild's actions in part two; traditional heroic *narrative* has generally been undone by female participation as combatants, and as serious and threatening combatants. Such being the

---

sterben. ė ich werde sin wip (" . . . mastery, then I will have intercourse with him / consummate the relationship. Otherwise he will die before I will be his wife.")

16. Despite the fact that the *Klage* is transmitted in such a large percentage of the manuscripts of the *Nibelungenlied* traditions, and thus may well have been viewed by its medieval audience as the sequel, or maybe even the *aventiure* that follows Kriemhild's death (although the *Nibelungenlied* does have a clear colophon), I am only allowing myself momentarily and playfully to pretend that the *Klage* is the finale of the narrative of the *Nibelungenlied*.

17. *Klage* 1878–1879; in 2004–2005 and 2039–2040, however, the perceived need of a crowned king, even if still a child, is emphasized.

case, heroic *epic* as conventionally defined seems almost to have disintegrated before our very eyes, as Kriemhild dies a heroic death still called *daz edele wîp* by the narrator, and as Brünhild reigns in Burgundy. Traditional heroism on several levels has not *disappeared,* but rather been displaced and rendered obsolete and socially and historically superfluous. It is small wonder that the *Nibelungenlied* became the high point, and, for some scholars at least, the end point of German heroic epic. Hereafter only epigones or ironists could approach the genre. Perhaps even Wagner's *tour de force* testifies to this status, for he too looked not to the "domestic" *Nibelungenlied* but to the Nordic versions of the legend as his primary source.

In a significant sense, then, at the conclusion of this extraordinary sequence of narrative events, played out over the course of decades and across the length and breadth of Northern Europe, Brünhild (re)mounts the throne of Burgundy (and perhaps also Iceland) and, lacking all rivals, male or female, rules her world. Perhaps it is time, after the work of a score of scholarly decades from around the globe first to recognize the fact that the text's author, audience and age were able to problematize such issues and were interested in doing so, and then to continue (or begin) our own reconceiving of the text and our understanding of its relationship to its social and historically overdetermined context. For that is precisely what the full-scale political counter-attack of *Kudrun* attempts to do — to reconceive and recast the gender issues as articulated by the *Nibelungenlied.* To this thirteenth-century "masculist backlash" we must now turn.

7. Women, Sovereignty, and Class in *Kudrun*

Let us begin this consideration of *Kudrun*[1] as we did the initial consideration of the *Nibelungenlied,* with an illustrative summary of the *fabula,* or rather with several alternatives, beginning with one derived from Karl Stackmann's summary of the narrative:

> In successive generations, a young prince, supported by loyal troops, obtains, after many and varied adventures, a wife who is married to him with all courtly honors.[2]

But since my understanding of *Kudrun* and of its main character's social role differs from the traditional scholarly view, let us change the accents of the suggested *fabula* right away, so as to tip my political hand immediately:

> Successive generations of individual nubile females from a single lineage are wed by various means, all traditional and all including massive, calculated violence as one of its integral elements; the bride of the last generation affirms the legitimacy of this cycle of male initiated bridal suit, the exclusion of the bride-to-be from her own marriage arrangements, and mass destruction and vengeance in the name of marriage negotiations.

Or again, this time viewed from the perspective of inevitable comparison with the *Nibelungenlied*: the *Nibelungenlied* is about what happens

---

1. While the scholarly convention of naming this text *Kudrun* is a long and broad one, many university libraries in German-speaking Europe catalogue the text and its scholarship under the entry "Gudrun," and many scholars use his name as well. The unique Austro-Bavario-Tirolian manuscript names the eponymous character *Chaudrûn,* which we might thus interpret as a reflex of thirteenth-century *Kudrun,* as is conventional in the scholarship. I have chosen to retain this conventional title of the text and the character's name: *Kudrun* / Kudrun.

2. Cf. Karl Stackmann, "Einleitung," *Kudrun,* ed. Karl Bartsch, rev. 5th ed. by Stackmann (Wiesbaden: Brockhaus, 1980), xix: "Ein junger Fürst, unterstützt von treuen Mannen, erringt nach allerhand Abenteuern eine Frau, die ihm unter höfischen Ehren angetraut wird." Here he is expounding his conception of "variierende Wiederholung" ("variable repetition") according to which this single motif is worked out recurrently throughout the whole of *Kudrun.*

when men steal women's property; *Kudrun* is about what happens when men steal men's property, that is, women. All of the larger narrative units of *Kudrun* deal with the same problematic, for which the German term *Brautwerbung* exists. The English approximations most often employed by medievalists, such as "bridal quest," are imprecise substitutes. For this reason I choose here to use the verbals "wive/wiving," which have a literary tradition dating back to the Old English translation of Boethius's *Consolatio*.[3] The terms are here used to designate the various modes and methods of obtaining and marrying a wife.

There are a number of related problematics that make an examination of *Kudrun* a logical continuation of a study of the *Nibelungenlied*. In recent decades it has become, as Barbara Siebert notes, almost a "Glaubensbekenntnis" ("credo") of *Kudrun* scholarship that this work is an "anti-*Nibelungenlied*."[4] There are serious limitations, both theoretical and practical to the value of such a view, but there are a number of levels on which a close comparative analysis can be useful. Clearly, in terms of the present articulation of relations of gender, property, and power distribution, *Kudrun* is, among other things, a response to the *Nibelungenlied*. In both texts the focus is on the female characters and their field of action. But it is not the case that *Kudrun* responds to all or even most points of analysis treated in the examination of the *Nibelungenlied* above. Understandably, *Kudrun* conceives of the problems rather differently and thus constructs and resolves them differently. The two do not offer opposing views of the same problem, but rather two radically differing conceptions of what can, from one perspective in the late twentieth-century, be constructed as a single problem: the potential for a woman's independent control of her own life. The *Nibelungenlied* problematizes a society in which such independence is systematically and systemically denied; *Kudrun*, on the other hand, affirms

3. According to the OED, the verb "wive" may be used both intransitively and transitively to mean "to take a wife, get married, marry, furnish with a wife, obtain a wife for, to marry *to* a wife." Despite the seeming stylistic clumsiness of the term, it is semantically quite appropriate to the situation: the term has historically carried both a transitive sense (a man "wives" an object — woman) and also a middle sense (a man "wives" for himself, that is, obtains a wife *for his own use*). Additionally, rather surprisingly, one may also "wive" for another.

4. Barbara Siebert, *Rezeption und Produktion. Bezugssysteme in der "Kudrun,"* p. 1. Franz Bäuml's measured comment here is pertinent: "the *Kudrun* was not committed to parchment in a vacuum, and no text is thinkable without the system of antecedent texts. From that standpoint — whatever the unascertainable and irrelevant 'intention' of its poet may have been — it is impossible to consider the function of *Kudrun* without reference to the *Nibelungenlied*, a reference which, I think, inevitably casts it as an anti-*Nibelungenlied*" (rev. of Campbell, pp. 788–789).

the legitimacy of such denial and engages the complicity of its primary⸴
female characters in explicit acts that restrict female independence. Thus,
rather than viewing *Kudrun* either as an epigonal variation on the earlier
text or as a point-by-point argumentative refutation of it, it seems far more
fruitful to view the relation of the two texts as Barbara Siebert suggests
concerning *Kudrun*: "Dichtung mußte eigentlichen Ort der Auseinander-
setzung über Dichtung werden, Kritik wurde ins Kunstwerk eingebettet"
("Literature had to become the appropriate site for the confrontation with
literature, criticism was embedded in the work of art").[5] *Kudrun* is a
response to the *Nibelungenlied*, not strictly narratively, nor even thematically, but rather politically. It responds, among other things, to the articulation of gender and power that the *Nibelungenlied* deploys. *Kudrun* recognizes and problematizes the radical potential for restructuring gender roles
that is articulated in the *Nibelungenlied* by rejecting *a priori* that potential
and suppressing direct reference to it.

The relationship between the *Nibelungenlied* and *Kudrun* is complex
and exists on multiple levels, among them those of citation: verbal, thematic, and motivic. Emil Kettner has catalogued in meticulous detail the
verbal citations and reminiscences by *Kudrun* of the *Nibelungenlied*.[6] Many
of the most interesting and telling similarities between the two works, however,
are those which are inexact. One could say that the "citation" is inaccurate,
the "parallel" actually on a tangent, that the *Kudrun*-poet somehow has
made a "mistake." Obviously such an evaluation would simply end discussion of the topic and hardly do justice to the sophistication that recent
scholars have begun to impute to the *Kudrun*-poet as critical commentator
of the *Nibelungenlied* (if not as stellar poet in his own right). Thus, for
instance, in both works, the initially introduced focal character at first
refuses to marry; unlike in the *Nibelungenlied* (where it is Kriemhild),
however, in *Kudrun* it is a male, Prince Siegeband, who like many medieval
literary kings and princes, must be persuaded of the dynastic necessity of
legitimate heirs and thus of marriage. In *Kudrun*, a character named Hagen,
unlike his namesake in the *Nibelungenlied,* is not initially the foe of the
bride-to-be (as with Brünhild) only then to become the champion of the

---

5. Siebert, *Rezeption und Produktion*, p. 8. Werner Hoffmann also observes that *Kudrun*,
whatever its aesthetic deficiencies, is, like the *Nibelungenlied*, an *Ideendichtung;* in *Kudrun: Ein
Beitrag zur Deutung der Nachnibelungischen Heldendichtung*, p. 280.

6. Emil Kettner, "Der Einfluß des Nibelungenliedes auf die Gudrun," *ZfdPh* 23 (1891),
145–217; table of correspondences by strophe, pp. 207–217. He probably goes too far even for
the positivistic paradigm in which he works when he suggests that *Kudrun* poet had the
Nibelungenlied open on his desk while he wrote (p. 285).

subdued and compliant courtly bride; nor is he the grim foe of the demonized independent female (Kriemhild). Instead, he is the defender of his daughter, the bride-to-be, and he rejects as a son-in-law anyone weaker than himself (201), the *valant aller künige*[7] ("devil of all kings"/"most devilish of all kings") who prevents suitors from marrying a nubile female under his control. He has, then, momentarily at least, assumed a function quite similar to Brünhild's in defending her own independence in the *Nibelungenlied*. Like the *Nibelungenlied*'s Brünhild, *Kudrun*'s Hagen actively discourages suitors; like her he earns the title *valant(inne)* "devil" (male/female). For him, however, it is clearly an epithet of praise, respect, honor; there seems to be no irony in the text's juxtaposition of Hagen's decapitation of eighty citizens, guilty of what he deemed *vnbillichß* ("wrong" 194,2), and the evaluation that he was *ein ritter guot* ("a good knight" 196).[8] Wate in Ireland provides an "oblique parallel" to Siegfried in Iceland: both are generally rowdy, deceptive, and take the primary role in the "games." But the deceptions in Iceland become the acknowledged root cause of the final international catastrophe in the *Nibelungenlied*, while those in Ireland, precisely because they do not so function, are in effect legitimized as proper, or at least allowable, techniques of patriarchal wiving praxis. As in the *Nibelungenlied*, so in *Kudrun*, within a few stanzas of the heroine's introduction (Kriemhild/Kudrun), the mating game begins with the introduction of the first suitor — who is in each case named Siegfried, and who is in each case willing to fight for the bride (580). In *Kudrun*, this Siegfried is characterized by an essential alterity, but it does not consist of the superhuman strength or astonishing wealth of the Siegfried of the *Nibelungenlied*, but rather in the fact that he is a non-Christian moor, whose skin is initially said to be the color of dirt (*salbe* "dirty" 583,3). Needless to say, he will not win the heroine as bride.

As oblique rhymes are jarring to the ear and call attention to themselves,[9] so too these oblique parallels indicate that systematic departures are

7. The text of *Kudrun* is cited from Franz H. Bäuml, ed., *Kudrun: Die Handschrift;* with dual apparatus, one of which indicates all substantive emendations in the varied editorial history of the text. Mention of "editorial emendation" or "general editorial practice" hereinafter may be understood to refer to information included in Bäuml's apparatus unless otherwise specified.

8. Hagen also *hangs* twenty ambassadors who have come to present marriage suits for their lords, if the general (but highly suspect) editorial emendation of 202,1 *haben* "have/hold" to *hahen* "hang" is accepted.

9. A classic case of phonological *Verfremdungseffekt*, à la Brecht, or better *ostranenie* in Viktor Šklovsky's usage [О теории прозы (Moscow: Federatsia, 1929)]; cf. also Fredric Jameson, *The Prison House of Language: A Critical Account of Structuralism and Russian Formalism* (Princeton, NJ: Princeton University Press, 1972), pp. 75–79.

made from the *Nibelungenlied*'s perspective. This widespread technique of
inexact citation or imprecise parallel is obviously not unique to the relationship between *Kudrun* and the *Nibelungenlied,* but is a common feature of
open intertextuality, functioning here as it often does elsewhere: to guide
the immediate receptive potential by the *informed* audience, i.e. those who
know the *Nibelungenlied.* Such oblique parallels immediately evoke in the
audience a sense of recognition which is then almost immediately to be
disappointed or revealed as misrecognition: this Siegfried is not that Siegfried, this Hagen not that Hagen, this *valant* not that *valantinne.* Often
such mistaken identities, of character as well as motif, have comic potential
in literature (as elsewhere). Perhaps this was also the case in the initial
reception of *Kudrun:* before its reception was a matter of literary historical
archeology, it is just possible to imagine the audience's laughter at its
parody and subversion of the *Nibelungenlied.* In any case, however, the
effect is to heighten the contrast between the expected identity of motif or
character and the disjunction actually represented.

Given the general view of *Kudrun* as a response to, or simply as an
anti-*Nibelungenlied,* it would seem reasonable here to analyze the key issues
of the articulation of *Kudrun* as response to the *Nibelungenlied,* except that,
as mentioned above, the basic issues of gender and power are differentially
articulated in *Kudrun.* This different case then must be examined on its own
merits, albeit with constant reference both to the *Nibelungenlied,* as its
necessary ante-text, and to the scholarship that has consistently constructed
Kudrun's politics as progressive.[10] In *Kudrun,* it can be said with little
qualification, women's property is lacking as a significant political issue.
While lavish clothes and the conventional feudal-aristocratic demonstra-
tions of wealth and luxury as power are as intrusively ubiquitous in this text
as in any other in medieval European courtly literature, wealth itself does
not constitute the concrete and acknowledged basis of *women's* power that it
does in the *Nibelungenlied.*

There is one instance in the poem, however in which the type of female
control of significant and politically deployable, movable property known
from the *Nibelungenlied* (and elsewhere) is thematized. Gerlind promises

---

10. In recent years there has been, relatively speaking, a great deal of excellent and
directly pertinent work on *Kudrun* so that the articulation of the present case for *Kudrun* as a
response to the *Nibelungenlied* is far more straightforward than was the presentation of the
initial argument concerning the *Nibelungenlied.* To be mentioned here, and dealt with at more
length in the course of the argument are Theodor Nolte, *Das Kudrunepos — ein Frauenroman?;*
Ian R. Campbell, *Kudrun: A Critical Appreciation* (Cambridge: Cambridge University Press,
1978); Inga Wild, *Zur Überlieferung und Rezeption des "Kudrun"-Epos.*

to give gold and silver *to vassals* who help to obtain Kudrun as a bride for Hartmut.

> *Da sprach die teufelinne. nu het Er grossen solt.*
> *Welt Ir reyten hÿnne. mein Silber vnd mein golt.*
> *das wil ich geben rechn̄. vnd wil es entsagen Fraẘen.* (738)

(The she-devil spoke: he[11] would have great reward, if you would ride hence, my silver and my gold. I wish to give to warriors,[12] and wish to deny it to women)

It is not altogether clear why she would deny the gifts to women, unless it is simply that the gold and silver that stands at her disposal is a strictly limited amount, an "allowance," as it were, for maintaining her retinue of ladies, which, if given to male vassals would logically be denied the ladies.

There are numerous other "oblique quotations" of the *Nibelungenlied*'s treatment of various property motifs. Wate, for instance, refuses Hagen's offer of rich gifts at the point of the false departure (that is, before they kidnap the bride) because it would, he claims, make Wate's lord never forgive them for having taken gifts from another (potential) lord (434), the putative result being the dilution or dissolution of feudal ties. A more interesting oblique reference here seems, however, to be to the distribution — as despoliation — of Brünhild's treasure at the departure of Brünhild and Gunther from Iceland and later the despoliation of Kriemhild first by Siegfried and then again later by Rüdiger, where treasure and its function is vastly different, depending on who has it, and who is giving and receiving it. There is a further, problematic, and quite intriguing twist on this treasure / treasurer motif in the claim made by Wate during the bloodbath he draws in Kassiane.[13] He proclaims: *Jch bin Cammerere. sust kan ich frawen ziehen. Er schlů̊g jr ab das haubet* ("I am the treasurer[14]; therefore I can train / lead / entertain / take care of ladies. He cut off her head" 1528,3–4). This juxtaposition of Wate / treasurer / *frawen ziehen* / decapitation is, on the

---

11. Or: perhaps *ir* instead of *er*, thus "you" pl., as in the next clause.

12. Or "give for the sake of retaliation" *recken / rechen*.

13. While his wild rampage may bear some resemblance to that of a *berserkr*, that designation alone neither explains nor justifies such behavior in this completely different literary (and cultural) context but simply functions to trivialize and deracinate the act from its social context and consequences.

14. The term also designates not just the general "treasurer" of a court, but also the overseer of the woman's chamber (cf. Lexer), which, however, adds to the semantic freight of the primary connotation without altering its basic load.

face of it, enigmatic. Since Fruote is identified in 280,1 as treasurer, we should probably take Wate's claim here as strictly metaphorical. It seems likely that there is an oblique citation here of Dancwart's role as Brünhild's momentary treasurer in Iceland. Wate's assigned role here, then, is to educate females in proper behavior; Gerlind and Hergard have transgressed the bounds of propriety and must be punished, that is, "paid" by the treasurer. Perhaps also we should simply understand Wate's role as patriarchal "treasurer" here in the way that it functions in the *Nibelungenlied* as well: to despoil females. Here he deprives them of their heads.

The absence of women's property as a significant issue in *Kudrun* does not mean it has no political function in the society of *Kudrun,* but rather simply that this topic is suppressed. Women do not, it seems, have access to property in the first place, as do Kriemhild and Brünhild. Hence, they need not be deprived of it in order to render them powerless and thus amenable to or complicit with the patriarchal order. Dowry, inheritance, feudal rights of property simply do not appear in the text. Instead of attention to the effects of female control of property, *Kudrun* represents females *as* property (cf. especially st. 566). Perhaps the most succinct expression of female as male property appears in Herwig's challenge to Ludwig, which, in many senses, summarizes the basic conflict of the whole poem: the possession of females, as a constituent aspect of the praxis of movable property and thus of all claims to sovereignty:

> *Ich bin gehayssen Herwigk du namest mir mein weib.*
> *die müst du geben widere. oder vnser aines leib.*
> *müss darůmbe sterben. dartzů der Recken mere* (1435)

(My name is Herwig; you took my wife away from me. You must give her back, or one or the other of us will die, as will many other knights in addition)

The absence in *Kudrun* of female property as a significant component of the political structure on the basis of which gender definitions are constructed would obviously not *necessitate* the addition of a replacement component. But the fact is that another component does assume a far greater importance in *Kudrun* than had been the case in the *Nibelungenlied*: class — or better, intra-class status.[15] While class and status are by no means

15. McConnell's remark that, with the exception of the Hartmut case, "criteria of class or rank are of secondary importance in this tale" (*The Epic of Kudrun: A Critical Commentary*

absent from the *Nibelungenlied* and are at times even of crucial importance in plot motivation (particularly in the Siegfried/*eigenman* motif), they play a far less significant role in gender construction itself. By contrast, in *Kudrun,* class is of crucial significance in the primary motivating issue of the entire narrative: obtaining a mate appropriate to class, rank, and feudal status. In fact it seems not too much to claim that in *Kudrun* as opposed to the *Nibelungenlied,* the issue of gender has been overlaid with, and in part systematically displaced by, issues of intra-class status. Kudrun accepts the powerless and subordinate gender role assigned her by her patriarchal society. Her thematized suffering, however, is not due to the strictures of that subordinated gender role, for the most blatant signs of that subordination have been suppressed and those still present as integral aspects of the narrative are deemphasized. Rather her suffering is strictly status/class-determined: (1) she spends thirteen years of her life as the kidnap victim of a previously rejected marriage suitor who is (from her point of view) her feudal subordinate, and (2) she is forced to perform menial labor during that time.

As might already be anticipated, since the feudal political formation is essentially patriarchal, then its enhanced or expanded role in the constitution of gender politics at the expense of the issue of female property rights results in a significantly reduced spectrum of possibilities for female power and a greatly increased automaticity of female subordination to a "naturalized" masculist authority in *Kudrun.* Class rigidity is not the ally of female emancipation. This problematic can best be illustrated by analyzing one of its primary instances in the text: the initial wiving-episodes involving Kudrun. The qualifications of her suitors and the expectations and direct responses of Kudrun and her guardians are of great importance in determining the shape of the plot.

The first suitor is Siegfried (ms. Seÿfrid) of Morland. He is not to marry Kudrun and will play a minor, but recurring, role in the remainder of the narrative. Perhaps it is for this reason that his entire suit comprises only eight stanzas; perhaps that also explains why the episode opens not with a general introduction of Siegfried, or even an identification of him by name (which does not take place until the subsequent stanza), but rather com-

[Göppingen: Kümmerle, 1988], p. 54) illustrates the difficulties that conventional *Kudrun* scholarship has with issues of class. As will become clear in the course of the discussion, "the Hartmut case" is not the only site of the preeminence of the issue of class. But even if that were the case, one might still expect some significant scholarly attention to class since "the Hartmut case" comprises two thirds of the narrative.

mences immediately with Hetel's rejection of the unnamed suitor: *Er versagt Sÿ ainem künige* ("he denied her to a king" 579,1). His qualifications: he is a king of Morland and has seven further kings as vassals; he is *also reiche. daz dhainer wäre der ye geparte mit seiner tugende also lobebare* ("so noble/powerful that no one had ever borne himself with such praiseworthy heroic behavior" 579,3–4), *in siten ellenthafften. was verren bekannt* ("with respect to courageous character/deeds, he was known far and wide" 580,2); *es kund ein Ritter edele nÿmmer gefarn bas* ("a noble knight could never have borne himself better" 583,1); and incidentally: *er phlag jr mÿnne gerne* ("he eagerly cultivated her *minne*/paid her court" 583,4). Kudrun's response to the suit is not without promise: *Sy trůg im holdñ willen. offt thet Sÿ das* ("she held him in great favor"[16] 583,2). But to no avail: *da gab ÿms nyemand ze weibe* ("no one gave her to him to wife" 583,4). On the basis of the narrator's description of Siegfried, there is no reason to suspect that he is less than an appropriate match for Kudrun: he is royal, wealthy, virtuous, and apparently devoted to Kudrun; she seems not averse to his suit. But, it should be noted, merely suitable biographical qualifications are not necessarily determinative in literature (as elsewhere); the demands of the narrative and historical conditions also play a role.

One further item among Siegfried's qualifications is most likely also significant here, for, as noted above, and as the name of his homeland suggests, Siegfried is a "Moor," and he is black: *wie salber varbe er ware ze sehenne an seinem leibe* ("however dirty was the color of his body" 583,3). Or rather—he is black at this point in the narrative. Later, when he is reintroduced into the grand marital finale, cultural rules dictate that his alterity be effaced or reduced, and it is thus revealed that he is not black at all. There, in juxtaposed stanzas, his men are still *salbe* ("dirty" 1663,4), while he, it is now revealed, being the son of a mixed marriage, has *varbe cristenliche* ("christian color" 1664,2) and hair like spun gold. It is not said whether he is in fact christian or muslim, but for a text that can change the ethnicity, skin, and hair color of a character so easily, religious conversion would hardly present a problem (cf. Feirifeiz in Wolfram's *Parzival*). In the episode in which he is introduced, however, Siegfried is (still) black.[17]

16. One could legitimately go so far as "loyal affection" here on the basis of the expression's permissible semantic field, but that seems too extreme, although it may also have resonated for a thirteenth-century audience.

17. A comprehensive study of the representation of non-whites in medieval European literature is still lacking, but a cursory acquaintance with the material indicates the condescension and exoticizing of basic and essential racism. That racism is clearly evidenced in Siegfried's miraculous narrative racial "conversion" for the sake of marital suitability, and it may also already play a role in the construction of this initial episode's abbreviated form, with truncations front and back.

The second marital suit — by Hartmut — unlike Siegfried's before and Herwig's after, is a full-scale conventionally structured literary wiving episode, including the suitor's hearing of the princess and her beauty from afar, his parents' participation in the preparations for the suit, the sending of an official wiving embassy, and so on. While Siegfried and Herwig initially appear as scarcely more than the names — without attendent personalities — of stereotypical suitors, Hartmut appears immediately in as full a contoured characterization as one can expect in such a narrative. As for his qualifications: prince and king (*vogt/künig* 587–588) of the royal house of Ormanie, which possesses such vast territories and vassals that the loss of thirty castles and four thousand warriors during the Hegeling siege and the subsequent "mopping-up" operation is apparently easily forgotten.[18] The kingdom has a thousand castles of its own (1625) and so many vassals that the share of them Princess Ortrun will bring with her into marriage with Ortwin is substantial enough for Fruote to mention as a primary reason for Ortwin's accepting the match (1623). But, of course, all this information comes only much later. In the two *aventiuren* that present Hartmut's initial suit, a relatively great number of descriptive details are given about him: he is in possession of *hohe züchte* "the highest courtliness," worthy to court noble ladies with *edeler mÿnne* "noble *minne*," tall, handsome, merciful (622–623), cultured (627,1). In fact it almost seems that Hartmut is more than merely a qualified suitor. Just before his private, incognito interview with Kudrun, even the narrator feels moved to interject: *ich wais nit wes Er entgalt. daz jn versprochen hette die schöne tochter herren Hetteln vnd fraẅen Hilden* ("I do not know why he had to endure it, that lord Hetel and lady Hilde denied him their lovely daughter" 623,2–4). Nonetheless, this suit's seeds of failure had been sown long before, their fruit already noted at the outset of the episode, when Hartmut's father, Ludwig, observed that Kudrun's mother, Hilde, was from Ireland. That she was the daughter of Hagen, from whom he had received a fief and to whom he had incurred feudal obligations, he does not and need not mention to his relations, for whom it suffices to say: *das Volck ist vbermůte. Chaudrůn mag auch sy verschmahe* ("that crowd/clan is full of pride; Kudrun might well despise them too" 593,4).[19] Hartmut's determination, even so, to take her by force at the head of an army (594) recalls Siegfried's initial discussion of his suit for Kriemhild in the *Nibelungenlied*. His ambassadors are well-attired, well-

---

18. It is actually not altogether clear whether these dead are solely Norman or the casualties of both sides (1538).

19. This is a vexed line; my translation of the second half of the line is as suspect as the various other emendations documented by Bäuml's editorial apparatus (ad loc.).

equipped, noble, and apparently perform their assignment adequately. Although no oral report of the content of their letters to the Hegelings is made until after their proposal has already been rejected (without immediate explanation: *do hette man sy vil schmähe* "one held them there in quite low esteem" 606,3), at their departure one of the ambassadors states that Kudrun would be queen and wear the crown, and that Hartmut, incidentally, is free of all shame (609). This finally prompts a Hegeling justification, which had not, we might recall, been necessary in the rejection of Siegfried of Morland's suit (nor will it be at Herwig's first suit):

> *Da sprach Fraw Hilde wie lage Sy jm beÿ.*
> *Es legt mein Vater Hagene. Hundert vnd dreÿ.*
> *seinem Vater pùrge da ze karadine*
> *die lehen namen üble. von Ludwiges hennde die mage meine.* (610)[20]

(Then lady Hilde said, "how could she lie with him? My father Hagen gave his father one hundred and three castles in fief, there in Karadie. It would be grossly improper for my relations to receive those fiefs from Ludwig")

The Hegelings initially reject Hartmut's suit not because of any putative defect in Hartmut's *royal* credentials, nor do they make an issue of any possible difference in the size and extent of Norman versus Hegeling holdings.[21] Rather, the sole identified cause lies in the Norman King Ludwig's feudal subordination via the reception of fiefs from, and the consequent obligation of service to, Hilde's father, Hagen. Now what precisely, if

---

20. Hartmut recognizes that his alleged low status is the reason for his rejection by Kudrun (796); Hetel later also repeats the Hegeling view of the issue:

> *darumb daz ich vertzech.*
> *Im mein schöne tochter. Wol weste ich. daz im lech.*
> *dem künige aus Ormanie Hagne sein landt.*
> *darumb war Chaudrun hin ze jm nach Eeren nicht gewant.* (819)

(For this reason I denied him my lovely daugher: I knew well that Hagen gave the king of Ormanie his land in fief. For that reason, Kudrun would not be appropriate to his rank)

21. When the plot is viewed in retrospect, the simple and perhaps simplistic measure of status as a function of one's military accomplishments weighs more heavily in favor of the Hegelings (the fact that theirs are accomplished in alliance with two other kingdoms simply indicates the further extent of their power to forge or force useful military alliances) who conquer Ormanie, than of the Normans who only manage a kidnapping raid on a single castle while its defenders are in large part absent.

anything, that feudal contract between Hagen and Ludwig has to do with Hagen's granddaughter and Ludwig's son, remains unspecified. Hilde's comment suggests nonetheless that the lands assigned in fief are still so held. Thus, according to the construction of the Hegelings (but apparently not the Normans), Hartmut is below the Hegelings' station, which would entail the general reduction of Hegeling status and in particular of Kudrun's own specific rank as well as that of her children, should she marry Hartmut, since the offspring of a union belong to the husband's rank.[22] The problem of multiple feudal ties and cross-obligations is hardly uncommon, particularly in the late Middle Ages, and the niceties of rank calculation could become far more picayune than the simple point insisted upon by Hilde here. Under certain conditions and for certain considerations, however, that point could have also been overlooked. The Hegelings do not do so. This issue of "status equality" ("Ebenbürtigkeitsmotif," Stackmann xxxiii), then, forms the basis of the enduring conflict between the Hegelings and Normans.

The primary confrontational roles in the conflict as staged are not those of, for instance, the actual participants in the feudal relationship, Hagen and Ludwig, nor of the ranking instances of authority present, Hetel and Ludwig, or Hartmut and Ortwin. Instead, the conflict is played out primarily by Gerlind and Kudrun, the one maintaining Hartmut's equality, the other disputing it. Thus here too, as with the *eigenman*-motif in the *Nibelungenlied,* as fought out between Brünhild and Kriemhild, the essentially patriarchal class/status conflict between male political instances is displaced onto their female appurtenances. Herewith a tenet of male privilege, status maintained through marriage appropriate to rank, is displaced onto the females who, since they are culturally denied definitive participation in such conflicts, cannot resolve them. Ultimately their restricted participation makes them liable to reduction to the petty bickering that so effectively functions to legitimize the conventional patriarchal denial of female political capabilities. Simultaneously the males continue to benefit from the preservation and continuation of the practice, without ultimately having to take responsibility for the conflicts resulting from it.

The report of the Norman ambassadors, including a description of Kudrun's beauty, strengthens Hartmut's determination, while Gerlind

22. Thus when males marry "down" the offspring are still of *his* original rank; viz. the lack of concern for the marriage of the Hegeling prince/king Ortwin with the Norman princess Ortrun, or of Hartmuot with the royal but "rootless" Hildeburg at the end of the poem.

weeps openly. At this point she has still not been demonized by the text (her only epithet so far is *die alte Gerlint* ("the elderly Gerlind" 592,1). She responds to the unsuccessful wiving embassy: *awe vil liebes kindt. daz wir vnnser potñ. hin nach jr ye gesanden. wie gern ich das gelebte. daz ich sy sähe in disen Lannden* ("alas, dear child, that we ever sent our ambassadors for her. How very much I would have liked to see her in this country" 616,1–4). There is still nothing untoward about Gerlind's behavior; her words seem rather clearly to indicate that for her the episode has now ended.[23]

Subsequently, in his incognito visit to the Hegeling court in the eleventh *aventiure*, Hartmut manages without any narrative ado to have what seems to be a private audience with Kudrun, despite the fact that, as seems to be almost the entire point of the plot at this point, she is all but immured to seclude her from suitors. Her words indicate that Hartmut — whether simply as a man in her presence, or perhaps because he is already a rejected suitor — is in mortal danger (*Sy gunnde im wol ze lebenne* "she was in favor of his escaping with his life" 625,2). Kudrun's response to Hartmut and his suit is warm and human, but in no sense an indication of her consent:[24] she simply wishes to prevent Hetel from killing him (*daz Ir Jr hertze riet* "this her heart counseled her" 626,1). Finally there is an obscure and overdetermined couplet that demands more interpretation than it admits: *Sy was im doch genedig. der Er im hertzen gerte. Wie Sy Hartmûten seines willen vil lützel icht gewerte* ("She was well-disposed toward him, the one whom he desired with all his heart; but she granted Hartmut nothing at all of what he wished" 626,3–4). Thus she does not grant him his desire, but she does give — let us be cautious — *some* indication of her lack of displeasure with his suit. In any case the concrete result of the interview is a further strengthening of Hartmut's resolve, which will now be executed in the form of an armed expedition.

In referring to the expedition, the narrator at this point identifies

---

23. Stackmann's note (ad loc.), that she regrets only that the process has begun in this particular way, implying a plan for future action, lacks textual support and serves, here too, to enable a construction of Gerlind as full-scale villain, based on her later actions.

24. As has occasionally been suggested, usually in order to disparage Kudrun's modesty, loyalty or morals. Cf., however, Nolte: "Daß die Frau sich dem aggressiv auftretenden Werber nicht entziehen kann und sich ihm in Minne unterwirft, wie dies Kudrun andeutungsweise allen drei Werbern gegenüber tut, ist das Produkt einer speziellen *männlichen Phantasie.* Männliches Imponiergehabe, Eitelkeit und die Neigung zum gewaltsamen Sexualkonsum schlagen hier in kaum verhüllter Form durch" ("That the woman cannot withdraw from / escape the aggressive suitor and subjugates herself to him, which Kudrun at least by way of suggestion does with all three suitors, is the product of a specifically *male fantasy.* The male affectation to impress, vanity and the inclination to violent sexual consumption show through here in scarcely disguised form" p. 39).

Hartmut's intent as revenge (627,3), designates him *der vil grÿmme* ("the furious one" 629,3) and Gerlind[25] for the first time is called *die alte Vallentinne* ("the old she-devil" 629,4), who *das riet im ze allen zeiten* ("who thus advised him at all times" 629,4), which in context seems best to interpret as "she was a constant source of encouragement to him in his plan." These terms signal a clear shift in the narrator's characterization of the Normans, but that shift is also a function of the narrative structure of the plot, for this *aventiure* brings to a close a narrative unit: the initial suits of the three kings have now all been rejected and thus the courting stage of the narrative is completed; action will now replace negotiation, as Herwig's immediately subsequent kidnapping raid indicates. That Gerlind, and to some extent also Hartmut, will figure as villains is then foreshadowed by their epithets here. There is no need to pretend, however, that Gerlind's "counsel" is the source of the plan to kidnap Kudrun. That plan had already been conceived two stanzas earlier, at an identifiable point in the narrative that occurred logically and logistically *before* Hartmut returned to Ormanie and the possibility of seeking the counsel of his mother. It may seem a trivial point, but it deserves some attention since it has sometimes been assumed that Gerlind is responsible for the transformation of the noble, handsome, gentle, lovable Hartmut into the dastardly instrument of "her" kidnapping raid.

The final suit for Kudrun, and the one that is ultimately successful, is Herwig's, sandwiched between Hartmut's two visits to the court. He is initially introduced simply as a young, praiseworthy king who took great pains to court Kudrun (617–618), but by the end of the second stanza his suit has already been rejected by Hetel without any reported response by Kudrun. A third stanza reports his disappointment, and that is the end of the episode. More details are given later, after the interposed episode concerning Hartmut's incognito visit to Kudrun. Here Herwig is said to long for Kudrun as much as did Hartmut but was rewarded only with condescension and disdain, which prompted his anger and a military invasion (630–633). Few further characterizing details are added here: his land is near the Hegelings, his relations aid him in his suit, he is *küene* and commands a force of three thousand (630–633). The narrator's hint — *seyt gelag Er Chaûtrunen vil nahen* ("since then he has lain quite near Kudrun" 631,4) — in the midst of the Hegelings' continued disdain for Herwig's suit helps to explain what might otherwise be an enigmatic duality in Hilde's reaction to the invasion:

25. *Gottelint* in the manuscript.

Was sol ich dartzů sprechen wann alles gůt.
es duncket mich nicht vnbillich. ob ain Ritter thůt.
mit liebe vnd auch mit laide. daz man auf ere preÿse.
wie möchte im misselingen. Herwigk ist piderbe vnd weÿse. (636)

(What should I say to that, if not my approval. It seems to me not unjust, if a knight does what is honorably to be praised, whether it is friendly or hostile. How could he go wrong/however much he might go wrong, Herwig is capable and wise)

This is hardly the response one might expect of the queen to the news that a massive armed force has invaded the kingdom and is already at the castle's ramparts. In the ensuing battle, it may be, as most editors have construed, that Herwig seems *biderbe* "capable" to the watching Kudrun, which both pleases and displeases her: *der helt der dûhtes biderbe;   daz was ⟨ir⟩ beide liebe unde leide* ("the warrior seemed capable to her; that both pleased and distressed her" 644,4, Stackmann's ed.). But such a reading requires substantial emendation of the manuscript, which reads: *der helt der daucht sich biderbe. daß was baide lieb vnd laide.* The manuscript's *sich* and lack of the editorial *ir* make the usual interpretation anything but certain, although in all honesty one must assume that Herwig has more than merely caught Kudrun's eye here; otherwise her subsequent actions might seem to lack sufficient motivation. In calling for her father to end the duel with Herwig, she calls the invader *ain übel nachgepaûre* ("a bad/nasty neighbor" 650,4) and requests that the battle be interrupted until she can establish *Wo der Fürst Herwigke habende seÿ. die aller peste mage* where Lord Herwig has his splendid kin" (651,4). Perhaps *wo* here is better understood in the sense of *woher*—"how/whence he has such splendid kin," that is: she wants to determine what has thus far, in the narrative at least, not been clarified, and what the Hegelings rather improbably do not know about their "neighbor," namely Herwig's pedigree. In her words for the first time, he is already identified as *Fürst* "leader/ruler/*princeps*," and in the introduction of his next words, the narrator for the first time designates him *edel* "noble." When he (with his hundred knights) appears before Kudrun and her retinue, she is *getzweÿet mit jr můte* ("of two minds" 654,2), one must imagine: both pro and contra the (thus far) young, praiseworthy, capable, noble Prince who almost killed her father and has splattered the castle walls with the blood of her vassals (650).[26] In the next several stanzas a number of further details

26. Stackmann's designation of Herwig as Kudrun's *Geliebten* "beloved" at this point (ad 654) lacks textual support.

are added to his portrait: he is *gût* "good/noble," exhibits *ellen* "bravery" and *grosse zucht* "fine breeding," pleases (*behaget*) both mother and daughter, is as handsome as a master artist could create. Kudrun seems to express as much willingness for the match as modesty would allow: *holder dann ich euch ware. ist dhain weib magt. die jr ȳe gesahet* ("no woman you have ever seen, whether married or maid,[27] is more well-disposed/ friendly/ loyal/ subservient to you than I would be" 657,4). *Sy trûge jn im hertzen* ("she bore him in her heart" 658,4), and concretely: *Wolten die mir deß gùnnen. die nachsten freŵnde mein. nach ewres selber willen. wolte ich bey euch sein* ("if my relations would allow it, I would wish to be with you according to your own will" 658, 1–2). Hetel and Hilde now immediately grant Herwig permission to present his suit for Kudrun (659,2), and they are expressly interested in Kudrun's view (*die wolten hören baide ob seiner lieben tochter wäre lieb der gewerb. oder laide* "they both wished to hear whether the deal/suit pleased or displeased his daughter" 659,3–4). She replies indirectly, in response to Herwig's asking *Gerûchet jr mich mȳnnen* ("do you have in mind to/do you grant to *minnen* me?" 661,1) and interestingly avoids the concept of *minne* altogether, replacing it with what *seems* a more general one, but which, I would argue, actually betrays quite clearly the two specific issues in this scene: she promises that she will be *holt* to him (which carries a range of significations, as noted above: "well-disposed/ friendly/ loyal/ subservient"; here, obviously, the concrete sense of this polysemic adjective is "to marry") *and* proclaims that this will be an end to the feud. The blatant terms of the exchange are clear: *daz mir nȳemand laiden du solt ȳmmer haben mit mir wûnne*[28] "so that you harm no one else among my people, you will henceforth have your pleasure with me" 662,4. Finally Hetel insists on a direct reply to *his* earlier question, whether she wishes to marry Herwig, and she replies with the magnificently ambiguous—*jch wil mir nicht pessers Frundes mûten* ("I cannot imagine a better friend/companion/lover"/"I'd rather not think about the possibility of a obtaining better lover"/"In the absence of a better offer, why not?" 664,4). I do not wish to pretend that Kudrun's words mean "no," nor do I wish to impute that or anything else to her unknown and (for us) unfathomable "intention," nor do I wish to imply that only prosaic bluntness can be unequivocal. But the fact is that a "yes"—however expressed—would have been so much sim-

27. The doublet *weib magt* is unusual; *weib* is commonly deleted by editors; cf. Bäuml's apparatus ad loc.

28. It seems legitimate here, as is not uncommon in Middle High German, to construe the subject and finite verb (here *du solt*) with both the preceding and the following clauses, and thus with both infinitives, *laiden* and *haben*.

pler, and it would in addition have provided precisely that solid and unequivocal basis for interpretation and action that Herwig, Hetel, Hilde, and
generations of scholars have assumed was present in Kudrun's all but
univocal words. Kudrun's answer here is assigned an affirmative sense,
which in context is the only reasonable one, and it is — we should note — by
contrast to the answers she later makes to Hartmut's proposal of marriage
rather clearly so.[29]

I have thus far deferred discussion of one problematic passage in the
episode — during the audience of Herwig with the ladies — that requires
attention and deserves to be quoted in full:

> *Herwigk sprach zu der Frawen mir ist das gesait.*
> *doch het es mich gerawen. von meiner arbait.*
> *das ewch verschmahe. durch mein leichtes kůnne.*
> *offt beý den reichen. haben arme leûte gute wůnne.*
>
> *Sy sprach wer wëre die frawe. der verschmahet das.*
> *dero ein Helt so diente. daz Sy dem trüege hass.*
> *gelauhet mir sprach Chautrůn. daz es mir nicht verschmahet* (656–
>   657,2)

(Herwig said to the ladies: "It has been said to me (though I would
regret it, because of all the trouble I've gone to) that you find my
inferior kin despicable/look down on my inferior status. Often poor
people have great pleasure with the wealthy and powerful." She said:
"What kind of woman would despise that, that a hero served her so
well, that she hated him. Believe me," said lady Kudrun, "that I do not
despise it/find it dishonorable.")

29. It is thus only when she is already married (to Herwig) that Kudrun rejects outright
the proposed match (with Hartmut) — *Ee ich Hartmůten näme. ich wolt Ee wesen todt* ("before I
would take Hartmut, I'd rather be dead" 959,2); cf. also *sy wolte ee selber ersterben. Ee sy geläge
ymmer an künig Hartmůtes armen* ("she would rather die herself than ever lie in King
Hartmut's arms" 1084,4). In one instance, however, she rejects *minne* with any and all men:
Wann mir die vbel Gerlint so vil ze laide tůt. daz mich nicht mag gelusten. dhaines Recken mÿnne
("because the evil Gerlind causes me such great distress that I do not desire the *minne* of any
hero" 1027,2–3). In the *Nibelungenlied,* Brünhild offers her suitors death instead of marriage,
while Kudrun "offers" death only to herself. Actually she also notes elsewhere an alternative
precondition to her marrying Hartmut, again requiring death — only if Herwig were
dead could she accept Hartmut's offer. For Kudrun death is both an alternative to and almost a
precondition of marriage. In any case Kudrun's rejection of Hartmut is as concrete and
unambiguous a denial as is, much later, Hildegard's, just before she is forced — by Kudrun — to
marry him.

My attempts to force some coherence onto these grammatically, phraseo-
logically, and logically problematic lines via translation are hardly successful
in disguising the clumsiness of expression. It may well be that the text is
damaged, but it might also be the case that the text's clumsiness reflects the
characters' inevitable difficulties in discussing such delicate subject matter.
In any case, the precise meaning is probably no longer recoverable, but it
seems that Herwig thinks the Hegelings' earlier rejection of him to have
been caused by his low status (*durch mein leichtes kûnne*). Kudrun hastens to
deny that *it* is dishonorable to a lady. But is it in fact the case that Herwig's
lineage is of lower status? And if so, then how low, relatively speaking, is it?
Lower or higher, for example, than Hartmut's? I fear that we can find no
satisfactory answers to such questions, although the general editorial emendation of 656,4, reversing the order of *reich* and *arm* attempts, it seems to
me, to force an answer to the first question in the affirmative. In any case,
Herwig's house stands in no vassalar relationship with the Hegelings.

It may well be the case that not all information relevant to the Hegelings' choice of a husband for Kudrun has been reported by the text,
especially in matters of personalities and emotions. But such matters play a
far less significant role in medieval than modern literature (and an even less
significant one in the medieval life of the royal class than in its literature).[30]
Let me then summarize the primary issues and qualities involved. There is
little to distinguish the three candidates' general qualities; they are all royal,
noble, and knightly. Siegfried, however, as the *narrator* observes, is from
Morland and is, at least initially, black and most likely muslim. Hartmut, as
Hilde insists, is a feudal subordinate to the Hegeling house. Herwig, as
(apparently) both *he himself* and *Kudrun* acknowledge, is of a lineage with
low status. Kudrun marries Herwig. Why? While I have already given more
emphasis to Siegfried's race and religion than does the narrator in the whole
tale, perhaps the culture's racism was sufficient for their mere mention to
justify his summary rejection. But why is the inferior Herwig preferred to
the inferior Hartmut? An immediate and unreflected answer might be that
Hartmut is — as the later course of the narrative develops — "unattractive"
because he kills Hetel, kidnaps Kudrun, and tries (for years) to force

---

30. Cf. Hindess and Hirst: "This naive egocentric mode of analysis [sc. Meillassoux,
Anthropologie, p. 223] is clearly inadequate; social relations cannot be explained by the feelings
of participants. The very possibility of these conflicting desires on the part of the elder are an
effect of the system of marriage exchanges and could not arise in the absence of that system.
The system itself cannot be the product of a contingent balance of forces between these
desires" (*Pre-Capitalist Modes of Production*, p. 78).

marriage on her. But then, after all, that takes place only after Herwig has married her.

Perhaps the best answer (for there may well be more than one legitimate one) is simply—in a realpolitical sense—Kudrun "willingly" marries Herwig because it seems rather likely at the moment in the battle at which she intervenes that otherwise her father will be killed, the castle destroyed, perhaps the entire kingdom plundered, *and* she will raped and forced into marriage with the victorious Herwig anyway. As her words at *the* key moment in the negotiations indicate, she is exchanged for peace. The answer to why she does not marry Hartmut is then simple, though double: when Hartmut with his army arrives on the scene, the military invasion to kidnap and force marriage on Kudrun has already been successfully carried out by Herwig.

But the case is, alas, not a simple one. On the one hand, the specific nature of Hartmut's class inferiority to the Hegelings—that he is (in some sense) a feudal subordinate—clearly outweighs, in the Hegeling view (which is, after all, the only one that counts when it is a matter of dealing out Kudrun as a bride), the vague and putative inferiority of Herwig. On the other hand, since the Hegelings refuse Kudrun to the entire lot of suitors (which, according to patriarchal convention, they have a perfect right to do), the apparently *only* possible means of gaining her as bride is by force, which, likewise according to convention, seems the logical if not necessary next step for any given rejected suitor. As Nolte points out, during some periods in the Middle Ages in central Europe bridal-kidnapping was often provoked by a feud and often provoked another one in its turn (pp. 14–17).[31] If the kidnapped woman was successfully retained, then she was usually married into the robber clan. The marriage was recognized as legal because of the publicly acknowledged consummation and cohabitation. The consent of the female was a possibility, but not necessary. If her guardians succeeded in getting her back from the kidnappers, the marriage was void. If the guardians accepted an atonement-payment, reconciliation and marriage could result. From the fifth to the ninth century, *Raubehe* was common; thereafter rulers no longer tolerated it. Lothar von Dargun further comments on a situation that will become important in *Kudrun*

31. On the legal status of bride-rape, see especially Rudolf Köstler, "Raub-, Kauf- und Friedelehe bei den Germanen," *Zeitschrift für Rechtsgeschichte,* germ. Abt. 63 (1943), 92–136; Paul Mikat, "Ehe," *Handwörterbuch zur deutschen Rechtsgeschichte,* ed. Adalbert Erler and Ekkehard Kaufmann (Berlin: E. Schmidt, 1971) I, 809–833; Lothar von Dargun, *Mutterrecht und Raubehe und ihre Reste im germanischen Recht und Leben* (Breslau: W. Koebner, 1883).

(p. 112): according to Lombard, Alemannic, and Frankish law, a prior betrothal is voided if the bride is subsequently kidnapped by a different bridegroom. According to Alemannic and Anglo-Saxon law, even a prior marriage is voided by such bridal-kidnapping. In any case, for Hartmut's marriage to Kudrun to be legal, she would have to consent, otherwise the engagement to Herwig could not be voided. Dargun notes that by 1000 such marriages were rare but not completely suppressed. Particularly widows with rich possessions were under the constant threat of such kidnapping by men who could thus seize their possessions.

In any case, bridal-kidnapping is the "method" employed by Herwig (with deflected, but ultimate success), by Siegfried (ineptly, since not directed at the female prize, but rather at her already *semi*-successful captor, Herwig), and by Hartmut (too late and ultimately without success). But then, if one takes stock of the situation at the mid-point, after Herwig has married Kudrun,[32] after he has responded to Siegfried's impotent raid, after Hartmut has killed Hetel and kidnapped Kudrun, then the "score" is hardly clear: Siegfried, Hartmut, and Herwig have all been rejected as peaceful suitors. Herwig has been successful as potential wiver-kidnapper — or rather, as noted above, only *semi*-successful, for in fact he goes home without Kudrun.[33] He possesses her "legally" but not in fact. Siegfried apparently misperceives either the demands of the system or the actualities of the situation, for his raid on Herwig either for the sake of revenge on the successful suitor or in order to kidnap the still desired bride is necessarily unsuccessful on the second count since Kudrun is not in Herwig's possession, and due to his newly gained alliances, Herwig is also able to repulse Siegfried's aggression and thwart the first desire as well. Hartmut, finally, because of Herwig's success, has himself no real hope of success, for the prize has already been bestowed, Kudrun already married. Thus he goes home without legal possession of a bride, but with actual

---

32. According to Gunther Grimm, Kudrun is not merely engaged but in fact already legally married to Herwig at the point when she is kidnapped by Hartmut ("Die Eheschließungen," in der Kudrun: Zur Frage der Verlobten-oder Gattentreue Kudruns," *ZfdPh* 90 [1971], 4 p. 69; cf. on this point also Frenkel, p. 343). Thus while she may still be praised for constancy, her subsequent refusal to marry Hartmut is not really a matter of free choice on her part: were she to accede to Hartmut's wishes, it would, from her perspective, constitute adultery (1043). In any case, her accomplishment is not less for her remaining faithful to her husband, but simply different than had she remained true to a marriage engagement or a "longed-for" beloved.

33. He is told that he should *mit schönen weÿben vertribe annderswo* ("fool around with beautiful women elsewhere" 667,2) for a year before returning to accept delivery of his bride.

possession of Kudrun. Possession is problematized; marriage suddenly becomes a quandary not a solution.

The focus on issues of class seems, in this complicated course of events, to have blurred, so that mundane praxis — physical possession — displaces all other considerations. But that would be succumbing to a simple empirical model. Herwig does not win Kudrun accidentally, not by chance, not because he *happened* to think of rape as the means to cut this Gordian knot, while Siegfried happened not to do so and Hartmut happened not to do so until it was too late. Rather, Herwig was successful both initially (or rather, secondarily, as it turns out) and finally in possessing Kudrun because he was somehow the narratively *appropriate* choice for Kudrun's husband, or as the mythic construct of the notion of courtly *aventiure* has it, the hero appropriate for this *aventiure*. The Homeric Achilles, for instance, is not a lesser hero because he has divine aid, but rather he receives divine aid precisely because and to the extent that he is a greater hero. Herwig is also the chosen one. His other positive attributes both contribute to that status and are simultaneously a direct result of it. To pretend that it is all only a matter of class and status considerations would be no more accurate than merely to affirm the legitimacy of the patriarchal right to traffic in women. Class bonds, however, to play the primary role and it clearly determines the course of Kudrun's future, both in the consequences of the Hegelings' rejection of Hartmut and their acceptance of Herwig.

The narratively and ideologically determinative deployment of class in *Kudrun* is found also in Kudrun's situation in Ormanie, which illustrates *in nuce* the issues of the entire narrative. It also seems that, because the Hegelings and especially Kudrun insist on the loss of status consequent on a marriage to Hartmut as the determinative issue, her further refusal to accept the *fait accompli* of her loss of father, home, husband, and independence, and her forced and actual presence at the Norman court under the control of Hartmut and his relations, Kudrun is condemned to a far greater loss of status than a marriage to Hartmut could ever have entailed. Instead of being queen in Ormanie, she has become laundress to the queen in Ormanie.[34] Generations of Germanists have praised Kudrun for her noble stand on principle and have even developed new definitions of heroic

---

34. Nolte remarks: "Die Dichtung nimmt hier, wie Gert Kaiser betont, reale Angste des Adels vor sozialer Deklassierung auf" ("The poem here takes up, as Gerd Kaiser emphasizes, actual anxieties on the part of the nobility concerning loss of class status"); *Das Kudrunepos — ein Frauenroman,* p. 50; cf. Kaiser, "Deutsche Heldenepik," in *Neues Handbuch der Literaturwissenschaft,* ed. Klaus von See, vol. 7: *Europäisches Hochmittelalter,* ed. Henning Krauss (Wiesbaden: Athenaion, 1981), pp. 181–216, here p. 211.

literature and heroism to encompass her loss of status and consequent suffering *as* heroism.[35] The text more than once reminds the reader of the class-based torture of the heroine. Condemned to do housework, the noble ladies do not "enjoy" their nobility: *ja mocht sy jrs adelß nicht geniessen* ("she [Hergard] could indeed not enjoy the benefits of her nobility" 1007,4);[36] *man het sy vnd kuniges kind nicht gleiche* ("she [Kudrun] was not treated like the daughter of a king" 1021,4). Kudrun recognizes that her humiliation, indeed transgression, at being found by the Hegelings as laundress will be unexpungeable: *das laster kunde ich nymmer überwinden* ("I could never overcome that dishonor" 1208,4). She immediately inquires of her companion Hildeburg *sol ich von hynnen weichñ. oder lassen mich hie vinden. in disen grossen schannden. Ee wolt ich hie ymmer haÿssen ingesinden* ("should I flee hence, or allow myself to be found here in this great dishonor? I would rather always be called a servant here" 1209, 3–4). Kudrun thus finds the prospect of being seen at her chores by someone other than her captors so horrendous that she considers something that, even in this restricted sense, she has apparently not considered in the previous thirteen years of her captivity: flight, not from her captors, but from her *liberators*. Such power does class consciousness have here. Furthermore, rather than undergo the humiliation of being found, as a queen, engaged in such work, she would prefer to renounce forever her status and become (or rather simply "be called") *ingesinde*. That is, she would finally acknowledge her present condition as a permanent one, for she *is* presently a servant. In fact she then does flee the intruders and must be coaxed into returning to talk to them. When they later learn of this scene, Kudrun's *mage* in the army weep because of how *her* humiliation shames *them* (*nu gedencket alle jr mage. ob vnns das sey ain schande* (1341,3).[37]

While it is generally difficult to carry out *detailed* analysis of class structures in medieval heroic and courtly genres because of their almost exclusive focus on the royal rank (often with some ancillary attention given to the high vassalar nobility), *Kudrun* offers slightly more of a purchase.

35. Cf., for instance, Roswitha Wisniewski, *Kudrun* (2nd ed, Stuttgart: Metzler, 1969), p. 64; McConnell calls her "defiance" heroism (*Epic of Kudrun,* p. 74); Hoffmann finds heroism in her patience (*Kudrun: Ein Beitrag,* p. 285).

36. This line refers to Hergard's carrying water to Ortrun's chamber. It is interesting that this humiliated noble Hegeling is later murdered by Wate because she *nam. des Jungen kuniges Schencken durch hohe mÿnne* ("accepted gifts from the young king for the sake of *hohe minne*" 1526,4), while Ortrun, the enemy she serves, is rehabilitated and annexed into the hegemonic domain of the Hegelings, by marriage to their "young king."

37. Wate immediately counters that they are weeping *allen weyben. vil gleiche* ("just like all women" 1342,3), which is, well, shameful.

Generally in such medieval literary genres, the vassalar ranks rarely play individual roles in the narrative, and in all cases in *Kudrun* and the *Nibelungenlied* their narrative lives are quite simply expendable. In *Kudrun* there are several illustrative instances of this issue. First, the masses of sub-royal battle casualties get predictably short shrift from the narrative and no more attention from the scholarly tradition. Siebert (among others), for instance, claims that Hegeling vengeance stops before it becomes "maßlos" ("extreme/immoderate" p. 170).[38] The corresponding female class issue arises with respect to the royal retinue of maidens. Whether Ortwin liberates Kudrun and Hildeburg on the beach or not, the Hegeling retinue remains captive — through the siege and its aftermath — without effective Hegeling protection. At no point in the narrative has their well-being been a matter of importance. Generally the queen's/princess's retinue in courtly literature is rather poorly treated, and that treatment is rarely the subject of comment either by narrator or modern scholar. Siebert suggests concerning the twenty maidens kidnapped along with Hilde in the previous generation that Hilde's ultimate consent to marriage is decisive (*entscheidend*), regardless of the wishes of the members of the retinue (p. 103); "decisive" obviously for the actions, for the narrator, and probably for (most of) the original audience of the narrative. But our assumption of that stance clearly makes us complicit in the class system and its obvious inequities that make political subordinates prey to such arbitrary acts of depredation. Nolte comments incisively on this problem that since the maidens of the retinue do not give their consent (indeed are not asked for it), then despite Hilde's consent, this *Brautentführung* simultaneously constitutes *Frauenraub* (*Kudrun*, pp. 35–36).

The potential fate of the members of the retinue also becomes clear to us in the case of Hergard. She is kidnapped along with Kudrun, is forced to perform manual labor as are the others, remains in captivity for thirteen years with, up to the eve of liberation, no end in sight and no reasonable expectation of a change or of liberation. Apparently somewhere along the way she decides to accept the fact that she is living in Ormanie, has been living in Ormanie for over a decade, and is likely to continue to do so for decades to come. She decides to make a life for herself in the land of her

---

38. Which opens numerous problematic issues, to be dealt with below. In any case, we should not misunderstand such claims as an apology for *feudal* class ideology of the thirteenth century, but rather as a twentieth-century bourgeois denial of the general significance of class analysis in literary criticism. In each case the privileged class, of which the "definers" are members, relieves itself of responsibility.

captivity. It is neither an unprecedented decision nor one that would lack legitimacy should Kudrun, the lady whom she serves, make the same decision, as, for instance, Hilde had done in the previous generation.[39] Thus Hergard has only two hopes for "happiness": either Kudrun relents and consents to marriage/adultery with Hartmut, which would then presumably legitimize the possibility of relations between members of her retinue and other Normans; or, if Kudrun continues to reject Hartmut, and Hergard nevertheless makes a life for herself in Normandy, then she can only hope that their captivity never ends. In either case the decision of Kudrun as her political superior is decisive for and binding on Hergard. Should she nonetheless attempt to free herself from the miseries of slavery by means of collaboration with the Normans, her greatest danger will be liberation by her countrymen, for then she will be seen as a collaborator, which — with respect to women — always carries with it a sexual charge, and thus constitutes a betrayal of a male proprietary relation. In this case, while the princess/wife remained "true" and sexually "untainted," the maid "succumbed to temptation," as it were and "accepted gifts from the young king for the sake of *minne*." Hergard, who may have enjoyed the sexual attentions of Hartmut (the text is delightfully ambiguous here),[40] then dies the same death as does Gerlind, who promoted the cause of Kudrun's marriage to Hartmut. Hildeburg, the only other of Kudrun's retinue in Ormanie who is named, does not accept Hartmut's gifts for the sake of *minne* before the liberation, and as a result of that loyal behavior is presented by Kudrun to Hartmut as a gift of *minne* after the liberation.

While we post-feudal readers can range from sentimental nostalgic sympathy for Kudrun's class humiliation to mild amusement to the savvy disdain of the *sans culottes,* such reactions too are generally also colored by gender considerations, for the corresponding genuflections before the conventions of class definition, as embodied in the knightly code of honor practiced by Ortwin, are, from a cynical post-feudal perspective no less ridiculous and no less disastrous. For despite the grief at the death of his father, the anguish at the kidnapping of his sister, the humiliation at her treatment in Ormanie, despite the years of waiting for the possibility of regaining Kudrun, Ortwin's honor does not allow him simply to take her and Hildeburg back to his camp from his encounter with them on the

39. Obviously the fact that Kudrun is already married here complicates matters.
40. The identity of her benefactor is rather clearly Hartmut (*des Jungen kuniges Schencken*), but it is not clear whether his gifts to her are for the sake of winning *her* affections or those of Kudrun via Hergard's influence.

beach; they must rather be sent back into the clutches of the enemy and then be liberated by force of arms. However contradictory this ethos and its pragmatic consequences may seem to the modern reader — rather than taking his sister now, he sends her back to the castle where she must survive both the siege and the predictible ire of the castle's defenders in their moment of defeat, should defeat come, and the blind rage and indiscriminate destruction that so often (here too) accompany the victors' final breaching of the walls[41] — the most remarkable aspect of Ortwin's action is his means of expressing his abhorrence of the idea of liberating Kudrun immediately on the beach: *Vnd het ich Hundert Swester. die liess ich sterben. Ee daz ich mich also starche in frombden lannden häle. die man mir mit sturme näme daz ich die meinen grymmen veinden stäle* ("and if I had a hundred sisters, I would let them die, before I would sneak around in a foreign country to the extent that I would steal from my hostile enemy what he had taken from me in battle" 1256,2–4).[42] He thus acknowledges that the entire thirteen-year-long affair is far less a matter of his sister's life and liberty than it is of his own honor. Just as the Hegelings plundered and kidnapped the pilgrims (and will now let them die in battle) for the sake of their cause, now Ortwin claims that he would also let a hundred (albeit fictive) sisters die rather than compromise his own honor. Thus his flesh and blood sister, who is freed from thirteen years of captivity and in his hands, is sent back into captivity and the uncertainties of a siege and its aftermath. Dare I recall here that not a few scholars have suggested that Kudrun is independent, indeed a model of the independent and sovereign woman?

To this issue we must now turn: the issue of female independence or sovereignty is the inevitable obverse of the displacement of female control of property and the insistence on intra-class status — *as dependent* on husband's status — as the defining feature of the female's own status, both feudal and general. Perhaps the most ubiquitous tenet of *Kudrun*-scholarship is that the female characters of the narrative are powerful,

---

41. The order to kill all the hostages does in fact come (1471), and when Kudrun sees the naked sword approaching, she, for the second time (understandably), wilts at the prospect of physical danger: *Sy vergasß ain tail jrer zucht. wie laůte sÿ schre. als ob sy ersterben solte. die angst tet jr wee* ("she forgot a part of her manners/decorum/courteous conduct. How loud she screamed, as if she were about to die; her fear distressed her" 1474,1–2).

42. A similarly illogical and seemingly counterproductive threat is made by Wate, when Kudrun refuses to betray Gerlind to him (this is Kudrun's second deliberate and blatant lie, the promise to marry Hartmut being the first; it too has a strategic, and here, humanitarian, purpose): he simply remarks that he will kill all the women, apparently Hegeling (including Kudrun?) as well as Norman, in order to ensure that Gerlind is among the dead (1520,3–4). Since this scene immediately follows his slaughter of the infants, there seems little reason to doubt his word.

independent, or sovereign; often this notion is expressed as a contrast with the putatively weak females of the *Nibelungenlied*. Sometimes this complex is an a priori assumption, sometimes an actual point of argument. Winder McConnell exemplifies the tendency:

> Unlike many of his contemporaries, the author of *Kudrun* appears to have assumed a stance towards women which allowed him to view them as more than objects. Regardless of who the poet was, the position taken is strikingly pro-female, the machinations of Gerlind notwithstanding. That, in itself, is remarkable in a work emanating from thirteenth-century Germany. While it is common in the literature of the period for a woman to display attributes that are thoroughly laudable in nature, the accent is invariably on the benefits, spiritual or otherwise, that her lover or husband might derive from his association with her. *Kudrun* most certainly contains edifying characteristics of this sort, but it stands out from other works in that it goes beyond them, allowing the women to assume a degree of sovereignty that was hardly to be expected in the literature of that time. (p. 4)
>
> One of the more unique [*sic*] characteristics of the work is the degree to which the female protagonist is *not* portrayed as a mere object, but rather as an individual whose independent judgment, inner strength, and uncompromising sovereignty over her own destiny stand in marked contrast to the object-status of so many of her counterparts in the fiction of the period.... [Kudrun] represents the culmination of a series of female figures, each of whom exhibits increasing levels of independence or sovereignty. (p. 90)

There are a number of important points to be made here, some obvious and not necessarily ones which McConnell or others of this school would oppose, others somewhat less obvious. First, since the primary theme of *Kudrun* is "wiving," there is nothing unusual about its focus on the females, although such a theme would not preclude a focus on male characters (as the wiving episodes of the *Nibelungenlied* demonstrate). In *Kudrun,* however, female characters play a major role through the generations. The mere fact of their significant *presence* as characters, however, does not in itself predispose them to be more or less "independent" or "sovereign" than, for instance, the narratively perhaps less prominent female characters of any other narrative, although the fact that they play more extensive roles *does*, as McConnell points out, calls our attention to what is still a narrative anomaly in thirteenth-century central Europe. Nonetheless, characterizing a female figure as "sovereign" makes very specific claims about her actions, her interaction with others, the social and political contexts of those actions, and their consequences. McConnell does not identify a character's mere presence with her actual independence, but his *conception* of the term "sovereignty" is vague, while the *practice* of *Kudrun* is quite specific, consistent, and completely at odds with his suggestions. His argument relates here to the notion that ruling kings in this text, as in a wide variety of narratives of this period, are depicted as ineffective. He refers to Edward Peters's excellent study of the "weak king topos" in medieval history and its representational texts,[43] where it is noted: "Secular literature is aristocratic rather than royal, and it reflects better than many other sources the aristocratic view of kingship in the twelfth century" (p. 95). This commonplace ineffectiveness of the king in medieval epic literature, from Hrothgar to Gunther to Etzel to Arthur (and beyond), however, does not in itself necessitate that this power vacuum be filled by a woman. Nor does the presence of extensive female roles in conjunction with ineffective kingship necessitate that the females be sovereign. While one might legitimately suggest that precisely this conjunction of weak male and extensive female roles offers the potential for and even a suggestion of an augmentation of female sovereignty, I would respond that it is precisely this potential that is then wholly rejected in *Kudrun*. The constructed potential for female sovereignty, when rejected, is then a starker denial of all female independence, than its tacit suppression in the first place would have been. To be specific: In the absence of strong kings, important female characters *could* take over the ruling roles, but in *Kudrun* they do not do so. Instead it seems that those issues over which they do assume control—in demonstrative and stage-filling fashion—are either precisely restricted to traditional spheres of female control or that their "sovereign" acts consistently reproduce that most insidious of all patriarchal gender-role constructs, in which men grant certain limited freedom of action to selected *conformist* females like Kudrun, thus creating a momentary, illusory sovereignty that serves in all contexts, literary and otherwise, to defuse further female demands for actual and broad-based independence. Kudrun in fact does very little for herself; men do it for her. And what she does is almost exclusively for the direct benefit of the men in her life, or the maintenance of the conventional gender structures of which each of those men is the automatic beneficiary. Her primary "sovereign" act—rejecting Hartmut's suit—is not performed in order to guarantee her own independence in any sense, but rather 1) because she is already party to a marriage contracted and executed; and 2) despite whatever participation Kudrun has in the pre-negotiations leading to that marriage—and she does participate at a *significant* level during that crisis situation—ultimately the conventions of normalcy again intrude and gov-

43. Peters, *The Shadow King: Rex Inutilis in Medieval Law and Literature 751–1327* (New Haven, CT: Yale University Press, 1970).

ern the remainder of the marital transaction, so that in the end she does little
more than accept her parents' offer of a husband.[44] This act seems neither
particularly sovereign nor indicative of independence or free will. And
certainly if one views this as an individual illustration of a societal pattern
(which necessarily must be the case, since the wiving thematic recurs nine
times in the work over the course of four generations), then Kudrun not
only does not break with conventional patterns of female subordination to
a male-dominated marriage system (Sanday's "traffic in women"), but
rather, like most other brides in the work,[45] participates wholeheartedly in
the system, even outdoing her predecessors, by assuming momentarily the
patriarchal role, insofar as, near the end of the narrative, she actively
engages in the practice of arbitrary wiving against, or regardless of, the will
of the brides. In her acting as "coupler," we must acknowledge some
measure of independence on her part, but if that action is directly support-
ive of conventional patriarchal wiving practice, then it is a deceptive or
simply self-destructive illusory independence so effective for and essential
to the long-term maintenance of male hegemony.[46]

There are other possible means to argue for sovereignty, however,
beyond *personal* independence. The most obvious one concerns whether
the given women of the royal class in a feudal society exercise power or
command authority in the political sphere. Much has been made of this
question by *Kudrun*-scholarship (albeit stated in other terms, as McConnell's example illustrates), but with the exception of Hilde's titular rule, no
female in *Kudrun* rules independently or as a significant partner to rule.
Particularly when one compares such roles in *Kudrun* with the corresponding roles in the *Nibelungenlied,* then the relative sovereignty of female
royalty in *Kudrun* is hardly worthy of mention. Let us first consider the
two supporting characters most often cited as examples of sovereign, ruling queens—Gerlind and Hilde—and then proceed to a consideration of
Kudrun herself.

Campbell, for instance, implies (pp. 202, 209) that Gerlind is the

44. Hoffmann takes Wolfgang Spiewok to task for claiming that Kudrun is abiding by
the traditional code of behavior for a feudal princess in letting her parents take care of her
marriage arrangements; he claims Spiewok does not know the text; Hoffmann, *Das Kudrunepos: Ein Beitrag,* p. 270; Wolfgang Spiewok, "Das Nibelungenlied," repr. in *Werkinterpretationen zur deutschen Literatur,* ed. Horst Hartmann (Berlin: 1986), pp. 12–33. They seem
perhaps both to be guilty of some exaggeration.

45. Hildeburg's and Herwig's unnamed sister are the text's only exceptions, in that they
openly reject the concrete offers to participate in the system, but are powerless to enforce that
rejection.

46. And, as we shall see in the next chapter, the actual independence of Kudrun's role as
"coupler" is minimal.

virtual ruler of Ormanie, the power behind the throne that manipulates Hartmut (and/or Ludwig). There is no evidence that this is the case. The only sphere in which she has any significant influence is traditionally female: the care and quasi-courtly "training" of royal maidens.[47] She is not responsible for (or, as conventional scholarship would have it, "guilty of") suggesting Hartmut's suit for and kidnapping of Kudrun, and even if she were, that in itself would hardly constitute ruling the kingdom (by proxy or otherwise). The single clear instance of her trying to influence the ruler (there is no example of her attempting to exercise direct power herself) — her astute military advice to Hartmut just before the disastrous defeat at the hands of the Hegelings — exemplifies the epic topos in which the male rejects the informed and critical advice of a female which would help to avert catastrophe (1323). Hartmut repeatedly and condescendingly tells Gerlind to stay out of men's business: *mûter geet hin dan. Jr mûgt nicht beweÿsen. mich vnd meine man. ratet ewren frawen. die mügenß sanffte leiden. Wie sy gestaine legen mit golde in seyden* ("Mother, go away! You may not instruct me and my men. Go advise your women — they ought to endure it patiently — how to decorate silk cloth with jewels inlaid in gold" 1379,1–4); *Da sprach in zorne Hartmût fraw nu geet hin. was mûget Jr mir geraten* ("Then Hartmut spoke in rage: 'Woman, now go away! What advice could you [possibly] give *me?*'" 1386, 1–2).[48]

Perhaps the scholarly interpretation of Gerlind as an independent ruler

47. Stephen Wailes argues that Gerlind functions as the courtly educator of Kudrun, as indicated in the course of the stanzas during which she receives her charge by the use of the terms *ziehen* "train," *zucht* "training/courtesy/punishment," *leren* "teach," *lere* "instruction" (993–995); see Wailes, "The Romance of Kudrun," *Speculum* 58 (1983), esp. p. 358. I concur in *strictly* limited fashion, and only insofar as Gerlind functions in a *structural* sense as courtly educator. She does not perform this task in conventional fashion: the maiden is already married, is not her daughter or legitimate ward, and her primary educative function — to prepare the maiden to be married to a king, as her primary role in life — is qualified by all the conditions that make the situation narratively interesting and personally catastrophic. Kudrun is a captive, being forced to marry, and thus commit adultery with, an unwanted husband. Gerlind's educative means are not courtly. It would seem then more accurate to deem this textual suggestion of the role of courtly educator not as an unmarked instance of that motif, but rather as an ironic subversion of it, as another oblique citation from the stock of conventional motifs.

48. Here we might recall Siegfried's and Hagen's treatment of women's advice and warnings in the *Nibelungenlied*. The man typically rejects the woman's advice and commits what we can only acknowledge as a tactical blunder (deriving at least in part from his desire to contradict the woman's advice) that leads directly to defeat. In the present instance, that is rather clearly the case. Later Wate too refuses to acknowledge the value or authority of female advice, even if conveyed by a warrior such as Herwig: *solt ich nu fraŵen volgen. wohin tet ich meinen syn* ("if I were now to follow/listen to women, I would have lost my wits" 1491,2).

or an approximation thereof derives simply from the fact that she more than once directly confronts and conflicts with the patriarchal order by which her engendered sphere of action has been defined and assigned (each time in the person of her son): in her mistreatment of Kudrun and in her attempt to give military advice to the military commander. In the first instance, however, the case is again ambiguous. It may well be that Hartmut's own conception of his mother's role in convincing Kudrun to marry him, and perhaps even his evaluation of her obvious mistreatment, vacillate. At one point he directs her to use whatever means necessary to ensure her compliance without at the same time destroying whatever *Freuntscheffte* ("friendship/affection") might exist (1003). Hartmut's inattention is also a problem. If we may make a brief foray into that hazy realm of psychological constructs, we might maintain that Hartmut must have known his mother well enough to have been able to predict how she would carry out her orders, should Kudrun remain obstinate/resolute. Regardless, however, of his insight into his mother's potential for abuse, the fact remains that after placing Kudrun in her charge, he simply ignores this highly desired and dearly bought potential mate for an inordinate length of time. It is not until three and a half years have passed that Hartmut again checks on Kudrun's willingness to marry, only to find that she has not changed her mind and that his mother's methods hardly conform to a courtly model (1014). Rather than rescuing Kudrun from his mother's abuse (as he had from his father's momentary, but murderous, response to her rejecting marriage), Hartmut simply expresses what we must in context view as mild dismay and returns her to his mother's control for several further years.[49]

It seems less likely that Gerlind plays a sovereign role here than that the extent to which she controls Kudrun's life is directly limited to what is minimally necessary for her to be represented as the effectively guilty party. As Hoffmann (p. 97) has pointed out, the narrative goes far to absolve Hartmut of his responsibility for Kudrun's suffering, and the depiction of Gerlind has certainly made it inviting particularly for masculist scholarship

---

49. Campbell notes on Hartmut's actions in defense of Kudrun: when he rebukes his father for throwing Kudrun into the ocean: "This is not chivalry speaking here, but ownership" (p. 205); and he rebukes his mother for her treatment of Kudrun because of its consequences, not its intrinsically abusive nature (p. 206). Cf. also Hartmut's words here: *die schone Chaudrun die ist mir als der leib* ("the beautiful Kudrun is as dear to me as/like my own body" 964,2), which echo Siegfried's appreciation/appropriation of Kriemhild as bride: *si wart im sô sîn lip* ("they became as one/she became for him as his own body" (*Nibelungenlied* 629).

to go yet farther and transfer all significant responsibility to her, by pretending that she is in control, thus effectively making her the scapegoat.[50] Thus another woman is made responsible for the suffering of the heroine, which hinders the identification of that suffering as a consequence of patriarchy or as a gender issue at all. Rather, it can be constructed simply as the result of yet another raging female out of control, wrecking havoc on the poor, innocent heroine. In this respect it clearly resembles the masculist construction of the feud between Brünhild and Kriemhild in the *Nibelungenlied* as the cause of Siegfried's death and, mediated by a further female obsession, the later Burgundian and Hunnic annihilation. That Gerlind actually represents the interests of patriarchy and that she is also made to bear the responsibility for patriarchy's control over the traffic in women are issues suppressed via the skillful construction of the situation to make her available as both guilty and executible. For Hartmut is most definitely *not* narratively and ideologically available for this role. She is thus — as the narrator designates her — the demon, the devil, the wolf-bitch, while her son who gave her this job and knows full well how she is performing it, is the "model of courtliness," "the ultimate king," according to scholars (and, to a lesser degree, the text).[51]

This is quintessentially one of the crucial points of the ideological problematic of the text. The ruler's "minister of wiving" openly and with the ruler's knowledge abuses her charge; she is condemned (by both the text and its scholars) and indeed dies a horrid death, while he is tacitly, spontaneously and without any recrimination rehabilitated and made part of the "harmonious" concluding round of marriages. Not surprisingly in this patriarchal world, although her military advice is sound, she is decapitated by the enemy's quasi-divine "executioner"; while he, the actual kidnapper and ineffective defender of the castle, is spared, survives, and ultimately regains his homeland and apparently his dynastic throne.[52] The roles of "hero" and (female) "villain" are overdetermined: women are simply available as villains, and can be designated "devilish," even if they do nothing in their own interest. Men, almost *regardless* of what they do, will be, in varying degrees, rewarded. Women obviously cannot be *rewarded,* since

---

50. Campbell, however, is well aware of the ideological move of the text to unburden Harmut of responsibility for Kudrun's kidnapping and mistreatment by imputing it to Gerlind (p. 201).

51. Campbell, p. 201 surveys some of the excessive examples of such views from the scholarship.

52. Although under the direct political hegemony of the Hegelings, and in a devasted kingdom.

they themselves constitute one of the primary types of reward, although they can occasionally share in the exercise of power, as long as it is exercised in a predefined, gender-specific manner.

Gerlind's quasi-counterpart in Hegeling-land, the queen mother, Hilde, like the other female characters in *Kudrun,* is a model of conformity, abiding strictly by her culture's gender code. She does no more than provide encouragement to her men to carry out their duties.[53] At the same time, however, Hilde is the text's only female who has any claim to the role of ruling queen.[54] After the death of her husband and at least for the number of years necessary for the new generation of Hegelings (including her son Ortwin) to attain majority, Hilde, apparently, rules. The qualification, "apparently," is neither gratuitous nor a denial. Rather, it is simply unclear from the text just how much it means to claim that Hilde rules. To insist on important state actions at her order as proof of her actual monarchical power would be unfair,[55] but it seems that most state actions are in fact initiated and executed not at her order, but at most with her assent. On the one hand, the exercise of monarchical power is not a trivial matter, nor one that merely requires an occasional act over the course of a generation. On the other hand, however, precisely that aspect of male as well as, on the rare occasion, female rule is of little moment in courtly literature. Otherwise there is *nothing* to report of Hilde's monarchy beyond her desire for vengeance on the invaders who killed her husband and kidnapped and still hold her daughter.

> *Da sprach die traurende. hey solte ich das gelebñ.*
> *alles daz ich hette. wolt ich darumb geben.*
> *daz ich errochen wurde. Wie so das geschahe.*
> *vnd daz ich vil goteß arme. mein tochter Chaudrun gesahe.* (929)

53. Her unremitting desire for revenge seems, in its cultural context, neither illegitimate nor excessive; in any case, since she at no point attempts to execute vengeance except by means of male warriors, she does not transgress gender strictures here either. See below.

54. Hoffmann attempts to contrast the *Nibelungenlied* with *Kudrun* by claiming that Uote of the *Nibelungenlied* is a narrative and political nonentity whose sons rule, while Hilde in fact rules after the death of her husband (p. 272). The observation is accurate as far as it goes, but it is rather self-serving in its proposal of inappropriate items of comparison: Uote and Hilde are both queen mothers and comparable as such. But if one wishes to compare examples of a *regens regina* in the two works, then obviously Uote is not the proper candidate, while Brünhild and, in an important sense also Kriemhild, are, and they both dwarf any restricted power that Hilde might be imagined to possess.

55. We do not, for instance, insist that the quintessentially weak king Arthur only rules if he spends his days judging legal cases. The representation of precisely this activity on the part of Hagen earlier in *Kudrun* hardly flatters the image of that ruler either.

(Then the sorrowful one said: "Oh, if only I could live to see that, I'd give everything that I own to get my revenge (however it should happen), and that I, God's poor little one, might see my daughter Kudrun.)

This desired vengeance is organized and executed by her son and son-in-law in command of Hegeling military vassals. Hilde participates insofar as she desires the same end, but does not, even though queen, apparently control the state coffers, for she is not said to provide any financial support (as such might be expressed in courtly literary guise—clothing, trappings). The men rather already have or simply take what they need without the narrator's noting Hilde's participation. When the time comes for the expedition, Fruote and Wate merely inform Hilde and in courtly manner request leave to depart; Hilde's replies are no more than the ceremonious granting of that leave (942–945). Just as patriarchy has historically defused potential objections to the exclusion of females from political power by inventing the concept of the wife or mother as "the power behind the throne," here Hilde's queenship avoids conflict with the patriarchal order by becoming the "throne behind the power."[56]

Kudrun herself, the most prominent character throughout two thirds of the multi-generational narrative, at no point possesses significant political power.[57] Kudrun's return from "class exile" to her royal status, as it were, after she has practiced her tactical deception of Gerlind and Hartmut on the eve of her liberation and return from geographical exile, restores her contact with and immediate command over her courtly serving maidens.

56. While it is tempting to designate Hilde simply a titular, *pro tempore* ruler during the Hetel-Ortwin interregnum, as I have done above, this "regency" lasts thirteen years. Ortwin already seems to be of age at the time of his father's death, but there may be some influence on this issue by the necessity for the Hegelings to postpone their expedition of vengeance until the next generation of potential warriors grows up: his majority may simply be narratively "contaminated" by this motif of the minority of the other Hegeling warriors-to-be. At any rate he arrives for the expedition from Nortland which seems already to be under his direct rule (1096–1100). While one might under such circumstances expect that Ortwin would assume the Hegeling throne upon his attainment of majority, or failing that, upon his marriage, the text makes no mention thereof, and it is not clear what to make of this silence: does he rule, or does Hilde continue on the throne?

57. Campbell notes that Kudrun is nonetheless referred to as *hêr* more than three times as often as any other character in the narrative (p. 21); the word is "an expressive term employed to telling effect. It often occurs, of course, as a stock epithet in the sense of 'most noble,' 'exalted,' particularly in address. It can include the idea of power conferred by very high birth and can pass readily to the idea of pride in one's social position, one's birth, one's power and authority. From here it is a small step to the idea of 'lordly,' 'grand,' 'imperious'" (p. 246). But as a title and/or epithet it can also function not to confer or even acknowledge power, but stand in its stead and offer merely the title (or the appearance) in place of actuality.

This reinstatement constitutes the greatest extent of her power, in fact the norm of her political status. She never commands armies, rules kingdoms, or exercises any effective control (authority) over vassals of her dynasty (consider, for instance, Wate's ignoring her will during the slaughter).[58] Nor does she have any control over her own person for any part of the work, which she spends under the direct protectorate of a succession of patriarchal instances of power: her father, her abductor, her husband. Here she regains "control" over her serving maidens and manages to make a suggestion to the king (about sending out messengers to announce the wedding). That is the extent of her sovereignty.

In the absence of political power on Kudrun's part, McConnell finds an "inner sovereignty" (p. 70) in her thirteen-year defiance of her captors: "Defiance, not passiveness, characterizes Kudrun's behavior, and it is precisely her inner comportment in the wasteland of Kassiane that comprises the essence of her heroism" (p. 74); and "Kudrun reaffirms her inner sovereignty when she defiantly throws the Norman's clothes into the water" (p. 77). There are a number of critical problems here. One might expect, for instance, in a "defiant," "sovereign" character some independence of action, some behavior that, even in such dire circumstances as those in which Kudrun finds herself, would indicate some measure of opposition. The primary scholarly claim of Kudrun's defiance of the Normans must concern her thirteen-year refusal to marry Hartmut. Despite its surface attractiveness, it is a problematic claim, however, for she may defy the Normans only insofar as *they* allow that behavior. As Hartmut's male counselors advise him, he may make her his wife simply by raping her at any

---

58. In a different context Werner Hoffmann makes a minor point that is also pertinent here, perhaps moreso than it initially seems, for it illustrates an essential problem in the masculist conception of female power and sovereignty. In fact he inadvertently undermines the argument for actual power or authority on Kudrun's part, for even in her dealings with Wate, her dynasty's vassal who at the moment in question is engaged in liberating her from Norman captivity, she has no control over his actions. Hoffmann attempts here to absolve Kudrun of any responsibility and guilt for the murders of Gerlind and Hergard, and remarks (p. 185) "Irgendeine Fürsprache wäre freilich ohnehin zwecklos gewesen" ("Any intercession would, of course, have been pointless anyway"); she does at about the same time, however, manage quite well to save Ortrun and her retinue. Why, one might wonder, if it is really a matter simply of Kudrun's authority, is she able to save the one group, but not the other? Those who would absolve Kudrun of all responsibility and control in this situation would do well to recall that she specifically tells Wate at one point that she now has under her protection those she wants, *nu thûe Wate waz er welle mit den gysel seinen* ("now let Wate do what he wants with his hostages" 1539,4). We have by this point in the narrative learned what Wate does with defenseless enemies in his power, and there is no reason to doubt that Kudrun knows it as well. Campbell notes that this aspect of the scene is "completely ignored by most critics" (pp. 188–189).

time. Based on his past acts of brutality, there is no reason to suspect that he is incapable of such an act. Thus Kudrun's "defiance" is simply another way to express Hartmut's "tolerance," neither of which is a very specific or critically very useful concept under the present circumstances.[59]

With this one qualified exception, however, Kudrun nowhere else and in no other respect behaves defiantly in Ormanie. She otherwise conforms, cowers, cringes, and at her most "defiant" merely complains: among other things she sweeps the floor, stokes the fire, and washes clothes on the beach for thirteen years without rebellion, without refusal, without defiance; only on the eve of her liberation, and after she has met with her brother and husband — the men who will effect that liberation — does she perform an act approaching defiance: she throws the laundry into the sea, which is, clearly, a rejection of her assigned task. But it is after all also a rather trivial act, not like storming a castle, slaying one's foe, demanding one's appropriated property. Rather, she simply refuses to wash the laundry *this single time* and throws it into the ocean: an act of defiance strictly circumscribed by the engendered sphere in which she finds herself (is narratively placed), and one which in contrast to the *thousands* of ignored opportunities for identical and similar acts of defiance over the course of the previous years calls more attention to its symbolic than to any defiant nature. Additionally, and most problematically for any interpretation of this act as illustrative of Kudrun as sovereign, is the fact that she then immediately covers up its potentially most significant aspect: instead of admitting to Gerlind that she threw the laundry into the ocean, she claims that she left the clothes on the beach: *ich han Sy ligen lan. da niden bey der flůte. do ich Sy wolte dan. mit mir heer ze hofe tragen. sy waren mir ze swäre* "I left them lying down there by the sea. When I wanted to bring them back with me to the castle, they were too heavy for me [to carry]" (1281,1–3).[60] Thus not only does she not cast her act of

---

59. While I feel no piety toward the morality of the character of Kudrun, nor any for the inviolability of the scholarly veneration of her, I at the same time have no interest in character assassination, nor do I wish to participate in the conventional ploy of masculist *Nibelungenlied/ Klage/Kudrun*-scholarship, in which one female character is chosen as villain and denigrated to the extent possible to make that characterization plausible. Thus my remarks should not be taken as an attack on the virtue of this literary figure, but rather as being in the same spirit as Campbell's attempt to achieve something of a better analytical balance.

60. I suppose it might be possible for Kudrun's defenders to argue that in this case the one constitutes the other, that is, that clothes thrown into the surf will soon enough be washed up on shore again. But obviously that is only the case on certain beaches with particular currents and tidal patterns. Additionally, if that were to be the case, then the "defiance" of this act is still further diluted. The fact too that this single act of defiance is, immediately and as a direct consequence of that act, followed by what can, from one perspective, be viewed as a cowardly lie — to avoid a beating Kudrun pretends to have changed her mind and now to want

"defiance" in Gerlind's teeth, not only does she not admit to Gerlind what she actually did with the laundry, she rather claims to have wished to comply with Gerlind's expectations, and even provides a plausible excuse for her noncompliance. It is difficult to imagine a less defiant response.[61] "Sovereignty" and "defiance" must be accompanied by an acknowledged responsibility for the acts so designated, otherwise the opposition required by the concept "defiance" is also jettisoned. In any case Kudrun's small act of "defiance" (with the laundry) vanishes in almost the same moment as does her large act of defiance. Whether in refusing to marry Hartmut for thirteen years, or now in pretending that she will marry him as soon as it can be arranged, her state of "not-marrying-Hartmut" does not change. However, when she now claims that she does wish to marry him, it is no longer possible to pretend that she defies by (apparently) concurring. Rather, she is now simply lying. The lie is made possible, even *caused,* not by any inner strength on Kudrun's part, but rather obviously by the presence of her legal male guardians' armies before the gates.

Let us return to McConnell's view in order to come to a conclusion:

> If *Kudrun* in any way reflects the status of noblewomen in mid-thirteenth century German, then it may be necessary to revise, however cautiously, our image of the totally dependent, usually subordinate female, whose welfare, both physical and spiritual, was very much dependent upon the good will of her spouse. It might be argued that *Kudrun* is actually a work concerned with the wielding of real, effective power by female rulers. Hagen of Ireland is, after all, the only male monarch in the work who enjoys any stature. The spotlight is otherwise constantly on the female protagonists: Sigeband's mother and later his wife as counselors; Hilde as the agent of reconciliation between the Hegelings and the Irish, and subsequently as the moving force behind the efforts to free her abducted daughter; Kudrun as heroine and reconciler of Normans and Hegelings as well as matchmaker for numerous figures at the conclusion of the work. (p. 96)

In fact Kudrun's welfare is, quite obviously, consistently and demonstratively, directly dependent on the good will of her male guardians, from her father's (vassals') failure to protect her from invading male kidnappers, to Ludwig's brutal attempt to drown her, Hartmut's momentary salvation

---

to marry Hartmut — does little to support a construction of a defiant character here. Siebert's claims that Kudrun here rebels (*rebellieren*) against her opponents is even less plausible than the claim that she is defiant (p. 192).

61. Which even her appended snarl/whine does little to strengthen: *beschawet jr Sÿ nÿmmer. daß ist mir auf mein trewe vil vnmäre* ("if you never see them again, it is in truth all the same to me" 1281,4).

of her, his control of her life in Ormanie, the Hegeling's liberation of her, and finally to her immediate transfer to Herwig's control after liberation. Nowhere is she in control of her life or her physical state. As noted above, the simple weakness or absence of male rulers does not of itself make of any given females either strong characters or ruling queens. And certainly the examples McConnell manages to glean as evidence not only do not support his argument, but actually are quite useful as evidence against the proposition of female sovereignty in *Kudrun*: the "wielding of real, effective power by female rulers" is, quite simply nonexistent in the narrative, as his examples ironically demonstrate: as counselor to the ruling king (with the recurring conventional rejection of female counsel by the male ruler), conciliatory negotiator, matchmaker. These are ancillary, "support" roles, that is, precisely those roles traditionally open to females and strategically placed close enough to the centers of power that patriarchy can always pretend that there is female participation. There is thus little revision of "our image of the . . . subordinate female" necessary, for there has been no transformation of the conventional patriarchally conceived gender roles. And as we shall see in the next chapter, transformation is in general a concept that has found too wide a currency in *Kudrun* scholarship for Kudrun's participation in the political realm is non interventionist, even, oxymoronically, when she intervenes.

8. *Suone* as Social (Trans)formation

Kudrun represents a society in which females of the royal class, compared with those of the *Nibelungenlied,* have no appreciable power or authority in the political sphere. One of the manifestations of this state of affairs is the narrative focus of *Kudrun*: the catastrophically dysfunctional conventions of feudal-aristocratic wiving, which, in the cases represented by this narrative, lead inevitably to murder and kidnapping on the personal scale and to the conquest and pillaging of kingdoms on the international scale. It is in such a milieu that Kudrun operates. While the scholarship on *Kudrun* has in general been less divisive than that on many other medieval texts, on one point there has been almost unanimity: that Kudrun effects a large-scale transformation of her society. This transformation (or rather the scholarly constructs of it), is expressed by means of various interpretive tropes, all participating in an idealist teleology. Some of these posited transformations are based on interpretive constructs generally no longer held to be valid; the remaining ones, I hope to demonstrate here, are no more plausible.

One of the keys to the scholarly constructs of social transformation is the concept of *suone,* particularly as it is associated with Kudrun. Werner Hoffmann suggests that in her imposition of *suone* near the end of the narrative, Kudrun sublates (*aufheben,* he specifies, in the Hegelian sense) the prior norm of conflict resolution, that is, vengeance.[1] This transformation from violence to reconciliation is then doubled or reproduced by a further demonstration of that transformation: the marriages that conclude the narrative. Further, that development from violence to peace and harmony is generally interpreted as a concretization of a deeper societal transformation from the Germanic past to a christian, courtly present. And finally, as one can imagine from this clearly teleological emplotment, *Kudrun* is held to demonstrate "progress" from barbaric to civilized, from primitive to sophisticated, from pessimism to optimism,[2] from political repression to

---

1. Hoffmann, *Kudrun: Ein Beitrag,* p. 232.
2. McConnell's remarks here are representative: "For the *Kudrun* poet, reconciliation and compromise are testimony to an optimistic world-view, in contrast to the nihilistic attitude conveyed by the author of the *Nibelungenlied*" (*Epic of Kudrun,* 1); "restoration of the

progressive freedom.[3] Furthermore, Kudrun herself is said to be exemplary of the good, virtuous, ethical woman, a "new woman," a proto-feminist who takes charge of her own life and even the "life" of her society and her age, to lead it/them into a new epoch of freedom, harmony, and justice. It is easy to get carried away with such idealist rhetoric, and many scholars have been. Each of these particular aspects of the teleological emplotment is a problem. The entire interpretive complex, in its various versions, is constructed either directly in opposition to the *Nibelungenlied* or with that text always as the subtext and guarantor of contrast. That scenario runs something like this: the plot of the *Nibelungenlied* is driven by vengeance, is peopled by heroic men and politically weak women, is ruled by a pre-Christian, Germanic ethic, is primitive, barbaric, pessimistic, destructive, nihilistic;[4] *Kudrun* is the calculated corrective thereto. Since my construction of the *Nibelungenlied* differs so dramatically from this conventional interpretation, it is no surprise that my interpretation of *Kudrun* as anti-*Nibelungenlied* will differ radically from the conventional construction of that intertextual opposition. The differences become even clearer with respect to the notion of social transformation.

In its various scholarly constructions this social transformation generally consists of several components. Many scholars have, like Hoffmann, used the term *suone* in their analyses, both because it is a significant concept in the narrative and because it is also a useful terminological rubric under which several types of transformations posited by scholars might be grouped. As the title of this chapter already indicates, I too will occasionally use this term as a generic designation of *posited* transformations in the text.

---

ordo of society in *Kudrun* contrasts with the triumph of chaos by the conclusion of the *Nibelungenlied*" (p. 92); the *Kudrun*-poet "underscores the importance of continuity, the merits of strength coupled with wisdom, of justice and vitality, the components of a productive society" (p. 98). The society of which he speaks demonstrates continuity insofar as it, with the regularity of a clock, goes on the bridal warpath that inevitably leads — in every such case represented — to slaughter and massive destruction; justice in any practical sense consists of thousand-fold vengeance in war; wisdom is represented only by Hagen's "rule of law," which is "comparatively benevolent," even when it extends to his beheading of eighty citizens whom he finds *vnbillich*.

3. Nolte thus suggests that "die produktive Konfliktlösung besteht in der Besiegelung des Friedens durch Eheschließungen" ("the productive conflict resolution consists in the sealing of the peace by marriage") and that this is "eine neue Konfliktlösungsstrategie" ("a new strategy for conflict resolution," Das *Kudrunepos* p. 12). Werner Hoffmann (p. 272) also uses the term *produktiv*, as opposed to destructive, about the reconciliation.

4. In the characterization of the *Nibelungenlied* as destructive, for instance, my own reading as detailed above, does not dissent, insofar, for example, as that text problematizes the necessarily destructive sexism that leads directly to the all but total destruction of several cultures. But in so specifying the grounds of my concurrence, I have already departed from the conventional scholarly emplotment.

But my view of *suone* as social transformation differs from that of the scholarly tradition, and thus it is necessary at the outset to reexamine the basic terms of this interpretive complex, the Middle High German *suone/ suon/süenen/versüenen.*[5]

Generally *Kudrun*-scholarship has simply and without a great deal of examination accepted the conventional interpretation of this complex of terms as *Versöhnung* "reconciliation." While this signification is one of the common ones in Middle High German literature, *suone* can also signify "atonement" or even "punishment," and in this respect resembles its modern German reflex, *Sühne.* That usage is somewhat more common in the medieval language than the sense of "reconciliation." But more common than either of these significations in Middle High German texts is *Urteil* "judgment"; rather less common, the very concrete *Gericht* "court of law." The term also can designate a more general "peace" or "calm." The verbal forms are more common in *Kudrun* than the nominals, and they too can signify the act of "(re)conciliation" but also both the more general *ausgleichen* "balance / compensate for," and (*süenen*) the less positive *abhelfen/ beseitigen* "redress [a wrong]." Obviously even so simple a semantic choice as which of these denotations, or which combination, or in what order, to "hear" in any given use or pattern of uses of *suone* rather clearly predetermines all subsequent interpretive gestures. For if one views the *suone* imposed by Kudrun after her recapture by her husband as altruistic and Christian reconciliation, then one's view of the slaughter that preceded it is different than if one views her *suone* as a quasi-court's judgment of her enemies, as the logically consequential atonement or final punishment following their brutal military defeat and the devastating pillaging of their country. Needless to say, such semantic choices also color one's evaluation of the marriages imposed by Kudrun as an integral component of the *suone* and their participation in the larger social structures of wiving. In any case, *Kudrun*-scholarship has deemphasized the "negative" denotations of the term.

Obviously of greater relevance than the general semantic range of *suone* in Middle High German is its specific use in *Kudrun.* The term is of some moment in the text, for it recurs at several key moments of conflict settlement in the narrative. The first instance is Hagen's proposal of a settlement between his father and the Graf of Garadie (*versüenen* 131,3); when the

5. A brief but representative selection of uses may be found in Matthias Lexer's *Mittelhochdeutsches Handwörterbuch*; my brief survey of general uses of the terms is based on Lexer's selective glosses.

settlement is later actually brought about, the unrequited losses of one of the parties to the settlement are noted in the same breath (*versüenen* 159,1–2). The next usage appears at the moment when the fictive conflict between Hetel and the exiled warriors (i.e., his bridal-raiding party led by Wate) is "settled" enabling the exiles to return home (*suone* 432,3). Here there is no explicit indication that such an obviously hierarchically defined settlement (i.e, between king and [albeit fictively] renegade vassals fleeing for their lives) would require, for instance, punitive damages from the vassals. The third instance occurs during the subsequent battle between Hetel and Hagen; here too the words are Wate's, as he interprets Hilde's plea to heal her father as one for *suone* (533,3), which, he claims, would first have to be ordered by Hetel. While the term may here simply signify "peace" or "the end of battle," Wate's hostile and defiant rejection of the suggestion may indicate that he attributes more and deeper significance to its usage at the juncture. The next instance of a cessation of hostilities, at which point one might expect the recurrence of *suone,* occurs in the conflict between Hetel and Sifrit; here the term is, interestingly, absent.[6] A cluster of uses is found at the settlement of the conflict between the forces of Siegfried and those of Herwig and Ortwin. Irolt offers a settlement (*süenen* 831,2) to Siegfried, accompanied, significantly, by a threat, if the offer is refused. After Siegfried makes a condition of his acceptance that it not compromise his honor (832,3), Fruote baldly counters that Siegfried's freedom depends directly on his agreement to serve Ortwin (833). That the condition was accepted and that it thus came to *suone/versüenen* (834,1&4) is duly reported by the narrator. In the subsequent occurrence (referring to the coming resumption of conflict with the Normans), Wate rather clearly opposes *versüenen* with *gestriten*; one is tempted to interpret the contrast as that between "peace" and "battle" (839,4). The final instances of the term in *Kudrun* occur in the train of the settlement imposed on the Normans by the Hegeling alliance. The first occurs in the hyperbolic claim that the *suone* (*versüenen* 1602,3) was so great that the opponents forgot that they had fought against each other only days before. In his approval of the proposed match between Ortwin and Ortrun and proposal of a further one between Hildeburg and Hartmut, Fruote subsumes such acts under the rubric

---

6. It is also accomplished without the direct peacemaking input of any female. It would be possible, of course, to argue that since Hetel and Siegfried stop fighting as a result of Kudrun's kidnapping they do so *for the sake of* a woman, or that they do so *at the request of* Hilde, who informs them of the kidnapping. But such connections are "causal" in a rather different and less direct sense.

versüenen (1624,1). Finally, the two last occurrences in the narrative offer what seems a clear semantic contrast: Wate makes *süenen* (1646,1) between the Hegelings and the surviving Normans, Ortrun and Hartmut, dependent on their obeisance (*biete sich ze füezen* 1646, 3) to Hilde. Kudrun views the fact that Hilde has provided the captive and despoiled Norman ladies with splendid clothing as proof of accomplished (or impending) *süenen* (1647).

These (relatively) few, but significantly placed, instances of the terminology of *suone* in *Kudrun* form a pattern of usage and suggest an emphasis of one semantic perspective over the other available ones. While all uses here *denote* the settlement of a conflict, there is in all cases a clear and often designated hierarchical rank of the parties to the settlement. In a significant number of the cases the conditions imposed on the weaker (or defeated) party to the settlement are noted; likewise in several of the cases the term is used in the context of a reminder of which party to the settlement most profited from it. There is no question that the term *suone* designates an action that ends (generally) military conflict in *Kudrun,* but the terms of such settlements are never irrelevant and here they are never excluded from the field of vision. *Suone* in *Kudrun* is not innocent, not egalitarian, not peaceful and harmonious. It is not "reconciliation" before or instead of conflict, but rather the settlement, including the victors' conditions of peace, imposed on the vanquished, after the conflict, often amid the mutilated dead and the smoking ruins (although in the case of the final *suone,* the physical site has been changed and the memory of the conflict almost magically erased, before *suone* can take place). In the subsequent argument of this chapter, then, there will be three strategic uses of the term *suone:* the cited conventional views of *suone* as "peace" and "reconciliation"; the counter-semantics I offer here; and the metaphorical use I (and others) make of *suone* as representative of the scholarly constructs of social transformation in *Kudrun.*

Probably the most common component of the conventional argument concerning *suone* as Kudrun's putative transformation of her world has to do with the ill-defined contrast between christian and Germanic. While recent work, especially by Theodor Nolte and Ian Campbell, has gone far toward laying to rest the extreme christian interpretation,[7] the larger proj-

---

7. Their work is groundbreaking in debunking the myth of "St. Kudrun" and has been fundamental in the following section: Nolte, *Das Kudrunepos*; and Campbell, *Kudrun: A Critical Appreciation.* Nolte, for instance subjects Hoffmann's idea that Kudrun's motives for *suone* are christian mercy and forgiveness to a brief examination and concludes that the idea is

ect of which the christian component is only the most prominent element can still be approached best via the structure of the christian thesis. Thus I will follow it here to the extent necessary to gain access to that larger critical project. The christianizing argument replaces a posited unethical and barbaric Germanic past with Kudrun's christian and ethical present. Most commonly the effective purpose of the almost hagiographic adulation by scholarship of Kudrun, particularly insofar as her virtues are (mis)represented as christian, is to contrast with the putatively less moral and ethical female characters of the *Nibelungenlied,* Brünhild and Kriemhild. The very fact that this issue is topicalized by the scholarship indicates its necessarily ideological nature. It forces one to the rather demeaning pseudo-empirical tasks of moral scorekeeping and toting up ethical and unethical points for the adversaries. Let us be content here to analyze the salient points at issue in such analyses, for they are almost without exception ambiguous, and thus by definition morally problematic.

Arguments for the significant role of christianity in the poem and for Kudrun's embodiment of the christian ideal generally deal with three significant issues: 1) the use of the word *got* in idiomatic phrases; 2) the explicit identification of the messenger bird as an angel (1167, 1169); 3) Kudrun's rejection of vengeance and introduction of reconciliation to resolve the final conflict.[8] The first two items indicate unambiguously that the text was produced by and for a christian society. They do not, however, constitute

---

untenable (p. 61). In his earlier and lengthier study Campbell provides a thorough analysis of the issue and, with a healthy dose of irony and no false piety, he comes to essentially the same conclusion as Nolte.

8. There is also a further topic, which is undeniably and explicitly christian, and christian-motivated, but awkward for both pro- or anti-christian positions: the despoiling of the pilgrims and the attendant kidnapping and forced military service of five hundred of them by the Hegelings (of whom *vil wenig* "very few" returned healthy, 844,4); their subsequent (from the perspective of the narrative — probably *consequent*) defeat; and their later repayment and atonement via the redundantly emphasized founding, funding, and apparently also staffing of a *spital* (st. 909, 916–918, 931–932, 949–950). Interestingly, however, this single example of an explicitly christian episode has no further resonance in the remainder of the work, particularly with respect to Kudrun and her behavior; and as a consequence it is not employed as key evidence by any pro-christian interpreters, perhaps because, one must admit, it reflects rather badly on the Hegelings as the narrative's heroes and thus, according to this scholarly construct, as representative christians. This is particularly true if the litotes of 844,4 is understood to mean that none of the five hundred captured pilgrims returned alive. If such is the case, then the Hegelings have not only disrupted a christian pilgrimage, stolen the ships and supplies of the pilgrims, and kidnapped and enslaved five hundred of them in military service, but also directly caused their deaths. Given the circumstances — that medieval christian pilgrims are almost by definition in a state of sin that must be expiated by means of an imposed pilgrimage — then no matter how many *spitale* the Hegelings build and equip, they may have sent five hundred souls to Hell. Small wonder this episode does not figure greatly in christian constructions.

evidence that the narrative's motivations are christian. While the messenger bird is unambiguously identified as an angel of god (1167), there is nonetheless a number of problems in an unnuanced christian interpretation, as has been pointed out by Campbell, for this angel is not particularly inspiring, since it "endorses without reservation Hilde's and the Hegelings' projected action on [Kudrun's] behalf, seems to have an almost morbid interest in the battle to come and expresses not one single Christian sentiment" (pp. 269–270). In his review of M. Weege's dissertation, Rainer Gruenter (not for the first time in the scholarly tradition) rejects the christian interpretation: " 'Gott' und 'Jenseits' interessiert das gesamte Personal der 'Kudrun'-Dichtung, grob gesprochen, nicht im geringsten" (" 'God' and 'the hereafter' is, to put it bluntly, of absolutely no interest to the entire personnel of the 'Kudrun' ").[9] Werner Hoffmann's response to Gruenter and defense of the text's christian nature is for the most part a very enlightening presentation of the textual evidence. He acknowledges that the formulaic use of *got*, the mention of mass and so forth, is neither meaningless — it demonstrates what we all know, that the text was written and initially received by a christian society — nor of great significance in determining the narrative motivation of the work: it is simply a basic aspect of the cultural context of thirteenth-century (christian) European literature.[10]

But what then *does* constitute the christianity of *Kudrun?* There are several prominent representatives of the pro-christian interpretation of what I above designated the third issue in the case of a "christian" *Kudrun:* the rejection of vengeance and introduction of reconciliation as the means of conflict resolution.[11] For Werner Hoffmann, primary proof is that:

9. Gruenter, in *Euphorion* 51 (1957), 324–330, here, p. 325; Magdalene Weege, *Das Kudrunepos, eine Dichtung des Hochmittelalters* (Diss., Mainz 1953).

10. Hoffmann notes that there is no mention of Christ except in formulae, such as *bey Criste* ("in Christ's name / for Christ's sake" 1178,3). But the usage in the stanza thereafter — *seyt dus von Crist gepeütest* ("since you ask for it from Christ" — often emended to *bî Krist*) seems not quite so formulaic, though still not indicative of christian motivation. The trinity is not mentioned in the text, as also acknowledged by Hoffmann (p. 235).

11. Werner Hoffmann is perhaps the most trenchant of the recent christian apologists: while he claims that there is ein tieferer, echterer religiöser Bezug, ja religiöser Gehalt spürbar" in *Kudrun* than in the *Nibelungenlied* ("a deeper, more authentic religious element, even a religious content perceptible," p. 233), he nonetheless inadvertently admits some doubt about the unequivocal christian nature of the text: "Daß der hier von Kudrun verwirklichte Gedanke, man müsse den Haß überwinden und die miteinander versöhnen, die Feinde waren, in seiner Wurzel christlich ist, sollte nicht zweifelhaft sein. Es braucht aber darum nicht bestritten zu werden, daß daneben auch die nüchterne 'realpolitische' Einsicht mitspricht, daß Versöhnung und Friede zweckmäßiger, besser seien als Feindschaft und Kampf" ("That the notion here realized by Kudrun, that one must overcome hatred and reconcile enemies with one another, is

Der von Kudrun verwirklichte Gedanke der Versöhunung wesenhaft (wenn auch nicht ausschließlich) von der christlichen Forderung der Nächstenliebe betragen und gespeist ist. . . . Hier gibt es agape, Erbarmung, Verzeihung, Versöhnung und damit den Geist des Christentums, gerade des gegenwärtigen Christentums. Denn sowenig es angeht, Kudruns Haltung und Wirken dem höfischen Harmoniewillen zuzuschreiben, sowenig auch einem 'natürlichen' Empfinden. Es mag mithelfen — das Wesentliche ist es nicht. Mit dem gleichen Recht, mit dem die Forschung Wates Weltbild und Handeln als im Kern germanisch zu bezeichnen pflegt, muß man dasjenige Kudruns christlich nennen (pp. 237–238)

(The concept of reconciliation realized by Kudrun is essentially (if not exclusively) defined and nourished by the christian demand for *caritas*. . . . Here there is *agape*, mercy, forgiveness, reconciliation, and thus the spirit of christianity. For it is no more legitimate to ascribe Kudrun's behavior and actions to the courtly will toward harmony than to a "natural" feeling. It may have assisted, but it was not the essence. With the same legitimacy with which scholarship has designated Wate's *Weltbild* and behavior as Germanic in their essence, one must call Kudrun's christian.

Herewith, however, Hoffmann sounds a note that rings through much of *Kudrun* scholarship (as it does in work on the *Nibelungenlied*): the Germanic vs. post-germanic ethos. Roswitha Wisniewski also relates an identification of Kudrun's behavior with christian virtue: "Kudrun verkörpert hier geradezu die christlichen Ideale der Vergebung und Feindesliebe" ("Kudrun embodies here precisely the christian ideals of forgiveness and love of one's enemy"; *Kudrun*, p. 68, *ad* 1644,1). She also contrasts a Germanic cult of vengeance with christian *suone*, suggesting that Kudrun "ist über das Rachedenken und damit über die germanische Ethik hinausgewachsen" ("has risen above vengeful thinking and thus also the Germanic ethic," *Kudrun*, p. 67). Ellen Bender assumes as well that the connection between crime and vengeance in the *Nibelungenlied* is the "Ausdruck einer vorchristlichen Auffassung der Sühnung von Schuld durch 'râche'" ("expression of a pre-christian view of the expiation of guilt by means of vengeance"), while Kudrun's *suone* is the "Ausdruck einer christlich geprägten Auffassung der Sühnung von Schuld durch Reue und Vergebung"

---

at root a christian one, should be beyond question. One need not, however, deny that the sober, 'realpolitical' insight, that reconciliation and peace are more purposeful and better than hostility and conflict, also plays a role," pp. 185–186). But this concession causes more problems than it solves, for it is based in a particular moral construct of "better" and "worse"; it is in any case unclear that a dominant political power possessed of devastating military superiority gains anything from *Versöhnung* as opposed to *Feindschaft*, since in either case political dominance is assured by the military dominance.

("expression of a christian-defined view of expiation of guilt by means of penitence and forgiveness").[12] If *Reue* were actually followed by forgiveness in the narrative, then Bender's case might be stronger, but in fact, with the sole exception of the restitution to the pilgrims by the Hegelings, there is no instance of the admission of guilt, penitence or anything of the kind. Unless one posits that the mere cessation of military hostilities constitutes the very specific acts of forgiveness and love of one's enemy, there is nowhere in the text any actual instance of the behavior deemed christian by Wisniewski. Specifically with reference to the Kudrun episodes, the only named enemies among the Normans to survive and thus be available for forgiveness and love are Ortrun and Hartmut. But since neither of them is ever really charged with wrongdoing by the narrator or his characters, there is never an actual opportunity to forgive them for anything.[13] And while Ortrun seems to enjoy (and return) the favor of Kudrun and while both Ortrun and Hartmut are both maritally appropriated into the sphere of Hegeling hegemony, there is nothing in the behavior of any of the participants to suggest "love" in any sense, and certainly no altruistic "love of one's enemy." Otherwise in Ormanie the enemy is simply slaughtered by the thousands, among them the king and queen, Ludwig and Gerlind, who thus have no opportunity to be forgiven and loved.[14]

Whatever the christian ornament attached to *Kudrun,* and it is hardly more (though without question more explicit) than in the *Nibelungenlied,* there is no christian narrative *movens.* The attempt to construct the concept of *suone* as essentially christian is no less problematic, for it is not explicitly so identified, and it seems just as likely that it could, on the one hand, be ethically or morally motivated, or on the other, politically motivated, as I will argue.

12. Ellen Bender, *Nibelungenlied und Kudrun: Eine vergleichende Studie zur Zeitdarstellung und Geschichtsdeutung* (Frankfurt: Lang, 1987), pp. 223–224.

13. It could conceivably be argued that such unconditional forgiveness, or rather simply forgetting of the wrongdoing, by Kudrun is even more 'christian' than would have been a demand for Hartmut's political confession and the imposition of some form of penance. But again, that would only be true in particular constructs of christianity, none directly relevant to this text or to thirteenth-century central Europe. While Campbell assumes that Kudrun forgives Hartmut, he also points out that her forgiveness "is not absolute but conditional upon his complying with the terms she stipulates . . . Christian forgiveness does not bargain" (p. 292). We might also note that rather than simply consenting unconditionally to Gerlind's plea for asylum from Wate's rampage, Kudrun makes sure that the queen knows precisely how great is her *caritas* before granting the request (1517–1518).

14. Viewed from the other perspective, the sacrilegious, murderous, thieving, kidnapping, vengeful, burning, pillaging Hegelings, as the narrative's heroes, do not admit any wrongdoing (and scholarship has been slow in acknowledging it as well), and there is no evidence that they are forgiven or loved by the surviving Normans.

The facile nature of the scholarly labeling of motifs as "Germanic" or "pre-christian" is demonstrated in Werner Hoffmann's comments on Wate's medical prowess (p. 225), which since learned from *wilde weibe* "wild/uncivilized women," is automatically assumed to be pre-christian and Germanic, and the "wild women," apparently, witches. The conception of the nonconformist female as *wildes weib,* as witch and demon, has been a long-standing and convenient masculist myth, quite effective in policing female attempts to break the bonds of patriarchal gender definition — the unmarried female living without male guardianship is necessarily suspect, and a potentially paradigm-threatening role. To assume that any and all *wilde weibe* in the thirteenth century, or the imagination of the thirteenth century (or in the sixteenth or eighteenth century, in France and North America, for that matter) were pre-, un- or anti-christian is to accept the terms of the conventional patriarchal demonization of the unmarried (i.e., to some degree, independent) adult female. Additionally we might recall that there has been a rich tradition of semi-, quasi- and often fully christian superstition and magic from the very beginning that makes the identification even as non-christian or extra-christian unnecessary. Furthermore, why is the necessary and immediate assumption that medically astute *wilde weibe* are non-christian at all? Need they be witches? In cultures without, for instance, penicillin or lasar surgery, a functional knowledge of pharmacological and not-yet-pharmaceuticalized healing plants and herbs constituted, for most of the world, "medicine." Interestingly no scholar stigmatizes Wate for having attained such expertise from the *wilde weibe,* nor do they disparage his actual, functional skill in healing the wounded which he learned from them. Here again we detect the conventional patriarchal double standard: as long as practiced by a male hero, such medicine is medicine; when practiced or taught by non-male non-heroes, then it must be pre-christian, Germanic, "wild," "lore," or simply black magic.[15]

15. A further assumption in pro-Germanic positions has long been that vengeance is necessarily Germanic. In the course of his own argument Werner Hoffmann points out — without acknowledging the damage that this admission does to his argument — that vengeance qua justice continued up through the seventeenth century in German-speaking Europe (p. 238). One might add that it has continued in some sections of Sicily, in Eastern Kentucky, in Saudi Arabia, and elsewhere up to the present, without anyone, I think, pretending that any such manifestations are cultural relics of a pre-Germanic social form. Cf. also Zacharias ("Die Blutrache im deutschen Mittelalter, *Zeitschrift für deutsches Altertum* 91 [1961/1962], pp. 210–211), quoted by Siebert (*Rezeption und Produktion,* p. 177), according to whom blood vengeance continued in Germany until the seventeenth century "ohne daß die Träger dieser Institution das Empfinden gehabt hätten, einem spezifisch heidnischen Brauch zu folgen" ("without the bearers of this institution having had the sense that they were following a

Any argument in favor of *Kudrun* as essentially christian must deal with a further issue that has conventionally forced intellectual and ultimately also ethical acrobatics onto its scholarly proponents: the problem of vengeance as represented in the narrative. The concept of vengeance and its literary praxis (far less its actual historical praxis) has been examined particularly by Adolf Beck and more recently by Barbara Siebert.[16] She identifies three types of vengeance in *Kudrun*: "1) Fraglos gerechte Rache — 2) Eskalation eines als gerecht angelegten Rachegeschehens — 3) Fälle von unbegründeter Racheausübung, die vom Dichter als ungerecht zurückgewiesen werden" (p. 144); ("1) unquestionably just vengeance — 2) the escalation of a vengeful event that is set up as just — 3) cases of unfounded vengeance rejected by the poet as unjust," p. 177). But in any case: "prinzipiell besteht das Recht, sich für ein zugefügtes Unrecht zu rächen" ("in principle there is a right to avenge oneself for an injustice suffered"), for the poet does not reject vengeance in principle, but rather problematizes only potentially excessive acts. A lengthy set of observations by Werner Hoffmann is worth quoting in full because it well illustrates the tangled interpretive web woven around the issue of vengeance in *Kudrun*:

---

specifically heathen custom"). This entire argument seems an instance of the fallacy of accepting the identity of *origin* as constitutive of definition. Despite, for instance, the obvious and demonstrably pagan origins of many aspects of various European christian celebratory rites, particularly Christmas, they neither function as nor are perceived by the millions of christian celebrants as Germanic festivals, as a Roman Saturnalia, as a winter solstice. The secularization and commercialization of that holiday in recent decades particularly in capitalist societies seems to be leading to a further paradigmatic change, such that the legend of the birth of Jesus as the christian god's divine son, and thus the entire christian significance of the festival, is being suppressed by the corporate media in favor of newly invented myths more conducive to commodification.

16. Adolf Beck, "Die Rache als Motiv und Problem in der 'Kudrun.' Interpretation und sagengeschichtlicher Ausblick," repr. in *Nibelungenlied und Kudrun,* ed. Heinz Rupp, Wege der Forschung 54 (Darmstadt: Wissenschaftliche Buchgesellschaft, 1976), pp. 454–501; Barbara Siebert, *Rezeption und Produktion.* Beck's essay is the most direct examination of the theory and practice of vengeance in *Kudrun.* He subscribes to the conventional interpretation of this motif in *Kudrun* as the transcendence of vengeance (pp. 454–455). Almost inevitably in the process of defending this position, Beck also stumbles on and over several unacknowledged problems; he claims, for instance, that "für Kudrun ist der Grundsatz der Sippenrache hinfällig. Das Individuum tritt, sofern es schuldlos ist, aus der kollektiven Verantwortung heraus" ("for Kudrun the principle of clan vengeance is invalid. The individual, insofar as she or he is innocent, separates her- or himself from the collective responsibility," p. 486). The interactionalist affinities are clear in the denial of an individual's social and class responsibility and pretense that all social behavior is merely personal. Beck recognizes that Kudrun is potentially co-responsible for the deaths of Gerlind and Hergard, but contends that "Gerlint und Hergard sind nicht zu retten, doch läßt der Dichter seine Lieblingin wenigstens nichts tun, sie der gerechten Strafe zuzuführen" ("Gerlind and Hergard cannot be saved, but the poet at least does not allow his favorite to do anything to bring about their deserved punishment" p. 483).

Der Vergebung und Versöhnung geht die Rache voraus, die Rache in einem Ausmaß, der nichts Christliches mehr innewohnt. Und diese Rache war notwendig, um überhaupt zu einer Versöhnung gelangen zu können. Ludwig und Gerlint mußten ihr zum Opfer fallen, damit Hartmut und Ortrun die Verzeihung und Versöhnung zuteil werden konnte. Bruno Boesch hat mit dem Satz: "Rache bleibt nach wie vor das Element, das die Ordnung der Großen dieser Welt ins Blei bringt" (Einl., S. liii), durchaus etwas Richtiges getroffen. Nur ist das, was auch Boesch, wenigstens andeutend, hervorhebt, nicht das Letzte—und darauf kommt es an. Die Auffassung, die Wate vertritt, wird überwunden. Aber der Dichter, der Wates Ansicht nicht teilt und sein Handeln im Schlußteil nicht billigt, hat die Stufe, auf der er steht, als notwendig betrachtet, und darum kann sich die Versöhnung nicht auf Gerlint und Ludwig erstrecken: die Gerechtigkeit verlangt Strafe, Vergeltung. Doch der Dichter tut dar, daß es nicht nur die strafende Gerechtigkeit gibt—die noch über die Talion des "Auge um Auge, Zahn um Zahn" hinausgeht—, sondern auch das Überhöhen der Gerechtigkeit durch das Verzeihen und die Gnade. Es geht dabei nicht um ein Entgegensetzen, sondern eben um ein Überhöhn oder um ein Aufheben im Doppelsinn des Wortes als Auslöschen und Bewahren. Die Haß- und Rachegesinnung wird überwunden, aber die Bereitschaft zum Kampf als Instrument der Ordnungs- und Friedenswahrung bleibt in ihrem Recht bestehen und hat nach wie vor ihre Notwendigkeit.[17]

There are a number of interconnected contradictions here. First, Hoffmann implies that there is nothing inherently un-christian about vengeance, but rather only about vengeance in excess.[18] If such a claim has a

---

17.
    Forgiveness and reconciliation are preceded by vengeance; the vengeance on such a scale that there is no longer anything christian about it. And this vengeance was necessary in order to be able to come to a reconciliation at all. Ludwig and Gerlint had to be sacrificed to it, so that Hartmut and Ortwin could have a share in the forgiveness and reconciliation. In the sentence: "vengeance remains now as ever the element that regulates the ranking of the powerful of this world" ("Einleitung," p. liii), Bruno Boesch has touched on something quite to the point. Only that which Boesch too, at least by implication, emphasizes, is not the ultimate point—and that is what matters most. The view that Wate represents is overcome. But the poet, who does not share Wate's view and does not approve his behavior in the final part, considered the stage at which he stands a necessary one, and thus the reconciliation cannot extend to Gerlind and Ludwig: justice requires punishment, retaliation. But the poet demonstrates that not just a punitive justice exists—which exceeds even the *lex talionis* of "an eye for an eye and a tooth for a tooth"—but also a transcendence of justice by means of forgiveness and mercy. In this regard it is not a matter of correspondence/opposition, but of transcendence or "Aufheben" in the double sense of the word "cancellation" and "preservation." The mentality of hate and vengeance is overcome, while the readiness for war as an instrument in its own right for preserving order and peace remains and retains now as ever its own necessity.
    18. Siebert remarks that it is characteristic of vengeance in *Kudrun* that once a vengeful act begins, it threatens to get out of control and to "burn until no fuel is left," that is, apparently until no potential victims of vengeance remain. She, like Hoffmann, claims that the vengeance in *Kudrun* is stopped before it becomes "maßlos" (p. 170). One wonders, however, how many more thousand deaths and dozens of castles in flames it would take to become *maßlos*.

basis in normative christian theology of some historical society relevant to the period of *Kudrun*'s composition, then that evidence would need to be adduced and analyzed, rather than merely tacitly assumed. Secondly, the assumption that Ludwig and Gerlind *must,* for any reason, be killed is rather astonishing in the context of an argument maintaining that the ethical focus of the text is on reconciliation, interpersonal harmony, and international peace.[19] Thirdly, it is not until Nolte's work that we find a scholar who does not just "describe" the insidious, indeed cynically duplicitous morality, inherent in the claim that there can be no forgiveness and reconciliation until there has been murderous vengeance, but identifies it as such.[20] We might also remark that if Kudrun were in fact acting on the idealized "christian principles" imputed to her, would she not have insisted on preventing the bloodshed *before* it occurred, that is when she met and freely conversed with the Hegeling commanders (Ortwin and Herwig) on the eve of the battle, rather than "reconciling" with the few enemy survivors *after* what we must acknowledge to have been a bloodbath. Hoffmann makes two further, related claims — that the quantity of vengeance exacted by the Hegelings is not excessive and that it is an essential element of the justice ("Gerechtigkeit") executed, that only in its *Überhöhen* and Hegelian *Aufheben* can it be culturally transcended. Finally and significantly, Hoffmann sees no contradiction in an insistence on this transcendence along with the narrative's obvious retention of war and cycles of vengeance in the function as guarantor of "order" and "peace."

Clearly one of the primary problems in such conceptions as Hoffmann's and Siebert's is their claim that the quantity of vengeance exacted is not excessive, for that logically requires a definition of what constitutes reasonable and legitimate as opposed to illegitimate and excessive vengeance in very specific terms. Ludwig's murder, for instance, might be said to "cancel" the murder of Hetel. But such quantifying obviously becomes tricky and almost embarrassing rather quickly, for there are a number of *categories* (as opposed to simple quantities within corresponding categories) of Hegeling violence that cannot be cancelled out, since they did not, apparently, take place in the prior Ormanian attack on the Hegeling castle: the slaughter of children, the murder of the queen, the destruction of castles other than the besieged focal residence. Two brief passages illustrate the controlling ethos of the Hegelings here. First, the blatant, all but glee-

---

19. Siebert also claims (p. 167) that Gerlind and Hergart are justifiably executed (*gerechte Rache* "just vengeance") as the primary guilty parties (*Hauptschuldige*).

20. Siebert too merely "notes" that *suone* becomes possible only after the thirst for vengeance has been quenched (p. 169).

ful looting and destruction by the Hegelings becomes almost parodic, for as soon as the capture of Kassiane is assured, Wate sings out: *Wo sind nu die knechte. mit den secken* ("'where are the young men/servants with the sacks?'" 1498,4); more than two ships full of loot were taken from this one castle (1500). On the slaughter of the innocents, it is laconically reported that *das Volck von dem Lannde grossen schaden nam. da slůg man darÿnne. Mann vnd weib. die kindel in den Wiegen. verloß maniges da seinen leib* ("the people of the land suffered great harm. Both men and women were killed; many a baby in the crib lost its life there" 1501,2–4). The exchange between Yrolt and Wate about the latter's slaughter of the infants is callous, witty, morbid, and essential: Wate explains that were they to live, they would grow up to become avengers (in fact precisely as have the Hegelings who make up their army, mention of which is tactfully omitted by Wate). In this context of the careful and precise slaughter of infants as potential future enemies, Wate slyly manages to fire off two jibes, first at Yrolt for having *kindeß mût* ("courage of a child" 1503,1) and then an ethnic slur as well: the babies, were they to survive, would be as untrustworthy as *ain wilder Sachse* ("a wild Saxon" 1503,4).

Whether the number represents the total casualties of the siege, only those of the Hegeling alliance, only Normans, or a combination of them is not clear, but after the siege of Kassiane, four thousand dead are dumped in the ocean nearby (1538).[21] After the mayhem at the capture of Kassiane, thirty thousand Hegelings rampage through the kingdom: *das fewr allenthalben hiesz man werffen an* ("it was ordered to cast fire onto everything/on all sides" 1545,2); *die prachten gûte Burge. was man der da vant. Sy namen weib den maistñ den yemand da mochte bringen* ("whatever good castles they found there, they destroyed. They took as many women[22] as anyone ever might bring" 1546,2–3); *Sechsundzwaintzigk purge. prachen Sy da nidere* ("they destroyed twenty-six castles" 1547,2–4).[23] They took a thousand hostages (1547), who suffered loss of freedom, exile, and as the text expressly claims, experienced what Kudrun and her twenty ladies had

21. One suspects that this form of sea burial will make what could never have been a very satisfactory laundry now completely unfit.

22. While ms. *weib* is grammatically a problem (generally emended to *roup* "booty"), the usage again demonstrates what was commonly assumed to be fair booty for the conquerors. This is especially interesting if *weib* is a textual "corruption" for *roub,* for that would mean that in the course of the text transmission a scribe (deliberately, unconsciously or indifferently) substituted the one type of war booty for the other.

23. The only reason that Kassiane is not also burned (as Wate counsels) is so that Kudrun and the Hegelings will have a suitable place to stay until they can return home (1534–1535; cf. also Siebert, p. 168).

suffered (1554–55).[24] The narrator reports on the generalized results of the expedition — *sy warn jr vrlauges vil stoltz. vnde here* ("they were very proud of and joyful about their war" 1547,3) — and Ortwin sums up: *Was sÿ vnns ye getaten. Wir nemen jn wol tausent mal mere* ("whatever they did to us, we took a thousand times more from them" 1550,4).

In any case, it seems only reasonable that if it is suggested that Hegeling vengeance is "not excessive," then the two analytical categories "excessive" and "not excessive" and a recognizable, quantifiable difference between them has been assumed. As a result, this unmistakably ethical valuation at least pretends to an empirical basis. Such being the case, it seems fair to expect both that empirical demonstration (e.g., the body-counts [burned castle counts, etc.] that have in recent decades become one means of publicly legitimizing military action) and the precise ethical criteria on the basis of which one might claim that neither the X deaths resulting from the Ormanian invasion nor the 1000 X deaths (according to Ortwin) resulting from the Hegeling expedition are excessive.[25]

Not all scholars have suppressed the excessive violence of the Hegelings. Nolte recognizes and analyzes the fact that the counterattack is more destructive than the initial causal attack (p. 10). In fact, as he further remarks:

> Die Rache der Hegelingen ist fürchterlich. . . . Um es noch einmal klar auszusprechen: Bei diesem Kriegszug der Hegelingen handelt es sich nicht nur um die "Rückentführung" Kudruns im Rahmen des literarischen Schemas, sondern um einen Rachefeldzug, der zum gewalttätigen Exzeß eskaliert und das Thema Frauenraub zu einer letzten Steigerung führt. Auch die versöhnungsstiftende Rolle Kudruns, die dem entgegensteuert, vermag diese Katastrophe vorerst nicht zu verhindern. Dies sollte man über dem versöhnlichen Schluß nicht vergessen." (p. 11)[26]

24. One should note, however, that after their bonds are loosed at the Hegeling court (1599), their conditions of exile and house arrest do not, apparently, include housekeeping chores.

25. Another of Hoffmann's remarks may, however, betray his real goal: "und wenn auch die Rache nie derart ins Maßlose wächst wie diejenige Kriemhilts" ("and even if the vengeance never becomes so excessive as Kriemhilt's" p. 234). Ultimately then it is a matter of the vengeance exacted *for* Kudrun not being as great or as despicable as that exacted *by* Kriemhilt. Here too, however, a pseudo-empirical claim is made.

26. "The Hegelings' vengeance is terrible. . . . To express it clearly once again: in this campaign of the Hegelings it is not just a matter of the 're-kidnapping' of Kudrun in the context of the literary model; it is rather also a campaign of vengeance that escalates to violent excess and brings the theme of bride-kidnapping to its highest level of intensity. Even the conciliatory role of Kudrun, which opposes all that, cannot for the time being prevent the catastrophe. Over and above the conciliatory conclusion, one should not forget this." McConnell also acknowledges, "Both the abduction and rescue of Kudrun involve war, mass destruction, and revenge" (p. 65).

The *suone* as such does not stop the battle, does not prevent what any modern conception would call war crimes, mass murder, atrocities, but rather:

> Die *suone* gelingt erst nach der Heimkehr der Hegelingen, *nach* der Stillung des Rachedursts. Zuerst muß der Boden mit Toten gedüngt werden (1415,4). Insofern hat das Kudrunepos durchaus die Unerbittlichkeit in der Auseinandersetzung, das Elefantengedächtnis der Rache (vgl. Kriemhilt!) und die Blindheit des Wütens, die das Nibelungenlied kennzeichnen, bewahrt. Die Gewalt, mit der man versucht, die Konflikte zu lösen, wird sogar noch schärfer pointiert als im Nibelungenlied. (p. 12)[27]

Another component in the construction of *suone* as reconciliation and Kudrun as the angel of peace is prescribed by Barbara Siebert in her claim that the potentially catastrophic vengeance in *Kudrun* is halted by the intervention of *Dritte*—third parties external to the conflict—and that these outsiders are usually female (p. 169). Such a conception of "the peace process" is common to the hegemonic political rhetoric of many periods and cultures. In such a conception the sponsor of peace negotiations is "neutral," without a stake in the outcome, without an interest in anything beyond the humanitarian aims of peace. It does not require a cynic to recognize that in international disputes (as in personal ones) settlements generally favor the party (the parties) with the power to bring them about, whether that party is an original party to the dispute or not. Certainly in the case of *Kudrun,* no one among the peacemakers is in any sense external to the conflicts at issue. Can Hagen be thought "external" to the conflict between his father and the prince of Garadie, who attempted to hold him at ransom in order to injure Hagen's father. Is it realistic to pretend that Kudrun—princess of the Hegelings, wife of Herwig, and former captive of Hartmut—is politically and personally disinterested in the disposition of the warring parties. Such altruism appears as far as I know only in myth and one of its subsets, hagiography, which I fear is the genre to which we must assign such claims concerning disinterested peacemaking in *Kudrun.*

The primary threat to a christian interpretation of Kudrun's character has generally been assumed by scholars to derive from her *list* "cunning/

---

27. "The *suone* succeeds only after the Hegelings' return home, *after* quenching the thirst for vengeance. First the ground has to be manured/fertilized with the dead (1415,4). In this respect the Kudrun-epic has thoroughly preserved the inexorability in conflicts, the memory of an elephant in matters of vengeance (cf. Kriemhilt!) and the blindness of rage that distinguishes the *Nibelungenlied*. The violence with which one attempts to resolve conflicts is even more pointedly represented than in the *Nibelungenlied*."

cleverness/slyness." Werner Hoffmann defends Kudrun from censure here
by suggesting that the *list* is, on the one hand, Kudrun's "Waffe . . . des
überlegenen Geistes" ("weapon of the superior spirit/imagination/intel-
lect")[28] but on the other, not an untruth, not even technically, he claims, for
she "grenzt an eine Unwahrheit" ("verges on an untruth" pp. 174–175)
only in 1285,2, where she says that she will now *minnen* Hartmut. Thus we
should rather speak of the *list* as a "Mentalreservation" rather than a lie
(p. 176). But the *list* and its effects are not exhausted in Kudrun's mental
processes, without external, social consequences, for it literally saves her
skin, causes joy among the Ormanians and grief among the Hegeling
maidens, and changes Kudrun's immediate status and material state from
indigent quasi-slave to "crown-princess."

It seems best here to abandon all defense of an idealized, perfect, and
pure Kudrun and simply admit that the lie is a lie, for otherwise Kudrun
nowhere betrays any intention of marrying Hartmut. Kudrun lies to save
herself and restore the concrete signs of her aristocratic status before her
liberators and their armies arrive to find her in rags, as her husband and
brother had already done. She lies to her archenemies who have murdered
her father, kidnapped her, and subjected her to almost a decade and a half of
what is, from her (and her class's) point of view, abuse (housekeeping:
lighting and maintaining fires, sweeping floors, washing laundry), and,
from most modern legal perspectives, sexual harassment and a type of
slavery.[29] Due to her astute handling of the situation, she also manages to

28. Hoffmann offers a useful analysis of the actual occurrences of the term *list* in the
work, by means of which he demonstrates that the use here approximates general Middle High
German practice in that *list* can signify either *astutia* or *dolus,* and is ethically indifferent or
rather ambivalent, with "good" and "bad" *list* differentiated only by means of an adjective
(p. 179).

29. Regarding her forced manual labor: so as to guard against sympathetic overreaction
here, we might remark that when Kudrun returns to her husband there will no doubt be
unfree, unpaid, and probably ragged females performing precisely these tasks *for* her and at
least in part *against* their will. On the other hand there are two sides to the "torture" motif
here. When Gerlind's methods have in the course of three-and-a-half years not persuaded
Kudrun to marry Hartmut, she mentions torture, but only to deny that it would have any
effect on Kudrun (1017). It is perhaps mildly amusing to modern readers accustomed to
housework to look across the centuries into another class formation and find housework
equated in *Kudrun* with abject humiliation, bordering on torture. (It is somewhat more than
mildly amusing to find the same attitude uncritically shared by modern, generally male,
scholars, who are, apparently, as aghast at the prospect of housework as was Kudrun.) There is
no need, however, to pretend that the dangers Kudrun faces in Ormanie are *exclusively* class
defined: despite the textual difficulties in st. 1282, it is clear that Gerlind intends to have
Kudrun bound to a bedstead and her skin whipped from her *beine* "bones/legs/thighs" with a
thorn-wrapped switch/rod; while it is certainly possible that such punishment could result in
death, as Wild (*Zur Überlieferung,* p. 62) would have us believe, there is no evidence in the
generalities of the text at this point to indicate the likely outcome of this mode of punishment,

turn this lie into a strategic advantage for the armies coming to liberate her, as the narrator observes, by having Hartmut dispatch enough messengers, with the news of the upcoming marriage, to reduce significantly the troops on hand to defend the castle.

To deny the nature of the *list* as a lie also denies Kudrun whatever political, strategic or military astuteness attaches to the stratagem. Here one can choose a compromised, idealist purity or a modicum of intelligence in one's heroine. In any case it seems unnecessary to disparage Kudrun's virtue because of this lie, and further it seems to misrepresent the function of the lie in the text, whose circumstances make it so useful. We might ask why scholarship has been so obsessed with this individual "immoral" act that is imbedded in the context of kidnapping, sexual harassment, mass murder, willful and capricious property destruction by the "heroes." Does its significance in the scholarship derive more from the attempt by scholars to defend a "good woman," (necessarily an idealized, pure, and morally unblemished woman), rather than from any objectively measurable or contextually relative immorality of the act itself? As Campbell points out, "critics have often felt that Gudrun's character is, or should be, without blemish, hence great embarrassment has been expressed when she makes these false promises" (p. 271).[30] Kudrun lies. Does this mean that she is no longer "worthy" not to be kidnapped, no longer noble, no longer the legitimate protagonist, no

---

whose result necessarily depends on its intensity and duration, especially since it is then not carried out. In contrast, however, when the text claims that washing laundry on a snowy beach while barefoot is life-threatening, there is every reason to believe it. On the issue of sexual harassment: during her thirteen years of captivity, Kudrun is subject to the constant threat of sexual violation. It seems as well that Hartmut's *freünde* counsel him to rape Kudrun in order finally to end the matrimonial limbo in which he hangs: *Da reiten seine freünde . . . daz Er die schone maid in seinen willen brächte. wo mit er künde* ("his friends advised . . . that he bring/bend the beautiful maiden to his will, by whatever means necessary" 1025,1–3).

30. And further: "Why should Gudrun not employ an 'offene Lüge' to ward off Hartmut's embrace and at the same time not undermine the credibility of her consent to wed him. . . . All the difficulties that critics have seen associated with Gudrun's 'list' would be resolved if only they would accept that Gudrun is not perfect according to their own understanding of perfection, just as Hagen and Hilde are not perfect" (p. 276). The tradition is too pervasive even for Campbell to evade at all times, however, for he imputes to an act of Kudrun's an interpretation that disintegrates under even casual inspection: he claims she regrets the blood spilled and to be spilled for her sake (pp. 281–282), which prompts her to lament: "Awe ich gotes arme. daz ich den leib ye gewan" ("alas, that I was ever born — I god's poor little thing!" 1359,3). If — and this is not altogether clear from context — this statement responds to the fact of others' suffering, then it seems that this is a typical response from a feudal, aristocratic character *and* a typical misinterpreting gesture on the part of a tradition of scholarship defined by bourgeois apologetics: she expresses "regret" for death of thousands of others by claiming that *she* is god's poor little thing!

longer virtuous, no longer christian? Or does it rather, as I would suggest, represent her as a more complex, less robotic character, one with an effective conception of her present situation at court and an ability to influence momentarily her immediate environment?[31]

To make the specific nature of my skepticism toward the pro-christian position clear: obviously Kudrun was conceived, written, and initially heard and/or read by a European christian audience; its characters are christian by definition, unless otherwise explicitly identified by the poem. But the same is true of the *Nibelungenlied,* where there is as significant a number of instances of "demonstrable" christianity—main characters attending mass or the presence of a priest in the Burgundian retinue, for example—as in *Kudrun.* But in the *Nibelungenlied* there is no evidence of (and indeed rarely a scholarly argument for),[32] a specifically christian motivation for any of the primary actions of the plot, let alone the main plot as a whole. The same is true of *Kudrun,* although obviously in such a tale it could conceivably have been otherwise. While we certainly must reckon with the all but ubiquitous importance of christianity in some form across much of Europe during the medieval period, for some of the populace,[33] and while we must also make certain allowances for our christian colleagues' attempts to appropriate as "christian" most motifs constructed as "ethical" or "virtuous" in medieval European literature, the time seems right to profit from recent research in historical and cultural criticism and to express some collegial skepticism about the idealized invention of a peaceful, loving character of historical christianity, especially in the high Middle Ages. Despite the relatively greater uniformity in institutional christianity in much of the Middle Ages than has been the case since the Reformation, "christian" is even then a term all but meaningless without some concrete historical specification of culture, sect, period, or theological foundation. It is in general difficult to discern the content of this "new" christian ethos— assumed by numerous scholars but defined by none—of which Kudrun is supposedly the exponent. Christianity is neither itself new in the mid-

31. For after all, the lie can only be temporarily effective: were the Hegelings *not* at the gates, then she would very soon have to marry Hartmut, unless she came up with a further ploy.

32. Cf., however, the work of H. B. Willson, for example the article "Concord and Discord: The Dialectic of the *Nibelungenlied,*" *Medium Aevum* 28 (1959), 153–166.

33. Not the Saxons until they were massacred and all but annihilated by Charlemagne's policy of imperial expansion; not the Swedes until almost the period when the *Nibelungenlied* and *Kudrun* were composed; not the Jews; not the Muslims of the Iberian peninsula or Sicily.

thirteenth century, nor is it new to the German-speaking inhabitants of central Europe, who had been christian for half a millennium by this time.[34] Otherwise, the posited conciliatory gestures of Kudrun (or Hagen) might well be better characterized without reference to an undefined religious ethos. This is particularly the case since such harmony and conciliation were hardly the norm and rarely even a recognized viable option for the resolution of political conflict in Europe of the bloody thirteenth century, especially if one looks beyond the borders of the continent to the extra-European imperialist enterprises (which were always allied with if not directly under the control of missionary christianity), and the resurgence of the fortress mentality in opposition to Islam. Just as christianity is not new in 1240, neither is there any historical evidence from the generation or two between the posited dates of the composition of the *Nibelungenlied* and *Kudrun* of a radical social change that might have been represented in mediated literary form as a move from vengeance as the norm of conflict resolution toward a more peaceful method.

In concluding this section on the long-standing tradition of constructing Kudrun as a model of ethical and particularly of christian behavior, let us turn to some final observations on Campbell's extensive analysis of this complex of issues. One of the most significant problems for the christian construction is the need to contextualize Kudrun's words and deeds. If, for instance, Kudrun and her acts at the end of the narrative are to be viewed as christian, there are grave problems, for her famous rebuke of her mother must be seen in context — *niemand mit übele. sol dhaines hasses lonen* ("no one should repay any hatred/hostility with evil" 1595,3). Campbell comments: "she is referring to an enemy who has been overcome already, she is not dealing, as Hilde is, with an enemy who is still powerful and quite unrelenting. Gudrun's policies are not inspired by a philosophy of turning the other cheek but by the idea of 'crush and then restore in reconciliation,' and this is precisely what Hagen did with the men of Garadie. This is also in accordance with the fact that Wate is . . . outmoded at the end of the work as far as treatment of defeated enemies is concerned, but indispensable when victory is yet to be won" (p. 232). Kudrun is politically pragmatic, and her political sense does not reject compromises for the sake of a modern idealization of a "medieval" christianity.

An analysis of Kudrun and *suone* must address as its primary focus the

---

34. Campbell too notes: "Not the least questionable aspect here is the insistence upon perpetuating the outmoded tradition of using the terms Germanic and Christian to set up mutually-exclusive categories" (p. 1).

motif of marriage *as suone,* as commonly employed at the conclusion of medieval courtly romance, for all Kudrun's previous deeds construed as conciliatory are overshadowed by the final episodes of marriage arrangement.[35] There is an unreflected assumption by conventional scholarship concerning the narrative's deployment of marriage: that it actually functions not just as a symbol of, but also as a cause of, stability and personal and social harmony. Loerzer, for instance, suggests: "Nach dem Sieg über Hartmut, der Wiedergewinnung Gudruns und der glücklichen Heimkehr bedeuten die Eheschließungen des Schlusses die Zusammenfassung des Ganzen in Freude und Glanz, im deutlichen Kontrast zum vorangegangenen Elend und Kriegsgeschehen. . . . Dies steht gleichsam als Programm über allem: das Verheiraten als Mittel der Versöhnung und Befriedung und des Harmonisierens" ("After the victory over Hartmut, the regaining of Kudrun and the happy return home, the marriages of the conclusion signify the bringing together of the whole in joy and brilliance, in clear contrast to the previous misery and war. . . . This is, so to speak, the determinative program: marriage as a means to reconciliation and pacification and harmonization," p. 132).[36] But it seems that the inevitable consequence of such a progression and intensification is not drawn by any scholar. Such happy endings of *structural* necessity, since of *societal* inevitability, lead to a new phase of identical conflict. The very fact of recurrence indicates that the problem is not resolved on any but an *individual,* momentary basis: by means of such a method, only the case at hand is, and can ever be resolved, and no solution for the inevitable social conflict arising from *future* wiving expeditions is proposed, nor is such a solution even conceived as necessary.

The importance of this motif is hardly surprising since wiving is the primary social activity represented in the poem. Nonetheless, nowhere is the proper means of marital arrangement theorized by the poem (which would probably be too much to ask of a work of imaginative literature), but likewise nowhere is the specific problem of wiving itself addressed as such, except in the one problematic claim by Kudrun, that marriage had traditionally only been allowed between mutually consenting men and women.[37] In terms of the history of Kudrun's culture as depicted in the

35. Scholarly attention has focused on none but the final marriage *as* transcendence and transformation of the prior conflictual state, which seems particularly peculiar, since they offer little that is new in *Kudrun*'s convention of wiving, except that they occur at the end of the narrative.

36. Wild notes that all conflicts arising in such a marriage quest in *Kudrun* lead to happy endings — a condition of stasis (pp. 55–56).

37. Nolte observes: "In der matrimonialen Praxis des mittelalterlichen Adels kann aber von einem ehelichen Selbstbestimmungsrecht des Mädchens keine Rede sein. Hier bestimmen

narrative, this claim is absurd. In historical terms it is at least problematic. Gunter Grimm notes that when Kudrun claims that consent is the "old way," she can only be referring to the tradition of *Friedelehe,* since ecclesiastical consent was a late-twelfth-century innovation ("Die Eheschließungen," p. 55).[38] But if *Kudrun* was written in the second quarter of the thirteenth century, then an ecclesiastical innovation from several generations earlier might well have been viewed as "old." The entire issue is further troubled, incidentally, by a problematic text here. What Kudrun actually says is: *Es ist noch heer der zeite. ain site also getan. daz kain fraw solte nemen ÿmmer man. Es war jr baider wille* "The times are long past that / up until now there has been a custom that/ no woman should ever take a man unless it were their common will" (1034,1–3). Generally the sense of *heer* in the first clause has been construed as "bisher" and of *war* in the third as *enwar.* As it stands, however, *noch heer der zeite* might just as legitimately be understood as "lange her"; the juggling of double and triple negatives in the second and third clauses, especially if one were to emend the texts, as most editors have, would, I fear, almost require a native speaker to decode.

It is not possible to extrapolate a transformation of wiving customs from the empirically accessible instances in the poem. There is in general no ⁇⁇⁇⁇⁇⁇⁇⁇⁇⁇⁇⁇ ⁇⁇⁇⁇⁇⁇⁇⁇⁇⁇⁇⁇⁇ ⁇⁇⁇⁇⁇⁇⁇ ⁇⁇⁇⁇⁇ ⁇⁇⁇⁇ ⁇⁇⁇⁇⁇ ⁇⁇ ⁇⁇⁇⁇ ⁇⁇⁇⁇⁇ fies four types of wiving in *Kudrun* and notes that the four parts of the narrative are all bridal-quests, and that there is an obvious intensification in their progression (*Steigerung*): the Sigeband episode is the simple schema

---

politische, dynastische und ökonomische Erwägungen die Gattenwahl. Diese wurde vom Pater familias geregelt, der für das Patrimonium Sorge zu tragen hatte. Innerhalb dieser matrimonialen Strategie, die der Allianz-Politik des Adels dient, ist die Frau ein Tauschobjekt" ("It is, however, out of the question to speak of a marital right of self-determination for unmarried females in the matrimonial praxis of the medieval nobility. The political, dynastic and economic considerations are determinative for the choice of a husband. Those were arranged by the *pater familias* who had to take care of the *patrimonium*. Within this matrimonial strategy, which served the alliance politics of the nobility, the woman is an object of exchange," pp. 27–28). He also notes (p. 29) Georges Duby's use of term "exchange value" for the analysis of the feudal traffic in women, whose marxist origins and specific connotation here seems entirely appropriate. Nolte cites from the English translation of Duby's text: *Medieval Marriage: Two Models from Twelfth-Century France,* transl. Elborg Forster, Johns Hopkins Symposia in Comparative History 11 (Baltimore: Johns Hopkins University Press, 1978), p. 99. Similarly, Joachim Bumke comments: "Theoretisch war eine Ehe zwar nur dann gültig, wenn beide Partner ihren Konsens gaben; aber in der Praxis hatte die Zustimmung der Frau oft nur formalen Charakter" ("Theoretically the marriage was only legal if both partners gave their consent; but in practice the consent of the woman often was merely a formality"), "Liebe und Ehebruch in der höfischen Gesellschaft," in *Liebe als Literatur: Aufsätze zur erotischen Dichtung in Deutschland,* ed. Rüdiger Krohn (München: Beck, 1983), p. 28.

38. "Die Eheschließung in der Kudrun. Zur Frage der Verlobten- oder Gattentreue Kudruns," *ZfdPh* 90 (1971), 55–56. Thomas Grenzler's recent claims that mutual consent and marital affection were the norms in medieval marriage are unsupported in his argument and in general untenable, in *Erotisierte Politik — Politisierte Erotik,* cf. esp. concluding chapter.

of wiving, the Hagen episode is "Erwerbung durch Taten" ("acquisition through deeds"), the Hilde episode represents "Entführung mit Einverständnis" ("abduction with consent") of the kidnapped bride, and the Kudrun episode represents the kidnapping of the bride without her consent (as treated in the previous chapter). As the narrative conclusion of each such episode, marriage assumes a further significance, normative for future episodes (marriage as *telos*) and lends significance to the individual current episodes as well: via the patriarchal myth of marriage as almost magically transformative of the male, changing boy to man, wild youth to responsible citizen, chaos to stability.[39]

The social transformation proposed by scholars is never articulated as one based in wiving-praxis, however, and thus traditional scholarship has never been able to solve that problem. If the final marriages *are* the solution, what do they solve? They change nothing about wiving praxis, but rather reinforce precisely those aspects of the inherited practice that recur in each of the four generations depicted and lead inevitably to chaos. The actual method by which the final marriages are brought about is somewhat unconventional, but hardly transformative. Hoffmann observes that some of the marriages at the end may appear "nicht ohne eine gewisse 'Künstlichkeit' oder 'Gewaltsamkeit'" ("not without a certain 'artificial or forced nature'" p. 287), but then, one might wonder, where might one expect non-arbitrary, non-artificial wiving in the context of such a system. Kudrun's method of "transformation" and *suone* is perhaps the most blatant example in the narrative of the dysfunctional and destructive mode of wiving: she forces marriage where either none was wanted or where the particular match she imposes was undesired; she does so without following the quasi-prescribed order of procedures; and she does so in blatant disregard of that element of wiving that she has earlier claimed to be of prime importance — mutual consent. But it is precisely in the arbitrariness and authoritarian manner in which she operates, that she participates directly in the inherited patriarchal praxis of wiving.

That Kudrun's marital *suone* is altruistic is a recurring scholarly assumption. Bender, for instance, speaks of "Kudruns freiwilliges Sich-Einsetzen auch für die Menschen, die ihr Leid zugefügt haben, begründet ihre selbstlose 'suone'-Haltung" ("Kudrun's voluntary engagement, even for those people who have caused her to suffer, is the basis of her selfless

---

39. The female, on the other hand, rarely is perceived to undergo a *corresponding* transformation, such as, for instance, Brünhild does in the *Nibelungenlied*; generally the female's transformation is either solely physical (putative rupture of the hymen) or vaguely almost mystically emotional (the experience of *vröude* "joy").

suone-attitude" p. 225).[40] On the one hand one must share the narrative's view of marriage as the (narrative) *summum bonum* of a society so structured, before one can assume that Kudrun's actions are so very munificent. On the other hand, however, I would suggest that there is little if anything selfless about her action: her forced marriages ensure some measure of Hegeling control over the defeated parties and attempt to bind them to a peaceful alliance so as to prevent their seeking counter-vengeance for the almost total devastation of their country. Kudrun's *suone* is not a political alternative to Wate's method of annihilation of the enemy in order to prevent further violence. It is rather a complement to it. Her method does not dis- or replace or transform Wate's method, but rather, as Hoffmann describes and Nolte critically analyzes, *may be practiced successfully* only as a result of the prior execution of his method. Only after the enemy is reduced to complete dependence is it possible to impose such ideological dominance as that which is manifested in these marriages. Such political acts are never selfless. When she speaks her famous line of harmony and conciliation to her mother — *niemand mit ûbele. sol dhaines hasses lonen* (1595,3), she refers *specifically* to the presentation of Ortrun and Hartmut to her mother, not, ostensibly at least, to life in general. In any case, it takes some effort not to find her words ironic.

The scholarly consensus has been that both in the fact and in the method of her composing peace via marriage, Kudrun transforms her society's customs and is thus the culmination of three generations of movement toward the enhancement of individual free will. After noting that Hartmut's consent to the match with Hildeburg is sought, Nolte, for instance, can already conclude: "Es geht also tatsächlich um die Herstellung des Willens des Anderen, um seine persönliche Integrität ("it is thus in fact a matter of the establishment of the will of the other person, of his personal integrity"). Campbell views Kudrun as "that champion of the individual's right to self-determination." Bender too speaks of "freie Willensentscheidung" ("decision of one's own free will") as a primary concern of the narrative at this point.[41] But in general this variation on the thesis of transformation has been less analyzed than conjured, accepted, and passed on. How is it, precisely, that Kudrun brings about these marriages that are obviously politically motivated and have less emotional basis or promise of

40. Siebert suggests: "daß Kudruns Friedenswerk vorbildlich ist und in der Qualität alle anderen vorausgegangenen Versöhnungen übersteigt, ist überflüssig zu betonen" ("it is superfluous to mention that Kudrun's peacemaking is exemplary and qualitatively superior to all the previous instances of reconciliation," p. 169).

41. Nolte, *Das Kudrunepos,* p. 66; Campbell, *Kudrun,* p. 156; Bender, *Nibelungenlied und Kudrun,* p. 224.

potential affection even than is customary in the typically political marriages of medieval literature and far less so than those motivated by preconceived *minne?* In none of the marriages that she arranges is there a mutually consenting couple, which she has claimed as the legitimate and traditional norm.

The legal definition of consensual marriage in the feudal period is complex, because it must be extrapolated from praxis. In his exemplary analysis of marriage practice in *Kudrun,* based on historical evidence for feudal marriage practice, Grimm suggests that the consensual act consists of three component elements: consensual discussion, promise of loyalty (*vestenunge*), and exchange of physical symbols (rings). Consummation follows immediately (p. 52). Clearly these categories do not exactly correspond to modern notions of "consent to marry," and we must be careful to guard against unwarranted, anachronistic assumptions of identity. Nonetheless, even if we hold to Grimm's categories, there is no unified picture of consent, so defined, in *Kudrun.* Of all the new marriage partners, in fact, only two — Hartmut (1640,4) and Ortwin, both men (1622,3) — actually might be said to consent in the modern sense. And, as we shall see, the medieval sense of consent, according to Grimm's analysis, is no better represented here. Siegfried is apparently not asked, has no opportunity to consent or not, but rather is only informed that the marriage will take place (he seems, *incidentally,* not to object). When the time comes for the marriage, Siegfried is ordered to the ring (1663,1).

Even those consulted, however, Hartmut and Ortwin, are in no sense in control of the situation. Hartmut's "consent" is such in only a restricted, perhaps "legal," but hardly volitional sense, for Kudrun's proposal to him is presented simultaneously as command, bargain, and threat, operating from a position of control, as wife/sister of the military victors:

> *wolt jr des volgen Hartmût. als ich euch lere.*
> *thuet jr das willikliche. so schaidet jr euch von aller hande sere.* (1635,3–4)

(If you would do as I tell you, Hartmut, [and] do it willingly, then you will depart from pain/ suffering/ wounds inflicted by anyone's hand)

> *so rat ich gernne dir*[42] *friste deinen leib* (1637,1)

(I eagerly advise you, by this means to save your life)

42. Ms. *die.*

The fiction of his free will (*willikliche*) is maintained, but the proposal is actually a command (*lere*) and blatant threat. He is presented with the "choice" of, on the one hand, marrying Hildeburg, retaining his throne (and honor, Kudrun points out), peace, the marriage of his sister Ortrun to Ortwin, and his physical well-being, or, on the other hand, death. Hartmut's response indicates both that he understands precisely the terms and "choices" offered and that the catastrophic turn his life has recently taken has done nothing to transform the codes of class and gender under which he operates: only if the match is not dishonorable in the eyes of his relations back home will he accept it. Otherwise he "chooses" death (1638). The open trafficking in women, and here also in politically subordinate men, is clearly expressed in Hartmut's repeating the terms of the "contract" at the end of the negotiations, simply reiterating what Kudrun has dictated to him: if Ortwin marries Ortrun, he will marry Hildeburg (1640). The exchange by two parties, one under duress, clearly illustrates and reenacts the political practice of hegemonic *do ut des*.

Just as important is the case of Hartmut's bride-to-be, Hildeburg. Siebert astutely observes that Hildeburg is an active participant in both the first and the last instance of *suone* in the tale and present at one middle one as well. "Als ist dies a *Daseinsform* of *suone* (p. 190), whose "Grunderfahrung ist es, gegen ihren Willen verschleppt zu werden, keine Kontrolle über ihr Schicksal zu haben. Mehr als alle anderen Gestalten im Roman ist sie Opfer von Fremdbestimmung" ("basic experience it is to be abducted against her will and have no control over her own fate. More than all other figures in the novel, she is the victim of non-self-determination" p. 192). At the end of the tale Hildeburg appears in her full epic development when she marries a man who doesn't love her for the sake of "Selbstaufgabe um eines Höheren willen" ("self-sacrifice for a sake of a higher cause" p. 196). Following Siebert's lead here, however, we might complete this catalogue by noting that just as Hildeburg was abducted by the griffin, by Hetel in his kidnapping of Hilde, and then by the Normans, here too she again is disposed of against her will—this time, however, by arrangement of her lifelong companion and "benefactress."[43] Hildeburg's only response to Kudrun's proposal of her marriage to Hartmut is a direct and unambiguous rejection,

43. Loerzer, *Eheschließung und Werbung in der "Kudrun"* (München: Beck, 1971), notes both that Kudrun has no "Verfügungsrecht" ("rights of disposal") or *Munt* over Hildeburg; in fact she has no clearly defined right to arrange a marriage for this princess of "Portigal," except perhaps insofar as she functions as the proxy for Hildeburg's currently effective male guardian (in the absence of an acknowledged one: Herwig or Ortwin). Despite Hildeburg's royal pedigree, Hilde at one point designates her as part of her *gesinde* (561,4).

which Kudrun just as directly and unambiguously dismisses without responding to its specific terms: she simply continues with her arrangements, which by this point have already become autocratic.[44] There is no *Selbstaufgabe* "self-sacrifice" on the part of Kudrun's lifelong (aristocratic) servant here, but rather a direct sacrifice of her by the beneficiary of that service — Kudrun — and for Kudrun's further benefit, as well for the sake of the Hegelings' political goals. Siebert can thus praise Hildeburg and her literary creator for a kind of self-denial and self-sacrifice that can only be a virtue for a class society that expects and commands such behavior on the part of its subordinates.[45]

The more extreme case of Herwig's unnamed sister is unusual even in this context of instant, imposed marriages. She is unconsulted and in fact not even present when the arrangements are made, but must be fetched from home in what functions as, and in fact may well have been experienced by her as, kidnapping or *Brautraub*.[46] For so we must designate the forced removal of a nubile female from her home and homeland for the purpose of marrying an unsought and undesired husband, in fact a husband who is her dynasty's hated enemy. In general the fetching of Herwig's sister conforms to the general actional pattern of *Brautraub* (1655–57) and is narrated in the same mode as any other military or kidnapping raid: Herwig observes that such an expedition will confront troubles (*arbait* 1652,4) unless or until (*ee*) he sends his own guide / retinue (*gelaite*); he then sends an armed party of a hundred of his own men for her, under the command of Wate and Fruote, the two most feared of the Hegeling warriors; despite Herwig's precautions and their own prowess, they do nonetheless suffer *arbait* in carrying out the assignment; they ride as fast as possible; prevent, only with great difficulty, Wate from attacking the (one must assume Herwig's) castle; take the sister and twenty-four ladies from the castle and return with

44. Campbell notes of Kudrun's response to Hildeburg's rejection of the marriage proposal: "This not unreasonable objection is peremptorily dismissed by Gudrun" (p. 295). While I think that the term "autocratic" here captures the essence of Kudrun's mode of action, we must bear in mind the tiny "realm" of matrimonial arrangements in which she is allowed to exercise such power; as will be treated farther on, there are further restrictions on what seems to be her complete control even of this restricted sphere.

45. Siebert comments on Hildeburg's *Deklassierung* and notes that the ostensibly joyous final departure of Hildeburg, that is, with Hartmut, is "nicht ganz frei von problematischen Aspekten" ("not altogether free of problematic aspects") in "Hildeburg im Kudrun-Epos. Die bedrohte Existenz der ledigen Frau," in *Der frauwen buoch: Versuch zu einer feministischen Mediävistik*, ed. Ingrid Bennewitz (Göppingen: Kümmerle, 1989), p. 222.

46. Nolte astutely comments on the inevitable functional similarity of *Brautraub* and *Brauttausch*: "Als literarische Fiktion aktualisiert der Raub die dem realen Frauentausch inhärenten raubartigen Momente" ("As a literary fiction, the kidnapping actualizes the rapacious factors inherent in the actual exchange of women," p. 35).

them at great speed in ships commandeered from the beach. Whether all this takes place against the maiden's will is both unclear to the reader and unproblematized by the narrative. In any case it certainly takes place without obtaining her consent to the action, for she seems utterly uninformed about its purpose even up to the point of the wedding. Loerzer's claim (p. 138), that she must have known why she was fetched, lacks support by the text, which makes it quite clear how shocked she was when the moment of her arrival at the Hegeling castle coincides with the conclusion of her marriage: *wes man da phlegen wolte. des nam Herwigeß Swester wunder* ("Herwig's sister was astounded by what they wanted to do/what was taking place there" 1662,4). The ritual request for consent takes place in public, in the ring, where it would be difficult if not impossible for this young women, this *kint*,[47] as she is called, to refuse (1661,1). It is difficult from a twentieth-century perspective to view this as an expression of her free will, and in terms of the thirteenth-century notions of legal consent it is hardly less troublesome. In the phrase *lobte sy jn träge* (1665,1), which, according to Grimm, functions as her expression of "consent" (p. 58), Loerzer interprets the word *träge* as the "zögernd-verschämte Haltung" ("hesitant-bashful pose") characteristic of a young girl (p. 138).[48] It seems just as likely that it is abject fear, the horror of powerlessness and the desperation of a young woman now traded to her peoples' enemy, exchanged on the orders of someone who has no traditional, legal authority over her and with the apparent but not explicit consent of her brother who does, but seems to have delegated it to Kudrun. When the text then reports that *da pot man Im jr mÿñe* ("there one [*man*] offered him her *minne*" 1665,2), it is not quite clear whom *man* — who has assumed control over her life, body, and *minne* — designates, although certainly not the bride herself. But by this point in this scene of marital terrorism, we are no longer surprised.[49]

Particularly problematic for the conventional interpretation of these marriages as Kudrun's consummate work of *suone* is the fact that three of the

47. This common Middle High German designation of females, whether adult, adolescent or otherwise, as *kint,* participates in the typical patriarchal tradition of trivializing — by infantilizing — women and their actions.

48. Elsewhere in *Kudrun,* Stackmann glosses *trage* as "sehr langsam, sehr wenig" (546,4).

49. There is a hint here as well of the property motif otherwise so carefully excluded from *Kudrun.* When Herwig protests that his sister does not have suitable clothing for court and wedding, since Siegfried (her husband-to-be) laid waste his land and burned his castles, Siegfried replies *daz er Ir wan in ainem hembde pate* "that he would sue for her even if [or "only if"] in nothing but a shift" (1654,4); thus her poverty either does not dissuade him, or is perhaps an outright incentive to marry her.

four unions are not, strictly speaking, her doing at all. Her own marriage to Herwig came about as a result of his instigation and Kudrun's parents' approval. Her own consent is present, although not unproblematic (as discussed in the previous chapter), but it is in no sense decisive in the matter. The marriage of Ortrun and Ortwin is suggested by Kudrun, at first rejected then accepted by Ortwin, rejected by Hilde (whose rejection is never recalled), and finally approved by Herwig and Fruote; it is this approval by the male counselors that seems primarily, if not exclusively decisive; this match is furthermore also insisted on later by Hartmut as a precondition to his accepting the match with Hildeburg. The instigation for *that* pairing is solely the responsibility of Fruote (1624), who simply appends to his approval of the marriage of Ortwin and Ortrun the suggestion of the next match: Hildeburg and Hartmut.[50] Only in the single case of Siegfried and Herwig's unnamed sister, both utterly subordinate to the central power of the Hegeling-Herwig alliance, does Kudrun initiate the marriage; and in this case it is most blatantly an imposed union in terms of the medieval conception of consent: Siegfried is not consulted but informed about his upcoming marriage, while his bride finds out about it only at the ceremony itself. Herwig has only a partial opportunity to approve.

Grimm attempts to account for these marriages in terms of thirteenth-century legal conventions. His summary of the legal status is both informative and problematic: there is no *desponsatio* in any one of this series of marriages; rather the *Ringakt* is itself the *Vertragsakt*; the sentence "die namen si ze wibe" ("they took them to wife" 1648,3) indicates the *Konsensakt,* whereafter the couples exchange rings without mentioning a *Treugelöbnis*; thereafter 1663–1116 the term *lobeten* constitutes the *Konsensakt* (p. 58). None of these is a *Muntehe,* but rather they all approximate Germanic *Friedelehe,* which consisted of two legal acts only — consent and consummation — and they even lean toward the consensual marriage instituted by the twelfth-century church (p. 62). The problems with this construction are obvious (and have nothing to do with Grimm's fine analysis): if these marriages are not examples of *Muntehe,* then they must, according to the restricted number of interpretive possibilities offered by Grimm, be *Friedelehe.* But the notion and practice of consent is decisive in *this* type of marriage, as it is not in the *Muntehe,* and precisely here is the

---

50. Fruote, incidentally, is also present at Kudrun's proposal to Hartmut of the match with Hildeburg, although she had just insisted to Hartmut that *daß sol nÿemand hören. Wann jch vnd Ir aine* ("that no one is to hear, except you and me alone" 1634,3).

problem. Neither Grimm's construction of the medieval sense of consent as consultation + vow + symbol, nor consent in the modern sense is present anywhere except in Kudrun's marriage, and even there numerous problems cloud the issue of mutual consent. "Consensual discussion," or consultation, takes place with only three of the six participants and in only one case with both partners to a pairing.[51] Let me recapitulate then to indicate why this ritual consent seems insufficient or at least problematic in context: the conquering/allied prince (Ortwin) is consulted about and consents to marrying the conquered princess (Ortrun); the conquered prince (Hartmut) is consulted and offered death or marriage to a subordinate, but allied princess (Hildeburg); the allied princess (Hildeburg) is consulted and rejects marriage; the previously conquered and now "rehabilitated" prince (a classic outsider, the "dirty" Moor) is not consulted; the conquered princess (Ortrun) is not consulted; a previously non-participating princess and sister of an allied prince (Herwig's sister) is not unproblematically consulted. It is quite clear that the attributes "male" and "allied" versus "female" and conquered "enemy" determine one's position on the scale of Nolte's "Herstellung des Willens des Anderen": currently powerful males are at one end of the spectrum and powerless females at the other end. Kudrun's putative championing of "free will" and "self-determination" is so very restrictive as to be almost nonexistent: only three of the six parties are consulted; one consents after persuasion, one other after he is offered the option of death for non-consent; the third directly refuses the offer. The only (free) will exercised here is Kudrun's.

While *Kudrun* has strong (though problematic) generic ties to romance that should not be dismissed here,[52] the treaty-marriages as enacted in *Kudrun* signal another strand of intertextuality that is perhaps more significant than the romance. Whatever the ultimate generic identity of *Kudrun,* it is clear that there are significant formal as well as thematic relations to that problematic generic category of "heroic" epic, where such political alliances via marriage are almost common enough to be a topos. Here such marriages function not as present evidence of future happiness, as generally in courtly romance, but rather as immediate and unambiguous signs of inevitable impending disaster: when the tribes are allied by mar-

---

51. Grimm claims that the marriage of Kudrun and Herwig is not a *Muntehe* (p. 63), and the absence of concrete indicators in the text supports his argument, especially since the marriage is a variation on *Brautraub.* At the same time, however, we should probably not build too extensive an interpretation on this argument *ex silentio.*

52. Cf. Wailes, "The Romance of Kudrun," 354–355.

riage in *Beowulf,* it is not for the sake of signifying a long-term alliance, but rather specifically to heighten the effect of the narratively inevitable violent disruption of the treaty. Even closer to home: marriage to the Burgundian princess does not *prevent* Siegfried's murder by a vassal of that house; nor does her later marriage to Etzel *prevent* a violent breakdown of Hunnic-Burgundian relations, but rather they in a significant way enable that murder and breakdown and signal their approach. Clearly the situations in *Kudrun* and in the *Nibelungenlied* are not identical; but the proposed *structural function* of marriage is the same.[53] Why then should the marriages in *Kudrun* be assumed "successful," while those of the *Nibelungenlied, Beowulf,* and other such narratives, which form the second intertextual "pre-text," consistently, as a thematic necessity, fail? Nolte significantly notes the use of marriage as the seal on a peace treaty: "Brach eine Familie den Ehe-oder Verlobungsvertrag oder kam es zur Scheidung, drohten u.U. gewalt-same Auseinandersetzungen. Mittelalterliche Eheschließungen waren et-was außerordentlich Prekäres, sie bargen immer schon den Casus belli in sich" ("If a family broke the marriage or engagement contract, or if a divorce ensued, then under certain conditions violent conflicts threatened. Medieval marriages were extraordinarily precarious and from the outset always already involved a *casus belli*" p. 36; cf. also here p. 44).

In this same vein, the characters' views of the future are tentative at best, often outright fearful. Kudrun's understanding of the exigencies of *Realpolitik* are demonstrated in her sending frequent and massive bribes of clothing and gold to Hartmut, so as to retain his good grace and treatment of Hildeburg (1681). We readers of the text have an unfair advantage over Kudrun here, however, for we "know" already that this couple is to live, as it were, "happily ever after"; the text has said as much thirty stanzas before: *die warn seyt mit trewen vngeschaiden* ("hereafter they were in truth unsepa-rated/inseparable" 1650,4). Or does the report of her bribing Hartmut at this point in the narrative serve to unsettle that assurance? Hilde too demands frequent and regular reassurance, for she requests that Kudrun send messengers three times a year to let her know that all is well (1699). As for the narrator's view of the future: the text partakes here also of a topos in denying any knowledge of what actually happened while the characters

53. Nolte notes that these final marriages function not as is commonly the case in medieval literature of sealing the end of a feud via a bilateral alliance (he notes the example of *Beowulf*), but rather by means of multilateral alliances among several dynastic families and states (pp. 67–68). He does not, inexplicably, also note that this common literary motif functions to heighten the tension before the inevitable breakdown of the alliance so forged and the consequent bloodbath (also the case in this foreshadowing motif in *Beowulf*).

were living happily ever after: they went their separate ways and saw each other rarely (*selten* 1690,3; litotes = "never"?), and thus neither they nor, apparently, the narrator can tell more about what happened to them. Concerning Hartmut the narrator openly admits: *Wie der der Lande phlage. das ist mir vnbekant* ("it is not known to me how he took care of the country" 1694,2). We readers, however, have additional information from the narrator, who says of Kudrun at least: *Ir sorge hette nu ennde* ("her sorrows were now at an end" 1700,4), much of the concrete significance of which disappears, however, since the immediately following phrase that concludes this line and stanza reports *man gesach nie nichtß so wol getanes* "no one had ever seen one so lovely." Are Kudrun's troubles — personal political, familial, dynastic, national, international — at an end, as the first half-line alone might suggest? Or is the first phrase only to be understood in light of the second: now she has returned to the sartorial luxury to which she was accustomed? Perhaps this latter interpretation is the more likely one, for only two stanzas later, Kudrun has been reduced to a caricature, whose only *laide* seems to be that anyone might live more sumptuously than her sister-in-law Ortrun (1702,4). The text's last two stanzas in fact point not toward a harmonious, peaceful future, but rather directly toward one that continues in the A night with previously and rather of chaos repre sented in the 1700 preceding stanzas. In the final stanza, for instance, despite the fact that in context the all but unanimous editorial emendation of the manuscript reading to *immer* makes sense, the fact is that the text actually maintains — just as sensibly — that *da sprach die küniginne. daz sys nymmer vngeniten ß liesse* "the queen said that she would never not begrudge it to her" (1704,4). In context it seems likely that this queen is Hilde, whose dedication to vengeance is strong and enduring.[54] That she might still

---

54. There has been a great deal of scholarly discomfort about Hilde's unrelenting desire for vengeance, which does not abate even after the Ormanian captives, including Ortrun and Hartmut, are brought back to the Hegeling castle. This scholarly concern most likely derives from two sources. First is the all but ubiquitous attempt to appropriate the "happy ending" of *Kudrun* into a conception of "christian" vs. Germanic culture. From this Manichean point of view, if vengeance is bad, the unrelenting desire for vengeance is worse, and female desire is the worst of all. Hilde is then either tainted or must be argued into purity. This argument has gone so far as to force the completely unwarranted text emendation in the final stanza of the poem. The second reason for scholarly unease with Hilde's will to vengeance is simply that it associates her with what is for conventional Germanistic a painfully embarrassing parallel to Kriemhild's revenge. Such a connection is tabu, for if Hilde is tainted, then so in part are Ortwin, Herwig, and of course Kudrun, for they all participate directly or are complicit. Furthermore, the fact is that vengeance as dire and destructive as that which concludes the *Nibelungenlied* (or more so) has already taken place. The "happy ending" of *Kudrun* attempts to mask this state of affairs by, among other things, imposing a change of venue back to Hegeling-land where there are no smoking ruins and no infant body parts inconveniently lying

entertain such thoughts is both possible and comprehensible. Finally, the text's concluding lines seem to point to things to come: *Ortrun vnd Herwigk. die swûrn baide ensambt mit trewen stâte einander . . . welhe in schaden wolten. daz sy die baide viengen vnnde slûgh* ("Ortwin[55] and Herwig swore with steadfast loyalty . . . that they would both catch and fight anyone who wanted to do them harm" 1705,1–4). The potential for future hostilities is probable enough that these two rulers have forged a concrete military alliance with that in mind, and Hilde and Kudrun have taken their conventionally "female precautions" as well.[56]

Two further problems undermine the security of the apparent optimistic conclusion. First, if my initial dissatisfaction, as described above, with the homogenized and imposed happy ending is plausible, then there is a problem with both the almost unanimously acknowledged "intention" of the poet and with the authority of any poet to impose an authorial interpretation on a text that does not otherwise support that interpretation. How does one deal critically with such a text? While the primary example here is the larger issue of the legitimacy of the "happy ending," several smaller, related issues elsewhere in the text well illustrate the problem. After the slaughter in, and mass destruction of Ormanie, peace—or rather absolute victory—is celebrated back in Hegeling-land. The poet comments: *mit vollen ward versûenet. der hasz. den sÿ da trûgen. daz sÿ des gar vergassen. daz jr Recken Ee einander in grossen sturmen ze tode schlûgen* ("the hatred was completely reconciled, so that they entirely forgot that their warriors had killed each other earlier in battle" 1602,3–4). Clearly this claim could be understood as rhetorical hyperbole for "the joy was very great indeed." But it does not seem legitimate to reduce its sense to that alone; some trace of its denotation remains. If so, then both heroes and villains (and by this point in the narrative, it is no longer unambiguously clear who is who) are—by medieval as well as modern ethical standards—abominable creatures. How could it be possible that the Normans—hostages under house arrest at the

---

around. Pro-christian, pro-Kudrun scholarship has followed the lead of the text here to dissociate the actual state of vengeance-achieved with the fiction of universal, harmonious reconciliation.

55. Ms. *Ortrun*. It seems rather likely here, for quite a number of reasons, that the partners to the treaty are *Ortwin* and Herwig; otherwise this would constitute the only evidence in the text for Ortrun's participation in political matters. Paleographically, the six quasi-minims of the one reading (*win*) could have conceivably been mistaken for the other (*run*) in copying a source manuscript in a variety of "Gothic" hands.

56. Nolte also notes that even after the appearance of the grand motif of *suone*: "Auch die Schlußstrophe des Epos zeigt, daß der Rachegedanke nicht grundsätzlich in Frage gestellt wird" ("Even the concluding stanza indicates that the concept of vengeance is not as a matter of principle called into question" p. 60).

court of the enemy who (apparently) only days before utterly destroyed their homeland and killed their king and queen (father and mother) — have forgotten those events? It seems almost that we have a choice: we accept what seems an impossibility, we refuse to believe the narrator, or we trivialize the whole by attributing it to the conventions of concluding tropes in the romance genre, where improbable and ideologically problematic reconciliations occur and impose closure often where least expected. A second similar example of almost magical transformation occurs in the act of Ortwin's placing the ring on Ortrun's finger: *da mit was verdrungen von Ir das michel ellennde* "herewith her great sorrow was banished" (1649,4). The ring as the concrete sign of marriage — a marriage to the leader of her people's archenemy and the slayer of her father — banishes the sorrow of loss of father, mother, home, sovereignty of the homeland, and so on. Such transformation is only believable within the realm of patriarchal myth as politics in which marriage is the ultimately defining and legitimizing experience for women.

Simply to claim that the narrator is "wrong" about the effect of Ortrun's ring or about the Norman's pro-Hegeling selective and collective amnesia, and consequently the legitimacy of the happy ending, would obviously be nonsense, for that would be abdicating the critic's task, which is to deal *with* the extant transmitted text, not pretend that altering it is necessary. The *contradictions* of the narrative must be the focus, for they point up the social contradictions that have been sedimented in the text.[57] If a narrative forces an improbable conclusion onto the conditions it has set up, the reader must both deal with that conclusion as narrative "fact" and still be free to problematize both the conclusion and its conditions beyond the borders of the specific text, as ideological documents in the larger cultural context.

Second, if in fact Kudrun effected a social transformation at the end of the narrative, one that would enable the peace to last beyond the (not very likely) personal happiness of the newlyweds, how would and how could that transformation be *represented* literarily? As noted above, it would be unrealistic to expect any in-depth theorization of the underlying social problem. Kudrun's one remark in this vein already seems inappropriate not just because it is inaccurate. In the same way, we can hardly expect new "legislation" or even monarchical proclamation as an indicator of political

---

57. The other side of this issue is represented by Werner Hoffmann's final abdication of his role as literary scholar, when he dismisses all those who see Kudrun's *list* as "ethisch Bedenkliches" ("ethically questionable" pp. 178–179): since the poet does not find the act contemptible, then the reader may not either: "dies ist die entscheidende Feststellung" ("this is the decisive factor").

transformation. Some smaller "transgressive" act would have to suffice in a literary work to signal a large-scale transformation. The closest thing to transgression here is perhaps *suone* itself, in its various manifestations, which are, I hope to have shown, hardly transformative.

But perhaps the formulation of the question regarding the happy ending, as posed above, makes it impossible to account for the inadequacy of the solution pro- and imposed by Kudrun. For the tale does *end* on a generally positive note, according to the conventions of the affiliated narrative genres, but it is possible that that conclusion is momentary. This may be the ultimate irony of the tale: that apparently despite the poet's "intention" — as divined by modern scholarship and imputed to him — or despite the actuality of the poem's happy ending, the tale's conclusion points to the inevitable cycle of recurring chaos that is attendant on wiving in the conventional and inherited pattern maintained and affirmed by that conclusion. Even if one accepts the conventional interpretation of the transformative effect of *suone* in *Kudrun,* then in fact the only thing that has prevented complete catastrophe is the single character Kudrun herself.[58] After the end of the tale with its several unions of conciliation, what is realistically to be expected in terms of the societies represented by the narrative? It is certainly not the case that the several societies have changed, certainly not that any of them has modified or reformed its wiving procedures. Rather, most certainly, each future bridal-quest-conflict (as has each past one) will tend toward the catastrophic cycle of suit-rejection-siege-capture-counter siege-recapture-vengeance. At any moment the whole cycle of chaos could begin anew.

In his efforts to go beyond the conventional limits of *Kudrun*-scholarship, Campbell poses questions of almost sufficient candor to reveal the problems concealed beneath the notion of the happy ending:

> What if a daughter of Gudrun's . . . were to be abducted against her will? Could anyone seriously suggest that Gudrun would be content to say: "niemen mit übele sol deheines hazzes lônen" (1595,3)? It is not unlikely that her attitude would be rather like her mother's, particularly if Herwig were, like Hetel, to

---

58. Wailes contends that the only tragedy in the entire poem is the death of Hetel, and further that "we may ignore the slaughter of anonymous masses in the many battles" (p. 363). I would counter that Hetel's death is a *tragedy* only in the vague lay sense of catastrophe, and further that there are numerous personal, familial, national, and even international catastrophes represented in the narrative, of which the death of a single person such as Hetel is, relatively speaking, of minimal significance. We may also remark that denying significance to "the slaughter of the anonymous masses" is a typical apology for the militaristic *Staatsraison* so devastatingly analyzed by Ekkehart Krippendorff (*Staat und Krieg*), and only a short step away from the New World Order's designation of dead humans in the Gulf War as "collateral damage."

fall during the pursuit. But on all these questions the poet remains silent. The epic comes to terms with problems of revenge and reconciliation after trouble has arisen, enmities have been born and enemies have been defeated. Nowhere, however, does it suggest a ready answer to the problem of future unwelcome or jealous suitors who might not shrink from violence to gain their ends. (p. 156)[59]

Hilde and Hetel learned no lessons from their youthful experiences. Is there any indication that Kudrun and Herwig have or will, and that they will accept any given qualified suitor for their daughter? Or will there again be threats, kidnapping, rape, and war? After a stunning victory and devastating conquest of the enemy, Kudrun imposes marriage as an attempted incentive to or guarantor of peace. This is not so much *suone* as it is simply the imposition of a peace treaty politically beneficial to the dictator of its terms, or the superimposition of one ideological structure over another (already accomplished) political and economic one, thus disguising the utter devastation and despoliation of the enemy land via "happy marriage" and the "happily ever after" motif. The problematic nature of such an imposed peace is starkly illustrated by Hilde's proclamation, noted above, after Ortrun and Hildeburg are led to the ring: *nu wil ich . . . daz so ymmer in fride beleibe* ("now I wish/will it that peace continues forever" 1684, 4). In this social context, with these existing conditions, it seems rather unlikely that peace is to be maintained by the queen mother's fiat.

Let us then take stock of Kudrun's *suone:* it is introduced not in place of, but rather after the utter devastation of the enemy; it is authoritarian; it transforms nothing except the marital status of a handful of the ruling elite; it is neither "productive" nor "optimistic" except insofar as it reproduces the conditions of production for feudal patriarchy. There seems little reason to retain "(re)conciliation" as a possible denotation of *suone* in interpretations of *Kudrun* except insofar as it resonates ironically: the settlement imposed by Kudrun is judgment, punishment, an iron-handed reestablishment of the *status quo ante* insofar as that benefits the Hegeling alliance. It is innovative only insofar as it recognizes and attempts to legitimize the enhanced political status of the Hegeling alliance as a result of its destruction of and both direct and hegemonic control over its enemies.

---

59. One might also reflect on the hypothetical case that the *Nibelungenlied* ended with Kriemhild's marriage to Etzel, whereupon the poet said that they lived happily ever after. What "likelihood" would that scenario evoke, and what literary response? After all, Kriemhild has only lost one man. In *Kudrun* almost everyone has lost relations (and significant property). How likely is peace and reconciliation?

9. Women's Epic and/as Masculist Backlash

Since, as argued in the previous chapter, *suone* aggressively affirms the status quo of the social mechanisms of wiving, dispute settlement, war, revenge, gender roles, and the relations of economic and gender structures, it is not a sign of transformation, nor is it conciliatory, innovative or progressive. Instead the effects of Kudrun's *suone* and her own participation in imposing it opposes clearly the anti-patriarchal and potentially more independent female roles represented in the *Nibelungenlied* and perverted by the masculist rigidity of feudal society there. Some recent scholars have come to similar conclusions: Nolte, for instance, pertinently remarks: "Permanent, am deutlichsten aber während der Krise, leisten die Frauen Zuarbeit zur Aufrechterhaltung der gesellschaftlichen Normen. . . . Das Recht und die gesellschaftlichen Normen, an deren Aufrechterhaltung die Frau einen derart großen Anteil hat, dienen wiederum zur Zementierung des Status quo, und das impliziert: der Unterdrückung der Frau" ("Permanently, but most clearly during the crisis, the women assist in the maintenance of social norms. . . . The law/privilege and the social norms in whose preservation the women play such an important role serve in turn to ensure the status quo, and that implies: the oppression of women" pp. 74–75).[1] In this

---

1. Two sentences later, however, he suddenly assumes that Kudrun has succeeded through precisely this type of anti-transformative activity in transforming this world of vengeance into one of peace. He nonetheless notes here: "Bei dieser Herstellung des Friedens [bleiben] die Frauen weiterhin Tauschobjekte. Die Frage, wie es um deren Autonomie bestellt ist, kommt gar nicht erst in den Blick. Die reale tagtägliche Unterdrückung der Frau . . . wird nicht ausdrücklich thematisiert" ("In this production of peace, the women remain objects of exchange. The question concerning the status of their autonomy is not one that is even considered. The actual, daily oppression of women . . . is not expressly thematized"). Barbara Siebert comments similarly: "Geht es im Hauptvertreter der mittelhochdeutschen 'Helden-dichtung,' im 'Nibelungenlied,' um die Zerstörung höfischer Werte durch die Protagonisten, so geht es in der 'Kudrun' wie im 'höfischen Roman' um deren Konstituierung und Ent-faltung" ("If it is a matter of the destruction of courtly values by the protagonists in the main representative of Middle High German heroic poetry, the *Nibelungenlied,* then in *Kudrun* and the courtly romance it is a matter of their establishment and development" p. 10). Among her tacit assumptions is a positive valuation of "courtly values," while I view such values as in significant part based on and determined by (that is, dialectically related to) the systematic and

context it might be useful to review the general relationship of the three texts under consideration here, insofar as they deal with issues of gender and power, for despite the fact that I have attempted to maintain a balance throughout the analysis, the interpretation I have offered could conceivably be susceptible to a disgruntled and reductive dismissal as: the *Nibelungenlied* and the *Klage* are "feminist," while *Kudrun* is "anti-feminist." As I noted at the outset, such terms are not just anachronistic, but culture-bound even in our own time, and are not of great value in coming to terms with these texts, which (like cultural products of other periods as well, our own included) deserve a more nuanced evaluation. While some who have suffered under the brutal excesses of patriarchal sexism might momentarily or otherwise delight in what seems the inexorable self-destruction of extremist patriarchy in the *Nibelungenlied,* few would recommend that scenario as a solution either to the concrete problems of that political formation or its sexist sedimentations. Neither does it seem to me that the *Nibelungenlied* itself presents this course of action as a remedy. Such an evaluation would simply recall one aspect of the conventional view of the "monstrous women" of the *Nibelungenlied* and recuperate their actions as those of social deviants and psychopaths.

Likewise, despite the regressive, repressive, and punitive politics of *Kudrun* (particularly with respect to gender issues), this text too must be seen in its thirteenth-century context. Which is not to say that that context diminishes the repressiveness of any of the characters' actions, but rather that we must guard against expecting action that the historical context could not provide us no matter what: not a reversal of the gender roles. An iron-fisted Queen Kudrun who summons a sniveling Hartmut to her court as bridegroom and laundryman, while plausible as modern satire, or, given some modifications, simply as modern fiction, is hardly conceivable even as medieval satire.[2] Not a redefinition of the gender roles: a strong, independent, self-reliant, politically conscious Kudrun who actively participates in locating, and negotiating a marriage with, a mate (who both is interested in

---

systemic oppression of the society's females, as grounded in its economic, political and ideological social formations. Thus also from my, albeit rather different, perspective, the problematization of precisely this conflict in the *Nibelungenlied does* in fact call into question, if not "destroy" such values; while *Kudrun* systematically reaffirms "courtly" society (among other similarly represented cultures) and its concomitant sexist repression.

2. For the fact is that we already know a similar text — in which a ruling warrior queen will marry only the man who accepts her conditions and beats her in combat — and it is neither satire nor an emancipatory manifesto, but — for much of its contemporary and also modern audience — a monster tale.

marrying her precisely because she possesses such qualities and is suitable to Kudrun for her own purposes), and then further participates in ruling their combined territories; this scenario is no more plausible in a medieval context than the other one, since all narrative factors that motivate the plot of *Kudrun* have herewith disappeared. The conception of gender-categories and the possibilities of their transgression are too narrow, and the narrative restrictions are likewise too rigid to allow for any such "feminist" narrative. Not surprisingly, thirteenth-century German epic for quite a number of reasons, all overdetermined, all dialectically articulated with the entirety of the literary-political society that produced the texts, hardly provides for our twentieth-century feminist search for emancipatory texts. What it does provide, or rather, what these three particular narrative examples provide is nonetheless a ruthless examination, with surprisingly little dissimulation, of gender issues that invites us to view them in the context of other literary and historical social formations.

With such qualifications in mind, then, it might be of interest to consider a final problem in the modern scholarly confrontation with *Kudrun*, in order to come to a conclusion. For almost all recent scholars who have written about *Kudrun* have had some observations on *Kudrun* as *Frauen-roman/Frauenepos*/"women's novel/epic," and some center their arguments around it. What is it about this work that makes it possible for a masculist scholarly tradition to acknowledge, or rather, as I see it, construct *Kudrun* such that this conception and designation can be "applied"? And, perhaps just as importantly, what does this term "Frauenroman" mean when so used? The initiator of this recent line of argument was Hugo Kuhn, who — one would do well to acknowledge — might well object to the direction it has since taken. In his celebrated conference address, he points out: "'Kudrun' ist ein Frauenroman, bis in erstaunliche politische Eingriffe hinein."[3] His use of the term "Frauenroman" indicates simply the text's focus on female characters. As Nolte elaborates, in taking Kuhn's prompt as the ostensible impetus for his essay: a *Frauenroman* is a literary text that may be of, by, and for women. *Kudrun* obviously focuses on female characters; courtly romance, he notes, had, as some scholars claim, a larger audience of women than other contemporaneous genres,[4] and thus

---

3. "*Kudrun* is a woman's novel, even as that extends into astounding political details/operations." Hugo Kuhn, "Kudrun," rpt. in *Nibelungenlied und Kudrun*, ed. Heinz Rupp (Darmstadt: Wissenschaftliche Buchgesellschaft, 1976), pp. 502–514, here p. 509.

4. His argument is based not on the (probably impossible) empirical study that would be necessary for audience identification, but rather is simply the logical consequence of the generic expectations conventionally accepted by modern scholarship.

Kudrun, as a work with strong romance affinities, likely had a significant female audience; only with the criterion of authorship is there then a problem, according to Nolte, who assumes that a male poet wrote the work (*Kudrunepos,* p. 56). Stephen Wailes, too, agrees with Kuhn that *Kudrun* is a *politischer Frauenroman* (pp. 364–365). Wild, too, *mutatis mutandis,* concurs: "Die 'Kudrun' ist ein Frauenroman" von den Hauptgestalten her gesehen und als dichterische Auffassung von weiblich tugendhaftem Handeln" ("In terms of its main characters and also as a poetic interpretation of female virtuous behavior, *Kudrun* is a 'Frauenroman,'" p. 62). Hoffmann too insists that *Kudrun* is in its essence a "Frauenroman." Not surprisingly in the context of such arguments, the *Nibelungenlied* is *not* designated a *Frauenroman,* or at least it is not so topicalized. In fact, with the exception of Wild's astute remarks on the placement of *Kudrun* and *Nibelungenlied* in the Ambraser manuscript, little if any scholarly attention has been directed to the *Nibelungenlied* as a "Frauenroman" *per se.*

But again, what does all this mean? Is there a kernel of shared sense in these various conceptions of *Kudrun* as a "Frauenroman"? Hoffmann claims that Kudrun's *Sein* "being" determines the *Geist des Werkes* ("spirit of the work," p. 274). But — to the extent that we want to join the idealist quest for spirits — could it not also be said that Kriemhild's *Sein* determines the *Geist* of the *Nibelungenlied*? Nolte's categories — of, by, and for women — are basic and common criteria of analysis, but are more than merely problematic for the literature of most of the European Middle Ages, for which most of the relevant information essential for the analysis of two of the three criteria (authorship and gender composition of the audience) is lacking.[5] Wild bases her claim for *Kudrun* as "Frauenliteratur" on the suggestion that "Frauen verkörpern sowohl böse als auch mit entscheidendem Akzent die bessernden Tugenden, die zugleich Maß und Vorbild für männliches Verhalten werden" ("women embody both bad as well as, with a decisive accent, the better traits, which become simultaneously the measure and the model for men's behavior" p. 62). There is, however, neither any instance in the text of female behavior actually functioning as a

5. Nonetheless, a great deal of very important research on the female audience of medieval literature is being carried out, based on the remnants of evidence that do survive. Joachim Bumke's brief chapter "Die Rolle der Frau im höfischen Literaturbetrieb," in *Mäzene im Mittelalter: Die Gönner und Auftraggeber der höfischen Literatur in Deutschland, 1150–1300* München: Beck, 1979), pp. 231–247, notes 409–418, with its extensive bibliography is an excellent introduction to the identified sector of the evidence from German-speaking Europe (and occasionally beyond), although, as could be expected, in the fifteen years since its appearance, much has changed, particularly insofar as many of the gaps in the scholarship have been filled.

model for men's, whether unconventional or otherwise; nor is there any indication in this text that women's behavior might ever legitimately so function. Furthermore, the women's behavior in the text is not so clearly good or bad (although Wild already acknowledges more nuance here than most). The women, as documented in the previous two chapters, simply reinforce the codes of conventional male political behavior, including the unquestioned patriarchal dominance over females. It also seems particularly inaccurate to suggest that Kudrun's patient suffering could function as a behavioral model for a man, who, if he could, then would and should immediately combat such humiliation by force of arms. Nolte's notions of the specific character of the "Frauenroman," and even of what seems on occasion in his essay to be a feminist argument, in the end all but disintegrate into conventional notions of *das ewig Weibliche*. Despite the fact that the author was male, he was able to take actually existent female abilities and proclivities ("solidarisch zu kooperieren" . . . to find "andere Strategeien der Konfliktlösung"; "To cooperate via solidarity" . . . to find "other strategies for the resolution of conflict") and represent them as exemplary. Kudrun and her companions overcome the "Abstraktionsprinzip" ("principle of abstraction") via *work*—"Ihre Arbeit ist Gegenproduktion, sie steht für das Produktions- bzw. Konkretionsprinzip" ("her work is counterproduction, she stands for the principle of production or concretization"). They work and produce concrete, useful, sensually tangible things, not abstracts such as are conventionally employed, for instance, as justifications for war (p. 56). This seems a particularly strange concept here: emancipation via menial labor, freedom via slavery. For whom, one might ask, is this work "productive," except at the lowest level of performance: that is, Kudrun's tending the stove keeps the room warm, her washing the laundry in the ocean provides (apparently) clean clothes.[6] But this work is performed under compulsion, and like slave labor and conventionally oppressed women's work, it is hardly productive in the unmarked or perhaps even positive sense deployed by Nolte. But if housework or marriage-coupling constitutes the narrative content that identifies and in its turn constitutes a "Frauenroman," then it is not just the emancipatory potential of this subgenre that is trivial. According to Nolte, the tale is a "Frauenro-

---

6. But it is precisely this level of *performance* that is demeaning and unmentionable for the nobility. The fact that she is caught at her work as laundress by her husband forces Kudrun to her only quasi-"defiant" act of thirteen years. In no sense could there be, for instance, pride in a job well done (which has been a recurring puritanical justification for menial labor that long predates the Puritans) as long as that job was inappropriate to the class of its performer.

man" insofar as it focuses on and praises the particular abilities of women: "Es geht . . . darum, angesichts gesellschaftlich-historischer Krisen sich der besonderen Fähigkeiten von Frauen zu erinnern. Es ist das Verdienst des Kudrunepikers . . . die spezifischen Arbeitseigenschaften von Frauen, die von jeher, seit dem Beginn des Patriarchats, am Werk waren (und es auch heute noch sind), ins Bewußtsein gehoben zu haben" ("In view of the socio-historical crises, it is a matter of recalling the special abilities of women. It is the accomplishment of *Kudrun*-poet . . . to have made us conscious of the specific traits / properties / qualities of women's working habits, which have been operative since time immemorial, from the onset of patriarchy, and still are even today" p. 73). Such statements, rare but recurring in the course of Nolte's argument, seem acknowledgements of gender as social construct, while at other points gender roles seem to be uncritically accepted as inevitable. He later specifies these particular abilities of women: "Kooperation, Solidarität, friedlicher Austausch, Integration von Fremdem, Umgang mit komplexen Beziehungsverhältnissen, Nichtan-erkennung des Raubbauprinzips, all dies gepaart mit der Fähigkeit, sich unendlich viel Mühe zu geben, zäh auf ihrer Position zu beharren (Kudrun vs. Gerlind) und übermenschlich scheinende Mühen und Leiden zu ertra-gen (Kudrun, Hildeburc)" ("cooperation, solidarity, peaceful exchange, integration of the Other, management of complex relationships, nonrecog-nition of the principle of excessive exploitation, all of this paired with the ability to take infinite pains, to persevere in one's position [Kudrun vs. Gerlind] and endure trouble and sorrow that appear superhuman [Kudrun and Hildeburg]" p. 76).

The limitations of such conceptions of the problem are crippling. If "Frauenliteratur" must be of, by, and for women; if "Frauenliteratur" must have a quasi-"saintly," eternally patient, and suffering heroine, who waits a dozen years for men to save and fulfill her, then gender analysis may be lim-ited to such concessions as Nolte's: "Ein mögliches Mißverständnis muß ausgeräumt werden. Das Kudrunepos ist kein Plädoyer für die Emanzipa-tion der Frau. Ihre Unterdrückung wird wohl punktuell deutlich (implizit in der gesamten Kudrunhandlung), sie wird jedoch nicht problematisiert" ("A potential misunderstanding must be removed. The *Kudrun*-epic is no plea for the emancipation of women. Their oppression is obvious in specific instances (implicitly in the entire plot of the Kudrun-section), but it is not problematized" p. 73). Similarly, Beck, whose work, unlike Nolte's, is not overtly sympathetic to feminism) states that Kudrun "Vertritt wohl ein neues Bild vom Sein der Frau in der Tatwelt des Mannes; aber sie kämpft nicht eigentlich für seine Verwirklichung, sie ist nicht Vorkämpferin einer Idee, und sie hat kaum das Bewußtsein eines Auftrags" ("represents to be sure a new image of the reality of the woman in the male realm; but she does not actually fight for its realization; she is not an ideological pioneer and scarcely is conscious of a mission" p. 487). It is, however, only in a limited and politically blindered context of the championing of *Kudrun* versus the *Nibelungenlied* that such concessive claims are necessary, for as soon as one views the *Nibelungenlied* not as (among other things) a political sermon against monstrous women, but rather an exploration of the terms of their socially imposed conventional dependence, then *Kudrun* must be seen as a response to that analysis. While the *Nibelungenlied* examines the economic basis of power, the patriarchal conventions of wiving, and the exclusion of women from political power, *Kudrun* "responds" by restricting the issues to conventional modes of wiving, particularly as based on rigid status-conscious class codes, as affirmed by the doubly insidious depiction in the final episode of the main female character's function as coupler.[7] In asking the question — is *Kudrun* a "Frauenroman" — one is, from my perspective, asking the wrong question, because it ensures a particular type of answer that functions primarily as obfuscation. One of the functions of such non-issues in the scholarship has been to mask the essential social and political issues represented in the text, especially as they respond to the *Nibelungenlied*.

The most essential argument in the conventional interpretation of *Kudrun*, as treated in the previous two chapters, concerns a further, perhaps more significant, issue of "transformation": besides the general scholarly consensus that Kudrun is a positive character, perhaps a model of virtue, and a political progressive, there is almost unanimity that the poem's conclusion — characterized by harmony, reconciliation, and joy — radically transforms the society. This conclusion follows after multiple wars, pillaging, kidnapping, general mayhem, mass murder, and the abduction and captivity of the main character for over a decade. According to the scholarly consensus, the conclusion transcends that chaos and replaces it with an ordered and "productive" harmony. As I have argued, however, the social

---

7. Bernhard Wurzer's observation is interesting here: "Bei der Siegesfeier entpuppt sich Gudrun als eine geschickte Kupplerin, die ihren Opfern in überzeugender Weise die Bedenken zu zerstreuen versteht" ("At the victory celebration, Kudrun reveals herself as a skillful procurer/coupler, who understands how to distract her victims persuasively from their objections"), in "Das Komische in der deutschen Heldendichtung von der Frühzeit bis zum hohen Mittelalter" (unpublished diss., Innsbruck, 1951), p. 211; quoted by Campbell, *Kudrun*, p. 290.

contradictions (as opposed to individual, personal conflicts) that recurringly led to chaos are never resolved or even topicalized in the poem. Instead, by means of the imposed resolution of the individual *personal* conflicts at the conclusion, they are simply displaced or deferred. If there is peace and harmony at the end of the poem, then it is a condition based not on transformed social formations but rather on ephemeral epiphenomena that have intruded into or have momentarily been forcibly imposed onto the inherited structures. The causal social problems remain unaddressed, unresolved, and will, there is little reason to doubt, logically and inevitably recur to plunge the several societies depicted into renewed chaos within a generation, if not before. Let me review these various transformations and the contradictions that undermine their stability.

Over the course of four generations scores of castles burn, thousands of warriors die, unarmed pilgrims are despoiled, infants slaughtered in their cribs, young women kidnapped and forced into marriage, all in the course of routine wiving practice. Is there any hint in the text that wiving practice is seen as destructive or even in need of reform? None. Any acknowledgment of the possibility that men are uncontrolled[8] during their regular rutting rituals? Never. Men — invaders as well as the blood-soaked avengers of invasions — are included among those who live happily ever after on their royal thrones at the conclusion of the tale. And in the end who or what is at fault? According to more than a mere suggestion in the text (and according to the thunderous approval of the text's scholars), it is, not surprisingly, a woman: Gerlind. And what precisely are her sins? She encourages her son's already conceived courtship, then pressures the woman (who has been kidnapped by the son) to marry her son by forcing her to do housework. Admittedly she is more than merely complicit in actually holding Kudrun and her retinue after their kidnapping by Hartmut. She places Kudrun and Hildeburg in a potentially life-threatening situation (doing laundry barefoot on a snowy beach), and she seems rather clearly about to have Kudrun flogged for "leaving the laundry on the beach." Gerlind is no angel, no saint, but hardly the villain that the text pretends and patriarchal scholarship has elaborated. She commits no murder, no kidnapping, no rape, no invasion, no theft, and at no point counsels anyone else to perform such acts. According to the text, however, Gerlind is *übel,* a *valantinne,* a *teufelinne,* and she is the only character in the narrative on whom such verbal abuse is

---

8. Not to say "out of control," which might be construed as lending credence to the longstanding conventional defense of rape (and other crimes) by patriarchy — men's putative loss of rational control due to passion and the overpowering influence of hormones.

routinely heaped,[9] the only one depicted as a monster, demon, and villain, and the only one so treated by conventional scholarship.[10] Hagen on the other hand may have hanged twenty of his countrymen, despite which (or in part as a result of which?) he is deemed a hero. And he is among the murderers, kidnappers, rapists, invaders, and robbers participating in the "harmonious," "peaceful" happy ending.

As treated in the previous chapter, Kudrun's arrangement of marriages at the conclusion of the narrative is prominent in arguments for her transformation of her society. In another context, Wild notes, for instance, that the marriages forced by Kudrun cross status boundaries and are executed without prior *Minnedienst* (p. 59). In her couplings Kudrun also preserves and affirms class structures by preserving the rule that no woman marries down the status scale. Nolte (p. 66) uncritically accepts the text's presentation here — that the marriage of Ortrun and Ortwin brings about an automatic enhancement of the status of the Norman house — thus conveniently (and only momentarily) forgetting that this issue of class has motivated the plot for two hundred pages. That Hartmut "marries down" is, within the terms of this system, his deserved comeuppance. It is, if nothing else, a clear indication of his present subordinate status: Kudrun dictates to him whom he is to marry. But is Ortwin's marrying down to the Norman dynasty not also a humiliation? It seems not that Kudrun thus changes or transcends the system in which class, mutual consent, and *Minnedienst,* are constituent elements, but rather simply that she bends but does not break particular rules of the larger code. The violation of individual rules of a code neither abolishes nor transforms it. Nor, if the violator has sufficient authority to ensure immunity from censure (as the Herwig-Hegeling alliance and Kudrun as its momentary proxy here clearly do), does violation constitute culpable transgression. In a definitive sense, then, Kudrun, unlike Kriemhild and Brünhild, is not in conflict with any basic practice of her culture. She does not transgress its rules and is not a threat to the system.[11] And

9. Cf. Campbell (*Kudrun,* p. 115) on the epithets of abuse.

10. Hoffmann denies that Gerlind is a demon (p. 97), but only so that he can reserve that epithet for his favorite foe: Kriemhild (p. 98).

11. Twice the text makes use of a potential or merely rhetorical transgression in order to express some exceptional quality of the heroine that apparently could not be so well expressed without momentary, implied, and then necessarily denied gender role transgression. In st. 577 there is an interesting ambiguity that depends on inscribed gender differentiation: either Kudrun grew up and attained the age at which she would have been knighted (had she been male), or she grew so large that she would have worn a sword had she been a knight. In st. 1033 Kudrun claims that if she were a knight then Ludwig would never be able to approach her unarmed. In each case the "unreal condition" conveniently contrasts with the actualities of Kudrun's case.

neither does she transform or reform that system. Rather, she *con*-forms and affirms the status quo, and further strengthens the existing system.[12] This is why she is not destroyed—as were Brünhild (insofar as she ceased to be wealthy, strong, sovereign, and independent) and Kriemhild. She offers patriarchy multiple opportunities to construct her as a strong, independent, resolute, defiant, sovereign, virtuous, powerful, and independent character, for in fact—in certain situations, in interaction with certain characters, under certain conditions—she is so. The important considerations are where, with whom, under what conditions, and to what end does she so act? And the necessary condition is that her field of action is so very restricted—in fact precisely to that sphere of traditional woman's action—that her "sovereignty" is all but meaningless even in her own world. She rules no state, no household, has no acknowledged direct relation to property (and thus all discussion of her potential access to power is effectively suppressed), and she at no point is in independent control of her own life. Her field of action and her sphere of sovereignty are strictly limited to remaining faithful to her husband and arranging other conventional marriages, although even here, as noted, her actual independence in these arrangements is also severely restricted. Men decide, they attack, they defend, they own, they rule. Regularly they also marry, and when they do, they occasionally allow some restricted female participation in the arrangements (by queen, mother, occasionally even bride).[13] If a literary work focuses on several instances of wiving praxis and particularly on one woman's experience of that praxis, as does *Kudrun,* then that momentary focus does not change the rigid social formations which may blur around that point of focus but do not thereby lose anything of their solidity or of their determinant control over the lives of the women. Thus without even granting exceptional independence to this one putative exception to that norm, the essentially debilitating sexist system that straitjackets all female independence can pretend that the system is both benign and reformed.

12. Cf. Fredric Jameson: "For Marxism, however, the very content of a class ideology is relational, in the sense that its 'values' are always actively in situation with respect to the opposing class, and defined against the latter: normally, a ruling class ideology will explore various strategies of the legitimation of its own power position, while an oppositional culture or ideology will, often in covert and disguised strategies, seek to contest and to undermine the dominant 'value system'" (*The Political Unconscious,* p. 84).

13. The extended but still strictly circumscribed roles in marriage arrangements for *other* women, exercised by female characters in *Kudrun,* represents the typical ideological carrot tossed to women by patriarchy, not in compensation for, but rather as a distraction from their losses elsewhere. *Kudrun*-scholarship has taken the bait as well as invested heavily in this patriarchal ploy.

But Kudrun as this putative champion of female independence and sovereignty is not independent and not sovereign. Her only vaguely independent acts serve directly to perpetuate precisely those practices of patriarchy that effectively prevent female independence. She marries a husband who was at the moment, in order to obtain her for marriage, engaged in killing her father, destroying her homeland, and raping her; this husband is then approved, as it were, by her parents; she remains "faithful" to him under adverse conditions and affirms without wavering the basic conditions for the reproduction of the gender and class roles that she has inherited. She does not learn politically as a result of her experience; she does not change her view of her world. She makes no attempt to change that world except as it benefits the political status quo. From the perspective of the still persisting patriarchy, what better heroine could there be than Kudrun? And — to step back and view the larger literary context in which Kudrun operates — what worse one than a Kriemhild or Brunhild, who insist on their economic, political, and personal independence; who — in what may be the most frightening aspect of their characters to patriarchy — recognize the necessary articulations of these three categories; and who constantly adapt to changing conditions as a result of their learning politically to control, to the extent possible, their own lives? In contrast, then, is it any wonder that Kudrun has been perceived and constructed by the *Kudrun* and its tradition of patriarchal scholarship as "virtuous," as "transformative," as "productive"? Kudrun is a patriarchal hero in a masculist *Frauenroman* and is thus an eminently comfortable hero*ine* for masculist scholarship. She has become its perennial darling, especially as contrasted with the constructed ogres Kriemhild and Brünhild.

The analysis of gender, property, and power relations in the *Nibelungenlied, Diu Klage,* and *Kudrun* elaborated in the preceding essays has resulted both in interpretations of the primary female characters that differ radically from conventional scholarship and ultimately also in a new paradigm of the political, narrative, and ideological relations among the three texts. That paradigm also redefines the provisional designation "women's epic," borrowed from conventional scholarship, which thereby gains an anti-conventional and strategically useful sense for politico-literary analysis of medieval narrative.

Bibliography

Admoni, V. G. [В.Г. Адмони]. "Песнь о Нибелунгах — ее истоки и ее художественная структура." In *Песнь о Нибелунгах*. Ed. V. G. Admoni et al. Leningrad, 1972.

Alexiou, Margaret. "Greek Philology: Diversity and Difference." *What is Philology.* Special Focus Issue of *Comparative Literature Studies* 27 (1990), 53–61.

Amira, Karl von. *Germanisches Recht.* 4th ed. by Karl August Eckhardt. Grundriß der germanischen Philologie 5/1–2. Berlin: Walter de Gruyter, 1960/1967.

Ancelet-Hustache, Jeanne. "La femme du moyen âge en Allemagne." In *L'Occident, des Celtes à la Renaissance,* undesignated vol. [2] of *Histoire mondiale de la femme.* Gen. Ed. Pierre Grimal. Paris: Nouvelle Librairie de France, n.d. [1966], pp. 55–78.

Anderson, Perry. *Passages from Antiquity to Feudalism.* London: Verso, 1974.

Anderson, Philip N. "Kriemhild's Quest." *Euphorion* 79 (1985), 3–12.

Andersson, Theodore M. "Why does Siegfried die?" In *Germanic Studies in Honor of Otto Springer,* ed. Stephan J. Kaplowitt. Pittsburgh: K and S Enterprises, 1978, pp. 29–39.

——. *The Legend of Brynhild.* Ithaca, NY: Cornell University Press, 1980.

——. *A Preface to the Nibelungenlied.* Stanford, CA: Stanford University Press, 1987.

Armstrong, Marianne Wahl. *Rolle und Charakter: Studien zur Menschendarstellung im Nibelungenlied.* Göppingen: Kümmerle, 1979.

Arthur, Marylin. "'Liberated' Women: The Classical Era." In *Becoming Visible,* ed. Bridenthal and Koonz. Boston: Houghton Mifflin, 1977, 60–89.

Baalsrud, Ellen Sofie, ed. *Free and Equal: Female Voices from Central and Eastern Europe.* Oslo: Equal Status Council, 1992.

Bal, Mieke. *Lethal Love: Feminist Literary Readings of Biblical Love Stories.* Bloomington: Indiana University Press, 1987.

——. *Murder and Difference: Gender, Genre, and Scholarship on Sisera's Death.* Trans. Matthew Gumpert. Bloomington: Indiana University Press, 1988.

——. *Death and Dissymmetry: The Politics of Coherence in the Book of Judges.* Chicago: University of Chicago Press, 1988.

Barrett, Michèle. *Women's Oppression Today: The Marxist/Feminist Encounter.* London and New York: Verso, 1988.

Bartels, Hildegard. *Epos — die Gattung in der Geschichte: Eine Begriffsbestimmung vor dem Hintergrund der Hegelschen "Ästhetik" anhand von "Nibelungenlied" und "Chanson de Roland."* Frankfurter Beiträge zur Germanistik 22. Heidelberg: Winter, 1982.

Bartsch, Karl, ed. *Die Klage: Mit den Lesarten sämtlicher Handschriften.* Leipzig: Brockhaus, 1875; repr. Darmstadt: Wissenschaftliche Buchgesellschaft, 1964.

Bataille, Roger. *Le droit des filles dans la succession d leurs parents en Normandie.* Paris, 1927.

Batts, Michael S. "Die Tragik des *Nibelungenliedes*." *Doitsu Bungaku* 16 (1960), 42–48.

———. *Die Form der Aventiuren im* Nibelungenlied. In *Gießener Beiträge zur deutschen Philologie* 29. Gießen: Wilhelm Schmitz, 1961.

———. "The *Nibelungenlied* (Thirteenth Century)." In *European Writers: The Middle Ages and the Renaissance, I: Prudentius to Medieval Drama,* ed. William T. H. Jackson, ed. in chief George Stade, New York: Scribner's, 1983, pp. 211–236.

Bäuml, Franz H., ed. *Kudrun: Die Handschrift.* Berlin: de Gruyter, 1969.

———. "Transformations of the Heroine: From Epic Heard to Epic Read." In *The Role of Women in the Middle Ages,* ed. Rosmarie Thee Morewedge. Papers of the Sixth Annual Conference of the Center for Medieval and Early Renaissance Studies, SUNY Binghamton, 6–7 May 1972. Albany: State University of New York Press, 1975, pp. 23–40.

———. Rev. of Campbell, *Kudrun: A Critical Appreciation. Speculum* 54 (1979), 787–789.

Bauschinger, Sigrid. "Weitere Perspektive." In *Die Frau als Heldin und Autorin. Neue kritische Ansätze zur deutschen Literatur,* ed. Wolfgang Paulsen. Bern: Francke, 1979, pp. 11–13.

Beck, Adolf. "Die Rache als Motiv und Problem in der 'Kudrun.' Interpretation und sagengeschichtlicher Ausblick." In *Nibelungenlied und Kudrun,* ed. Heinz Rupp. Wege der Forschung 54. Darmstadt: Wissenschaftliche Buchgesellschaft, 1976, pp. 454–501.

Becker, Claudia. "Spatial, Societal, and Personal Distance Among the Protagonists in the *Nibelungenlied*." Typescript, 15 pp. 1988.

Becker, Gabriele, Helmut Brackert, Sigrid Brauner, and Angelika Tümmler. "Zum kulturellen Bild und zur realen Situation der Frau im Mittelalter und in der frühen Neuzeit." In *Aus der Zeit der Verzweiflung. Zur Genese und Aktualität des Hexenbildes,* ed. Gabriele Becker et al. Frankfurt: Suhrkamp, 1977, pp. 11–128.

Bekker, Hugo. *The Nibelungenlied: A Literary Analysis.* Toronto: University of Toronto Press, 1971.

Bell, Susan Groag, "Medieval Women Book Owners: Arbiters of Lay Piety and Ambassadors of Culture." In *Women and Power in the Middle Ages,* ed. Erler and Kowaleski, pp. 149–187.

Bender, Ellen. *Nibelungenlied und Kudrun: Eine vergleichende Studie zur Zeitdarstellung und Geschichtsdeutung.* Frankfurt: Lang, 1987.

Bennett, Judith M. "Public Power and Authority in the Medieval English Countryside," in *Women and Power in the Middle Ages,* ed. Erler and Kowaleski, pp. 18–36.

Bennewitz, Ingrid, ed. *Der Frauwen buoch: Versuch zu einer feministischer Mediävistik.* Göttingen: Kümmerle, 1989.

Bernal, Martin. *Black Athena: The Afro-Asiatic Roots of Classical Civilization.* Vol. 1,

The Fabrication of Ancient Greece, 1785–1985. New Brunswick, NJ: Rutgers University Press, 1987.

Beyschlag, Siegfried. "Das Motiv der Macht bei Siegfrieds Tod." *Germanisch-Romanische Monatsschrift* 33 (1951/1952), 95–108.

———. "Die Funktion der epischen Vorausdeutung im Aufbau des *Nibelungenlieds.*" *Beiträge zur Geschichte der deutschen Sprache und Literatur* 76 (1954), 49–54.

———. "Das Nibelungenlied als aktuelle Dichtung seiner Zeit." *Germanisch-Romanische Monatsschrift* 42 (1967), 225–231.

Blackburn, Robert, ed. *After the Fall: The Failure of Communism and the Future of Socialism.* London: Verso, 1991.

Bloch, Marc. *La société feodale.* Paris: Michel, 1939.

Blumstein, Andrée Kahn. *Misogyny and Idealization in the Courtly Romance.* Studien zur Germanistik, Anglistik, und Komparatistik 41. Bonn: Bouvier, 1977.

Bornstein, Diane. *The Lady in the Tower: Medieval Courtesy Literature for Women.* Hamden CT: Archon, 1983.

Bostock, J. K. "The Message of the *Nibelungenlied.*" *Modern Language Review* 55 (1960), 200–212.

Bowden, Betsy. "The Art of Courtly Copulation." *Medievalia et Humanistica,* n.s. 9 (1979), 67–86.

Bowker, L. H. "Marital Rape: A Distinct Syndrome?" *Social Casework: The Journal of Contemporary Social Work* (June 1983), 347–352.

Brackert, Helmut. *Beiträge zur Handschriftenkritik des Nibelungenliedes.* Quellen und Forschungen, n.s. 135. Berlin: Schmidt, 1963.

———. "Nibelungenlied und Nationalgedanke. Zur Geschichte einer deutschen Ideologie." In *Mediævalia litteraria: Festschrift für Helmut de Boor zum 80. Geburtstag,* ed. Ursula Hennig and Herbert Kolb. München: Beck, 1971, pp. 343–364.

———. "Androgyne Idealität: Zum Amazonenbild in Rudolfs von Ems 'Alexander.'" In *Philologie als Kulturwissenschaft: Studien zur Literatur und Geschichte des Mittelalters Festschrift für Karl Stackmann zum 65. Geburtstag,* ed. Ludger Grenzmann, Hubert Herkommer, and Dieter Wutke. Göttingen: Vandenhoeck & Ruprecht, 1987, pp. 164–178.

Bridenthal, Renate and Claudia Koonz, eds. *Becoming Visible: Women in European History.* Boston: Houghton Mifflin, 1977.

Brietzmann, Franz. "Die böse Frau in der deutschen Literatur des Mittelalters." *Palaestra* 42 (1912), 120–236; rpt. New York 1967.

Brooke, Christopher N. L. *The Medieval Idea of Marriage.* Oxford: Oxford University Press, 1989.

Browne, Angela. *When Battered Women Kill.* New York: Free Press/Macmillan, 1987.

Brownmiller, Susan. *Against Our Will: Men, Women and Rape.* New York: Simon and Schuster, 1975.

Brüggen, Elke. *Kleidung und Mode in der höfischen Epik des 12. und 13. Jahrhunderts.* Heidelberg: Winter, 1989.

Brundage, James. "Rape and Marriage in the Medieval Canon Law." *Études offertes à Jean Gaudemet = Revue du Droit Canonique* 28 (1978), 62–75.

Bücher, Carl. *Die Frauenfrage im Mittelalter.* Tübingen: H. Laupp, 1882.

Bumke, Joachim. "Sigfrids Fahrt ins Nibelungenland: Zur achten Aventiure des *Nibelungenliedes.*" *Beiträge zur Geschichte der deutschen Sprache und Literatur* (Tübingen) 80 (1958), 253–268.

———. "Die Rolle der Frau im höfischen Literaturbetrieb." In *Mäzene im Mittelalter: Die Gönner und Auftraggeber der höfischen Literatur in Deutschland, 1150–1300.* München: Beck, 1977, pp. 231–247, 409–418.

———. "Liebe und Ehebruch in der höfischen Gesellschaft." In *Liebe als Literatur: Aufsätze zur erotischen Dichtung in Deutschland,* ed. Rüdiger Krohn. München: Beck, 1983, pp. 25–45.

Burger, Bernhard. *Die Grundlegung des Untergangsgeschehens im Nibelungenlied.* HochschulSammlung Philosophie, Literaturwissenschaft 11. Freiburg: HochschulVerlag, 1985.

Burns, E. Jane and Roberta Krueger. "Introduction" to *Courtly Ideology and Women's Place in Medieval French Literature,* special issue of *Romance Notes* 25 (1985), 205–219.

Campbell, Ian R. *Kudrun: A Critical Appreciation.* Cambridge: Cambridge University Press, 1978.

Carby, Hazel. *Reconstructing Womanhood: The Emergence of the Afro-American Woman Novelist.* Oxford: Oxford University Press, 1987.

Carlé, Birte, Nanna Damsholt, Karen Glente and Eva Trein Nielsen, eds. *Aspects of Female Existence: Proceedings from the St. Gertrud Symposium Women in the Middle Ages.* Copenhagen, September 1978. København: Gyldendal, 1980.

Carles, Jean. *Le poème de Kûdrun: Étude de sa matière.* Paris: Presses Universitaires de France, 1963.

Casey, Kathleen. "The Cheshire Cat: Reconstructing the Experience of Medieval Women." In *Liberating Women's History: Theoretical and Critical Essays,* ed. Berenice A. Carroll. Urbana: University of Illinois Press, 1976, pp. 224–249.

Chojnacki, Stanley. "The Power of Love: Wives and Husbands in Late Medieval Venice." In *Women and Power in the Middle Ages,* ed. Erler and Kowaleski, pp. 126–148.

Classen, Albrecht. "The Defeat of the Matriarch Brünhild in the *Nibelungenlied,* with Some Thoughts on Matriarchy as Evinced in Literary Texts." in *Waz sider da geschach: German-American Studies on the Nibelungenlied Text and Reception,* ed. Werner Wunderlich and Ulrich Müller. Göppingen: Kümmerle, 1992, pp. 89–110.

Cocalis, Susan and Kay Goodman, eds. *Beyond the Eternal Feminine: Critical Essays on Women and German Literature.* Stuttgarter Arbeiten zur Germanistik 98. Stuttgart: Akademischer Verlag Hans-Dieter Heinz, 1982.

Collier, Jane Fishburne. "Women in Politics." In *Woman, Culture, and Society,* ed. Rosaldo and Lamphere, pp. 89–96.

Colloquio italo-germanico sul tema: I Nibelunghi. Atti dei Convegni Lincei. Organizzato d'intesa con la Bayerische Akademie der Wissenschaften. Roma 14–15 maggio 1974. Roma: Accademia Nazionale dei Lincei 1974.

Culler, Jonathan. *On Deconstruction: Theory and Criticism After Structuralism.* Ithaca, NY: Cornell University Press, 1982.

——. "Anti-Foundational Philology." *What is Philology,* Special Focus Issue of *Comparative Literature Studies* 27 (1990), 49–52.

Curschmann, Michael. "'Nibelungenlied' und 'Nibelungenklage.' Über Mündlichkeit und Schriftlichkeit im Prozeß der Episierung." In *Deutsche Literatur im Mittelalter. Kontakte und Perspektiven. Hugo Kuhn zum Gedenken,* ed. Christoph Cormeau. Stuttgart: Metzler, 1979, pp. 85–119.

Czerwinski, Peter. "*Das Nibelungenlied.* Widersprüche höfischer Gewaltreglementierung." In *Einführung in die deutsche Literatur des 12. bis 16. Jahrhunderts.,* ed. Winfried Frey, Walter Raitz, Dieter Seitz, et al., Vol. 1: *Adel und Hof — 12./13. Jahrhundert.* Opladen: Westdeutscher Verlag, 1979, pp. 49–87.

Dargun, Lothar von. *Mutterrecht und Raubehe und ihre Reste im germanischen Recht und Leben.* Breslau: W. Koebner, 1883.

Davis, Natalie Zemon. "Introduction," In N. D., *The Knight, the Lady and the Priest: The Making of Modern Marriage in Medieval France,* trans. Barbara Bray. New York: Pantheon, 1983, pp. vii–xv.

——. "Women on Top." In N. D., *Society and Culture in Early Modern France.* Stanford, CA: Stanford University Press, 1975, pp. 124–151.

Delaney, Sheila. "Undoing Substantial Connection: The Late Medieval Attack on Analogical Thought." In S. D., *Medieval Literary Politics: Shapes of Ideology,* Manchester: Manchester University Press, 1990, pp. 19–41.

——. "Women, Nature and Language: Chaucer's *Legend of Good Women.*" In S. D., *Medieval Literary Politics: Shapes of Ideology.* Manchester: Manchester University Press, 1990, pp. 151–165.

Dickerson, Harold D., Jr. "Hagen: A Negative View." *Semasia: Beiträge zur germanisch-romanischen Sprachforschung* 2 (1975), 43–59.

Dobash, R. Emerson and Russell Dobash. *Violence Against Wives: A Case Against the Patriarchy.* New York: Free Press, 1979.

Donahue, Charles, Jr. "The Canon Law on the Formation of Marriage and Social Practice in the Later Middle Ages." *Journal of Family History* 8 (1983), 144–158.

duBois, Page. *Centaurs and Amazons: Women and the Prehistory of the Great Chain of Being.* Ann Arbor: University of Michigan Press, 1982.

Duby, Georges. "Le mariage dans la société du haut moyen âge." In *Il matrimonio nella società altomedievale.* Settimane di studio del centro italiano de studi sull'alto medioevo 24. Spoleto: Presso la sede del centro, 1977, pp. 15–39.

——. *Medieval Marriage: Two Models from Twelfth-Century France.* Trans. Elborg Forster. Johns Hopkins Symposia in Comparative History 11. Baltimore: Johns Hopkins University Press, 1978.

——. *The Knight, the Lady and the Priest: The Making of Modern Marriage in Medieval France.* Trans. by Barbara Bray. New York: Pantheon, 1983. (Orig.: *Le chevalier, la femme et le prêtre.* Paris: Hachette, 1981).

——, ed. *De l'Europe féodale à la Renaissance.* Vol. 2 of *Histoire de la vie privée,* under the direction of Philippe Ariès and Georges Duby. Paris: Éditions du Seuil, 1985.

Duby, Georges and Jacques Le Goff, eds. *Famille et parenté dans l'occident médiéval*. Actes du Colloque de Paris (6–8 juin 1974) organisée par l'École Pratique des Hautes Études (VIe section) en collaboration avec le Collège de France et l'École Française de Rome: Communications et débats. Collection de l'École Française de Rome 30. Rome: École Française de Rome, 1977.

Dürrenmatt, Nelly. *Das Nibelungenlied im Kreis der höfischen Dichtung*. Bern: Lang, 1945.

Eckhardt, Karl August, ed. *Die Gesetze des Karolingerreiches 714–911*. 3 vols. Germanenrechte 2 = Schriften der Akademie für deutsches Recht, Gruppe 5. Weimar: Böhlau, 1934.

———, ed. *Lex Salica. Monumenta Germaniae historica, Legum sectio IV, Constitutiones et acta publica imperatorum et regum, tomus IV, pars 2*. Hanover: Hahn, 1969.

———, ed. *Lex Salica 100 Titel-Text*. Germanenrecht, neue Folge [kritische Ausgabe] Abt. Westgermanisches Recht 3. Weimar: Böhlau, 1958, pp. 233–235.

———, ed. *Sachsenspiegel*. Germanenrechte, neue Folge Land- und Lehnrechtsbücher. Landrechte in hochdeutscher Übertragung V. Hannover: Hahn, 1967.

———, ed. *Schwabenspiegel*. Normalform. Studia iuris Suevicis, vol. 5. Bibliotheca rerum historicarum = Studia 8. Aalen: Scientia, 1972.

Ehrismann, Otfrid. *Das Nibelungenlied in Deutschland: Studien zur Rezeption des Nibelungenlieds von der Mitte des 18. Jahrhunderts bis zum ersten Weltkrieg*. Münchner Germanistische Beiträge 14. München: Fink, 1975.

——— *Nibelungenlied: Epoche   Werk   Wirkung*. München: Beck, 1907.

——— "Disapproval, Kitsch, and the Process of Justification: Brünhild's Wedding Nights." In *Waz sider da geschach: German-American Studies on the Nibelungenlied Text and Reception*, ed. Werner Wunderlich and Ulrich Müller. Göppingen: Kümmerle, 1992, pp. 167–177.

Eilts, Hilda. *Die Frau in den deutschen Großerzählungen des hohen Mittelalters*. Diss., masch. Leipzig, n.d. [1926].

Ennen, Edith. *Frauen im Mittelalter*. München: Beck, 1984.

Erickson, Carolly. *The Medieval Vision: Essays in History and Perception*. New York: Oxford University Press, 1976, "The Vision of Women," pp. 181–212.

Erler, Mary and Maryanne Kowaleski, eds. *Women and Power in the Middle Ages*. Athens: University of Georgia Press, 1988.

Ertzdorff, Xenja von and Marianne Wynn, eds. *Liebe-Ehe-Ehebruch in der Literatur des Mittelalters*. Beiträge zur deutschen Philologie 58. Gießen: Schmitz, 1984.

Estrich, Susan. *Real Rape*. Cambridge, MA: Harvard University Press, 1987.

Facinger, Marion F. "A Study of Medieval Queenship: Capetian France, 987–1237." *Studies in Medieval and Renaissance History* 5 (1968), 1–48.

Falk, Walter. *Das Nibelungenlied in seiner Epoche: Revision eines romantischen Mythos*. Heidelberg: Winter, 1974.

Fechter, Werner. *Siegfrieds Schuld und das Weltbild des* Nibelungenliedes. Hamburg: Toth, 1948.

Fehr, Hans. *Die Rechtsstellung der Frau und der Kinder in den Weistümern*. Jena: Gustav Fischer, 1912.

Ferguson, Ann. "Sex and Work: Women as a New Revolutionary Class in the

United States." In *An Anthology of Western Marxism: From Lukacs and Gramsci to Socialist Feminism,* ed. Roger S. Gottlieb, Oxford: Oxford University Press, 1989, pp. 348–372.

Ferrante, Joan M. *Woman as Image in Medieval Literature: From the Twelfth Century to Dante.* New York: Columbia University Press, 1975.

——. "Public Postures and Private Maneuvers: Roles Medieval Women Play." In *Women and Power in the Middle Ages,* ed. Erler and Kowaleski, pp. 213–229.

——. "Male Fantasy and Female Reality in Courtly Literature," *Women's Studies* 111 (1984), 67–97.

Finke, Heinrich. *Die Frau im Mittelalter.* Kempten and München: Josef Kösel und Friedrich Pustet, 1913.

Finkelhor, David and Kersti Yllo. *License to Rape: Sexual Abuse of Wives.* New York: Holt, Rinehart and Winston, 1985.

Fleet, Mary. "Siegfried as Gunther's Vassal." *Oxford German Studies* 14 (1983), 1–7.

Fossier, Robert. "La femme dans les sociétés occidentales." *Cahiers de Civilisation Médiévale* 20 (1977), 93–104.

Fourquet, Jean. "Réflexions sur le Nibelungenlied," In J. F., *Recueil d'études.* Études Médiévales 1. Amiens: Centre d'Études Médiévales Université de Picardie, 1979, I, 279–290.

——. "Un *Nibelungenlied* féministe: la *Lied*fassung." In *La Chanson des Nibelungen hier et aujourd'hui: Actes du Colloque Amiens 12–13 janvier 1991,* ed. Danielle Buschinger and Wolfgang Spiewok. Amiens: Centre d'Études Médiévales Université de Picardie, 1991, pp. 71–79.

Frakes, Jerold C. "Kriemhild's Three Dreams: A Structural Analysis." *Zeitschrift für deutsches Altertum* 113 (1984), 173–187.

Frenkel, R.V./Р.В. Френкель, ed. *Кудруна.* Moskva: Nauka, 1983.

Frieze, Irene H. "Investigating the Causes and Consequences of Marital Rape." *Signs: Journal of Women in Culture and Society* 8 (1983), 532–553.

Funk, Nanette and Magda Mueller, eds. *Gender Politics and Post-Communism: Reflections from Eastern Europe and the Former Soviet Union.* London: Routledge, 1993.

Gamarnikow, Eva, David H. J. Morgan, June Purvis, and Daphne Taylorson, eds. *The Public and the Private.* London: Heinemann, 1983.

Gamarnikow, Eva and June Purvis. "Introduction." In *The Public and the Private.* ed. Gamarnikow et al. London: Heinemann, 1983, pp. 1–6.

Gellinek, Christian. "Marriage by Consent in Literary Sources of Medieval Germany." *Studia Gratiana* 12 (1967), 555–579.

Gentry, Francis G. "Trends in 'Nibelungenlied' Research Since 1949: A Critical View." *Amsterdamer Beiträge zur älteren Germanistik* 7 (1974), 125–139.

——. Triuwe *and* vriunt *in the* Nibelungenlied. Amsterdam: Rodopi, 1975.

Gerhards, Gisela. *Das Bild der Witwe in der deutschen Literatur des Mittelalters.* Diss., Bonn 1962.

Gillespie, Cynthia. "Cruel and Usual Punishment." Review of Lenore E. Walker, *Terrifying Love: Why Battered Women Kill and How Society Responds. Women's Review of Books* 7/3 (December 1989), 24.

Gillespie, G. T. "'Die Klage' as a Commentary on 'Das Nibelungenlied.'" In *Probleme mittelhochdeutscher Erzählformen. Marburger Colloquium 1969,* ed. Peter F. Ganz and Werner Schröder. Berlin: Schmidt, 1972, pp. 153–177.

Göhler, Peter. *Das Nibelungenlied: Erzählweise, Figuren, Weltanschauung, literaturgeschichtliches Umfeld.* Diss., Berlin (Humboldt) 1985. Berlin: Akademie-Verlag, 1989.

Gold, Penny Schine. *The Lady and the Virgin: Image, Attitude, and Experience in Twelfth-Century France.* Chicago: University of Chicago Press, 1985.

Goody, Jack. *The Development of the Family and Marriage in Europe.* Cambridge: Cambridge University Press, 1983.

Goody, Jack and S. J. Tambiah. *Bridewealth and Dowry.* Cambridge Papers in Social Anthropology 7. Cambridge: Cambridge University Press, 1972.

Göttner-Abendroth, Heide. "Wissenschaftstheoretische Positionen in der Frauenforschung (Amerika, Frankreich, Deutschland)." In *Methoden in der Frauenforschung. Symposium an der Freien Universität Berlin vom 30.11-2.12.1983,* ed. Zentraleinrichtung zur Förderung von Frauenstudien und Frauenforschung an der Freien Universität Berlin. Frankfurt: R. G. Fischer, 1984, pp. 250–267.

Gramsci, Antonio. *Quaderni del Carcere.* Ed. Istituto Gramsci, under the direction of Valentino Gerratana. 4 vols. 2nd ed. Torino: Einaudi, 1975.

Gravdal, Kathryn. "Chrétien de Troyes, Gratian, and the Medieval Romance of Sexual Violence." *Signs: Journal of Women in Culture and Society* 17 (1992), 558–585.

Grenzler, Thomas. *Erotisierte Politik — Politisierte Erotik. Die politisch-ständische Begründung der Ehe-Minne in Wolframs "Willehalm," im "Nibelungenlied" und in der "Kudrun."* Göppingen: Kümmerle, 1992.

Grierson, P. "Election and Inheritance in Early Germanic Kingship." *Cambridge Historical Journal* 7 (1941), 1–22.

Grimm, Gunther. "Die Eheschließung in der Kudrun: Zur Frage der Verlobten- oder Gattentreue Kudruns." *Zeitschrift für deutsche Philologie* 90 (1971), 48–70.

Grundmann, Herbert. "Die Frauen und die Literatur im Mittelalter," in *Ausgewählte Aufsätze,* Teil 3: *Bildung und Sprache.* Schriften der MGH, vol. 25,3. Stuttgart: Hiersemann, 1978, pp. 67–95. Originally in *Archiv für Kulturgeschichte* 26.2 (1935), 129–161, entire vol. dated 1936.

Günzburger, Angelika. *Studien zur Nibelungenklage: Forschungsbericht — Bauform der Klage — Personendarstellung.* Europäische Hochschulschriften 685. Frankfurt: Lang, 1983.

Hallissy, Margaret. *Venomous Woman: Fear of the Female in Literature.* New York: Greenwood Press, 1987.

Hamburger, Käte. "Zur Erzählerhaltung im *Nibelungenlied.*" In *Kleine Schriften,* ed. Ulrich Müller et al. Stuttgarter Arbeiten zur Germanistik 25. Stuttgart: Heinz, 1976, pp. 59–73.

Hannawalt, Barbara A. "Lady Honor Lisle's Networks of Influence." In *Women and Power in the Middle Ages,* ed. Erler and Kowaleski, pp. 188–212.

Hansen, Elain Tuttle. "The Powers of Silence: The Case of the Clerk's Griselda." In *Women and Power in the Middle Ages,* ed. Erler and Kowaleski, pp. 230–249.

Hansen, Hilde E. *"Das ist Hartnäckigkeit in einer verwerflichen Sache; sie selbst nennen es Treue": Literatursoziologische Untersuchungen zum Nibelungenlied.* Diss. Bonn 1990. Frankfurt: Lang, 1990.

Hartmann, Heidi. "The Unhappy Marriage of Marxism and Feminism: Towards a More Progressive Union." In *An Anthology of Western Marxism: From Lukacs and Gramsci to Socialist Feminism,* ed. Roger S. Gottlieb, Oxford: Oxford University Press, 1989, pp. 316–337.

Haymes, Edward R. *The Nibelungenlied: History and Interpretation.* Urbana: University of Illinois Press, 1986.

——. "Dietrich von Bern im Nibelungenlied." *Zeitschrift für deutsche Altertum* 114 (1985), 159–165.

Hays, H. R. *The Dangerous Sex: The Myth of Feminine Evil.* New York: Putnam, 1964.

Hazen, Don, ed. *Inside the L.A. Riots: What Really Happened and Why It Will Happen Again.* N.p.: Institute for Alternative Journalism, 1992.

Heinzle, Joachim. *Das Nibelungenlied: Eine Einführung.* Artemis Einführungen 35. München: Artemis, 1987.

Hempel, W. "*Superbia* als Schuldmotiv im *Nibelungenlied.*" *Seminar* 2 (1966), 1–12.

Hennig, Ursula. "Herr und Mann—Zur Ständegliederung im Nibelungenlied." In *Hohenemser Studien zum Nibelungenlied,* ed. Achim Masser and Irmtraud Albrecht. Dornbirn: Vorarlberger Verlagsanstalt, 1980 [= *Montfort: Vierteljahresschrift für Geschichte und Gegenwart Vorarlbergs* Heft 3/4 (1980)], pp. 349–359.

——. "Die Heldenbezeichnung im Nibelungenlied." *Beiträge zur Geschichte der deutschen Sprache und Literatur* (Tübingen) 97 (1975), 4–58.

Herlihy, David. "Land, Family, and Women in Continental Europe, 701–1200." *Traditio* 18 (1962), 89–120. Reprint in *Women in Medieval Society,* ed. Stuart, pp. 13–45.

——. "The Making of the Medieval Family: Symmetry, Structure, and Sentiment." *Journal of Family History* 8 (1983), 116–130.

——. *Medieval Households.* Cambridge, MA: Harvard University Press, 1985.

Heusler, Andreas. *Lied und Epos in germanischer Sagendichtung.* Dortmund: F. W. Ruhfus, 1905.

——. *Nibelungensage und Nibelungenlied: Die Stoffgeschichte des deutschen Epos.* Dortmund: F. W. Ruhfus, 1921. 5th ed. 1955.

Hindess, Barry and Paul Q. Hirst. *Pre-Capitalist Modes of Production.* London: Routledge and Kegan Paul, 1975.

Hobsbawm, Eric J. "Introduction." In *Karl Marx: Pre-Capitalist Economic Formations,* ed. Eric J. Hobsbawm, trans. Jack Cohen. London: Lawrence and Wishart, 1964.

Hoecke, Willy van and Andries Welkenhuysen, eds. *Love and Marriage in the Twelfth Century.* Leuven: Leuven University Press, 1981.

Hoffmann, Werner. "Die Hauptprobleme der neuren 'Kudrun'-Forschung." *Wirkendes Wort* 14 (1964), 183–196, 233–243.

——. "Die englische und amerikanische Nibelungenforschung 1959–1962: Überschau und Kritik." *Zeitschrift für deutsche Philologie* 84 (1965), 267–278.

——. *Kudrun: Ein Beitrag zur Deutung der Nachnibelungischen Heldendichtung.* Stuttgart: Metzler, 1967.

——. "Die Fassung *C des Nibelungenliedes und die 'Klage.'" In *Festschrift Gottfried Weber: Zu seinem 70. Geburtstag überreicht von Frankfurter Kollegen und Schülern,* ed. Heinz Otto Burger und Klaus von See, pp. 109–143. Frankfurter Beiträge zur Germanistik 1. Bad Homburg: Gehlen, 1967.

——. *Das Nibelungenlied.* München: Oldenbourg, 1969.

——. "Die 'Kudrun': Eine Antwort auf das Nibelungenlied." In *Nibelungenlied und Kudrun,* ed. Rupp, pp. 599–620.

——. *Das Siegfriedbild in der Forschung.* Erträge der Forschung 127. Darmstadt: Wissenschaftliche Buchgesellschaft, 1979.

Hollander, Anne. *Seeing Through Clothes.* New York: Viking, 1978.

Howell, Martha C., "Citizenship and Gender: Women's Political Status in Northern Medieval Cities." In *Women and Power in the Middle Ages,* ed. Erler and Kowaleski, pp. 37–60.

Howell, Martha C., with Suzanne Wemple and Denise Kaiser. "A Documented Presence: Medieval Women in Germanic Historiography." In *Women in Medieval History and Historiography,* ed. Stuard, pp. 101–131.

Hughes, Diane Owen. "From Brideprice to Dowry in Medieval Europe." *Journal of Family History* 3 (1978), 262–296.

Ihlenburg, Karl Heinz. *Das Nibelungenlied: Problem und Gehalt.* Berlin: Akademie-Verlag, 1969.

——. "Die gesellschaftliche Grundlage des germanischen Heldenethos und die mündliche Überlieferung heroischer Stoffe." *Weimarer Beiträge* 17/2 (1971), 140–169.

Imray, Linda and Audrey Middleton. "Public and Private: Marking the Boundaries." In *The Public and the Private,* ed. Gamarnikow et al., pp. 12–27.

Jaeger, C. Stephen. *The Origins of Courtliness: Civilizing Trends and the Formation of Courtly Ideals 939–1210.* Philadelphia: University of Pennsylvania Press, 1985.

Jameson, Fredric. *The Political Unconscious: Narrative as a Socially Symbolic Act.* Ithaca, NY: Cornell University Press, 1981.

——. *The Prison House of Language: A Critical Account of Structuralism and Russian Formalism.* Princeton, NJ: Princeton University Press, 1972.

Jaquette, Jane S. "Power as Ideology: A Feminist Analysis." In *Women's Views of the Political World of Men,* ed. Judith Hicks Stiehm. New York: Transnational Press, 1984, pp. 7–29.

Johnson, Barbara. "Philology: What is at Stake." *What is Philology,* Special Focus Issue of *Comparative Literature Studies* 27 (1990), 26–29.

Johnson, L. P. "Down with *hohe Minne!*" *Oxford German Studies* 13 (1982), 36–48.

Kahn Blumstein, Andrée. *Misogyny and Idealization in the Courtly Romance.* Studien zur Germanistik, Anglistik und Komparatistik 41. Bonn: Bouvier, 1977.

Kaiser, Elsbet. *Frauendienst im mittelhochdeutschen Volksepos.* Breslau: Marcus, 1921; rpt. Hildesheim: Olms, 1977.

Kamuf, Peggy. *Fictions of Feminine Desire: Disclosures of Heloise.* Lincoln: University of Nebraska Press, 1982.

Keitel, Evelyne. *Die gesellschaftlichen Funktionen feministischer Textproduktion.* In

Weiblichkeit oder Feminismus, ed. Claudia Opitz. Weingarten: Drumlin, 1984, pp. 239–254.

Kellermann-Haaf, Petra. *Frau und Politik im Mittelalter: Untersuchungen zur politischen Rolle der Frau in den höfischen Romanen des 12., 13. und 14. Jahrhunderts.* Diss., Cologne, 1983. Göppingen: Kümmerle, 1986.

Ketsch, Peter. *Frauen im Mittelalter.* Ed. Annette Kuhn. Vol. 2: *Frauenbild und Frauenrechte in Kirche und Gesellschaft: Quellen und Materialien.* Düsseldorf: Schwann, 1984.

Kettner, Emil, "Der Einfluß des Nibelungenliedes auf die Gudrun." *Zeitschrift für deutsche Philologie* 23 (1891), 145–217.

King, K. C. "The Message of the *Nibelungenlied*—A Reply." *Modern Language Review* 57 (1962), 541–550.

Klein, Hans-Adolf. "Rüdiger und Dietrich von Bern als christliche Neuinterpretation des *êre*-Begriffs im Nibelungenlied?" In *Erzahlabsicht im Heldenepos und im höfischen Epos. Studien zum Ethos im "Nibelungenlied" und in "Flore und Blanscheflur."* Göppingen: Kümmerle, 1978, pp. 213–243.

Knäpper, Marie-Theres. *Feminismus-Autonomie-Subjektivität: Tendenzen und Widersprüche in der neuen Frauenbewegung.* Bochum: Germinal, 1984.

Kochendörfer, Günter. *Das Stemma des Nibelungenliedes und die textkritische Methode.* Diss., Freiburg. Freiburg: Johannes Krause, 1973.

Köhler, Erich. "Über die Möglichkeiten historisch-soziologischer Interpretation (aufgezeigt an französischen Werken verschiedener Epochen)." In E. K. *Esprit und arkadische Freiheit. Aufsätze aus der Welt der Romania.* Frankfurt: Athenäum, 1966, pp. 83–103.

Körner, Josef. *Das Nibelungenlied.* Leipzig: Teubner, 1921.

Konecny, Sylvia. "Das Sozialgefüge am Burgundenhof." In *Österreichische Literatur zur Zeit der Babenberger: Vorträge der Lilienfelder Tagung 1976,* ed. Alfred Ebenbauer, Fritz Peter Knapp, and Ingrid Strasser. Wien: Halosar, 1977, pp. 97–116.

Köstler, Rudolf. "Raub-, Kauf- und Friedelehe bei den Germanen." *Zeitschrift für Rechtsgeschichte,* germ. Abt. 63 (1943), 92–136.

Kralik, Dietrich von. *Das Sigfridstrilogie im Nibelungenlied und in der Thidrekssaga,* vol. 1. Halle: Niemeyer, 1941.

Krippendorff, Ekkehart. *Statt und Krieg: Die historische Logik politischer Unvernunft.* Frankfurt: Suhrkamp, 1985.

Krogmann, W. and U. Pretzel. *Bibliographie zum Nibelungenlied.* Berlin: Schmidt, 1966.

Kroes, H. W. J. "Kudrunprobleme." *Neophilologus* 38 (1954), 11–23.

Kroeschell, Karl. *Deutsche Rechtsgeschichte 1 (bis 1250).* 7th ed. Reinbek bei Hamburg: Rowolt, 1985.

Kuhn, Hans. "Kriemhilds Hort und Rache." In *Festschrift Paul Kluckhohn und Hermann Schneider gewidmet zu ihrem 60. Geburtstag.* Tübingen: Mohr/Siebeck, 1948, pp. 84–100. Also in H. K. *Kleine Schriften,* Vol. 2. Berlin: de Gruyter, 1971, pp. 65–79.

———. "Brünhilds und Kriemhilds Tod." *Zeitschrift für deutsches Altertum und deutsche Literatur* 82 (1950), 191–199.

———. "Der Teufel im Nibelungenlied: Zu Gunthers und Kriemhilds Tod." *Zeitschrift für deutsches Altertum und deutsche Literatur* 94 (1965), 280–306.

———. Rev. of G. Weber, *Das Nibelungenlied: Problem und Idee. Anzeiger für deutsches Altertum* 76 (1965), 1–18.

Kuhn, Hugo. "Brunhild und das Kriemhildlied." in *Frühe Epik Westeuropas und die Vorgeschichte des Nibelungenliedes,* ed. Kurt Wais. Tübingen: Niemeyer, 1953. *Zeitschrift für romanische Philologie,* Beiheft 95, pp. 9–21.

———. "Kudrun." In *Text and Theorie: Kleine Schriften,* Vol. 2. Stuttgart: Metzler, 1969, 200–216. Reprint in *Nibelungenlied und Kudrun,* ed. Rupp.

Kump, Otto. *Frauengestalten mittelhochdeutscher Epen des 12. und 13. Jahrhunderts.* Diss., masch. Graz 1934.

Lachmann, Karl. *Der Nibelunge Not mit der Klage.* 2nd ed. Berlin: Reimer, 1841.

Laubacher, A. "Die Entwicklung des Frauenbildes im mittelalterlichen Heldenepos." Diss. Würzburg 1954.

Lehmann, Andrée. *Le rôle de la femme dans l'histoire de France au moyen âge.* Paris: Berger-Levrault, 1952.

Leicher, Richard. *Die Totenklage in der deutschen Epik von der ältesten Zeit bis zur Nibelungen-Klage.* Germanistische Abhandlungen 58. Breslau: Marcus, 1927; rpt. Hildesheim: Olms, 1977.

Lévi-Strauss, Claude. *Anthropologie structurale.* Paris: Plon, 1958.

Levine, M. M., ed. *The Challenge of Black Athena.* Special Issue of *Arethusa* (Fall 1989).

Lewis, Gertrud Jaron. "'Daz vil edel wîp': Die Umkung zeitgenössischer Kritiker zur Frauengestalt der mittelhochdeutschen Epik." In *Die Frau als Heldin und Autorin. Neue kritische Ansätze zur deutschen Literatur.* Ed. Wolfgang Paulsen. Bern: Francke, 1979, pp. 66–81.

Lexer, Matthias. *Mittelhochdeutsches Handwörterbuch.* 3 vols. Leipzig: Hirzel, 1872–1878; repr. Stuttgart: Hirzel, 1979.

Lisak David. "Sexual Aggression, Masculinity, and Fathers." *Signs: Journal of Women in Culture and Society* 16 (1991), 238–262.

Loerzer, Eckart. *Eheschließung und Werbung in der "Kudrun."* München: Beck, 1971.

Lösel-Wieland-Engelmann, Berta. "Verdanken wir das *Nibelungenlied* einer Niedernburger Nonne?" *Monatshefte* 72 (1980), 5–25.

———. "Feminist Repercussions of a Literary Research Project." *Atlantis: A Women's Studies Journal* 6 (1980), 84–90.

Mackensen, Lutz. *Die Nibelungen: Sage, Geschichte, ihr Lied und sein Dichter.* Schriften zur Literatur- und Geistesgeschichte 1. Stuttgart: Ernst Hauswedell, 1984.

Mackinnon, Catherine. "Feminism, Marxism, Method, and the State: Toward Feminist Jurisprudence." *Signs: Journal of Women in Culture and Society* 8 (1983), 635–658.

McConnell, Winder. "Marriage in the *Nibelungenlied* and *Kudrun,*" in *Spectrum Medii Aevi: Essays in Early German Literature in Honor of George Fenwick Jones,* ed. William C. McDonald, Göppingen: Kümmerle, 1983, pp. 299–320.

———. *The Nibelungenlied.* Twayne World Authors Series 712. Boston: Twayne, 1984.

——. "The Passing of the Old Heroes: The *Nibelungenlied, Kudrun,* and the Epic Spirit." In *Genres in Medieval German Literature,* ed. Hubert Heinen and Ingeborg Henderson. Göppingen: Kümmerle, 1986, pp. 103–113.

——. "Kriemhild and Gerlind. Some Observations on the *vâlandinne*-concept in the *Nibelungenlied* and *Kudrun.*" In *The Dark Figure in Medieval German and Germanic Literature,* ed. Edward R. Haymes and Stephanie Van d'Elden. Göppingen: Kümmerle, 1986, pp. 42–53.

——. *The Epic of Kudrun: A Critical Commentary.* Göppingen: Kümmerle, 1988.

McNamara, JoAnn and Suzanne F. Wemple, "Sanctity and Power: The Dual Pursuit of Medieval Women." In *Becoming Visible: Women in European History,* ed. Renate Bridenthal and Claudia Koontz. Boston: Houghton Mifflin, 1977, pp. 90–118.

——. "The Power of Women Through the Family in Medieval Europe, 500–1100." *Feminist Studies* 1 (1973), 126–141. Rpt. in *Women and Power in the Middle Ages,* ed. Erlen and Kowalski, pp. 83–101.

——. "Marriage and Divorce in the Frankish Kingdom." In *Women in Medieval Society,* ed. Stuard, pp. 95–124.

Mahlendorf, Ursula R. and Frank J. Tobin. "Legality and Formality in the *Nibelungenlied,*" *Monatshefte* 66 (1974), 225–238.

Maurer, Friedrich. "Das Leid im *Nibelungenlied.*" In *Angebinde: John Meier zum 85. Geburtstag.* Ed. Friedrich Maurer. Lahr: Schauenberg, 1949.

——. *Leid: Studien zur Bedeutungs- und Problemgeschichte besonders in den großen Epen der staufischen Zeit.* Bern/München: Francke, 1951, pp. 13–28.

Mauss, Marcel. "Essai sur le don: "Forme et raison de l'exchange dans les sociétés archaïques" *L'Année Sociologique* 2 ser. 1 (1923–24). Reprint in M. M., *Sociologie et anthropologie.* Paris: Quadrige/Presses Universitaires de France, 1950; 5th ed. 1993, pp. 143–279.

Mergell, Bodo. "Nibelungenlied und höfischer Roman." *Euphorion* 45 (1950), 305–336.

Merschberger, Gerda. *Die Stellung der Frau im Eherecht und Erbrecht nach den deutschen Volksrechten.* Mannus-Bücherei 57. Leipzig 1937.

Meyer, Herbert. "Friedelehe und Mutterrecht," *Zeitschrift der Savigny-Stiftung für Rechtsgeschichte,* Germ. Abt. 47 (1927), 198–286.

Mikat, Paul. "Ehe." *Handwörterbuch zur deutschen Rechtsgeschichte.* Ed. Adalbert Erler and Ekkehard Kaufmann. Berlin: Schmidt, 1971, I, 809–833.

Miller, Nancy. "Arachnologies: The Woman, the Text, and the Critic." In N.M., *Subject to Change: Reading Feminist Writing.* New York: Columbia University Press, 1988, pp. 77–101.

——. "Changing the Subject: Authorship, Writing and the Reader." In N.M., *Subject to Change: Reading Feminist Writing.* New York: Columbia University Press, 1988, pp. 102–121.

Modleski, Tania. *Loving with a Vengeance.* Hamden, CT: Archon Books, 1982.

Moos, Peter von. *Mittelalterforschung und Ideologiekritik.* München: Fink, 1974.

Moser, H. and H. Tervooren, eds. *Des Minnesangs Frühling* 36th ed. 2 vols. Stuttgart: Hirzel, 1977.

Mowatt, D. G. "A Note on Kriemhild's Three Dreams." *Seminar* 7 (1971), 114–122.

Mowatt, D. G. and Hugh Sacker. *The Nibelungenlied: An Interpretive Commentary.* Toronto: University of Toronto Press, 1967.

Müller, Jan-Dirk. "SIVRIT: *künec-man-eigenholt.* Zur sozialen Problematik des Nibelungenliedes." *Amsterdamer Beiträge zur älteren Germanistik* 7 (1974), 85–124.

Mueller, Werner Achilles. *The Nibelungenlied Today: Its Substance, Essence and Significance.* Chapel Hill: University of North Carolina Press, 1962. Rpt. New York: AMS, 1966.

Murdoch, Brian. "Interpreting Kudrun: Some Comments on a Recent Critical Appreciation," Rev. of Ian R. Campbell, *Kudrun: A Critical Appreciation. New German Studies* 7 (1979), 113–127.

Nagel, Bert. *Das Nibelungenlied: Stoff - Form - Ethos.* Frankfurt: Hirschgraben, 1965; 2nd ed. 1970.

Naumann, Hans. "Brünhilds Gürtel." *Zeitschrift für deutsches Altertum und deutsche Literatur* 70 (1933), 46–48.

Nelson, Charles G. "Virginity (De)Valued: Kriemhild, Brünhild, and All That." In *Waz sider da geschach: German-American Studies on the Nibelungenlied Text and Reception,* ed. Werner Wunderlich and Ulrich Müller. Göppingen: Kümmerle, 1992, pp. 111–130.

Nelson, Janet L. "Queens as Jezebels: The Careers of Brunhild and Balthild in Merovingian History." In *Medieval Women,* ed. Derek Baker. Oxford: Blackwell, 1978, pp. 31–77.

Neubecker, Friedrich Karl. *Die Mitgift in rechtsvergleichender Darstellung.* Leipzig. Deichert, 1909.

Neumann, Friedrich. "Kudrun." *Die deutsche Literatur des Mittelalters: Verfasserlexikon.* Vol II. Berlin: de Gruyter, 1936, coll. 961–983; vol. V (1955), coll. 572–580.

———. *Das Nibelungenlied in seiner Zeit.* Göttingen: Vandenhoeck and Ruprecht, 1967.

Newman, Gail. "The Two Brunhilds?" *Amsterdamer Beiträge zur älteren Germanistik* 16 (1981), 69–78.

Das Nibelungenlied. Ed. Helmut de Boor. (nach der Ausgabe von Karl Bartsch). 21 ed., rev. by Roswitha Wisniewski. Wiesbaden: Brockhaus, 1979.

Das Nibelungenlied: A Complete Transcription in Modern German Type of the Text of Manuscript C from the Fürstenberg Court Library Donaueschingen. Ed. Heinz Engels, with an Essay on the Manuscript and Its Provenance by Erna Huber. New York: Praeger, 1969.

Nolte, Theodor. *Das Kudrunepos—Ein Frauenroman.* Untersuchungen zur deutschen Literaturgeschichte 38. Tübingen: Niemeyer, 1985.

Otto, Eduard. *Deutsches Frauenleben im Wandel der Jahrhunderte.* Aus Natur und Geisteswelt 45. Leipzig: Teubner, 1918.

Owen, Stephen. "Philology's Discontents: Response," *What is Philology.* Special Focus Issue of *Comparative Literature Studies* 27 (1990), 75–78.

Panzer, Friedrich. *Das Nibelungenlied: Entstehung und Gestalt.* Stuttgart: Kohlhammer, 1955.

———. *Studien zum Nibelungenlied*. Frankfurt: Diesterweg, 1945.

Paulsen, Wolgang. "Vorbemerkung." In *Die Frau als Heldin und Autorin.*" *Neue kritische Ansätze zur deutschen Literatur*, ed. Wolfgang Paulsen. Bern: Francke, 1979, pp. 7–10.

Peters, Edward. *The Shadow King: Rex Inutilis in Medieval Law and Literature, 751–1327*. New Haven, CT: Yale University Press, 1970.

Peeters, Leopold. *Historische und literarische Studien zum dritten Teil des Kudrunepos*. Diss., Utrecht 1968. Meppel: Boom en Zoon, 1968.

Pfaff, Volkert. "Das kirchliche Eherecht am Ende des zwölften Jahrhunderts." *Zeitschrift der Savigny-Stiftung für Rechtsgeschichte*. Kanon. Abteilung 63 (1977), 73–117.

Pomeroy, Sarah B., *Goddesses, Whores, Wives, and Slaves: Women in Classical Antiquity*. New York: Schocken, 1975.

———. "A Classical Scholar's Perspective on Matriarchy." In *Liberating Women's History: Theoretical and Critical Essays*, ed. Berenice A. Carroll. Urbana: University of Illinois Press, 1976, pp. 217–223.

Portmann, Marie-Louise. *Die Darstellung der Frau in der Geschichtschreibung des früheren Mittelalters*. Basler Beiträge zur Geschichtswissenschaft 69. Basel & Stuttgart: Helbing and Lichtenhahn, 1958.

Post, J. H. "Ravishment of Women and the Statutes of Westminster." In *Legal Records and the Historian*, ed. J. H. Baker. London: Royal Historical Society, 1978, pp. 150–160.

Power, Eileen. "The Position of Women." Chapter 7 in *The Legacy of the Middle Ages*, ed. C. G. Crump and E. F. Jacob. Oxford: Clarendon Press, 1926, pp. 401–433.

———. *Medieval Women*. Ed. M. M. Postan. Cambridge: Cambridge University Press, 1975.

Renoir, Alain. "Levels of Meaning in the *Nibelungenlied*: Sifrit's Courtship." *Neuphilologische Mitteilungen* 61 (1960), 353–361.

Rezak, Brigitte Bedos, "Women, Seals, and Power in Medieval France, 1150–1350." In *Women and Power in the Middle Ages*, ed. Erler and Kowaleski, pp. 61–82.

Riché, Pierre. "La femme dans la société germanique païnne." In *L'Occident, des Celtes à la Renaissance*, undesignated vol. [2] of *Histoire mondiale de la femme*. Gen. Ed. Pierre Grimal. Paris: Nouvelle Librairie de France, n.d. [1966], pp. 27–34.

———. "La femme à l'époque barbare." In *L'Occident, des Celtes à la Renaissance*, undesignated vol. [2] of *Histoire mondiale de la femme*. Gen. Ed. Pierre Grimal. Paris: Nouvelle Librairie de France, n.d. [1966], pp. 35–46.

———. "La femme à l'époque carolingienne." In *L'Occident, des Celtes à la Renaissance*, undesignated vol. [2] of *Histoire mondiale de la femme*. Gen. Ed. Pierre Grimal. Paris: Nouvelle Librairie de France, n.d. [1966], pp. 47–53.

Rings, Lana. "Kriemhilt's Face Work: A Sociolinguistic Analysis of Social Behavior in the *Nibelungenlied*." *Semiotica* 65 (1987), 317–325.

Rosaldo, Michelle Zimbalist. "The Use and Abuse of Anthropology: Reflections on Feminism and Cross-Cultural Understanding." *Signs: Journal of Women and Culture in Society* 5 (1980), 389–417.

———. "Women, Culture and Society: A Theoretical Overview." In *Woman, Culture, and Society,* ed. Rosaldo and Lamphere, pp. 17–42.

Rosaldo, Michelle Zimbalist and Louise Lamphere, "Introduction." In *Woman, Culture, and Society,* ed. Rosaldo and Lamphere, pp. 1–15.

Rosaldo, Michelle Zimbalist and Louise Lamphere, eds. *Woman, Culture, and Society.* Stanford, CA: Stanford University Press, 1974.

Rose, Peter W. *Sons of the Gods, Children of Earth: Ideology and Literary Form in Ancient Greece.* Ithaca, NY: Cornell University Press, 1992.

Rowbotham, Sheila. "Through the Looking Glass." In S. R., *Women's Consciousness, Man's World.* New York: Penguin Books, 1974. Also in *An Anthology of Western Marxism: From Lukacs and Gramsci to Socialist Feminism.* Oxford: Oxford University Press, 1989.

Rubin, Gayle. "The Traffic in Women: Notes on the 'Political Economy' of Sex." In *Toward an Anthropology of Women,* ed. Rayna R. Reiter. New York: Monthly Review Press, 1975, pp. 157–210.

Ruether, Rosemary Radford and Eleanor McLaughlin, eds. *Women of Spirit: Female Leadership in the Jewish and Christian Traditions.* New York: Simon and Schuster, 1979.

Rupp, Heinz. "'Heldendichtung' als Gattung der deutschen Literatur des 13. Jahrhunderts." In *Volk, Sprache, Dichtung. Festgabe für Kurt Wagner,* ed. Karl Bischoff and Lutz Röhrich. Gießen: Wilhelm Schmitz, 1960, pp. 9–25.

———, ed. *Nibelungenlied und Kudrun.* Wege der Forschung 54. Darmstadt. Wissenschaftliche Buchgesellschaft, 1976.

———. "Das 'Nibelungenlied'—eine politische Dichtung." *Wirkendes Wort* 35 (1985), 166–176.

Russell, Diana E. H. *Rape in Marriage.* New York: Macmillan, 1982.

Sacker, H. "On Irony and Symbolism in the *Nibelungenlied:* Two Preliminary Notes." *German Life and Letters* 14 (1961), 271–281.

Salmon, P. B. "Why does Hagen Die?" *German Life and Letters* 17 (1963–1964), 10–13.

Sanday, Peggy Reeves. "Female Status in the Public Domain." In *Woman, Culture, and Society,* ed. Rosaldo and Lamphere, pp. 189–206.

———. *Female Power and Male Dominance: On the Origins of Sexual Inequality.* Cambridge: Cambridge University Press, 1981.

———. "The Socio-Cultural Context of Rape." *Journal of Social Issues* 37 (1981), 5–27.

———. "Rape and the Silencing of the Feminine." In *Rape: An Historical and Social Enquiry,* ed. Tomaselli and Porter, pp. 85–101.

Sayce, O. L. "Abortive Motivation in Part I of the *Nibelungenlied.*" *Medium Aevum* 23 (1954), 36–38.

Schäufele, Eva. *Normabweichendes Rollenverhalten: Die kämpfende Frau in der deutschen Literatur des 12. und 13. Jahrhunderts.* Göppingen: Kümmerle, 1979.

Schlauch, Margaret. *Chaucer's Constance and Accused Queens.* New York: New York University Press, 1927.

Schmidt-Wiegand, Ruth. "Kriemhilds Rache. Zu Funktion und Wertung des

Rechts im Nibelungenlied," In *Tradition als historische Kraft: Interdisziplinäre Forschungen zur Geschichte des früheren Mittelalters,* ed. Norbert Kamp und Joachim Wollasch, with collaboration of M. Balzer, K. H. Krüger, and L. von Padberg. Berlin: de Gruyter, 1982, pp. 372–387.

Schneider, Hermann. *Die deutschen Lieder von Siegfrieds Tod.* Weimar: Böhlau 1947.

Schramm, Gottfried. "Der Name Kriemhilt." *Zeitschrift für deutsches Altertum und deutsche Literatur* 94 (1965), 39–57.

Schröbler, Ingeborg. *Wikingische und spielmännische Elemente im zweiten Teile des Gudrunliedes.* Halle: Niemeyer, 1934.

Schröder, Franz Rolf, *Nibelungenstudien.* Rheinische Beiträge und Hülfsbücher zur germanischen Philologie und Volkskunde 6. Bonn und Leipzig: Kurt Schroeder, 1921.

——. "Sigfrids Tod." *Germanisch-Romanische Monatsschrift* 41 (1960), 111–112.

Schröder, Richard. *Geschichte des ehelichen Güterrechts in Deutschland.* 2 pts., 4 vols. Stettin/Danzig/Elbing 1863–1874; rpt. 2pts. in 4 vols. in 2. Aalen: Scientia Verlag, 1967.

Schröder, Walter Johannes. "Das Nibelungenlied: Versuch einer Deutung." *Beiträge zur Geschichte der deutschen Sprache und Literatur* (Halle/Saale) 76 (1954), 56–143.

Schröder, Werner, "Das Leid in der 'Klage.'" *Zeitschrift für deutsches Altertum und deutsche Literatur* 88 (1957/1958), 54–80. Rpt. in W. S. *Nibelungenlied-Studien.* Stuttgart: Metzler, 1968, pp. 185–225.

——. "Die Tragödie Kriemhilts im Nibelungenlied." *Zeitschrift für deutsches Altertum und deutsche Literatur* 90 (1960–61), 41–80, 123–160.

——. "Zum Problem der Hortfrage im *Nibelungenlied.*" In W. S. *Nibelungenlied-Studien.* Stuttgart: Metzler, 1968, pp. 157–184.

Schulenburg, Jane Tibbetts, "Female Sanctity: Public and Private Roles, ca. 500–1100." In *Women and Power in the Middle Ages,* ed. Erler and Kowaleski, pp. 102–125.

Schulze, Ursula. "Nibelungen und Kudrun," in *Epische Stoffe des Mittelalters.* Ed. Volker Mertens and Ulrich Müller. Stuttgart: Alfred Kröner, 1984, pp. 111–140.

Schwarze, M. "Die Frau in dem *Nibelungenliede* und der *Kudrun.*" *Zeitschrift für deutsche Philologie* 16 (1884), 385–470.

Schweikle, Günther. "Das 'Nibelungenlied' – ein heroisch-tragischer Liebesroman?" In *De poeticis medii aevi quaestiones: Käte Hamburger zum 85. Geburtstag,* ed. Jürgen Kühnel et al. Göppingen: Kümmerle, 1981, pp. 59–84.

See, Klaus von. "Die Werbung um Brünhild." *Zeitschrift für deutsches Altertum und deutsche Literatur* 88 (1957/1958), 1–20.

——. "Freierprobe und Königinnenzank in der Sigfridsage." *Zeitschrift für deutsches Altertum und deutsche Literatur* 89 (1959), esp. pp. 164–172.

——. *Deutsche Germanen-Ideologie: Vom Humanismus bis zur Gegenwart.* Frankfurt: Athenäum, 1970.

Seitter, Walter. *Das politische Wissen im Nibelungenlied.* Berlin: Merve Verlag, n.d.

——. *Versprechen, Versagen: Frauenmacht und Frauenästhetik in der Kriemhild-Diskussion des 13. Jahrhunderts.* Berlin: Merve Verlag, 1990.

Shahar, Shulamith. *The Fourth Estate: A History of Women in the Middle Ages.* Trans. Chaya Galai. London: Methuen, 1983.

Shorter, Edward. "On Writing the History of Rape." *Signs: Journal of Women and Culture in Society* 3 (1977), 471–482.

Siebert, Barbara. *Rezeption und Produktion: Bezugssysteme in der "Kudrun."* Diss., Freiburg. Göppingen: Kümmerle, 1988.

——. "Hildeburg im Kudrun-Epos. Die bedrohte Existenz der ledigen Frau." In *Der frauwen buoch: Versuch zu einer feministischen Mediävistik,* ed. Bennewitz, pp. 213–226.

Siefken, Hinrich. *Überindividuelle Formen und der Aufbau des Kudrunepos.* München: Fink, 1967.

Soeteman, C. "Das schillernde Frauenbild mittelalterlicher Dichtung." *Amsterdamer Beiträge zur älteren Germanistik* 5 (1973), 77–94.

Spelman, Elizabeth V. *Inessential Women: Problems of Exclusion in Feminist Thought.* Boston: Beacon Press, 1988.

Spiewok, Wolfgang. "Das Nibelungenlied." In *Werkinterpretationen zur deutschen Literatur,* ed. Horst Hartmann. Berlin, 1986, pp. 12–33.

Spivak, Gayatri Chakravorty. *In Other Worlds: Essays in Cultural Politics.* New York: Methuen, 1987.

——. "The Politics of Interpretations." In *The Politics of Interpretation,* ed. W. J. T. Mitchell. Chicago: University of Chicago Press, 1983. 347–366.

Stackmann, Karl. "Kudrun." *Die deutsche Literatur des Mittelalters. Verfasserlexikon.* 2nd ed. Kurt Ruh. Berlin: de Gruyter, 1983, V, 410–426.

——. "Einleitung." *Kudrun.* Ed. Karl Bartsch. Revised 5th ed. by Stackmann. Wiesbaden: Brockhaus, 1980, vii–civ.

Stafford, Pauline. *Queens, Concubines, and Dowagers: The King's Wife in the Early Middle Ages.* Athens: University of Georgia Press, 1983.

Strauß und Torney, Lulu von. *Deutsches Frauenleben in der Zeit der Sachsenkaiser und Hohenstaufen.* Jena: Diederichs, 1927.

Stuard, Susan Mosher, ed. *Women in Medieval Society.* Philadelphia: University of Pennsylvania Press, 1976.

——. "The Annales School and Feminist History: Opening Dialogue with the American Stepchild." *Signs: Journal of Women in Culture and Society* 7 (1981), 135–143.

——, ed. *Women in Medieval History and Historiography.* Philadelphia: University of Pennsylvania Press, 1987.

Szklenar, Hans. "Die literarische Gattung der *Nibelungenklage* und das Ende 'alter maere.'" *Poetica* 9 (1977), 41–61.

Szövérffy, Josef. "Das Nibelungenlied: Strukturelle Beobachtungen und Zeitgeschichte." *Wirkendes Wort* 15 (1965), 233–238.

Thelen, Lynn. "The Internal Source and Function of King Gunther's Bridal Quest." *Monatshefte* 76 (1984), 143–155.

Thieme, Hans. "Die Rechtstellung der Frau in Deutschland." In *La Femme,* ed. John Gilissen. Vol. 2. Brussels 1962, pp. 351–376 = *Recueils de la Société Jean Bodin* 12 (1962), 351–376.

Thorp, Mary. *The Study of the Nibelungenlied: Being the History of the Study of the Epic and Legend from 1755 to 1937.* Oxford: Clarendon Press, 1940.

Tomalin, Magaret. *The Fortunes of the Warrior Heroine in Italian Literature: An Index of Emancipation.* Ravenna: Longo Editore, 1982.

Toman, Lore. "Der Aufstand der Frauen. Ein strukturalistischer Blick auf die Brünhild-Sage." *Literature und Kritik* 14 (1979), 25–32.

Tomaselli, Sylvana and Roy Porter, eds. *Rape: An Historical and Social Enquiry.* Oxford: Blackwell, 1986.

Tonnelat, Ernest. *La chanson des Nibelungen. Étude sur la composition et la formation du poème épique.* Publications de la Faculté des Lettres de l'Université de Strasbourg 30. Paris: Les Belles Lettres, 1926.

Tyrrell, Wm. Blake. *Amazons: A Study in Athenian Mythmaking.* Baltimore: Johns Hopkins University Press, 1984.

Verdon, Jean. "Les sources de l'histoire de la femme en Occident aux Xe–XIIIe siècles." *Cahiers de Civilisation Médiévale* 20 (1977), 219–251.

Vesterguard, Elisabeth. "Gudrun / Kriemhild, søster eller hustru?" *Arkiv för nordisk filologi* 99 (1984), 63–78.

——. "Continuity and Change in Medieval Epic and Society." In *Continuity and Change: Political Institutions and Literary Monuments in the Middle Ages: A Symposium,* ed. Elisabeth Vestergaard. Odense: Odense University Press, 1986, pp. 119–131.

Vogelsang, Thilo. *Die Frau als Herrscherin im hohen Mittelalter: Studien zur "consors regni" Formel.* Göttinger Bausteine zur Geschichtswissenschaft 7. Göttingen: Musterschmidt, 1954.

Voorwinden, Norbert. "Nibelungenklage und Nibelungenlied." In *Hohenemser Studien zum Nibelungenlied,* ed. Achim Masser and Irmtraud Albrecht. Dornbirn: Vorarlberger Verlagsanstalt, 1980 [= *Montfort: Vierteljahresschrift für Geschichte und Gegenwart Vorarlbergs* Heft 3/4 (1980)], pp. 276–287.

Wachinger, Burghart. *Studien zum Nibelungenlied: Vorausdeutung, Aufbau, Motivierung.* Tübingen: Niemeyer, 1960.

——. "Die 'Klage' und das Nibelungenlied." In *Hohenemser Studien zum Nibelungenlied,* ed. Achim Masser and Irmtraud Albrecht. Dornbirn: Vorarlberger Verlagsanstalt, 1980 [= *Montfort: Vierteljahresschrift für Geschichte und Gegenwart Vorarlbergs* Heft 3/4 (1980)], pp. 264–275.

Wailes, Stephen L. "Bedroom Comedy in the *Nibelungenlied.*" *Modern Language Quarterly* 32 (1971), 365–376.

——. "The Romance of Kudrun." *Speculum* 58 (1983), 347–367.

Walker, Lenore E. *Terrifying Love: Why Battered Women Kill and How Society Responds.* New York: Harper and Row, 1989.

Walker, Lenore E. *The Battered Woman.* New York: Harper & Row, 1979.

Ward, Donald J. and Franz H. Bäuml. "Zur Kudrun-Problematik: Ballade und Epos." *Zeitschrift für deutsche Philologie* 88 (1969), 19–27.

Ward, Donald J. and Franz Bäuml. "Nochmals Kudrun: Ballade und Epos. Eine Erwiderung." *Jahrbuch für Volksliedforschung* 17 (1972), 70–86.

Washington, Ida H. & Carol E. Washington Tobol. "Kriemhild and Clytemnestra:

Sisters in Crime or Independent Women?" In *The Lost Tradition: Mothers and Daughters in Literature,* ed. Cathy N. Davidson and E. M. Broner, New York: Ungar, 1980, 15–21.

Weber, Gottfried. *Das Nibelungenlied: Problem und Idee.* Stuttgart: Metzler, 1963.

Weber, Gottfried and Werner Hoffman. *Nibelungenlied.* 3rd ed. Stuttgart: Metzler, 1968.

Weege, Magdalene. *Das Kudrunepos, eine Dichtung des Hochmittelalters.* Diss. Mainz, Lemgo 1953.

Wehrli, Max. "Die 'Klage' und der Untergang der Nibelungen." In *Zeiten und Formen in Sprache und Dichtung. Festschrift für Fritz Tschirch zum 70. Geburtstag,* ed. Karl-Heinz Schirmer & Bernhard Sowinski. Köln/Wien: Böhlau, 1972, pp. 96–112.

Weigand, Edda. "Historische Sprachpragmatik am Beispiel: Gesprächsstrukturen im *Nibelungenlied.*" *Zeitschrift für deutsches Altertum* 117 (1988), 159–173.

Weinhold, Karl. *Die deutschen Frauen im Mittelalter.* 2 Vols. Wien 1882; rpt. 1 vol. Amsterdam: Rodopi, 1968.

Wemple, Suzanne Fonay. *Women in Frankish Society: Marriage and the Cloister, 500 to 900.* Philadelphia: University of Pennsylvania Press, 1981.

Wenzel, Horst. *Frauendienst und Gottesdienst. Studien zur Minneideologie.* Philologische Studien und Quellen 74. Berlin: de Gruyter, 1974.

Wesle, Carl. "Brünhildlied oder Sigfridepos?" *Zeitschrift für deutsche Philologie* 51 (1926), 33–45.

Westphal Wihl, Sarah. "The Ladies' Tournament: Marriage, Sex, and Honor in Thirteenth-Century Germany." *Signs: Journal of Women in Culture and Society* 14 (1989), 371–398.

Weydt, Harald. "Streitsuche im *Nibelungenlied:* Die Kooperation der Feinde: Eine konversationsanalytische Studie." In *Literatur und Konversation: Sprachsoziologie und Pragmatik in der Literaturwissenschaft,* ed. Ernest W. B. Hess-Lüttich. Wiesbaden: Athenaion, 1980, pp. 95–114.

White, Hayden. *Tropics of Discourse: Essays in Cultural Criticism.* Baltimore: Johns Hopkins University Press, 1978.

Whyte, Martin King. *The Status of Women in Preindustrial Societies.* Princeton, NJ: Princeton University Press, 1978.

Widén, Solveig. "Morgengåvan som grund för änkeförsörjning." In *Förändringar i kvinnors villkor under medeltiden: Uppsatser framlagda vid ett kvinnohistoriskt symposium i Skálholt, Ísland, 22.–25. juni 1981,* ed. Silja Aðalsteinsdóttir and Helgi Þorláksson. Reykjavík: Sagnfræðistofunun Háskóla Íslands, 1983, pp. 71–81.

Wild, Inga. *Zur Überlieferung und Rezeption des "Kudrun"-Epos: Eine Untersuchung von drei Europäischen Liedbereichen des "Typs Südeli."* Teil 1. Diss. München 1976. Göppingen: Kümmerle, 1979.

Willson, H. B. "Concord and Discord: The Dialectic of the *Nibelungenlied.*" *Medium Aevum* 28 (1959), 153–166.

Wis, Marjatta. "Zu den 'Schneiderstrophen' des *Nibelungenliedes:* Ein Deutungsversuch." *Neuphilologische Mitteilungen* 84 (1983), 251–260.

Winkler, John H. "The Education of Chloe." In *Rape and Representation,* ed. Lynne Higgins and Brenda Silver. New York: Columbia University Press, 1991.

Wisniewski, Roswitha. *Kudrun.* 2nd ed. Stuttgart: Metzler, 1969.

Wunderlich, Werner, ed. *Der Schatz des Drachentödters: Materialien zur Wirkungsgeschichte des Nibelungenliedes.* Literaturwissenschaft-Gesellschaftswissenschaft 30. Stuttgart: Klett, 1977.

Wynn, Marianne. "Hagen's Defiance of Kriemhilt." In *Mediaeval German Studies Presented to Frederick Norman.* London: Institute of Germanic Studies, 1965, pp. 104–114.

Zacharias, Rainer. "Die Blutrache im deutschen Mittelalter." *Zeitschrift für deutsches Altertum* 91 (1961/1962), 167–201.

Zallinger, O. *Die Eheschließung im Nibelungenlied und in der Gudrun.* Wien: Hölder-Pichler-Tempsky, 1923.

——. "Heirat ohne 'Trauung' im Nibelungenlied und in der Gudrun." *Veröffentlichungen des Museum Ferdinandeum in Innsbruck* 8 (1928), 337–359.

Zeitlin, Froma. "Configurations of Rape in Greek Myth." In *Rape: An Historical and Social Enquiry,* ed. Tomaselli and Porter, pp. 122–151.

Ziolkowski, Jan, ed. *What is Philology?* Special Focus Issue of *Comparative Literature Studies* 27 (1990).

Zumthor, Paul. *Parler du Moyen Âge.* Paris: Éditions du Seuil, 1980.

Index

University of Pennsylvania Press
MIDDLE AGES SERIES
Edward Peters, General Editor

F. R. P. Akehurst, trans. *The* Coutumes de Beauvaisis *of Philippe de Beaumanoir.* 1992

Peter L. Allen. *The Art of Love: Amatory Fiction from Ovid to the* Romance of the Rose. 1992

David Anderson. *Before the Knight's Tale: Imitation of Classical Epic in Boccaccio's* Teseida. 1988

Benjamin Arnold. *Count and Bishop in Medieval Germany: A Study of Regional Power, 1100–1350.* 1991

Mark C. Bartusis. *The Late Byzantine Army: Arms and Society, 1204–1453.* 1992.

J. M. W. Bean. *From Lord to Patron: Lordship in Late Medieval England.* 1990

Uta-Renate Blumenthal. *The Investiture Controversy: Church and Monarchy from the Ninth to the Twelfth Century.* 1988

Daniel Bornstein, trans. *Dino Compagni's* Chronicle *of Florence.* 1986

Maureen Boulton. *The Song in the Story: Lyric Insertions in French Narrative Fiction, 1200–1400.* 1993

Betsy Bowden. *Chaucer Aloud: The Varieties of Textual Interpretation.* 1987

Charles R. Bowlus. *Franks, Moravians, and Magyars: The Struggle for the Middle Danube, 788–907.* 1994

James William Brodman. *Ransoming Captives in Crusader Spain: The Order of Merced on the Christian-Islamic Frontier.* 1986

Kevin Brownlee and Sylvia Huot, eds. *Rethinking the* Romance of the Rose*: Text, Image, Reception.* 1992

Matilda Tomaryn Bruckner. *Shaping Romance: Interpretation, Truth, and Closure in Twelfth-Century French Fictions.* 1993

Otto Brunner (Howard Kaminsky and James Van Horn Melton, eds. and trans.). Land *and Lordship: Structures of Governance in Medieval Austria.* 1992

Robert I. Burns, S.J., ed. *Emperor of Culture: Alfonso X the Learned of Castile and His Thirteenth-Century Renaissance.* 1990

David Burr. *Olivi and Franciscan Poverty: The Origins of the* Usus Pauper *Controversy.* 1989

David Burr. *Olivi's Peaceable Kingdom: A Reading of the Apocalypse Commentary.* 1993

Thomas Cable. *The English Alliterative Tradition.* 1991

Anthony K. Cassell and Victoria Kirkham, eds. and trans. *Diana's Hunt/Caccia di Diana: Boccaccio's First Fiction.* 1991

John C. Cavadini. *The Last Christology of the West: Adoptionism in Spain and Gaul, 785–820.* 1993

Brigitte Cazelles. *The Lady as Saint: A Collection of French Hagiographic Romances of the Thirteenth Century.* 1991

Karen Cherewatuk and Ulrike Wiethaus, eds. *Dear Sister: Medieval Women and the Epistolary Genre.* 1993

Anne L. Clark. *Elisabeth of Schönau: A Twelfth-Century Visionary.* 1992

Willene B. Clark and Meradith T. McMunn, eds. *Beasts and Birds of the Middle Ages: The Bestiary and Its Legacy.* 1989

Richard C. Dales. *The Scientific Achievement of the Middle Ages.* 1973

Charles T. Davis. *Dante's Italy and Other Essays.* 1984

Katherine Fischer Drew, trans. *The Burgundian Code.* 1972

Katherine Fischer Drew, trans. *The Laws of the Salian Franks.* 1991

Katherine Fischer Drew, trans. *The Lombard Laws.* 1973

Nancy Edwards. *The Archaeology of Early Medieval Ireland.* 1990

Margaret J. Ehrhart. *The Judgment of the Trojan Prince Paris in Medieval Literature.* 1987

Richard K. Emmerson and Ronald B. Herzman. *The Apocalyptic Imagination in Medieval Literature.* 1992

Theodore Evergates. *Feudal Society in Medieval France: Documents from the County of Champagne.* 1993

Felipe Fernández-Armesto. *Before Columbus: Exploration and Colonization from the Mediterranean to the Atlantic, 1229–1492.* 1987

Jerold C. Frakes. *Brides and Doom: Gender, Property, and Power in Medieval Women's Epic.* 1994

R. D. Fulk. *A History of Old English Meter.* 1992

Patrick J. Geary. *Aristocracy in Provence: The Rhône Basin at the Dawn of the Carolingian Age.* 1985

Peter Heath. *Allegory and Philosophy in Avicenna (Ibn Sînâ), with a Translation of the Book of the Prophet Muhammad's Ascent to Heaven.* 1992

J. N. Hillgarth, ed. *Christianity and Paganism, 350–750: The Conversion of Western Europe.* 1986

Richard C. Hoffmann. *Land, Liberties, and Lordship in a Late Medieval Countryside: Agrarian Structures and Change in the Duchy of Wrocław.* 1990

Robert Hollander. *Boccaccio's Last Fiction: Il Corbaccio.* 1988

Edward B. Irving, Jr. *Rereading* Beowulf. 1989

C. Stephen Jaeger. *The Envy of Angels: Cathedral Schools and Social Ideals in Medieval Europe, 950–1200.* 1994

C. Stephen Jaeger. *The Origins of Courtliness: Civilizing Trends and the Formation of Courtly Ideals, 939–1210.* 1985

William Chester Jordan. *The French Monarchy and the Jews: From Philip Augustus to the Last Capetians.* 1989

William Chester Jordan. *From Servitude to Freedom: Manumission in the Sénonais in the Thirteenth Century.* 1986

Richard Kay. *Dante's Christian Astrology.* 1994

Ellen E. Kittell. *From Ad Hoc to Routine: A Case Study in Medieval Bureaucracy.* 1991

Alan C. Kors and Edward Peters, eds. *Witchcraft in Europe, 1100–1700: A Documentary History.* 1972

Barbara M. Kreutz. *Before the Normans: Southern Italy in the Ninth and Tenth Centuries.* 1992

E. Ann Matter. *The Voice of My Beloved: The Song of Songs in Western Medieval Christianity.* 1990

María Rosa Menocal. *The Arabic Role in Medieval Literary History.* 1987

A. J. Minnis. *Medieval Theory of Authorship.* 1988

Lawrence Nees. *A Tainted Mantle: Hercules and the Classical Tradition at the Carolingian Court.* 1991

Lynn H. Nelson, trans. *The Chronicle of San Juan de la Peña: A Fourteenth-Century Official History of the Crown of Aragon.* 1991

Charlotte A. Newman. *The Anglo-Norman Nobility in the Reign of Henry I: The Second Generation.* 1988

Joseph F. O'Callaghan. *The Cortes of Castile-León, 1188–1350.* 1989

Joseph F. O'Callaghan. *The Learned King: The Reign of Alfonso X of Castile.* 1993

David M. Olster. *Roman Defeat, Christian Response, and the Literary Construction of the Jew.* 1994

William D. Paden, ed. *The Voice of the Trobairitz: Perspectives on the Women Troubadours.* 1989

Edward Peters. *The Magician, the Witch, and the Law.* 1982

Edward Peters, ed. *Christian Society and the Crusades, 1198–1229: Sources in Translation, including* The Capture of Damietta *by Oliver of Paderborn.* 1971

Edward Peters, ed. *The First Crusade: The* Chronicle of Fulcher of Chartres *and Other Source Materials.* 1971

Edward Peters, ed. *Heresy and Authority in Medieval Europe.* 1980

James M. Powell. *Albertanus of Brescia: The Pursuit of Happiness in the Early Thirteenth Century.* 1992

James M. Powell. *Anatomy of a Crusade, 1213–1221.* 1986

Jean Renart (Patricia Terry and Nancy Vine Durling, trans.). *The Romance of the Rose or Guillaume de Dole.* 1993

Michael Resler, trans. Erec *by Hartmann von Aue.* 1987

Pierre Riché (Michael Idomir Allen, trans.). *The Carolingians: A Family Who Forged Europe.* 1993

Pierre Riché (Jo Ann McNamara, trans.). *Daily Life in the World of Charlemagne.* 1978

Jonathan Riley-Smith. *The First Crusade and the Idea of Crusading.* 1986

Joel T. Rosenthal. *Patriarchy and Families of Privilege in Fifteenth-Century England.* 1991

Teofilo F. Ruiz. *Crisis and Continuity: Land and Town in Late Medieval Castile.* 1994

Steven D. Sargent, ed. and trans. *On the Threshold of Exact Science: Selected Writings of Anneliese Maier on Late Medieval Natural Philosophy.* 1982

Robin Chapman Stacey. *The Road to Judgment: From Custom to Court in Medieval Ireland and Wales.* 1994

Sarah Stanbury. *Seeing the* Gawain-*Poet: Description and the Act of Perception.* 1992

Thomas C. Stillinger. *The Song of Troilus: Lyric Authority in the Medieval Book.* 1992

Susan Mosher Stuard. *A State of Deference: Ragusa/Dubrovnik in the Medieval Centuries.* 1992

Susan Mosher Stuard, ed. *Women in Medieval History and Historiography.* 1987

Susan Mosher Stuard, ed. *Women in Medieval Society.* 1976

Jonathan Sumption. *The Hundred Years War: Trial by Battle.* 1992

Ronald E. Surtz. *The Guitar of God: Gender, Power, and Authority in the Visionary World of Mother Juana de la Cruz (1481–1534).* 1990

William H. TeBrake. *A Plague of Insurrection: Popular Politics and Peasant Revolt in Flanders, 1323–1328.* 1993

Patricia Terry, trans. *Poems of the Elder Edda.* 1990

Hugh M. Thomas. *Vassals, Heiresses, Crusaders, and Thugs: The Gentry of Angevin Yorkshire, 1154–1216.* 1993

Frank Tobin. *Meister Eckhart: Thought and Language.* 1986

Ralph V. Turner. *Men Raised from the Dust: Administrative Service and Upward Mobility in Angevin England.* 1988

Harry Turtledove, trans. *The* Chronicle *of Theophanes: An English Translation of* Anni Mundi *6095–6305 (A.D. 602–813).* 1982

Mary F. Wack. *Lovesickness in the Middle Ages: The* Viaticum *and Its Commentaries.* 1990

Benedicta Ward. *Miracles and the Medieval Mind: Theory, Record, and Event, 1000–1215.* 1982

Suzanne Fonay Wemple. *Women in Frankish Society: Marriage and the Cloister, 500–900.* 1981

Jan M. Ziolkowski. *Talking Animals: Medieval Latin Beast Poetry, 750–1150.* 1993

This book has been set in Linotron Galliard. Galliard was designed for Mergenthaler in 1978 by Matthew Carter. Galliard retains many of the features of a sixteenth-century typeface cut by Robert Granjon but has some modifications that give it a more contemporary look.

Printed on acid-free paper.